Openly Gay Openly Christian

SAMUEL KADER, a graduate of the University of Pittsburgh (1973, 1978), received his call to ministry in 1976. After training as clergy in the Metropolitan Community Church of Detroit, within UFMCC, he began actively pastoring in 1980 as the founding pastor of Reconciliation Metropolitan Community Church in Grand Rapids, Michigan. After pastoring in Michigan, he moved to Ohio to pastor the MCC Church in Dayton. It was here that he met his lifemate, Robert, in 1983. In 1984 Pastor Kader accepted the pulpit of Metropolitan Community Church of Melbourne, Australia. Due to the challenges of immigration, it took a year to arrive on the shores of Australia, where he pastored throughout 1985. Back in Ohio, in July, 1986, Rev. Kader founded Community Gospel Church, the full-gospel, independent church he currently pastors. During the 3 years from 1992–1995 Pastor Kader's sermons reached out to the greater Dayton metropolitan area through a televised program called "Eunique (sic) Perspectives of Hope." Community Gospel Church is known as "A house of prayer for all people."

Community Gospel Church is a charter member of the Alliance of Christian Churches, and in 1996 Pastor Kader was elected as a member of the Executive Council of the Alliance. Currently Rev. Kader is also a faculty member and vice president of the Dayton, Ohio satellite campus of Grace Institute, a Bible college in Panama City, Florida.

Since 1975, and prior to active pastoral ministry, Rev. Kader has spoken on many college campuses, written numerous articles in the gay press, and hosted a Pittsburgh radio program called "Lambda, the gay wavelength." Samuel serves as a clergy volunteer to the Miami Valley AIDS Foundation. He currently resides in Dayton, Ohio with his spouse Robert, their dog Trip, and their cat, Mrs. Clay.

Openly Gay
Openly Christian

HOW THE BIBLE REALLY *IS* GAY FRIENDLY

Rev. Samuel Kader

Leyland Publications
San Francisco

First edition 1999
Front cover design by Stevee Postman. Cover photo: *Christ Blessing*, detail of the painting by Bellini, ca. 1500 from the book *The Golden Century of Venetian Painting* copyright 1979 by Museum Associates of the Los Angeles Museum of Art, p. 37. Original painting in Kimball Art Museum, Ft. Worth, TX.

Library of Congress Cataloging-in-Publication Data

Kader, Samuel.
  Openly gay openly Christian : how the Bible really *is* gay friendly / by Rev. Samuel Kader.
    160 p. 22 cm.
    ISBN 0-943595-78-9 (alk. paper)
    1. Homosexuality in the Bible. 2. Homosexuality—Religious aspects —Christianity. 3. Homosexuality—Biblical teaching. I. Title.
BS680.H67K33 1999   99-12808
220.8'306766—dc21   CIP

Leyland Publications
P.O. Box 410690
San Francisco, CA 94141

TABLE OF CONTENTS

DEDICATION

This book is dedicated to the glory of God and to Jesus Christ His Son. It was the vision God gave for the book that prompted its beginnings. It was the constant encouragement of the Holy Spirit that kept me working at this book when time constraints seemed impossible to make it happen.

I want to give special acknowledgment to my Christian sisters Elaine and Pam who believed in this project when it was only a vision, as well as Faith Fellowship Church. I want to thank them for their commitment to the completion of this goal. I want to thank my spouse, Robert, who gave me the extra encouragement and love I needed, and my church family, Community Gospel, for providing their love, prayers and support during this time.

It is my sincere desire that the truth and content of this book will be of benefit to many people trying to please God, walk in love, and be Christ's disciples. I hope many will discover that *homosexuality* and *holiness* have been and still are biblically compatible states. My hope is also that the truth will set people free; knowing they are free to be who God made them to be: whether gay, lesbian, bisexual, heterosexual or otherwise. I pray readers will soon discover how it is possible to be gay, Christian, responsible, and holy all at the same time.

God bless you as we study God's word together.

REV. SAMUEL KADER

OPENLY GAY, OPENLY CHRISTIAN

AN INTRODUCTION

Over the last several years, there has been a great deal of verbal, preached and printed rhetoric against the gay, lesbian and bisexual community coming from various segments of the Christian Church. In some cases this stems from blatant homophobia. But I believe in many cases this stems from a sincere desire to see others "get right with God." Yet by not fully understanding what they are talking about, people are only badgering the lesbigay community with the very Book that was designed to bring freedom. This stems from an ignorance of what the Bible actually says about homosexuality as well as relying on traditions of Biblical interpretations handed down through the ages. These traditions are often steeped in ignorance of both scientific data, as well as ignorance of the new discoveries from the Word of God itself.

It is my desire to dispel the myths, bring the truth to light, and open our hearts to the understanding that fosters love. It is not necessary to draw all of the same conclusions that I do, nor to necessarily agree with me on all points. I am presenting the conclusions I have drawn after two decades of research. It is my desire to see people get revelation from the Word of God for themselves, and my task is to help you along that journey.

I have been a pastor in the gay community since 1980. I have pastored four churches, spoken in countless others, been to a variety of Christian conferences both within and without the identified gay Christian community. I have taught, preached, and served on denominational committees in a variety of capacities. I have been on task forces, chaired committees, and in general have been very involved in the Christian community. It is my life.

Over the years, I have certainly met thousands of sincere Christians, who also happen to be gay, or of another sexual minority. I have seen only the tip of the iceberg. There are millions of gay, lesbian and bisexual Christians already serving God and their local congregations in churches and in denominational committees. Many church elders are gay. Many pastors are gay, even in organizations that would immediately revoke their credentials if their orientation were to become public knowledge or even suspected.

The Christian Church is in bondage to a tradition that has no basis in fact. Countless lives are being battered, bruised and damaged by maintaining this tradition. In order to maintain membership in good standing within innumerable congregations, many gay people try to do everything they can to keep the secret in their hearts quiet and out of public view. They have been to Christian counselors, they have had hands laid on them in prayer, they have fasted, prayed, and begged God to remove the desire in their heart. They have suffered abuse and mistreatment. When all else failed, they have been ostracized, removed from membership, shunned, even physically thrown out of the church and told to never return. Had there been a way to change their orientation they would have done so. With their prayer to change unanswered, I personally know of gay Christians who have taken their lives because they could no longer bear the pressure to conform.

Chapters of so-called self-help groups have sprung up overnight within churches and as parachurch ministries to help homosexuals get "out of the lifestyle." The most they have been able to offer is support for a gay person to remain as celibate as possible and offer forgiveness when they have slipped. Occasionally a person who can sexually function as a bisexual opts to get heterosexually married. Then that "cure" and "deliverance" from the homosexual lifestyle is highly advertised within the church.

I have a pastor friend named Karl. He is gay. Karl's brother-in-law is also a pastor. Karl's brother-in-law said one time that the only thing gay people have to do is come to the altar, pray, and they will be delivered from homosexuality. Karl's own sexual orientation was unknown to his brother-in-law, and Karl posed this question to his brother-in-law. "If that were so, then suppose a person in your church came for prayer, repented of their sins, and for the next year were a model Christian member of your church. After a year had gone by, if they wanted to take your 16-year-old son on a camping trip would you let them go?"

The brother-in-law said, "No!"

"Then you see," Karl replied, "you don't really believe that a person's orientation changes if they are prayed for and become a Christian.''

Many people who have tried everything the church offered, discovered their innate feelings have never gone away. These feelings are as much a part of who they are as the heterosexual's feelings are innate in them. In so many cases the Church is not offering help and hope; it is offering bondage and legalism— bound to a tradition that has no power to help. But people are incredibly resilient. When situations dictate, heterosexuals and homosexuals alike can keep their sexual urges in check, without acting upon them. But nothing they do can stop them from being attracted to another person. Sexual attraction does not go away with prayer and fasting. That is a person's orientation, and it is innate. It can be sublimated, it can be denied, but it cannot be driven out.

Steve Parker, for example, is a young man who discovered that his Christianity and homosexuality are compatible. He consented to share his testimony. Steve writes:

I became a Christian at age 20 after a spiritual experience convinced me of the existence of God. I was eager to learn all about my new faith, and earnestly tried to live a life which I felt would be pleasing to God. I joined a church and eagerly adopted the lifestyle of those around me whom I felt to be godly individuals. I quit drinking, smoking, and cursing. I started a daily regimen of prayer and Bible study. At the age of 23 I was licensed as a minister in my denomination and started a campus ministry at a local college. I became active in conservative politics. On the outside, I looked like the perfect candidate to join the Christian Coalition. There was only one problem: I was gay.

I had known I was gay since I was thirteen years old. When I became a Christian, I was told that Christians could not be gay and that God could change me. Not knowing any better, I believed them. I spent hours fervently praying for God to change me. I studied scriptural principles and applied them to my life. I fasted. And I waited for God to change me. It didn't happen.

For five years, I lived a celibate life. Yet, inside, I knew that

I was attracted to men. I met a wonderful woman to whom I became very close. I asked her to marry me, feeling that surely that would finally "cure" me. It did not. Two months into the marriage, I told her about my secret feelings. She was devastated. Our marriage ended in divorce. My denomination would not renew my credentials. My life came to a screeching halt.

In the months that followed, I tried to make sense of what had happened in my life. I felt God had abandoned me. Meanwhile, my sexual desires grew stronger. Finally, with a sense of utter frustration and despair, I quit fighting. On a cold winter night in January, 1988, I went to a gay bar. This marked the beginning of a steady descent into a world of alcoholism, drugs, and meaningless sex.

For the next seven years, my life slowly deteriorated. By January of 1995, I stayed drunk nearly all the time and was struggling with an addiction to crack cocaine. In March of that year, I lost my job and totaled my car. My father, who had never been one to offer much advice, came to me and said what were probably the wisest words he had ever uttered: "You need help." I really couldn't disagree.

I entered a substance abuse treatment center. Once there, my counselor designed my treatment program to help me deal with the fact that I was gay, something I had never come to terms with. As I began to accept that I was a homosexual, something else began to happen as well. I came to a very real awareness that the God that I had run away from seven years previously was still there, and even more amazingly, still loved me! This went against everything that I had believed and everything I had been taught.

Yet, as I began to be more comfortable with being gay, I began to sense God's presence even more strongly. I began to pray on a daily basis again. Then, one morning after I had been there for about two weeks, I was in prayer and felt a tremendous power flow through my body. Suddenly, the cocaine addiction that I had been struggling with for years was gone. Inside my head, I heard a voice as clear as a bell say, "I died for you." Jesus Christ had set me free. From that moment on, I knew that I was okay with God. And I knew it was okay to be gay.

During the five weeks I spent in that treatment center, I learned more about the love of God than in the entire five years I had spent in church so many years before. Because I had come to accept myself and love myself as I was, homosexuality and all, I could now accept God's unconditional love for me. And just as importantly, I could love other people as they were, just as God does.

Before, I had thought that my sexual nature was perverse, twisted and evil. Because of that, I was constantly critical of myself and others. I felt it was necessary to compensate by being a super-Christian, praying more than anyone else, reading the Bible more than anyone else, being more holy than anyone else. Nothing I did was ever enough to please God; there was always a need to do more. Now, realizing that my sexuality was God-given and God-ordained, I could freely accept Christ's unmerited favor.

Since that time, my relationship with God has grown and prospered. God has blessed my life in numerous ways. I am back in school, quickly approaching a degree in sociology. I am conducting research that I will continue in graduate school next fall, exploring the role that negative images of God play in keeping gays from coming to terms with their sexuality, and how that can lead to substance abuse in order to dull the pain that results. What started as a part time job in a small business on the verge of failure has grown into part ownership of a company that grossed approximately three-quarters of a million dollars in 1996. I have met a wonderful Christian man and am engaged to be married to him this spring. I feel closer to the Lord than I ever have. My life is truly rich and full by every measure.

God is very active in my life, calling me to higher levels of honesty and personal integrity. The fruits of the Spirit are manifest as I find love, joy, peace, etc. becoming ever more evident. This is something I never knew before. I think it should be obvious why I feel that being gay and being a Christian are not incompatible.

Steve's testimony is like that of so many others. After accepting the "party line," the tradition that said homosexuality and Christianity were incompatible, many did everything they thought was possible to forget the secret desires in their hearts. And they did those things for years. Finally it dawns on them; this orientation is not going away, and it is not going to change.

Many people over the years have telephoned or made counseling appointments who were on the verge of suicide, frustrated because everything they had been taught did not stop their orientation from manifesting itself in their feelings and desires. They can't help whom they find attractive. Why do people seek a mate with one characteristic over another? No one taught them to prefer a person of a certain sex, height, or eye color. They just do.

When the topic of sexuality hits the Church there are few or no answers that work. There are platitudes. There are plenty of traditional theologies based on scriptural interpretations. But when those traditions fail, the person seeking help is considered a moral failure and is asked to leave. The *tradition* is never questioned.

The tradition declares that all non-heterosexual orientations are evil, and must be changed. This tradition however has never brought freedom; instead it has brought bondage, legalism, ostracism, depression, psychiatric institutional admissions, despondency and suicide. It has driven people from God and the Church and offered no hope.

Nevertheless, there are countless numbers of gay people and others who are experiencing a meaningful relationship with God and Jesus Christ in spite of the Church and the tradition. A similar phenomenon happened in the early first century Church as well. Tradition, to the newly created Jewish sect, meant gentiles could not be a part of the Church unless they first converted and became just like the Jewish believers. They had councils over the issue. Peter was called on the carpet for going to visit non-Jews. Yet in spite of what people thought, God was moving in the earth and bringing gentiles to Christ anyway, without the written consent of the Jews. Today, without the written consent of pastors, church boards, or deacons, God is drawing gay people to Himself, raising up churches faster than anyone can count, and adding them to the Body anyway. God is way ahead of His people, and the

Church is lagging behind God by decades. It is time to examine the tradition that keeps the rest of the Body from following the Shepherd who has already gone into the highways and byways and compelled them to come in. He is already adding gay people to His Church roster daily whether heterosexual Christians know it or not.

It has too long been assumed a person could not be gay and Christian. Too many gay people have experienced a genuine encounter with the Holy Spirit through faith in Christ to accept this fallacy any longer. Also it has been assumed that if a gay person became a Christian they would no longer be gay, or at very least would remain forever celibate. Again this fallacy is not borne out in the everyday experiences of gay Christians. Believers who are also gay are asking and discovering what God requires of them. They discover it is neither heterosexuality nor celibacy.

They are finding it possible to be both holy and homosexual with no discrepancy in lifestyle. The two states are totally compatible. The Holy Spirit is the reliable source to lead a person through their conscience into right and wrong behaviors. Many are even finding a helpmate as they walk with the Lord. Many are discovering that promiscuity is not an option, but that a stable love life with a lifetime partner is the place they best honor the Lord. Many such Christian couples will testify that their relationship came about through their walk with God. It is time to challenge false stereotypes, and see what God is and has been saying to His people.

In an age when people are dying of AIDS, and are in need of love and compassion, the Church, or many who call themselves the Church, have gotten themselves entangled in a web of legalism and bondage. Rather than helping people discover the Savior, the Church is alienating people and pushing them further away. The Church is not called to be the judge of the world. The Church has been given the ministry of reconciling the world to God.

Galatians 5:1 tells us to stand fast therefore in the liberty wherewith Christ has made us free. So the Gospel is *good* news. It brings liberation, it doesn't bring bondage. If we're really listening to the Gospel and paying attention to the *good* news of Jesus Christ, it is going to set us free. It is going to bring us joy. It is going to bring us peace, an increase of love, and the fruits of the Spirit. God's good news will not bring hatred for the people God loves. And He loves the world!

So God has given to us, the Church, the ministry of reconciliation, not the ministry of alienation. Matthew 15:6 tells us that religious traditions can make the Word of God ineffective and unable to work. If you bring people a false religious tradition in place of the truth, it has no enduring effect on the listener for Good. The Word of God is *good* news, and it is alive and active in our lives, unlike empty traditional religious words of bondage. John 8:32 says the truth will set people free. The tradition does not bring freedom, but rather bondage and legalism.

The Church has been wrong before. Its interpretation of scripture has been abused to maintain a traditional status quo that needed to be challenged.

In America's 19th century and the century prior, slave owners would assemble a church service for their slaves, and they would provide the preacher. The text used consistently by these white preachers was that slaves should be subject to their masters. Week after week the topic would be expounded upon. But after the preacher would leave, that sermon topic never brought any liberty to the souls of the hearers. After the preacher would leave, then the slaves would really have church! It was from these clandestine services that we got so many of the spirituals that the Church enjoys today. I believe it was the fervent prayers of these enslaved righteous folks that brought about the Civil War, resulting in their freedom. The biblical texts often used in the slave quarters were the ones about God delivering the children of Israel from the slavery of the Egyptians, with God raising up a Moses in their midst. Only in recent times has the Southern Baptist Convention apologized for its theological tradition that helped maintain slavery during and prior to the Civil War in the United States.

Women have long heard preaching that said they were not to speak in the Church. They were told to keep quiet and ask their questions at home. They were told that a woman has no place in the pulpit, pastoral ministry. Those traditions did not bring liberty, but bondage. They hindered God from bringing about ministry in the lives of many women. Maria B. Woodworth-Etter had a large healing, signs, wonders and miracles ministry with crowds of up to 25,000 people in a single service in the late 1800's and early 1900's. Yet women were still being told there was no place for them in the pulpit ministry. God obviously thought differently as He continued to pour out His Spirit on all flesh. It was the tradition that was hindering the Word of God and making it ineffective for so many. In the early part of Etter's life, she did not begin ministry because she said, "How can I, I'm not a man."

It wasn't until her husband died, her children died and she was left alone in life that she decided she had nothing else she could do but follow God. Then she began to preach, and 20,000 people at a time would come to her meetings. People would be overpowered by the Spirit, healings took place, and many were set free.

Had it not been for the Spirit of God bringing forth the truth of the Word, thus setting women free, we would have missed out on Aimee Semple McPherson, Kathryn Kuhlman, and countless others who have blessed and edified the Body of Christ.

The issue we are looking at is not the first time God had to bring revelation to set people free within the Church. Historically, this is not the first time scripture traditionally used to keep people in bondage has been challenged. The challenge has always come as the Spirit brought about revelation. Scripture tells us that in the last days knowledge will increase. Knowledge is increasing. Revelations and discoveries about God's Word are coming too quickly to catalog.

We know from John 3:16 that God loves people, and is not just loving certain kinds of people to the exclusion of others. God loves the world. So people who say, "Well God doesn't love *those* kinds of people," don't know what the Bible is talking about in this area, nor do they really understand God's love.

According to John 3:16 God so loved the world that He gave His love; not just to the Church, but to the world.

John 12:47 says that Jesus did not come to judge the world, but to save the world. Yet there have been many who have said that AIDS is God's judgment on the gay community. But the Bible said that Jesus did not come to judge. He didn't come to bring AIDS. He came to bring salvation. The word that means *to save* in Greek, is the same word that means *to heal*. So if He came to heal the world, He would be inconsistent if He came to heal the world and at the same time judge with AIDS. God is not inconsistent.

Hebrews 13:8 shows us that Jesus Christ is the same yesterday, today, and forever. He came to heal and save then, and it's what He does now. AIDS is not a judgment; it is a disease. If God were bringing AIDS here on Earth as a judgment, that would be inconsistent with the gospel. Jesus had compassion on the multitudes and healed them all. Jesus showed the purpose and character of God in His earthly ministry. What God brings are good things like love, joy, peace, liberty, and hope into our lives.

AS WE STUDY THE BIBLE

I will discuss first the primary tools we will be using in order to demonstrate how we arrive at conclusions. We will often make reference to the numbering system found in *Strong's Concordance*. *Strong's* has been the standard, solid concordance and dictionary for the last century. Every translated word in the Bible is assigned a number which corresponds to the Hebrew or Greek word actually used in the original language. In the dictionary in the back of *Strong's*, you can then look up the number for the word you want to research. The number will lead you to the actual word in the original language and give you a definition.

Strong's Concordance was written in conjunction with the wording used in the King James Version of the Bible. So by using the *Strong's Concordance* and the King James Version, we will be able to code and discuss any word used in the Bible from the original languages. But for the sake of readability, in most cases the *New International Version* of the Bible (NIV) will be quoted and any differences in the two translations pointed out.

When we look at traditional beliefs surrounding a topic like homosexuality, we have to ask these questions:

1. Where did these traditions come from?
2. Do they have any validity?
3. What does the Word of God really say?

We will begin by looking at the story of Sodom.

SODOM REVISITED

We have all heard many things about the story of Sodom and Gomorrah, and not simply from one source. What most of us have been told is that Sodom was destroyed because of homosexuality. But, is that true? Is that the case? Is that the only reason the Bible gives, if it even gives that particular reason at all, for Sodom's judgment? How do we decide if what we have been told is true? Should we look at the footnotes in our Bible for the answer?

Probably not. Footnotes are not scripture. There are footnotes in some Bibles, for instance, that try to explain passages according to a particular doctrinal slant or tradition. Be aware that footnotes are comments about scripture, they are not themselves scripture. The Bible is its own best interpreter and the best way to see what God is saying in a scriptural passage is to discover what else God says on that topic in the Bible. And the only way we can discover what is actually going on in the story of Sodom and Gomorrah is to look at the story itself.

As we look at the story, there are two numbers in *Strong's Concordance*; two words of which to take note.

1.   The first is #3045 (in Hebrew) *yada'* (yaw-dah'); *to know, to be acquainted*; to know (properly, to ascertain by seeing); used in a great variety of senses, figuratively, literally, euphemistically and inferentially (including observation, care, recognition; and causatively, instruction, designation, punishment, etc.)

2.   The second is #7901 (in Hebrew) *shakab* (shaw-kab'); *to lie down. It can be used in a sexual connotation heterosexually, homosexually, in bestiality, or to ravish, to seize, to carry away and to rape*; to lie down (for rest, sexual connection, decease or any other purpose)

Now these two words are both in the Bible. We find out that the first word, #3045, *yada*, meaning *to know*, is used over 900 times in the Bible. In all but ten times, it means to be acquainted with, to observe, to recognize, to have an understanding. Some examples of this word *yada* being used are:

> *Gen. 27:2*
> Isaac said, "I am now an old man and don't *know* [#3045] the day of my death.
> *Isa. 1:3*
> 3 The ox *knows* his master, the donkey his owner's manger, but Israel does not *know*, my people do not understand."

This obviously doesn't mean the ox has sex with its master; only that it knows its master.

For some reason people want to translate that word *yada*, #3045 as if it were #7901, *shakab*. *Shakab* means to lie down; and this word can mean to lie down for a sexual connection. If *shakab* is being used to lie down in a sexual way, it could mean, based on its context, a heterosexual, homosexual or bestial sexual connection. But it also means to lie down for any purpose. It means to lie down for rest, like you were going to take a nap. It also means to lie down because you are a corpse. In addition it means to ravage.

Depending on the form of the verb used, #7901, or its derivatives #7902, #7903 in Leviticus 18:20,22,23, can be found. So this word *is* in the Bible, and if indeed the people of Sodom wanted to homosexually molest the visitors at Lot's house this word *shakab* should have been used. That's the Hebrew word that means to rape, to carry away by force, homosexually, heterosexually, or for bestiality. But #7901 *shakab* is *not* the word that is used in Genesis 19, referring to Lot's visitors. We have instead, the word *yada* #3045.

Having said that, we begin our look at the story in Genesis 18:16.

> *Gen. 18:16–17*
> 16 When the men got up to leave, they looked down toward Sodom, and Abraham walked along with them to see them on their way.

17   Then the LORD said, "Shall I hide from Abraham what I am about to do?"

The men referred to are the angels who are with the Lord and Abraham.

Gen. 18:20–22

20   Then the LORD said, "The outcry against Sodom and Gomorrah is so great and their sin so grievous
21   that I will go down and see if what they have done is as bad as the outcry that has reached me. If not, I will know."
22   The men turned away and went toward Sodom, but Abraham remained standing before the LORD.

Gen. 18:23–26

23   Then Abraham approached him and said: "Will you sweep away the righteous with the wicked?
24   What if there are fifty righteous people in the city? Will you really sweep it away and not spare the place for the sake of the fifty righteous people in it?
25   Far be it from you to do such a thing—to kill the righteous with the wicked, treating the righteous and the wicked alike. Far be it from you! Will not the Judge of all the earth do right?"
26   The LORD said, "*If* I find fifty righteous people in the city of Sodom, I will spare the whole place for their sake."

What we find here is that in chapter 18, long before there is any altercation with the angels and the people of the city, God has already determined to destroy the city of Sodom.

Sodom is so wicked, God can hear its cry; He is sending His angels to find out if all of this is so. Abraham begins to bargain with God, saying, if you find fifty righteous there will You spare the city? God says yes. Then Abraham goes on in this chapter and says what about forty-five? If You find forty-five that are righteous will You spare the city? Again God says yes. Well, what if You find thirty, Abraham asks God. The Lord says yes. Eventually, through this bargaining with God, Abraham has God agree that He will not destroy it for the sake of ten righteous.

So now we're looking at a city that has to be completely wicked *minus ten people*, if it is to be spared. Many people try to say that Sodom was destroyed because of homosexuality. If the city of Sodom were to be destroyed because of *homosexuality*, then that means that out of the entire valley that encompasses Sodom as well as Gomorrah, *every person must be a homosexual*, every man, woman and child *minus nine individuals must be gay*. This valley with all its surrounding cities must have ten heterosexuals to be spared, *if* the reason it is being destroyed is for homosexuality. God *doesn't* tell Abraham the reason is homosexuality. *He merely says that it is wicked.*

Now we will find out what is going on. We go to Genesis, chapter 19.

Gen. 19:1-5

1   The two angels arrived at Sodom in the evening, and Lot was sitting in the gateway of the city. When he saw them, he got up to meet them and bowed down with his face to the ground.

2   "My lords," he said, "please turn aside to your servant's house. You can wash your feet and spend the night and then go on your way early in the morning." "No," they answered, "we will spend the night in the square."

3   But he insisted so strongly that they did go with him and entered his house. He prepared a meal for them, baking bread without yeast, and they ate.

(For clarity in literal translation, we look at the next two verses in the King James Version):

4   But before they lay down, the men of the city, even the men of Sodom, compassed the house round, both old and young, *all* the people from every quarter:

5   And they called unto Lot, and said unto him, Where are the men which came in to thee this night? Bring them out unto us, that we may *know* [*yada* (#3045)] them.

Some translations will say they want to *know sexually, know carnally, have carnal knowledge*. But the word *yada* is used here: *to be acquainted with*. It is *not* the Hebrew word #7901 in Strong's, *shakab: to have sexual knowledge, to lie down with*.

Continuing on with the Genesis account:

Gen. 19:6-17

6   Lot went outside to meet them and shut the door behind him

7   and said, "No, my friends. Don't do this wicked thing.

8   Look, I have two daughters who have never slept with a man. Let me bring them out to you, and you can do what you like with them. But don't do anything to these men, for they have come under the protection of my roof."

9   "Get out of our way," they replied. And they said. "This fellow came here as an alien, and now he wants to play the judge! We'll treat you worse than them." They kept bringing pressure on Lot and moved forward to break down the door.

10   But the men inside reached out and pulled Lot back into the house and shut the door.

11   Then they struck the men who were at the door of the house, young and old, with blindness so that they could not find the door.

12   The two men said to Lot, "Do you have anyone else here—sons-in-law, sons or daughters, or anyone else in the city who belongs to you? Get them out of here,

13   because we are going to destroy this place. The outcry to the LORD against its people is so great that he has sent us to destroy it."

14   So Lot went out and spoke to his sons-in-law, who were pledged to marry his daughters. He said, "Hurry and get out of this place, because the LORD is about to destroy the city!" But his sons-in-law thought he was joking.

15   With the coming of dawn, the angels urged Lot, saying, "Hurry! Take your wife and your two daughters who are here, or you will be swept away when the city is punished."

16   When he hesitated, the men grasped his hand and the

hands of his wife and of his two daughters and led them safely
out of the city, for the LORD was merciful to them.

17   As soon as they had brought them out, one of them
said, "Flee for your lives! Don't look back, and don't stop
anywhere in the plain! Flee to the mountains or you will be
swept away!"

Then skipping to verse 24 we read:

Gen. 19:24-25
24   Then the LORD rained down burning sulfur on Sodom
and Gomorrah—from the LORD out of the heavens.
25   Thus he overthrew those cities and the entire plain, including all those living in the cities—and also the vegetation
in the land.

In this story we must look at some things in order to dig out the
truth. By the time we get to verse 4 in Genesis 19, we see that Lot
has already come upon the two angels as he sat in the entrance gate
of Sodom. The angels have said that they were going to sleep in
the city streets, and Lot won't hear of it. He invites them back to
his house, to feed them and give them lodging. Lot is offering
hospitality according to the custom of the day.

Gen. 19:4
4   Before they had gone to bed, all the *men* from every
part of the city of Sodom—both young and old—surrounded
the house.

The word for *men* does not mean *men*, as in a *male human being*. It is #582 *'enowsh* (en-oshe'); from #605; properly, *a mortal*; hence a *person* in general (singly or collectively).

So a proper translation is to say:

Gen. 19:4
4   Before they had gone to bed, all the *mortals* from every part of the city of Sodom—both young and old—surrounded the house.

Thus we have a gathering of *all* the mortals. Men and women, young children and aged senior citizens are *all* present. The Bible is *not* talking about a crowd of homosexual men. It is talking about a crowd comprised of every human being who lives in this city: the men, the women, the children, *all* the people, verse four says, from every quarter. Every citizen is present.

What is occurring is a mob scene. Is this a mob scene of *all homosexuals*? Some people obviously think so.

In verse five, we read the words of this mob.

Gen. 19:5

And they called unto Lot, and said unto him, Where are the *men* [#582] which came in to thee this night? Bring them out unto us, that we may know them. (KJV)

The word for *men* is also #582 *'enowsh* (en-oshe'); *a mortal.* In other words, the people of the town show up at Lot's door, and they don't know whether Lot has men in his house or whether he has women in his house. They ask where are the mortals? All they know is that Lot has somebody in his house, and they don't know who it is. So they say bring them out that we might *yada (to know, to be acquainted with)* them. If this word is used to mean to "have sex," then why are all the people (the men, the women, and the children saying, bring out these *mortals*, not knowing whether they are men or women, to have sex with them? It doesn't make much sense does it? It is far more likely that what is recorded is that the townspeople want to become acquainted with whoever it is Lot had taken into their city.

Have you ever seen *this* scenario in human history: a cross burning on the lawn, while a mob demands those inside the house come out for a confrontation?

I can picture a few generations or even a few decades ago in America, a person from up north, like New York City, having moved into the deep south, finding himself suspect just because he's a Yankee. Then he invites into his home an old friend of another race. Before long, the hooded mob is on his lawn burning a wooden cross and demanding to see the unwelcome visitor, demanding to deal with this unacceptable visitor because "We don't allow that kind in our city!''

This is a far more likely scenario in the realm of human behavior than everyone in town going to Lot's house for sex with a person of unknown gender. This is a violent mob scene. Sex is not the issue, but is more likely murder by lynching or stoning. When the mob demands that Lot bring out his visitors that they might *know them*, this mob is in a furor and they want to know who is in the house! Lot goes out to the door, shuts the door behind him and speaks to these townspeople.

Gen. 19:6–8
6   Lot went outside to meet them and shut the door behind him
7   and said, ''No, my friends. Don't do this wicked thing.
8   Look, I have two daughters who have never slept with a *man* [#376 in *Strong's* meaning a *male person*]. Let me bring them out to you, and you can do what you like with them. But don't do anything to these *men* [#582 in *Strong's* meaning *mortal*; he still does not identify the gender of these angelic visitors], for they have come under the protection of my roof.''

The word used by Lot to say his daughters had never known a *man* is the word available in Hebrew to state a male human or a group of male persons [#376 in *Strong's*]. If the mob at the door were all men, then this is the word the Bible would have used to say only men were at the door. But it didn't. It used the word for *mortals*, meaning the mob was a mixed crowd of both sexes. It gets pretty hard at this point to make a case that Sodom was destroyed because of homosexuality.

Lot then goes on to say:

Gen. 19:8
8   Look, I have two daughters who have never slept with a man. Let me bring them out to you, and you can do what you like with them. But don't do anything to these men, for they have come under the protection of my roof.''

Lot thought for some reason that if he would push his daughters out there, this would quiet down all the mortals of the city. Are these men gay who are going to be so quickly appeased by two daughters coming out, *if* their intention was to *have sex* with these two visitors? The interpretation that Sodom was destroyed for homosexuality does not make sense in light of what is actually recorded. Also we read in

2 Pet. 2:6

6   if he condemned the cities of Sodom and Gomorrah by burning them to ashes, and made them an example of what is going to happen to the *ungodly* [#765];

The word for *ungodly* in the New Testament Greek: #765 in *Strong's*: asebes (as-eb-ace´); from #1 (as a negative particle) and a presumed derivative of #4576; worship irreverent, i.e. (by extension) impious or wicked.

Therefore the word could literally be translated they were *without worship*, making Sodom and Gomorrah an example to all others who would in the future live *without worship*. What Lot saw day after day was not homosexuality but a people who did not worship God. It greatly distressed his righteous soul, just as Acts 17:16 points out that Paul the Apostle was greatly distressed in his soul to see that the city of Athens was full of idols.

So we see Sodom was destroyed as an example for every group of people from that point on who live *without worship* of the true and living God. Sodom was a town that did not worship God. It is apparent, these people were *daily* lawbreakers. This is important to remember.

Picking up again at Genesis 19:9

Gen. 19:9–11

9   "Get out of our way," they replied. And they said, "This fellow came here as an alien, and now he wants to play the judge! We'll treat you worse than them." They kept bringing pressure on Lot and moved forward to break down the door.

10   But the men [*the angels*] inside reached out and pulled

Lot back into the house and shut the door.

11   Then they struck the men [*the mortals; the men, the women, the children, everyone in town*] who were at the door of the house, young and old, with blindness so that they could not find the door.

In verse 9 it is obvious that the people of Sodom are determined to get to those angels.

Consider this thought. Imagine you were feeling very amorous. You were determined you were going to have sex with a certain person, but then they slammed the door in your face. How would you feel? Don't you think the act of slamming the door would cool your amorous feelings? But people still say this was a homosexual city and God judged Sodom because they wanted to have sex with the angels. Then consider this out of your own experience, perhaps. Suppose you were about to have sex with someone you love, and you were just about to actually engage in a sexual encounter. Imagine your sexual energy just racing through your heightened nervous system, and just as you were getting involved, suddenly you went blind! Do you think that would get your attention? Do you think you'd be concerned about the blindness? Don't you think that this sudden occurrence of blindness would take precedence over a sexual encounter?

Yet the Word says these mortals, not just the men, but these men, women, and children are struck with blindness. Yet they struggle to get to the door! They are obsessed with getting those angels! They are not interested in sex, any more; they never were. Under any normal circumstances, now that the townspeople are all blind, they should all stop and try to find out what happened! But no, they are wearying themselves to get to the door, scratching and digging, clawing and grasping to find the door! In fact they do it all night long! It is not until the morning [v. 15] that the angels take Lot and his family out of town. All night long they are scratching, clawing, grasping for the door, trying to find those angels. This does not sound like a sexual encounter to me! Newly struck blind people, consumed with only one thought, to get the angels, are not thinking about a sexual encounter. This is neither a story about sex nor homosexuality. It is the story of a pagan stronghold and the oppression of a town.

Therefore the angels say to Lot in verse 13, to get out of town because they are about to destroy it.

Gen. 19:12–13

12   The two men said to Lot, ''Do you have anyone else here—sons-in-law, sons or daughters, or anyone else in the city who belongs to you? Get them out of here,

13   because we are going to destroy this place. The outcry to the LORD against its people is so great that he has sent us to destroy it.''

God sent angels to destroy the city; because it was a wicked, idol filled town. This passage should be interpreted metaphorically: a town that was turning away from real spirituality. According to 2 Peter 2:6–8 the Word of God declares that Sodom stands forever as an example of those who would live ungodly. *Ungodly* means literally *without worship* towards God.

2 Pet. 2:6

6   if he condemned the cities of Sodom and Gomorrah by burning them to ashes, and made them an example of what is going to happen to the *ungodly* [*without worship*] . . .

That's the problem. They were *without worship*. They were not serving the God of all creation. They were serving only materialism.

Many times, when Bibles have footnotes on Genesis 19 they will refer you to Judges 19 for a similar story. The assumption is, by traditional interpretation, that homosexuality destroyed Sodom, and it also had similar consequences for a city in the tribe of Benjamin named Gibeah. If we look at the story in Judges 19, it has nothing to do with Sodom, because Sodom doesn't exist any more. It is about Gibeah, a city within the borders of Benjamin, a tribe of Israel. In other words, this is a story about God's people, a part of Israel. It is important to realize whom we are talking about when we look at any of these biblical accounts.

Judges 19 is the story of a man whose wife ran away and went back to her father. The man travels to win his wife back, and to bring her home. He stays several days at his father-in-law's house eating and drinking, and enjoying his father-in-law's hospitality. After several days, the man saddles his donkey, takes his wife and leaves. On the journey, it gets late. He could turn in to the city of the ungodly, the Jebusites, but decides instead to continue to God's people by traveling on to Gibeah. They felt certain that when they got to Gibeah, they would find hospitality, a place to room for the night. They even had plenty of supplies with them, and did not plan to be an imposition on anyone. They merely needed shelter. As they arrive in Gibeah, an old man sees them sitting in the town square, just as Lot found the angels. The scripture relates the following:

Judg. 19:16–29

16   That evening an old man from the hill country of Ephraim, who was living in Gibeah (the men of the place were Benjamites), came in from his work in the fields.

17   When he looked and saw the traveler in the city square, the old man asked, "Where are you going? Where did you come from?"

18   He answered, "We are on our way from Bethlehem in Judah to a remote area in the hill country of Ephraim where I live. I have been to Bethlehem in Judah and now I am going to the house of the LORD. No one has taken me into his house.

19   We have both straw and fodder for our donkeys and bread and wine for ourselves your servants—me, your maidservant, and the young man with us. We don't need anything."

20   "You are welcome at my house," the old man said. "Let me supply whatever you need. Only don't spend the night in the square."

21   So he took him into his house and fed his donkeys. After they had washed their feet, they had something to eat and drink.

22   While they were enjoying themselves, some of the wicked men of the city surrounded the house. Pounding on the door, they shouted to the old man who owned the house,

"Bring out the man who came to your house so we can have sex with him."

23   The owner of the house went outside and said to them, "No, my friends, don't be so vile. Since this man is my guest, don't do this disgraceful thing.

24   Look, here is my virgin daughter, and his concubine. I will bring them out to you now, and you can use them and do to them whatever you wish. But to this man, don't do such a disgraceful thing."

25   But the men would not listen to him. So the man took his concubine and sent her outside to them, and they raped her and abused her throughout the night, and at dawn they let her go.

26   At daybreak the woman went back to the house where her master was staying, fell down at the door and lay there until daylight.

27   When her master got up in the morning and opened the door of the house and stepped out to continue on his way, there lay his concubine, fallen in the doorway of the house, with her hands on the threshold.

28   He said to her, "Get up; let's go." But there was no answer. Then the man put her on his donkey and set out for home.

29   When he reached home, he took a knife and cut up his concubine, limb by limb, into twelve parts and

A closer look at *Judges 19:22* in the King James Version will reveal a few more details:

22   Now as they were making their hearts merry, behold, the *men* [here again is the word for *mortals* #582] of the city, certain *sons* [#1121, which means children, descendants, members of a group] of *Belial*, beset the house round about, and beat at the door, and spake to the master of the house, the old man, saying, Bring forth the man that came into thine house, that we may *know him*. (KJV)

Again we are not looking at an exclusively male crowd, at least based on the words chosen in the original language. These people are called sons of Belial.

> *Belial*: #1100 in *Strong's*, Old Testament: *beliya'al* (bel-e-yah'-al); from 1097 and 3276; without profit, worthlessness; by extension, destruction, wickedness; Belial, evil, naughty, ungodly (men), wicked.

Furthermore they surrounded the house, and beat at the door, and spoke to the master of the house, the old man, saying, Bring forth the man that came into your house, that we may *know him*.

Again here is the word *yada'* (yaw-dah'); [#3045 in *Strong's*] a primitive root; *to know* (properly, *to ascertain by seeing*).

"We want to know him," they say.

Now let me reveal something else here. The Bible shows us what the man who was traveling with his wife thought they meant when they said, "Bring him out that we might *know* him."

In Judges 20:5, he says, "During the night the *men* of Gibeah came after me and surrounded the house, intending to kill me. They raped my concubine, and she died."

This word for *men* is a different word altogether than previous words we have looked at. This word is #1167 in *Strong's* Old Testament. This word doesn't really mean *men* as in a plural for male people. It is the word *Baal* (or lord).

The man talks about the lord or the Baal. Baal is a pagan god. "*The master of Gibeah* rose against me," is what this statement is literally saying. In other words, the man declares there was an outright pagan attack against him.

> *Judg. 20:5*
> 5   During the night the *men* [#1167, *Lord, Baal, Master*] of Gibeah came after me and surrounded the house, intending to kill me [not thought *to have had sex with me*, but thought *to have murdered me!*] They raped my concubine, and she died.

He realizes why the people are outside the door. They have one thing in mind, and it is not a casual sexual encounter between consenting adults. Their evil intent is murder! Murder, not sex. So there is no homosexual activity involved in this story at all, but in fact it is the story of a man about to be murdered.

Back to the story line in Judges 19:22 we read

Judg. 19:22–24
22   While they were enjoying themselves, some of the wicked men of the city surrounded the house. Pounding on the door, they shouted to the old man who owned the house, "Bring out the man who came to your house so we can have sex with him." (King James Version more accurately translates: "Bring forth the man that came into thine house, *that we may know him.*")
23   The owner of the house went outside and said to them, "No, my friends, don't be so vile. Since this man is my guest, don't do this disgraceful thing.
24   Look, here is my virgin daughter, and his concubine. I will bring them out to you now, and you can use them and do to them whatever you wish. But to this man, don't do such a disgraceful thing."

The mob outside speaks to the master of the house, the old man, saying bring out the man that came into your house that we might *know him*, meaning that they might *kill* him! They are saying to the old man, bring out your guest that we might know him, be acquainted with whom you have in your house, that we might know who it is. Their intent, however, is to kill him. This is an enraged mob scene.

The master of the house went out to the mob and said, "Don't do this! Don't be so wicked. Seeing this man has come under the protection of my house, do not do this folly. Behold here is my daughter, and his wife, his concubine."

Does he think this is a group of homosexual men if he is offering two women in exchange for the man? He says "them [these two women] I will bring out now, and humble them, and do with them what seems good to you; but unto this man do not so vile a thing."

Judg. 19:25
25   But the men would not listen to him. So the man took

his concubine and sent her outside to them, and they raped
her and abused her throughout the night, and at dawn they
let her go.

The meaning of the words used shows us these are pagans, enslaved to a false god. They are not gay men.

At daybreak the woman went back to the house where her
master was staying, fell down at the door and lay there until daylight. There she died, and was not discovered until later that morning. The man takes his dead wife home, divides her body into
sections and sends them to the tribes of Israel which begins a war
of revenge against these mad men of Gibeah. Gibeah is destroyed.
That is why in Judges 20:5 the man is telling his story to explain
his behavior in sending the sections of his dead wife's body to the
tribes of Israel.

Many times people try to show that Sodom and Gomorrah are
cities of homosexuals by using Judges 19 as a proof text. If there
is any similarity between the Gibeah of the book of Judges and
the Sodom of the book of Genesis it is not homosexuality. Gibeah
had people who worshipped idols. According to 2 Peter 2:6-8, the
city of Sodom also had people who were without worship of the
true and living God. Verse 6 says they were made an example for
those who would live ungodly. *Ungodly* means *without worship*
in the original language.

The Bible gives even more references to Sodom and exposes even
more clearly the real problem there. In Deuteronomy Sodom is
mentioned, but Israel is really being discussed and rebuked for a
descent into idolatry.

Deut. 32:32
32   Their vine comes from the vine of Sodom and from the
fields of Gomorrah. Their grapes are filled with poison, and
their clusters with bitterness.

By the time the Old Testament book of Deuteronomy was written, historically, Sodom was long gone as a city. It was destroyed
in Genesis, and we're now into the exodus period of Israel. So we
know God is not talking about the literal town of Sodom which

has been wiped out for a long time. In Deuteronomy 32, God is not talking about Sodom, but He's talking about Israel and comparing the two. In verse 32 God says their vine is of the vine of Sodom, and of the fields of Gomorrah; their grapes are grapes of gall, their clusters are bitter. Whose vine is the vine of Sodom? Israel's vine is the vine of Sodom. God was saying Israel was from the same vine as Sodom. They are the same plant. They are connected. God was saying to ancient Israel, that they were as if they came from the same stock as Sodom.

Deut. 32:17
They sacrificed to demons, which are not God—gods they had not known, gods that recently appeared, gods your fathers did not fear.
[You can see Sodom was a town being referred to that was pagan in worship, and Israel is being admonished for becoming the same way!]

Israel is under the same condemnation at this point, because they were doing the same thing as Sodom: worshipping idols. It is clear therefore, that when God's Word says the children of Gibeah in Judges 19 are the children of Belial, He was saying they were idolaters, not homosexuals. Idolatry is always condemned in the Bible.

A similar theme is picked up in Ezekiel 16. Here the Word of God is again correcting Israel of antiquity, but in the same breath, comparing it to Sodom. This time the Word not only says by comparison to Israel's folly in idolatry, Sodom was a saint, but also gives a complete rundown of all the sins of Sodom. Homosexuality is clearly missing from the list! If God had ever wanted to say that Sodom was condemned for homosexuality, here is the logical place to include it, but it is conspicuously absent as a problem in Sodom. Peruse the list of the sins of Sodom, and see that homosexuality is not on the list!

Ezek. 16:49-50
49   " '*Now this was the sin of your sister Sodom*: She and her daughters were arrogant, overfed and unconcerned; they

did not help the poor and needy.

50   They were haughty and *did detestable things* before me. Therefore I did away with them as you have seen.

Doing *detestable things* (or *abominations* in the King James Version), listed above, is a word that means to commit idol worship, or idolatry. It is #8441 *tow'ebah* (to-ay-baw') in the Old Testament dictionary of *Strong's Concordance*. The meaning of committing abomination means they were idolaters.

Verse 49 says "*Now this was the sin of your sister Sodom.*" It is obvious the Ezekiel author intends to spell out the sin of Sodom. Here is the list. Nowhere is homosexuality mentioned!

In the New Testament Jesus makes a reference to Sodom in Luke 10:3–12. Verse 12 says that cities not hospitable to God's ambassadors will be more severely judged than Sodom.

The issue for Jesus is that these cities are showing inhospitality to His sent ones, just as Sodom showed inhospitality to God's sent ones, the angels. In Sodom, they were full of bread, and had abundance, yet had a haughty attitude, and would not feed the hungry, show hospitality, or strengthen the hand of the weak. In the day of Sodom travelers needed to stop in the cities for protection. They not only would need to replenish their supplies but come within the walls for safety from robbers, as well as lions, bears, and other wild animals. Showing inhospitality is next to manslaughter in the effects it could have on the one left unprotected and without nutrients and supplies. Jesus felt it would be even worse if cities treated His ambassadors this way than it was when Sodom treated the angels that way. Inhospitality, along with pride, was the main issue. They were apathetic about helping those in need.

God always takes an attitude of benevolence towards the downtrodden. Yet the cities of Sodom and its environs would not help the helpless, though they were able to do it. In the book of Isaiah,[1] God clearly shows He favors those who help people in need.

So God's way is to be helpful and hospitable, not to kill, steal, destroy, ruin. If we won't be hospitable, we're held back from blessings. God's way is to help the oppressed. If we won't help the downtrodden in society or be helpful to the oppressed, we're held back from our potential in God. Where in the Word does it say that Sodom was destroyed for the sin of homosexuality? It is simply not there.

CONCLUSION

That's it! Being gay or lesbian had nothing to do with Sodom's judgment. It had to do with a city in bondage to idolatry, a city that refused to help the oppressed, the orphan, the widow, the poor, hungry or naked.

Sodom was not destroyed for homosexuality. This church-perpetuated tradition has kept talented, God-loving lesbians, gays and others in bondage and off the membership rolls of many churches. Many have been told they could never be acceptable to God unless they changed something they could no more change than their eye color! Yet the myth goes on, damaging more and more lives, and fragmenting the Body of Christ. This travesty and tragedy has done more harm than could ever be calculated.

Jesus came to set people free. Once a gay person comes to Christ, their orientation does not change any more than does a heterosexual's. But in both cases, as the Holy Spirit begins to change the character of the individual through the process of sanctification and the growth of the fruit of the Spirit, the way one expresses their sexuality is done in a more responsible manner. God's love is revealed in all their interpersonal relationships. The thought of gay Christians storming a neighbor's house to kill their houseguest is not even tenable.

The people of Sodom were not gay. They had plenty, were prosperous, and yet were arrogant and inhospitable. In many ways, the inhabitants of Sodom were like much of the Church's treatment of gays today. There are no scriptural grounds in this story for Christian cruelty to gay people. In the upcoming chapters we will look at the other scriptures people use to justify this inhospitality toward the gay neighbor in their midst.

NOTES

[1]Isa. 58:6–8.

LEVITICUS AND THE LAW

The Book of Leviticus was written for the people of Israel to follow. It was the law. Leviticus is not the only place the law is found. Deuteronomy and Exodus also contain portions of the law; but, by and large, most of the Jewish legal codes are listed in Leviticus.

In Leviticus there are two passages that are frequently employed to condemn gay people. These passages are almost identical, and they are found in chapters 18 and 20:

Lev. 18:22
22   Do not lie with a man as one lies with a woman; that is detestable.
Lev. 20:13
13   If a man lies with a man as one lies with a woman, both of them have done what is detestable. They must be put to death; their blood will be on their own heads.

If we were to take this at face value, with no further investigation, we could only come up with one probable conclusion. That would be any time a man had sex with another man the way he would have had with a woman there is only one thing we can do. We must kill him. That's what the Bible seems to say we should do. There are people who take this attitude.

But we have to look at the New Testament concept of the law if we're going to understand the law. 2 Corinthians 3:5-6 gives us insight into how Christians perceive the law. It states that we have been made into administrators of a new covenant, empowered by the Spirit of God. Whereas enforcement of the old covenant meant death, enforcement of the new covenant brings liberty. Keeping the letter of the law kills, but keeping the spirit of the law gives life.

So if we're going to live by the law, and try to get everyone to live by the letter of the law, we find that the letter of the law brings death. But the Spirit gives life. Therefore in order to understand the law you need to understand the spirit in which it is written. We have to ask: what is the intent of the law, and what was God trying to say to the people of God when God gave the law?

In Galatians 3:1-3 is another important concept. These Galatian believers were initially gentiles. First century Christian Judaizers came along and said, "Even though you are Spirit-filled followers of Christ, you really are not a Christian until you also follow the Jewish rituals and the laws of Moses. The apostle Paul addresses that situation when he wrote the following letter to the Galatians.

Gal. 3:1-3

1   You foolish Galatians! Who has bewitched you? Before your very eyes Jesus Christ was clearly portrayed as crucified.

2   I would like to learn just one thing from you: Did you receive the Spirit by observing the law, or by believing what you heard?

3   Are you so foolish? After beginning with the Spirit, are you now trying to attain your goal by human effort?

In other words he is asking, "How did you receive the Holy Spirit? Did you receive Him because you followed all of the rituals and rules, and by having finally obtained the right degree of goodness? Or was it simply by faith you received the Holy Spirit?"

Then having received the Holy Spirit by faith, were they going to be perfected by going back into the ancient traditions of laws and rituals? Or were they going to go on with God being perfected by faith through the Holy Spirit? Paul says in essence that if they want to go back to the law, they are really fools.

In the book of James, we are told a little bit more about the law.

James 2:10

10   For whoever keeps the *whole law* and yet stumbles at just *one point* is guilty of breaking *all of it* [all of the law].

Here it says if a person keeps the whole law—all of it—all of it in Leviticus, all of it in Exodus, and all of it in Deuteronomy, yet misses *one single point*, they are guilty of having broken all of the law in its entirety. So if a person were to condemn a gay man because he had had sex with another man, according to what they believe Leviticus to say, and yet they themselves had not kept all of the law, they are guilty of that same sin in Leviticus. If you keep all of it, yet miss it in one little, tiny item, you are guilty of everything in there. You're guilty of murder, guilty of adultery, guilty of *everything* in the law! So if people demand you live by the law, they themselves must also be living by the law.

The Gospels come along and declare no one ever lived by the law, no one ever could, except Jesus. That is why we all need a Savior. The purpose of the law is to show us our deep need for a Savior!

Humanity has always tried to get into God's grace through their own good works. One religious system after another is built on systems of laws to follow. They are designed for us to think we are good persons on our own. Many people reason, therefore, they don't need God's help, or the cross of Jesus at Calvary. God responded by saying if we think we can earn eternity with God by our behavior, then here are the rules to follow. But we were required to follow all of them or we were disqualified from eternal life. No one could do it. We need help. Romans 3 shows us how desperately we all need a Savior.

Rom. 3:10–23

10 As it is written: *"There is no one righteous, not even one,* . . .

12 All have turned away, they have together become worthless; there is *no one* who does good, *not even one."* [This is by God's standard. Remember, if you miss one point, you are guilty of all!] . . .

19 Now we know that whatever the law says, it says to those who are under the law, so that every mouth may be silenced and the whole world held accountable to God.

20 Therefore *no one will be declared righteous in his sight by observing the law*; rather, through the law we become conscious of sin. . . .

23 *for all have sinned and fall short of the glory of God,*

Based on this word, if someone wants to judge another based on the law, they become accountable to that very same law. We know already that if they have missed anything in the law themselves, then they become guilty of the very thing for which they are judging someone else.

You can't just pull out a verse from Leviticus 18 or Leviticus 20 and say, "Well look right here, God hates homosexuals." To utilize the law properly you have to live by the whole thing. Therefore it behooves us to see what else it might say, and see how well we measure up. Now let's look at the law, and some of the demands people are expected to keep.

Deut. 23:20
20   You may charge a foreigner interest, but not a brother Israelite, so that the LORD your God may bless you in everything you put your hand to in the land you are entering to possess.

If you ever lend money, you cannot charge interest if they are related to you by nationality.

Deut. 24:5
5   If a man has recently married, he must not be sent to war or have any other duty laid on him. For one year he is to be free to stay at home and bring happiness to the wife he has married.

Whenever a person gets married, they can't go to work for a full year. Could you live without that paycheck? How would your creditors like that? How do you think the military would react whenever a soldier marries and says, I have to go home now, I can't work for a year, because I just got married. Do we actually live by this? So to anyone who wants to condemn someone else, ask if they are married. If they are, did they stay home the first year? If not, they not only broke the law, but are guilty of the whole law—all of it.

Lev. 19:14
14   Do not curse the deaf or put a stumbling block in front of the blind, but fear your God. I am the LORD

Even if a deaf person makes you angry, we can't ever say a mean thing to a deaf person. No matter what! If we do, we have broken all the law.

Lev. 19:17

17   Do not hate your brother in your heart.

Don't ever feel hatred toward your siblings, even while growing up, or you are guilty of breaking *all* the law of God.

Lev. 19:19

19   Keep my decrees. Do not mate different kinds of animals. Do not plant your field with two kinds of seed. Do not wear clothing woven of two kinds of material.

Don't ever plant a garden with more than one crop in it. If you plant tomatoes and green peppers in your vegetable garden, you're guilty. Only one kind of seed can go on any one piece of property. If you plant two kinds of grass seed, you're guilty of breaking the whole law!

Don't ever wear a garment of clothing made of a blend of fabrics or you have broken all the law! Check your label. If it is not 100% cotton, or linen, or wool, but is a blend, you are guilty. Or if you have ever worn a blend of fabrics in your lifetime, you are guilty of breaking the law! If you're going to wear polyester, it must be 100% polyester, the whole thing, or your neighbors can throw stones with God's permission!

Lev. 19:27

27   Do not cut the hair at the sides of your head or clip off the edges of your beard.

Don't shave!

Lev. 19:32

32   Rise in the presence of the aged, show respect for the elderly and revere your God. I am the LORD.

Honor *all* elderly folks. If you get a little snippy with an older person, you've broken the law!

Deut. 23:1-2
1   No one who has been emasculated by crushing or cutting may enter the assembly of the LORD.
2   No one born of a forbidden marriage nor any of his descendants may enter the assembly of the LORD, even down to the tenth generation.

No male who has been emasculated or injured in his private area can ever come to church. Who stands at the door and does the checking? If they don't have someone assigned to this task, the whole church is guilty of breaking the law if such a fellow gets in the doors.

No child born out of wedlock can ever come to the house of worship. Nor can any of his children or descendants down to ten generations. Do we know the genealogy of every church member that far back? Is there a skeleton in the church closet up to ten generations ago?

Lev. 20:9-10
9   If anyone curses his father or mother, he must be put to death. He has cursed his father or his mother, and his blood will be on his own head.
10   If a man commits adultery with another man's wife— with the wife of his neighbor—both the adulterer and the adulteress must be put to death.

Anyone who says something nasty to his/her parents: kill them!
Everyone who cheats on their mate must be executed! No exceptions, no mercy!

Yet in the New Testament we see that someone was caught in adultery, in the very act. In John 8:3-7 Jesus's response to the woman caught in adultery was not, "That's right, it's in the law of Moses, stone her!" His response was, "Let the one among you who has never sinned cast the first stone."

Of course there was no one who had never sinned. All were

guilty. We are all guilty. Jesus asked the woman where were her accusers. They had all left. She no longer had accusers. Previously, they thought they could be her judge, but instead, the sins of the accusers were judged. Jesus then told her, go now and sin no more. Quite a bit different than the death penalty.

Deut. 22:5
5   A woman must not wear men's clothing, nor a man wear women's clothing, for the LORD your God detests [the *King James Version* calls this an *abomination*] anyone who does this.

If a woman is married, and the doorbell rings, and she grabs her husband's flannel shirt to go answer the door, she's guilty under the law! Likewise, if a barefoot husband grabs his wife's high heels to go answer the door, he's guilty also! If either one wears the clothing of the opposite sex, under any circumstances, they are guilty under the law and here, a detestable *abomination*! We'll look at that word later.

The only dress code seemingly mentioned in the New Testament has more to do with hats for church members, or the lack thereof. The apostle Paul told the Corinthians in 1 Cor. 11:4-6 that they should not bring dishonor to their community of faith by their standard of dress. His point was that their local society's customary standards of dress should not be ignored when doing so implied a lack of morals on their part. This could bring disgrace on the entire Christian witness in Corinth.

Ministers were mentioned under the law also.

Lev. 21:17-21 states that no minister who has a defect may come near to present the offerings made to the LORD. No man who has any defect may come near: no man who is blind or lame, disfigured or deformed, no man with a crippled foot or hand, or who is hunchbacked or dwarfed, or who has any eye defect, or who has festering or running sores or damaged testicles.

The priest was not allowed to minister if he had *any* blemish! A pimple, a wart, an age spot, *anything* superficial. Who checks out the minister before the Sunday morning service to make sure he is a perfect being, with nothing superfluous? No flat nosed ministers allowed in church! Flat nosed ministers need not apply. Nor ones who wear glasses, because they have an eye defect. If a minister breaks a hand or a foot, slips on ice and breaks an ankle, it is time to retire, or at least take a leave of absence. If he has damaged testicles, that's too bad, he can't be a minister under the law! Someone needs to be assigned, as the minister robes up, to make sure there are no pimples, warts, blemishes of any kind, then break the news, "I'm sorry but you'll have to sit it out another week or more, pastor."

Leviticus 15:19-20, 28-30 declares a host of rules about a woman's monthly menstrual flow. She becomes unclean and untouchable for seven days, and then she has to bring in a guilt offering.

Eight days after her period stops she has to sacrifice a couple of birds to be free from her guilt of having been unclean. This becomes a monthly event.

It is obvious no one is free from the condemnation under the law! No one is guilt free!

So I find it a curiosity that people will single out one passage and say: "Here's the sin that God hates." Well what about all these other things? James says if you miss one thing, you've missed all of it. You are guilty of all of it if you're guilty of any one thing. Therefore you're guilty of being a minister with a scab, as well as everything else, even if you've never been a minister. You're guilty of having charged interest to your relatives. You're guilty of having married someone and not stayed home for a year, even if you're single, because you've broken the whole law, if even one detail was missed. That's how the law is set up.

Men Lying with Men

Now we can look at Leviticus 18:22.

> *Lev. 18:22*
> 22 Do not lie with a man as one lies with a woman; that is *detestable*. [*King James Version* says it's an *abomination*.]

Also, looking at Leviticus 20:13 which says:

> *Lev. 20:13*
> 13 If a man lies with a man as one lies with a woman, both of them have done what is *detestable*. They must be put to death; their blood will be on their own heads.

What did the word translated as *detestable* or *abomination* mean in ancient Hebrew? Many people might assume the word means what the English implies. But the Bible was not written originally in English, so we need to know what the word meant in Hebrew:

> #8441 *tow'ebah* (to-ay-baw'). *Tow'ebah* has a primary meaning of an association with idolatry, or concretely of an idol itself; according to *Strong's*: *especially idolatry* or (concretely) an idol.

It means things which belong to the worship of idols, or the idol itself.

When we look at either of these Leviticus passages, it says these men have committed an abomination. What it literally says is they have committed idolatry. Now why does it say they have committed idolatry? You might think it would say they have committed a lustful act, or perhaps an unlawful act. But instead it says they have committed idolatry. Both these chapters [Leviticus 18 and 20] go on to say for Israel not to defile themselves in any of the things listed in those chapters. It was in these behaviors listed that the nations around them defiled themselves.

Lev. 18:24-27

24   Do not defile yourselves in any of these ways, because this is how the nations that I am going to drive out before you *became defiled.* . . .

26   But you must keep my decrees and my laws. The native-born and the aliens living among you must not do any of these detestable [idolatrous] things,

27   for all these things [idolatries] were done by the people who lived in the land before you, and the land became defiled.

Lev. 20:23

23   You must not live according to the customs of the nations I am going to drive out before you. Because *they did all these things*, I abhorred them.

In other words, God's covenant, and God's law, are dealing with God's covenant people. These covenant people are supposed to be the people who walk with Yahweh, with God Almighty. They are not supposed to do the things that the idolatrous heathen nations had been doing.

It's idolatry because their religious practices of worship involved fertility cults.

As part of their worship of fertility gods and goddesses, they believed that the high priests/priestesses of their religion could ensure the fertility of their ground, crops, cattle, livestock, their spouse and children. The worship act involved a sexual encounter in the temple with the priest or priestess as an offering to that deity. The priest was a representative of that deity. Sex with the priest, it was believed, was passed on to the deity, which insured the fertility of crops, livestock and house. Since this was an agricultural society, having your ground, crops and livestock fertile was very important. This was a part of their religious ceremony. The Old Testament authors said, on the contrary: if you do these things, you are doing the same idolatrous things the non-covenant heathen did. Don't do them because it is idolatry. In other words, it is a part of their worship.

Many contemporary scholars dismiss Leviticus from any discussion of homosexuality for several reasons. In its context it is clear that the law is dealing with idolatrous forms of worship, and God was calling out a people to be separated unto Him. Leviticus was really spelling out a legal and holiness code for a newly formed covenant people. The people of Israel stated again and again they would follow this code but found it was impossible to do so. They fell short even in the wilderness on their way to the Promised Land. All of Israel was under condemnation and lost a battle they should have won when one man, Achan, brought trouble on the whole nation by disobeying the law. Many kings of Judah reinstituted revival of the law, and the people all agreed again to live under it. They still could not do it, however, and found that they were carried away into captivity to Babylon. Even in Ezra's day all the people again agreed to live under the law, and were unable to keep that commitment.

The point of the law was to show each person their need for God and God's mercy in their life. No one could claim personal holiness by following the rules because everyone broke them. There was none righteous, no not one.

These are some things we know. There are other things probably indicated in these passages, besides idol worship, that are not as obvious when you read the passages in English. But they raise further questions in Hebrew.

Leviticus 20:13, when looked at word by word in Hebrew, using *Strong's Concordance*, appears to unfold an even more complex meaning than simply condemning male to male impersonal sexual anal intercourse as part of an act of idolatrous worship.

Lev. 20:13
If a *man* [#376] also *lie* [#7901] with *mankind* [#2145], as he *lieth* [#4904] with a *woman* [#802], both of them have committed *an abomination* [#8441] [idolatry]: they shall surely be put to death; their blood shall be upon them (KJV)

If this passage were trying to make a case about homosexual behavior in general, it would have talked about a man with a man, or a woman with a woman. If it was talking about a man with a man, or a woman with a woman, the *same numbers* in *Strong's*

Concordance would have been used to talk equally about the same sex partners; a *man* with a *man*. But looking at the actual numbering in *Strong's Concordance*, we see that is not the case. For the Leviticus author to say a man should not lie with a man, just in general, both men listed would be #376, *man*, in the Old Testament.

Instead it says a *man* [#376] who lies with a *mankind* [#2145] as one would lie with a woman [#802] has committed idolatry, [#8441] *tow'ebah* (to-ay-baw').

What's the point? To make a case against homosexuality, the *Strong's* numbers would have read if a man [#376] lies with a man [#376] as one lies with a woman [#802] then it would be something other than #8441, idolatry; maybe perhaps, it is wrong.

The word for *woman* [#802] is an identically comparable word to [#376], *man*. It is the feminine, irregular plural version of the same word. The word [#376] is the word *'iysh* (eesh); which merely means: a man as an individual or a male person. It means just a man in general; a mortal, a male human being.

The word [#802] means an identical thing in a feminine context. It is the word [#802] *'ishshah* (ish-shaw'); feminine of #376 or #582; irregular plural, *nashiym* (naw-sheem'); a woman: each, every, female. It means each and every woman, any woman. It does not specify who she is or anything about her. It is the same word that can be translated for a harlot. Sexually, she is just a generic female, according to this Hebrew word. Any woman will do. We're not going to get to know her, only take up a few moments of her time, then move on to the next [#802] female mortal.

The male version of the word is identical. He is just a [#376], a man.

Scripture could easily have said if a man [#376], any man, lie with any other man whatsoever [#376], whoever he is doesn't matter, the way he lies with any woman whatsoever; but it doesn't say that. Because the second word for male is not [#376], but [#2145]!

2145 *zakar* (zaw-kawr'); remembered, i.e. a male (of man or animals, as being the most noteworthy sex): its root word #2142 zakar (zaw-kar') means: to mark (so as to be recognized), i.e. to remember; by implication, to mention; also to be male: (make) mention (of), be mindful, recount, record, remember, make to be remembered, bring (call, come, keep, put) to (in) remembrance, think on.

The word #2145 in *Strong's Concordance*, *zakar*, in Hebrew, is a very specific word. It is not the generic word for man, meaning any man. But this word means *to be remembered*. This is someone special, and you need to remember who he is! Its root word is translated as a remembrance. God remembers us, or God remembers our situation and shows His mercy. God remembered Abraham, etc. Many times it is translated as a remembrance because it is an important thing. In other words you're not to lie with this person (to be remembered), somebody very important, the way that you would lie with a common harlot or prostitute. There is a difference in the way one could lie with a prostitute, and the way someone would lie with someone very important, and you better remember who they are.

Someone important, like a president or a king of a nation, would not be treated the way you would lie with [#802] *any woman*, a common harlot, or anyone you do not need to know anything about. You cannot treat this high ranking official this way because it is *idolatry*, [#8441] *tow'ebah* (to-ay-baw').

In these well documented sexual idolatrous worship encounters, you don't care who the priest is personally, or what their name is. All you care about is that your fertility is guaranteed for whatever you're wanting to be fertile (crops, family, livestock). All that matters is that the religious ritual is satisfied, to please the fertility god(s/dess/es). You don't need to know the name of the priest/priestess, you don't care who their family is, you don't need their phone number so you can call them up again sometime. This sexual encounter is not to build a loving relationship between the people involved. It is a religious business transaction.

All the things condemned in Leviticus 18 and 20 were what the idolatrous nations were doing. They did treat *zakar, to be remembered* as if he were a common prostitute, and did it in the name of idolatrous religion.

In 1 Samuel 31:1–13, Saul was king of Israel, and he lost the battle with the idolatrous Philistines.

Saul was injured and he knew in a matter of time the Philistine army would find him. Saul opted for suicide, rather than let the Philistines find him still alive. Saul asked his armorbearer to kill him, "lest these uncircumcised Philistines come and . . . abuse me." The word *abuse* [*Strong's* Old Testament #5953] is the same word used in Judges 19:25 when the men of Gibeah abuse and rape and torture the visitor's wife all night.

In abusing a defeated king this way, it humiliated the king and the defeated nation. It also was a declaration that the triumphant nation had a god more powerful than the defeated nation's god. It was a common practice well known to Saul, and he would rather die than suffer through it. Leviticus says not to treat *zakar* that way, because it is the way the heathen nations around Israel behave, and Israel was to be different. They were to be a separated nation unto God. Their laws and statutes, if followed, would make them merciful, as God is merciful.

1 Sam. 31:6–10
6   So Saul and his three sons and his armor-bearer and all his men died together that same day. . . .
8   The next day, when the Philistines came to strip the dead, they found Saul and his three sons fallen on Mount Gilboa.
9   They cut off his head and stripped off his armor, and they sent messengers throughout the land of the Philistines to proclaim the news in the temple of their idols and among their people.
10   They put his armor in the temple of the Ashtoreths and fastened his body to the wall of Beth Shan.

The Philistines had no intention of taking someone *to be remembered* and treating him with any dignity, they had no intention of burying his headless corpse. They even took his head and went from temple to temple in town after town to show their god what they were bringing as a sacrifice.

These were fertility gods, and sex and temple prostitution was part of their worship. King Saul knew that, and he pleaded with his armorbearer to please kill him before the Philistines had a chance to abuse him. Since the armorbearer could not kill the wounded king, Saul opted for suicide rather than rape at the hands of this idol worshipping nation.

If we look at the passage in chapter 18 of Leviticus that deals with a man lying with *zakar*, we see something else when placed in its context with the verse before it.

Lev. 18:21-22
21   Do not give any of your children to be sacrificed to Molech, for you must not profane the name of your God. I am the LORD.
22   Do not lie with a man as one lies with a woman; that is detestable.

Look at Leviticus 18:21, in the King James Version:

Lev. 18:21
21   And thou shalt not let any of thy seed pass through the fire to Molech, neither shalt thou profane the name of thy God: I am the LORD. (KJV)

This says in essence:
And you shall not let any of your seed [or semen] pass through the fire to Molech [Molech is a god, small "g," an idol], neither shall you profane the name of your God: I am the LORD.

Although the worshippers of Molech sometimes passed their seed through the fire by sacrificing their children as burnt offerings, they also had cultic sexual liaisons with the fertility god's priest/priestess, thus passing on their seed in this manner also.

Therefore the statement here, "the semen should not pass on to Molech" can also mean that you should not have sex with the priest/priestess of Molech, as part of the idol worship ceremony. The thinking was that when having sex with the priest/priestess of the fertility god, the semen passed right on through the priest to the god itself.

Therefore you shall not let any of your seed pass on to Molech. Neither shall you profane the name of your God. I am the Lord . . . you shall not lie with mankind [*zakar*] as with womankind;

it is *abomination, idolatry* [#8441] *tow'ebah* (to-ay-baw'). Right after telling His people not to pass their seed on to Molech, God says don't have these cultic sexual worship experiences because it is idolatry. It is all wrapped up in idolatry.

CONCLUSION

We have looked at all the verses that are used to condemn gay people in Leviticus, out of the law. There are only two, and they say essentially the same thing. They are both talking about *zakar*.

God says that is abomination. That is idolatry.

But clearly, the situation described in Leviticus 20:13, is not talking about two gay men who have fallen in love and have set up a home and are having a love relationship with mutual respect for one another. The Levitical situation in modern times is more similar to prison rape, in which case one proves superiority over the other. It is idolatry. My god (strength, prowess, virility) is greater than your god. I have power over you, and your feelings don't count. It doesn't matter who you are or even what your name is. I win. It is power. It builds and feeds my god of self and ego.

Nonetheless, for Christians, the Old Testament law is not the code we live by. We are not saved by deeds. We are saved by grace. For it is by grace we have been saved through faith, and that is a gift of God. No matter what laws we look at in Leviticus, no one has ever been able to keep them all. Everyone falls short of perfection somewhere.

We know from the New Testament that in God's eyes everyone needs to be treated with respect, as *zakar*. Everyone ought to be remembered because they are important in their own right, and in God's eyes. No one should be treated as a mere sex conquest, someone whose name doesn't matter. Their name does matter. Sex for sex's sake, taking selfish advantage of someone, whether to insure the fertility of one's crops, to give an offering to a false god, or just for hedonistic pleasure could all fall in the same category of idolatry. In the latter case, we set our self up as the god whose appetites must be satisfied, treating someone important in God's eyes as a sexual business encounter. We are all fearfully and wonderfully made, the Psalmist tells us. When the scripture says we should not lie with *zakar* as if *zakar* were just a generic human, it calls us to responsibility. It calls us to being responsible to know the person because they matter. It does not allow us to cheapen the encounter just because the big I, the big god of self, demands a sexual offering. It does not allow us to get away with a slam bam affair just because all the other heathen nations around us are doing it that way.

Lev. 20:23-26

23   You must not live according to the customs of the nations I am going to drive out before you. Because they did all these things, I abhorred them.

24   . . . I am the LORD your God, who has set you apart from the nations . . .

26   You are to be holy to me because I, the LORD, am holy, and I have set you apart from the nations to be my own.

Just because everyone else is doing it doesn't make it right. God calls His people to a higher standard than merely living like the worst of this world, or even after our lower baser nature. God calls us to responsible living with one another, in love.

Leviticus is a mirror. It was written as a legal code for the ancient nation of Israel. But it was also written to show all of us that if we were going to get into God's grace by being especially good, we will all fall short somewhere. No one has ever been able to keep all the law. If one part was not kept, it was all broken. God's answer was always to show us our need for His solution, a Savior. Through that Savior we would be restored to our original purpose. It was not that we would all be heterosexuals, but that we would all come into relationship with God through Jesus Christ the Lord.

QADESH REVEALED

There is a Hebrew word used in the Old Testament that we would never even look at in a discussion of homosexuality, except that one translation, and one alone, unfortunately mistranslates the word as sodomite. The word in Hebrew is *Strong's* #6945 in the Old Testament:

> #6945 *qadesh* (kaw-dashe′); from #6942; a (quasi) sacred person, i.e. (technically) a (male) devotee (by prostitution) to licentious idolatry, sodomite.

The King James Version appeared in 1611, and when they translated this word as sodomite, it had ramifications for centuries to come in the legal codes of English speaking nations.

Many newer translations point out the much more specific and technical meaning of this word *qadesh*. It is in reality a male cult temple prostitute. In other words this person is a high priest of a cultic god's temple. Part of the religious ceremony in a fertility cult involved sexual acts to ensure the fertility of crops, livestock and family. Sex was engaged in with the priest/priestess representing the particular idolatrous deity.

It is interesting that the word in question translated as sodomite in the King James Version, is the masculine version of the concept. There is a feminine word that corresponds to the masculine *qadesh*. The feminine word is the word #6948 in *Strong's Concordance*,

> #6948 *qedeshah* (ked-ay-shaw′); feminine of #6945; a female devotee (i.e. prostitute).

That is *Strong's* definition. However, in the Lexical Aids to the Old Testament provided at the end of the *Hebrew-Greek Key Study Bible*,[1] Bible and language scholar Spiro Zodhiates, Th.D., defines #6948 *qedeshah* (ked-ay-shaw′); as follows:

> . . . This is the feminine form of the Hebrew #6945 . . . it

means harlot, whore, sacred temple prostitute. Prostitution received official sanction from the Canaanite religion which made reproduction part of its summum bonum. As in India today, at the Holi festival, there were seasons of sexual orgy associated with Astarte. The temple precincts became an inglorious brothel. . . .[2]

Zodhiates also says of the masculine word *qadesh*:

. . . this Hebrew adjective derives from #6942. It means a consecrated one, a devoted one, a sacred person; a devotee to a licentious idolatry, a cultic prostitute or priest of Astarte . . .[3]

The following Old Testament passage in question uses both the masculine and feminine words for the concept of qadesh/qedeshah in this one passage. Compare how the King James translates the words, as well as the more modern NIV.

Deut. 23:17

17   There shall be no *whore* [#6948] of the daughters of Israel, nor a *sodomite* [#6945] of the sons of Israel. (KJV)

Deut. 23:17

17   No Israelite *man or woman* is to become a *shrine prostitute*.

Both the masculine and feminine words were used in this passage. According to the King James Version, it would imply a female Israelite merely was not to be a prostitute. But as the NIV translation points out, the issue is far deeper than that. Neither male nor female Israelites, covenant people of God, were to become temple prostitutes to these false Canaanite gods. No Israelite was to take part in an idolatrous worship orgy, much less to become the priest or priestess of these false fertility gods! They were to be holy and set apart for God alone.

All the following Old Testament passages use this one word *qadesh*. I show the King James Version where it translates the word as *sodomite*, then a more correct rendering in a modern English translation.

1 Kings 14:24
24   And there were also *sodomites* in the land: and they did
according to all the abominations of the nations which the
LORD cast out before the children of Israel. (KJV)
1 Kings 14:24
24   There were even *male shrine prostitutes* in the land; the
people engaged in all the detestable practices of the nations
the LORD had driven out before the Israelites.

1 Kings 15:12
12   And he took away the *sodomites* out of the land, and
removed all the idols that his fathers had made. (KJV)
1 Kings 15:12
12   He expelled the *male shrine prostitutes* from the land
and got rid of all the idols his fathers had made.

1 Kings 22:46
46   And the remnant of the *sodomites*, which remained in
the days of his father Asa, he took out of the land. (KJV)
1 Kings 22:46
46   He rid the land of the rest of the *male shrine prostitutes*
who remained there even after the reign of his father Asa.

2 Kings 23:7
7   And he brake down the houses of the *sodomites*, that
were by the house of the LORD, where the women wove hang-
ings for the grove. (KJV)
2 Kings 23:7
7   He also tore down the quarters of the *male shrine
prostitutes*, which were in the temple of the LORD and where
women did weaving for Asherah.

Job 36:14
14   They die in youth, and their life is among the *unclean*.
(KJV)
Job 36:14
14   They die in their youth, among *male prostitutes of the
shrines*.

The false religious systems and culture of the nations around Israel had fertility as its focus; therefore, sexual rituals were seen as a way to insure this fertility of their crops and cattle, etc. The utilization of this cultic shrine prostitute was part of an act of worship of these local deities. Other practices of these religions included the murder of one's children as burnt sacrifices.

The sacred instruction, therefore, was clear that the people of Israel were to have no male or female cultic shrine prostitutes. The concept in Hebrew is clearly translated in modern translations as a practice of forbidden idolatry.

If the word in question were really trying to say *sodomite*, meaning someone from Sodom, then in light of Biblical references such as Ezekiel 16:49, they would have to say there shall be no inhospitable person among Israel, since the sins of Sodom boiled down to inhospitality, pride, arrogance, abundance with a life of ease, and yet not helping the less fortunate. If sodomites were the issue, then they'd translate these passages to say there shall be no inhospitable person allowed to live in Israel. But that was not the question with this word. The issue is idolatry.

In spite of the fact that we see in the law, the book of Deuteronomy, for instance, that the ancient Israelites were told not to set up temples to these gods or worship them, what do you think they did? They set them up anyway. In fact King Solomon set up many of those shrines in Israel to appease his 700 wives and 300 concubines.[4]

These shrines were set up even within the Temple of God itself. They remained in Israel for hundreds of years until King Josiah of Judah brought reform and tore them down.[5] Between Solomon and Josiah, there were only a few good kings who sought even partial reform.

The very thing God commanded the people of Israel not to do, they did anyway, and it drew them from worshipping God to worshipping idols and false gods. This was serious, and it caused the nations of Israel and Judah to be defeated and carried into captivity. They set up these idolatrous altars on every high hill. Occasionally a good king would drive out the cultic priests and priestesses, but the false religions would flourish again after only a short time. Kings Asa, Jehoshaphat, Hezekiah, and Josiah removed the false religions from the land, at least partially, and removed the cult shrine prostitutes. They brought reform to the nation, for a time. It is clear the idolatry they stopped was the idol worship utilizing the adoption of fertility cults.

CONCLUSION

We only find the word #6945 *qadesh* used in the previously listed six passages, and never is it referring to gay people, the gay community, or gay couples. So if the King James Version had not translated this word as sodomite, implying in the English language a certain form of sexual expression, we would never have had to address any of these passages at all. They are not dealing with homosexuality.

NOTES

[1]Spiro Zodhiates, comp. and ed., *The Hebrew-Greek Key Study Bible* (Chattanooga, TN: AMG Publishers, 1984).
[2]Ibid., 1633.
[3]Ibid.
[4]1 Kings 11:1–10.
[5]2 Kings 23:7, 13–25.

NEW TESTAMENT PASSAGES USED
TO CLOBBER GAY PEOPLE:
A FRESH LOOK

1 CORINTHIANS / 1 TIMOTHY

Although I have already referred to a number of verses in the New Testament that I thought would be helpful in our discussions surrounding Sodom and Leviticus, it is now time to focus exclusively on the New Testament itself as a source for misinterpretation. Depending upon the Bible translation one is reading, there are two passages in the New Testament that are frequently cited against homosexuality. It is interesting to note that both of these passages use the same two words in Greek that are sometimes translated as the word *homosexual*. These passages are found in 1 Corinthians 6:9 and 1 Timothy 1:10.

In the King James Version they read as follows:

1 Cor. 6:9–10
9   Know ye not that the unrighteous shall not inherit the kingdom of God? Be not deceived: neither fornicators, nor idolaters, nor adulterers, nor effeminate, nor abusers of themselves with mankind,
10   Nor thieves, nor covetous, nor drunkards, nor revilers, nor extortioners, shall inherit the kingdom of God. (KJV)

1 Tim. 1:9–10
9   Knowing this, that the law is not made for a righteous man, but for the lawless and disobedient, for the ungodly and for sinners, for unholy and profane, for murderers of fathers and murderers of mothers, for manslayers,
10   For whoremongers, for them that defile themselves with mankind, for menstealers, for liars, for perjured persons, and if there be any other thing that is contrary to sound doctrine; (KJV)

In these passages, there are two words used that come into question. Some translations combine the words into one word as if they were one concept. Other translations give a plethora of options in their choice of translating these two words into English. Since this is the New Testament, the words are originally written in Greek, and the corresponding numbers for them in the *Strong's Concordance* are:

#3120 *malakos* (mal-ak-os'); of *uncertain affinity*; *soft*, i.e. fine (clothing); and
#733 *arsenokoites* (ar-sen-ok-oy'-tace); from #730 and #2845.

When researching these Greek New Testament words, it becomes apparent they are rarely used at all in the Bible.

The word *malakos* [#3120] literally means *soft*.

The other word, *arsenokoites* [#733], is a word Paul made up. The first time this word is used in ancient Greek literature is in 1 Corinthians. Paul's word *arsenokoites*, is a compound word like Reaganomics or lady-killer as pointed out by Daniel Helminiak.[1] This compound word created by Paul is one he expects his readers to understand. But other than these two cited texts, this word is not used anywhere else in the Bible. The two words Paul compounded together were the words #730 which means *lifting*, and the word #2845 which means *couch*. Therefore the literal meaning of these two words is: *lift couch: arsenokoites*. The word *arsenokoites* is not seen in literature for another four hundred years.

Today if we said God is "awful," people would think you were angry with God and you better watch what you say. Yet four hundred years ago the word awful meant awe inspiring, full of awe. In four hundred years the word has had a complete reversal of meaning, from something good to something bad.

Paul assumed his hearers would understand the word he was coining. But today, there is great debate about the meaning of *lift couch* (*arsenokoites*). English Bibles today translate this word in a myriad of ways. We will look at some of these conflicting translations.

We will break down 1 Corinthians 6:9, using the *Strong's* numbers, to note the location of these words.

1 Cor. 6:9

9   Know ye not that the unrighteous shall not inherit the kingdom of God? Be not deceived: neither fornicators, nor idolaters, nor *adulterers*, nor *effeminate*,[2] nor *abusers of themselves with mankind*[3] . . .

Notice that the words in question, *malakos* [#3120] and *arsenokoites* [#733], are together in sequence and follow the word *adulterers*. That is important to notice because in some translations you will never recognize the words unless you know they are whatever follows *adulterers*. Many times the translation will combine both words into one word as if they convey the same concept. In such a case I list it under the first word since only one is given. Also, if the translators change their definition/translation of a word between 1 Corinthians 6:9 and the same word #733 *arsenokoites* in 1 Timothy 1:10, the difference is noted.

Many pastors, Christian writers, and church leaders (those who follow what they believe to be a literal interpretation of Scripture) conclude that the words *soft* and *lift couch* (which literally follow the word *adulterers*) condemn all homosexuals under all conditions and that under no circumstances can a gay person ever get into Heaven. They state that as long as a person is a homosexual they can never be Christian. They make that assumption from stating that neither the *effeminate*, nor the *abusers of themselves with mankind*, etc., shall inherit the kingdom of God.

As we list and study the various English translations, we will see that the translators rarely agree among themselves on what these two words mean. Often they ignore the one word, *malakos* as if it were not there, and even within the same translation, the word *arsenokoites* is not translated as the same thing consistently. It seems to mean one thing in 1 Corinthians, and another in 1 Timothy. One thing is clear, though. In ancient Greek, there was no noun to express homosexuality. If the ancient world wanted to talk about homosexuality, they would have used verbs expressing specific sexual activity. Therefore any time one of these words is translated as homosexual, it is a mis-translation since the word *homosexual* did not even exist until the nineteenth century. Let's look at several of the translations we have in English. They are

ENGLISH TRANSLATION	#3120 MALAKOS	#733 ARSENOKOITES
King James Version	Effeminate	Abusers of themselves with mankind
		1 Tim. 1:10: Them that defile themselves with mankind
NIV	Male prostitutes	Homosexual offenders 1 Tim. 1:10: Perverts
Living Bible	Homosexuals	
Interlinear Bible	Abusers	Homosexuals
Revised	Sexual perverts	1 Tim. 1:10: Sodomites
J.B. Phillips	Effeminate	Pervert
		1 Tim. 1:10: Sexually uncontrolled or perverts
Amplified	Those who participate in homosexuality	1 Tim. 1:10: Those who abuse themselves with men
New English Bible	Homosexual perversion	1 Tim. 1:10: Perverts
New King James	Homosexuals [explained as *catamites* in footnotes]	Sodomites [explained as *male homosexuals* in footnotes]
New American Standard Bible	Effeminate	Homosexuals
Barclay	Sensualists	Homosexuals
Good News	Homosexual perverts	1 Tim. 1:10: Sexual perverts
St. Joseph New Catholic Edition	Effeminate	Sodomites

conveniently placed in a table to identify how the two Greek words are translated.

Remember in each case we're looking at the two words that follow *adulterers* in 1 Corinthians 6:9.

The King James Version translates the word #3120 *malakos, soft* as *effeminate*. The NIV translates this same word as a *male prostitute*. Those are totally different concepts. For the word #733 *arsenokoites, lift couch*, the King James Version calls them *abusers of themselves with mankind*. The NIV calls them *homosexual offenders*. These are also different concepts. If I said a person was an abuser of themselves with mankind, that might imply that they somehow abuse their bodies with men. That could be a male or a female person. Abuse is the issue. If I say the same person is a homosexual offender, I could mean they are a gay person who got a traffic violation. A homosexual offender is a person who breaks the law, and also happens to be gay. That may not be what the NIV had in mind but nonetheless the definition still applies.

The Living Bible says *adulterers*, and then it says *homosexuals*. It only gives one word, so it combines *malakos* and *arsenokoites* into one word, the word *homosexuals*. As far as they are concerned, both words, both individuals being spoken about, are homosexuals.

The Interlinear Bible translates *malakos*, the word *soft* as *abusers*. You would not think that the person called *soft* would be the person who would be an abuser. Usually an abuser is someone who is hardened and rough and abuses others verbally or physically. Someone who has been abused would not think their abuser was soft, or milquetoast, or a pushover. Then they take the word *arsenokoites* and translate it *homosexuals*. Those are two different groups of people: *abusers* and *homosexuals*.

They do not even specify what these abusers abuse. Are they wife beaters? Are they drug abusers? Do they belong to over-eaters anonymous because they are abusers of food? What do they abuse? All this from the word *soft*.

Then we have the Revised Version. They put the two words together after adulterers and call them *sexual perverts*. Sexual perverts brings up a completely different concept. If I said to you that a person is a sexual pervert, what would you think I meant? A sexual pervert often refers to someone who perhaps molests little girls. That would usually be a heterosexual male, since statistically by far they have the greatest numbers of child molestation cases in the courts. Homosexuality is not a perversion per se, since it occurs naturally among not only humans but in the animal kingdom as well. Dogs, mice, ducks, and countless other species have seen homosexuality occur randomly among them. So, though it is not the majority, it is a variation among the norm. Child abuse is not a norm, whether it is sexual or otherwise. Serial rapists would also be among the sexual perverts. These again in the majority of cases would be heterosexual men.

The J.B. Phillips translation translates *malakos*, *soft*, as *effeminate*, and the word *arsenokoites*, lift couch as *pervert*. The word pervert brings up a totally different concept again. If I were to ask a police officer to show me the records of all the perverts they have on file, they probably would have lots of individuals to bring up, but they would not necessarily be homosexuals. What is a pervert? What would be the definition among different groups of people in different cultures throughout the centuries?

Some people might consider the cultures of their neighboring nations as perverted. For instance ancient Israel's neighbors worshipped Molech, and sacrificed their children as burnt offerings in fire. In the days when the ancient nation Israel was walking in obedience to God, like under King David or Hezekiah, the practice of worshipping Molech and burning their children certainly seemed perverted.

The word *soft*, *malakos*, being translated *effeminate*, makes you wonder what are the translators trying to convey? Do they mean that if a man is just a little effeminate that he can never get into Heaven under any conditions? There are many happily married heterosexual men who are a little bit effeminate. They might be the househusband and a nurturing caretaker of their children. They might just walk in an "unmanly" way, whatever that is. Maybe they don't like football, sports, or fixing cars, but do like to take care of the house and are generally more sensitive, nurturing, and considerate. What is implied in translating this word as *effeminate*, is that every effeminate man, no matter to what degree, is going to hell! As Christians mature, they become more gentle and meek. Paul said when he was weak, then he was strong. Does that make Paul effeminate? If so he never could get to Heaven according to this mistranslation.

The word *effeminate* does not imply any sexual behavior whatsoever! Neither does it mean a homosexual! Furthermore, the Bible is not implying that an effeminate person is going to hell! Even modern Bible translations cannot agree on what these ancient words meant. Preachers walk on thin ice if condemning homosexuals based on these two scriptural passages.

The Amplified Bible lumps the two words together and says *those who participate in homosexuality*. There is a world of difference between people who participate in homosexuality, meaning to have same gender sexual activity, and those who are homosexual. Someone can be a homosexual and never have a sexual experience. Likewise, a predominantly heterosexually oriented person could end up in a homosexual or homogenital sexual encounter. It is a common event among heterosexual men in prison. Being a homosexual is not talking about sexual activity. It is talking about whom they are attracted to, likely to fall in love with, and want to spend their life with. A person's sexual orientation defines which gender they gravitate towards. For some that is exclusively someone of the opposite sex. For others that is never the case. When the Amplified says *those who participate in homosexuality*, it does not have to refer to a gay person at all.

The New English Bible lumps *malakos* and *arsenokoites* together and says those who are guilty of *homosexual perversion* will not inherit God's kingdom. My question is, what is *homosexual* perversion? It would imply that a homosexual who is not a pervert is okay. But one who is a pervert is condemned in this passage. Who is that person? Would it be perverted for a homosexual to act like a heterosexual, since that perverts their innate nature?

The New King James Version does something different. They translate the first word following adulterers, *malakos, soft*, as the word *homosexuals*, and the second word, *arsenokoites, lift couch* as *sodomite*. In the footnotes of the New King James Version, *Spirit-Filled Life Bible*[4] the footnote for the word translated *homosexual* helps explain how *malakos, soft* became *homosexual* by defining it as *catamite; those submitting to homosexuals*. I wonder if that footnote was for clarification or confusion. This definition in their footnote now changes the word *homosexual* to a *catamite*, or as they say, *one who submits to a homosexual*. Again there is a big difference between a homosexual and someone who submits to one. Children when molested by a relative may submit out of fear and intimidation by the adult, but that does not mean they were willing participants. People can submit without giving consent. The latter person identified as a catamite, is not identified any longer by sexual orientation. There is no longer a clue as to whether they are heterosexual, gay or something else.

Then the word *sodomite* is explained in their footnote as *male homosexuals*. The biblical book of Ezekial explained Sodomites as people who were inhospitable[5] and arrogant. In fact, the people of God are referred to as the rulers of Sodom in Isaiah 1:10. Then the instruction God gives for them to redeem themselves is found in verses 15-20. In the midst of that passage, in Isaiah 1:17, they are told to relieve the oppressed.

The New American Standard Bible translates the first word in 1 Cor. 6:9 following *adulterers*, the word *malakos, soft*, as *effeminate*; and they translate the second word, *arsenokoites, lift couch*, as *homosexuals*. This of course is *homosexuals*, unqualified. Any homosexual is referred to, whether or not they have ever participated in homogenital activity of any kind or not. It does not differentiate between a monogamous loving relationship and stable loving home life, or a series of one night stands, serial weekend affairs, or half hour incognito escapades in the dark. Yet a true homosexual is not a verb, a description of sexual activity, but a noun—a person. It is a person who lives their life out as does any other human being, but realizes they are attracted to someone of the same sex, rather than, or more than, the opposite sex. A bisexual is a person who is attracted to both men and women. This noun does not mean any of these attractions are acted upon.

In ancient Greek, the concept of homosexuality was unknown as a noun but was expressed as a verb. It is expressed as a behavior, as certain specific sexual activities, rather than as a specific kind of person. So to state that *lift couch* is a homosexually oriented person, with no more description than that, is a gross injustice.

In the Barclay translation *malakos* is translated *sensualists* and *arsenokoites* is translated *homosexuals*.

The Good News Bible combines both words in 1 Cor. 6:9 to call them *homosexual perverts*, then changes their mind about the word *arsenokoites* in 1 Timothy 1:10 and calls them *sexual perverts*.

Homosexual perverts are not the same as *sexual perverts* [Good News]. *Those who participate in homosexuality* are not the same as *those who abuse themselves with men*, which could be female prostitutes, or a variety of other life situations [Amplified]. As you can see, Bible translators are not consistent even within their own translations, much less as various different translations are checked. It leads to a great deal of confusion. No wonder when these two obscure words are used so rarely, and then as in the case of *arsenokoites*, the word Paul coined to describe a particular situation in Corinth.

When some Christians try to say, "Well the Bible says homosexuals are not getting into heaven!" the question then remains, which Bible translation are you referring to?

Sometimes translators look at a word and try to figure out what it means by looking at its usage in other secular writings of the time. But that option is not available for *arsenokoites* since it is only used twice.

The word *malakos* is used a few other places in the Bible. In each other case the word #3120 in *Strong's* New Testament is translated *soft* in both the King James Version and the New American Standard Version.

Matt. 11:8

8   But what did you go out to see? A man dressed in *soft* clothing. Behold, those who wear *soft* clothing are in kings' palaces. (NAS)

The word means soft. It is not translated that they are wearing sexually perverted clothing. It is not translated they are wearing male prostitute clothing in kings' houses. It is not abusive clothing. This clothing in kings' houses does not participate in homosexuality. It is not catamite clothing. It is not effeminate clothing. So why is it translated as all these other things in 1 Corinthians, or ignored altogether as it is coupled with the word *arsenokoites*, as if *malakos* doesn't matter?

WHO ARE THE PEOPLE SO DESCRIBED?

When Paul wrote to the church at Corinth in the first century, it would have been obvious to them what he was talking about. His coined new word had meaning to those in that day. Paul then went on to say that this included some in his parish. They would have been able to look around the congregation and nod their heads in agreement; yes, some of us were like that. They would know from personal experience and be able to say yes, I was that. They would know whether they had been a *lift couch* or not.

So now we go back into archeology and anthropology, and look at first century Greek and Roman culture to see what Paul could have been addressing.

Some people think the Bible and its writers were homophobic, especially Paul. To coin a word, I think they were homo-ignorant. Attempting to reconcile first and second century understanding of sexuality into a modern framework is virtually impossible. What the apostle Paul, his Christian contemporaries, and the society around him believed about sexuality would be rejected as ridiculous myth by even the most conservative, prudish Christian today. Though homosexuality existed, it was not scientifically understood. Human sexuality itself was steeped in myth. For instance, the Epistle of Barnabas was written about the same time as the New Testament epistles,[6] and was widely circulated along with Paul's writings. In the second and third century it was often regarded as part of the Christian scripture, and held credibility for early Christians as part of the sacred writings of the early church. Yet commentary in the Epistle of Barnabas about sexual beliefs, which were widely held by first century culture, are dismissed as myth today.

A modern understanding of a so-called "homosexual lifestyle" was not what Paul was talking about. He was not addressing gay couples living together, setting up a home, checking account, and life with one another. But he was addressing something the Corinthians all knew about. Many of them could indeed say they had been very familiar with the life Paul was talking about. Paul said such were some of you, and they agreed.

The social norms of the first century Greek and Roman cultures are well documented in the writings from that era, as well as by many noted historians such as John Boswell[7] and Robin Scroggs.[8] It has long been established historically that in that era adolescents were considered sexually desirable by older men. The culture glorified the youthful male body. Once they grew a beard the attraction was over and the desirability was gone as an object of romanticized sex. Youth was a more established requirement for the male than for the female among prostitutes; for women could be considered desirable in middle age whereas before the age of twenty a boy already ceased to be desirable. Greek men seem to have regarded the presence of hair upon the cheeks, thighs and hindquarters of maturing youth with intense sexual distaste. Once the boy became a teenager, started to sprout facial hair, and no longer looked boyish but started to develop as a man, his sexual desirability to other men was over except to those homosexuals who liked mature men (the Emperor Galba, 68 A.D., is an example). The boy was also expected to get married, raise his own children, and work at a trade. He was not expected to continue on in homogenital liaisons with other men, unless he in turn took a younger lover.

Although the activity was homosexual in its genital arrangement, neither partner was actually considered to be a gay person in the modern sense of that word. The man in fact would probably be heterosexually married, expected his marriage to remain intact, and often expected the seduction of the boy to be a transient affair. In many cases, however, the affair was not a transient one. Roman Emperor Hadrian (ruled 117–138) began his affair with the handsome youth Antinoüs when the latter was in his early teens. They stayed together for many years until Antinoüs' untimely death by drowning at the age of about nineteen. Their love relationship (doubtless similar in its positive dynamics to many other same-sex relationships in the Ancient Graeco-Roman world) seems to have involved a mutual giving and taking: for Antinoüs, the wisdom and stability of an older man; for Hadrian, the youthful energy and sexual attractiveness of his lover.

Royston Lambert in his superbly written and scholarly researched book *Beloved and God: The Story of Hadrian and Antinous* describes this dynamic:[9]

> The older male lover (or *erastes*), aged between twenty and forty, was expected not only to provide his beloved (or *eromenos*), aged between twelve and eighteen, with unstinting affection but to encourage and oversee his development of mind and body and his training in the morals, customs and responsibilities of civic society. In return the boy was expected to respond by devotion, if not love, and by gratifying the older man's sexual desires. . . . [This arrangement] provided a loving and caring relationship not found within the family and acted as a means of initiation into the male-dominated society of the Greek city. . . . The boy, beautiful in body and filled with unspoilt promise and unsullied idealism, was conceived as incarnating qualities of the divine . . ."

It was the adult who selected the partner and determined what happened in the sexual encounter, although the sexual and emotional gratification was often mutual.

In addition to voluntary sexual encounters between the free born men and boys, there existed various forms of slave prostitution: brothels taxed by the city in Athens, for instance. Some slave boys were sold into these brothels. Other household slaves were also used sexually by their masters. Scroggs notes how it was common to castrate these youths to keep their youthful appearance, increasing their usefulness for sexual activity.[10] A famous example was Nero's treatment of his slave boy Sporus. He had Sporus castrated, dressed in women's clothes, given a woman's name, and publicly married the slave as a wife. The society of Rome did not think the relationship was all that uncommon or unusual. But since Nero was so widely hated, his opponents often lamented it was too bad Nero's father had not married a lad as Nero had done, instead of Nero's mother.

Beyond the situations cited with youth who were seduced for their charms or slaves who were forced into brothels or sexually compromising situations, there were still other well known situations in ancient Greece and Rome. One was the free born male hustler. This situation was not socially looked upon with favor. It seems that once a boy got used to gifts and money for selling his body, it became an easy way to continue in a lucrative financial exchange. Scroggs cites a case made against Timarchus[11] in which the young man is portrayed to the jury as an insatiable lustful degenerate who prostitutes himself over and over to older men. The prosecutor, Aeschines, admits he himself is a lover of beautiful young boys, but makes a distinction between what is socially acceptable and how Timarchus has crossed the line. The prosecutor states "to be in love with those who are beautiful and chaste is the experience of a kind-hearted and generous soul; but to hire for money and indulge in licentiousness is the act of a man who is wanton and ill-bred."

Additionally, Cicero accused Mark Antony of being a wanton hustler. Apparently, according to Cicero's version, this great lover of Cleopatra was a male prostitute in his earlier days. Both Cicero and the Jewish historian Josephus report this to be true.[12]

In all these cases we are mostly not talking about homosexual orientation, but about heterosexuals or bisexuals acting upon homogenital erotic behavior, although men who would today be considered "gay" existed, too.

Once a person becomes a Christian, however, they come under a new law. No longer are we under survival of the fittest, but we are commanded to love our neighbor as ourselves. It is very difficult, with the Holy Spirit guiding you, to maintain an exploitative power relationship over someone. It doesn't take too long to understand, considering the magnitude of this socially approved exploitative relationship, that this is likely what Paul is addressing.

They could nod in agreement when Paul said, such were some of you, but now you're changed, you're different. Now perhaps the older man is taking the boy under his wing as a son, and genuinely caring for him as well as gently making love to him, instead of exploiting his young apprentice or slave.

Therefore it is possible, not totally conclusive, that *arsenokoites* could have been this adult heterosexual male who had temporary sexual encounters with a male adolescent. And *malakos, soft,* could be the youth who was being used sexually. He could be soft, because he was not yet developed as a man.

So *malakos* and *arsenokoites* could have been referring to the relationship between this adult male and adolescent. Even so, the relationship was not considered a homosexual affair in their society.

That's one possibility. Remember, though, the word *arsenokoites* was not used as a word except by Paul initially. It shows up four hundred years later, being translated by the early Church father, Jerome. Interestingly enough, in 383 A.D., Jerome translates the word as *male prostitute*.

When Jerome lived, the Roman empire was still intact. Much of the society that Jerome was looking at was similar to the society that Paul was looking at. So Jerome, in retranslating the word *arsenokoites* would think it referred to something obvious to him. Male prostitution as part of pagan religious ritual also was very common in the early Roman empire. Male prostitution in Paul's day was often associated wtih pagan religious rites within the pagan shrines. It was a prevalent part of pagan worship rites in certain Roman temples, especially those of the eastern "dionysian" traditions. In the city of Rome alone, there were 420 temples to different gods and goddesses. Each deity had its own temple.

Therefore when Jerome in 383 A.D. translated *lift couch*, to him it seemed obvious it was a male temple prostitute. That is another possibility. However, to equate male prostitution with homosexuality per se is in as much discord and as inaccurate as equating all female heterosexuality with female prostitution.

Though *arsenokoites* could have been a temple prostitute, the word *malakos*, *soft*, could have been something else, totally unrelated, that was very real in Paul's day. The word *soft* can also legitimately be translated as *jelly-like* or *spineless*.

What was happening in the Roman empire in Paul's day? Christians were being persecuted. Paul himself helped in the persecution in the earlier days of his life. More than once a great persecution arose against the Church.

These were times of trouble. Saul made havoc of the Church. Christians were hauled to prison. Christians were crucified, beaten, thrown to lions and gladiators for public sport. Herod the king had James, the brother of John, killed with the sword. He proceeded to arrest Peter also. [Acts 12:1-5].

Persecution continued long into Paul's ministry. He mentioned how many ways he was in danger. He was in danger from false brethren, or spies in the Church. He had been beaten with thirty-nine lashes several times. Several times he was stoned. He was left for dead. This volatile atmosphere caused even the apostle Peter to back down from the truth, not only at Calvary, but also in Antioch, for fear of the persecution. [Gal. 2:11-20]. Barnabas also was carried away with Peter for fear of public opinion. Many became opponents of the truth from within the ranks of the Church. Diotrephes, mentioned in 3 John, as well as Hymenaeus and Alexander, who Paul said made a shipwreck of their faith, are a few among the many who are mentioned.[13]

Several of these converts fell away and became traitors. Persecution caused people to behave in weak willed ways. When a Roman soldier had his sword at your throat demanding to know whether or not you were a Christian, lots of believers lied and said no. Some people were *soft*. Some people were spineless. Some people were *jelly-like*, because with a sword at their throat they too ran away from Christ and denied Him as in the garden of Gethsemane.

In the meantime others were asked if they were Christians, with a sword at their throat, and they said yes. They faced the gladiators. They faced the lions. They were burned alive. They were crucified. They were thrown in jail to be held for a trial of injustice. They lost their homes, their lives, all worldly possessions. There were many martyrs, as in Smyrna and Pergamos [Rev. 2:8-17].

Some of those spineless ones came under conviction of the Holy Spirit. They repented. They realized they could not afford to deny Christ. Because they repented they came back to the Church. But they came back to those who have now lost their loved ones as martyrs for their confession while these others had denied Christ. This was a very real issue faced by the early Church. Should they forgive these deniers of Christ and bring them back into full fellowship, or deny them access to the secret meetings of the Church? The early Church at first did not trust Paul after he had seen Jesus. How much more did they possibly distrust these others? Yet if *malakos*, *soft*, meant spineless, Paul could have been saying to the Corinthians, and such were some of you. But now you are changed. They could easily look around the meeting room and nod, yes that's so.

In all these instances, whether it was the man who sexually exploited his slave boys, or seduced the free born youths, the idolatrous male priest-prostitute, the young male hustler, as Mark Antony was said to be, or the spineless as *malakos*, they were changed. And in any of these cases they would no longer be who they once were.

SANCTIFIED GAYS

Reading again from 1 Corinthians 6:9–11,

1 Cor. 6:9-11
9   Do you not know that the wicked will not inherit the kingdom of God? Do not be deceived: Neither the sexually immoral nor idolaters nor adulterers nor [*malakos*], nor [*arsenokoites*] nor thieves nor the greedy nor drunkards nor slanderers nor swindlers will inherit the kingdom of God.
11   And that is what some of you were. But you were washed, you were sanctified, you were justified in the name of the Lord Jesus Christ and by the Spirit of our God.

Whoever Paul is talking about as *malakos* and *arsenokoites* will not inherit the kingdom of God if they stayed in their former state. If the words malakos and arsenokoites were referring to homosexuals, as many churches and traditions insist, then what would a washed, sanctified and justified homosexual be? Would a washed, sanctified, justified homosexual be a heterosexual? If these words meant homosexual, unqualified, then you would have to say that every homosexual who came to Christ became a heterosexual. But we know this is just not so. A washed, sanctified, justified homosexual is a homosexual who has been washed, just like anybody else who has come to Christ, but a homosexual nonetheless.

Ask the parallel question: what is a heterosexual who is washed and sanctified and justified? Do they stop being sexual after they get saved? No. But the way they live out their heterosexuality changes. They become more responsible. Now they don't follow every lustful thought, but act according to the leading of their conscience, as the Holy Spirit leads them.

They don't find the need to go into singles bars every night to make a new sexual conquest, or cheat on their spouses and commit adultery. Although these things do occur even among Christian heterosexuals, if they are living for Christ, they come under conviction, and know they're not acting properly in a way that now honors God. They still function heterosexually, but differently, because they're washed.

The same would apply for gays and lesbians.

As was reported in the May, 1990 edition of *Keeping in Touch*, the publication newsletter of the Universal Fellowship of Metropolitan Community Churches,

> Michael Bussey and Gary Cooper, the founders of Exodus International, a Church-based coalition of "ex-gay" ministries have denounced all such programs seeking to convert homosexuals into heterosexuals, according to articles in *The Sentinel* (2/2/90) and *The Bay Area Reporter* (2/8/90).
>
> Bussey remarked of the programs: "I had no success with them. I counseled . . . hundreds of people . . . who tried to change their sexual orientation, and none of them were successful. If you got them away from the Christian limelight and asked them, "Honestly now, are you saying that you are no longer homosexual, and you are now heterosexually oriented?" . . . not one person said, "Yes, I am actually now heterosexual."
>
> Bussey is now a family counselor for gay and lesbian couples. He admits that his past work did "psychological damage. . . . There may very well be out there people that I talked to who are dead, having committed suicide because of the guilt I inadvertently heaped on them. I feel guilty about that. It was well intentioned. I was getting brainwashed by the church; this is what I was supposed to be doing. But it

damaged me; it damaged the people I talked to.''

One man, according to the pair, suffered such psychological damage that he mutilated his own genitals with a razor blade in a desperate attempt to rid himself of his sexual desires. Another impulsively underwent an incomplete sex-change operation because he believed his sexual desires might receive divine approval if he were biologically a woman.

But at the time ''I was convinced it was working,'' Bussey said. ''Every once in a while a crack in that conviction would occur. I'd ask, 'How come I'm still having these feelings?' '' I'd see a Christian psychologist, and he'd say, ''Oh, that's just temptation. Ignore it or suppress it. You are different. You are now ex-gay. You're no longer gay. Those feelings don't mean anything.'' But the feelings didn't go away for either of the men. In fact, even during their tenure with Exodus, some ''ex-gay'' counselors actively engaged in gay sex, even after a full day of ''ex-gay'' counseling.

Both said they experienced such inner conflict that they decided to leave the organization in 1979. They altered a talk they were scheduled to give before the general synod of the United Church of Christ. To the shock of the audience they called for the acceptance of gays and lesbians as they are. That stand spelled a rapid end to their involvement as speakers to organized evangelical Christianity. Soon after, they moved in together.[14]

When people try to define *arsenokoites* as unqualified homosexuality, they see it doesn't work. But whatever Paul was referring to does work. It couldn't have been homosexuality, per se, otherwise homosexuals would *all* be ex-gays once they became Christians. That would be it. They wouldn't have to worry about it any more. It just doesn't happen that way. A lot of gay people try to fool themselves, but one day they wake up and realize they are still gay, though Christian, as Mr. Bussey points out.

INHERITING THE KINGDOM OF GOD

Another question this passage in 1 Corinthians raises is what does it mean to *inherit the kingdom of God*?

1 Cor. 6:9-11
Know ye not that the unrighteous *shall not inherit the kingdom of God*? Be not deceived: neither fornicators, nor idolaters, nor adulterers, nor [*malakos*], nor [*arsenokoites*], nor thieves, nor covetous, nor drunkards, nor revilers, nor extortioners, *shall inherit the kingdom of God.* (KJV)

Some people interpret this passage to say that gay people cannot go to heaven. When we first taught this series in Community Gospel Church, the very day we were going to look at this passage, a prominent radio evangelist stated that "there will be no homosexuals or lesbians in heaven." He was basing his statement on this passage that "these people shall not inherit the kingdom of God." But ask this question: what did Paul mean by *inherit the kingdom of God*? Does it mean getting into heaven after you die? Some people would glibly say yes. Yet the Bible is talking about something different in its references to the kingdom of God. It doesn't mean just slipping into heaven eventually.

Looking at the Bible itself to see what it means to inherit the kingdom of God, we find these scriptures:

Rom. 14:17
17   For *the kingdom of God is* not a matter of eating and drinking, but of *righteousness, peace and joy in the Holy Spirit,*

From this passage, we see what the kingdom is not. It is not eating and drinking. Eating and drinking are things that you do. When we eat or drink, we are responsible for those actions and behaviors. We don't obtain the kingdom by our deeds, but by our faith. We can't work our way into the kingdom, but when we have the kingdom within us, good deeds follow.

The kingdom of God is three things.

1. It is *righteousness*. We are not the author of our own righteousness. Jesus paid the price. It is His righteousness.

2. The kingdom of God is *peace*. This is the peace of God that passes understanding. It is the peace of God that guards our heart and our mind in Christ Jesus. Where does that come from? It is in fact a fruit of the Holy Spirit.

3. The kingdom of God is also *joy* in the Holy Spirit. We see this is also something God gives us.

If we look at these three things: *righteousness, peace* and *joy in the Holy Spirit*, which are the kingdom of God, how do we know if we have these attributes or not?

Looking at *righteousness*, how do I know if I have righteousness? I have righteousness if I belong to Jesus. I need to be committed to Christ as my Savior. I have to choose Jesus for myself. Does that mean then, that if a person is heterosexual, and does not choose Jesus they have righteousness just because they are a heterosexual? Of course not. If a person is gay or lesbian, but has Jesus as their Savior do they have righteousness? Yes, because it is not their own righteousness, but His, which He gives to everyone who belongs to Him by choice.

How about *peace*? By looking at someone, can I really determine if they have peace or not? Part of my perception will be colored by my own emotions and experience. Suppose they have peace, and there is a contented smile on their face. But I have just had bad news from my family, am worried sick about something, everything is going wrong and I walk by their smile. My emotions may internalize their expression as a smirk. How do you know what they are feeling if it is not expressed?

I might tell you I have peace, but I might put on a mask, wear a facade, and say, "I have the peace of God that passes understanding!"

You might believe me. But the only one who really knows whether I have peace, outside of God, is me.

So I can't judge whether you are a Christian and whether you have inherited righteousness and peace unless you can witness that you have peace. You'll have to tell me.

The third item in the inheritance of the kingdom of God, is *joy in the Holy Spirit*. Who knows best whether someone has joy in the Holy Spirit? The person who has received it. If a lesbian or gay man has righteousness because they belong to Christ, and if they have peace, and if they have joy in the Holy Spirit, have they inherited the kingdom of God? According to the Bible they have!

Now that's not all. If I look up the word *kingdom* in the Bible, I find out that in the New Testament it is #932 in *Strong's*, and there are columns of references to the kingdom in the Bible. These references give me additional clues of what to watch for to determine if someone has inherited the kingdom. So to determine whether someone has inherited the kingdom, I have to rely on their testimony, and what the Word also shares in Matthew 7:21.

Matt. 7:21
21   Not everyone who says to me, "Lord, Lord," will enter the kingdom of heaven, but only he who does the will of my Father who is in heaven.

I must also watch to see if they do the will of the Father. Watching a person's behavior to see if it matches up with the will of God is another clue. We know God commanded Christians to walk in love and to love one another. There will also be fruit borne over the long haul.

Gal. 5:22–23
But the fruit of the Spirit is love, joy, peace, patience, kindness, goodness, faithfulness, gentleness and self-control.

There will be a change in character noticed over a duration.
Luke 17:21 says the kingdom of God is within you. So inheriting the kingdom of God is not merely slipping into Heaven when our Earth suit, or body, is thrown in a grave. Getting the kingdom of God is getting it right here, right now, because I'm God's child.

1 Cor. 4:20
For the kingdom of God is not in word, but in power. (KJV)

The kingdom is not just in word. It is not just in my saying I have the kingdom, but in power. There ought to be a changed life. That's what the Bible says, "Such were some of you, but you have been washed . . ." Your life has been changed. No one internally knows that better than the person who has been changed.

Gal. 5:25
25   Since we live by the Spirit, let us keep in step with the Spirit.

Here Paul had to admonish the Galatians to live in the Spirit, and to walk in the Spirit. Even though a person may have the kingdom within them, they can still falter, and still need to choose to follow God on a daily and moment-by-moment basis. We might see them in a moment of weakness and judge according to that, yet they still might be a Christian. Otherwise, Paul would never have to instruct the Church to choose to walk in the Spirit. This instruction was given to the believers in the Church in Galatia.

These are people who have inherited the kingdom of God and they still have to be told to get their act together! If I judge others only by what I see, I might misjudge them because they might be missing it momentarily, but the kingdom is still in there doing its work to change them into a pearl of great price.

I don't know what they say to God out of a repentant heart in the middle of the night. So I cannot judge their current standing with God.

Peter denied the Lord three times, but he went to Heaven. King David committed adultery, then successfully plotted the murder of his pregnant girlfriend's husband. Yet God did not take the Holy Spirit or the kingdom from him. Abraham lied about his wife to foreigners, out of fear, yet he is called the father of faith.

Why? Because God's grace is sufficient for us all. We sin, we falter, we miss the mark. But God does not give up on us. The Master is still at work smoothing off the rough edges and creating a masterpiece out of a marred lump of clay. There is only one Savior, and we don't qualify. We are not our own savior. We have need of salvation. Our glaring shortcomings only point out our great need for a great Redeemer. This doesn't have a thing to do with our sexual orientation, but how we live our lives before God.

CONCLUSION

Colossians 1:12 says God made us qualified to be partakers of the inheritance. God alone qualifies us to inherit the kingdom of God. It is not up to us. We can't do it. We can't make ourselves fit. We can't save ourselves, we need God to make us qualified to be partakers of the inheritance of the saints in light. God furthermore delivered us from the power of evil. God did this. We couldn't, whether heterosexual, homosexual, bisexual, or whatever. We all need God to get us out of the clutches of death and God did it! Then God transferred us into the kingdom of His dear Son. Not because we deserved it. But because of His love for us.

Who put us into the kingdom? Who puts anyone into the kingdom? The Father does. He does it for everyone whether male or female, black or white or yellow or red, by the same process, coming to Him through faith in Christ. The Father translated us into the kingdom of His dear Son.

Such were some of you, the Scripture states in 1 Cor. 6:9–11.

And *such were some of you*, fornicators, or idolaters, or adulterers, or *malakos* [spineless perhaps] or *arsenokoites* [maybe involved in idolatrous practices, maybe exploiters of children] or thieves, shoplifters, stealing for drugs, or covetous, or drunkards, or revilers, or extortioners: but ye are washed, but ye are sanctified, but ye are justified in the name of the Lord Jesus, and by the Spirit of our God. (KJV)

Whatever it was we were, we are changed and transformed. Not by our power but by God's as the kingdom works God's nature into ours. None of us stays the same. We grow from glory to glory. Our orientation remains the same, but how we live out our lives is transformed as we were snatched out of the oppression of evil to the liberty of the Son of God. We are known by a new name, written in the Lamb's book of life. We are the whosoevers and the redeemed of the Lord and we say so.

We are washed by the Blood of Calvary. Without the shedding of blood there is no remission of sins. But there was Blood. It washes, it sanctifies, and it causes us to be overcomers in the trials and fiery darts of the wicked one. Thank God, He did it all, and it is freely given to whoever will receive! Praise God.

ROMANS I

If a Bible has a concordance at the back, and if among the topics listed is the topic of homosexuality, then usually Romans chapter one will be the reference cited, particularly verses 26–27. Romans 1:26 is the only verse in the whole Bible that deals with women being sexually active with women. There is no other such verse anywhere.

It is important also to note that the Bible says that out of the mouth of *two or three witnesses* let every word be established.[15]

Therefore to make a case about lesbianism in the Word of God, there should be *at least* one other scripture to deal with the topic of women being sexually involved with other women. But there isn't.

There are other topics in the Bible as well, about which conclusive doctrines cannot be built. This is because these topics are merely mentioned once. Paul makes only one passing reference about baptism for the dead, and that is to the Corinthians.[16] We don't know what he was talking about in that situation, and his one reference is not enough information upon which to build a solid doctrine about the issue. Yet this is the only reference in the entire Word of God that talks about women being with women.

When we read the Bible we have to ask questions. It is truly recorded in Matt. 27:5 that Judas went and hanged himself. Can we build a doctrine around that as truth though? No. It is truly recorded, but does that make it right? Is it a truth for us to live or die by? No. These are important issues to consider whenever you want to do an exegesis, or study of the Bible to get at its truth. It is also truly recorded in Luke 10:37 that Jesus said go and do likewise. I can pull scripture out of context, and state that the Bible says Judas went and hanged himself. And that Jesus said, "Go and do likewise." Does that mean Jesus was saying to hang ourselves? No, no, no! What Jesus is telling us to go and do likewise in Luke 10, is to be like the Good Samaritan: give help to our neighbors, and show mercy. You can't take scripture out of context, and arrive at its truth. Yet if I were to tell people who knew little or nothing about the Bible that the Bible says Judas went and hanged himself, and Jesus says in the Bible to go and do likewise, therefore the Bible condones suicide by hanging, it is obvious I am twisting the scriptures by taking them out of context. What I do in such a case is actually an abortion to the intent and truth of the Word, even though I am quoting the truly recorded words of the Bible. Yet this process is exactly what occurs when people try to make Romans 1:26–27 a condemnation of homosexuality.

When a scripture verse begins with *therefore* it is important to know for what purpose it is there. It is obviously connected in thought to the previous verses. When the word *therefore* or a similar type of connective word is used to start a verse, it is important to see what came before this verse, since it is obviously attached in thought, content, and context to the previous thought. It is there to build a case, and it is important to see why they are using the connective word. We need to ask ourselves, "What is the point the writer is trying to make?" We need to know. Even simple verses like "Jesus wept"[17] do not stand alone. It is necessary to read the rest of the story in John 11 to find out why He wept. What was going on, what were the circumstances, to whom and about what was He talking when He wept? The verse needs its context. This is important to understand in any kind of Bible exegesis. And it is especially true here in Romans chapter one.

We will start by taking these two verses out of context to see what they say when they stand alone, and see why people say these verses are against homosexuals, and then try to make their case that God hates homosexuals.

Rom. 1:26–27
26   Because of this, God gave them over to shameful lusts. Even their women exchanged natural relations for unnatural ones.
27   In the same way the men also abandoned natural relations with women and were inflamed with lust for one another. Men committed indecent acts with other men, and received in themselves the due penalty for their perversion.

Note that in spite of the version being read, verse 26 starts out by saying something similar to *therefore*, or another word that means "because of what you just read." The NIV states "Because of this . . ." You can't read those three words without asking the question, Because of *what*? These verses are also attached to the verses before them and the verses after. The next verse, verse 28, begins with the word *and*, which also means there is more than what we've just read.

We can see there is more than an isolated scripture here, so we ask, to whom is Paul writing? He is writing to the first century Christian church at Rome. He is not writing to an organized church for and by gays in metropolitan ancient Rome. He is not writing to gay people at all. He is writing to an audience that is both heterosexual and Christian.

This verse 26, written to the heterosexual church at Rome, says: "Because of this [we still need to see because of *what*] God gave them up unto vile affections: for even their women did *change* [or *exchange*] the natural use . . ."

The word *change* is #3337 in *Strong's*.[18] It means to *exchange*. What does exchange mean? It means I must already have something that I will let go of in order to trade it for something else. If I have a shirt, and I take it back to the store to *exchange* it, I have to have an original shirt in the beginning in order to trade, or exchange, for a different shirt. But in order to *exchange* anything, I have to have something initially.

These women exchanged the *natural* use. The word *natural* is #5546 in *Strong's*.[19] It means *instinctive*. So what they are exchanging is their instinctive use. In other words, a heterosexual woman has basic instincts to have sexual relationships with a heterosexual man. These are her instincts. As a little girl perhaps she thinks about boyfriends, and having a husband, playing house and playing mommy. You look at her childhood to see what instincts she has and see what is ingrained in her. If a nonheterosexual woman is going to *exchange* what is natural or *instinctive* to her, it means she would have to exchange what is natural to her, what is instinctive in her, for what is not natural to her, and what is not instinctive in her. These women did exchange the natural use into that which is against their own nature, as heterosexuals. So they exchanged their heterosexual *orientation* for homosexual *activity*. Not for a homosexual orientation, because a heterosexual person cannot make themselves have a different orientation, but they could pick up a different behavior that is not instinctive to them. They exchanged their orientation for certain sexual behavior.

The next verse says "and likewise also the men. . . ." This tells us that whatever we can infer about the women, we can likewise infer about the men. It is likewise, or the same way, for the men as for the women. Likewise the men leaving the *natural* use. Again it's the same word, *natural* or *instinctive*, meaning their own instincts as heterosexuals. They left their own instinctive use of a woman. Which man would have an *instinctive* use of a woman; a *heterosexual* man or a *homosexual* man? A heterosexual man. He has a natural instinctive use of a woman.

He *leaves* that. To *leave*, #863 in *Strong's,*[20] means *having forsaken*, to *send away*, to *lay aside* the instinctive use, to *leave* their natural use or to *yield up* their natural use of the woman.

They *burned* in their lust. To *burn* is #1572 in *Strong's,*[21] and it means to *inflame deeply*. If you look in *Strong's* or *New Englishman's,*[22] you discover there are other Greek words for burn, but the difference in this word is that it has a prefix which shows that it is more than a simple burning, it is an all consuming burning; it burns deeply. The person is consumed with this lust. It is a deeply burning inflammation of lust. It is lust at the point of orgasm where there is no turning back. At that point it doesn't matter what consequences follow.

They are burning in *lust*. The word lust is interesting. It is a consuming craving, and a lust as we might expect the word to say. It is #3715 in *Strong's,*[23] meaning lust, excitement of the mind, longing after, craving. What the Bible does not say is also interesting. It does not say they are burning in their *love* for one another. It is pure raw sexual lust for the sake of sex alone.

NOTES

[1] Daniel Heminiak, *What the Bible Really Says about Homosexuality* (San Francisco: Alamo Square Press, 1994), 89.

[2] #[3120] malakos

[3] #[733]arsenokoites

[4] *Spirit-Filled Life Bible*, 1726.

[5] Ezek. 16:49–50.

[6] Estimated to be written between 70–135 A.D.

[7]John Boswell, *Christianity, Social Tolerance and Homosexuality: Gay People in Western Europe from the Beginning of the Christian Era to the Fourteenth Century* (Chicago: University of Chicago Press, 1980).

[8]Robin Scroggs, *The New Testament and Homosexuality: Contextual Background for Contemporary Debate* (Philadelphia: Fortress Press, 1983).

[9]Royston Lambert, *Beloved and God: The Story of Hadrian and Antinous* (New York: Viking, 1984), 78.

[10]Scroggs, 39.

[11]Ibid., 40.

[12]Ibid., 41 / Cicero, *Philippics* II.44f. / Josephus, *Antiquities XV.23–30.*

[13]1 Tim. 1:19–20.

[14]"Ex-Gay Ministry Founders Recant," *Keeping in Touch*, Universal Fellowship of Metropolitan Community Churches Newsletter, May 1990.

[15]2 Cor. 13:1.

[16]1 Cor. 15:29.

[17]John 11:35.

[18]*Strong's Exhaustive Concordance of the Bible*, see dictionary section of New Testament Greek Words.

[19]Ibid.

[20]Ibid.

[21]Ibid.

[22]Wigram-Green, *New Englishman's Greek Concordance and Lexicon* (Peabody, MA: Hendrickson Publishers, 1982).

[23]*Strong's.*

THE VERSES YOU DON'T HEAR ABOUT

INTRODUCTION

Up to this point I have concentrated on Scriptural passages that have been wrongly used to condemn homosexuals and homosexuality. But since it is my desire to dispel myths *and* bring truths to light, I think it is equally important to examine some passages in the Bible that are actually speaking a clear word of hope and love to the gay community. To that end, we will shift our focus in this section to a discussion of Scriptural stories that are all too often conveniently overlooked when studying the Bible to see what God has to say on this topic.

EUNUCHS ARE UNIQUE

Looking at the topic of *eunuchs* is certainly very interesting. There are two words used for eunuch in the Bible: one in the Hebrew and one in the Greek. In the Old Testament, the word for eunuch is the word *cariyc*.

#5631 *cariyc* (saw-reece'); meaning to castrate; a eunuch; by implication, valet (especially of the female apartments), and thus, a minister of state.

In the New Testament the word for eunuch is *eunouchos*.

#2135 *eunouchos* (yoo-noo'-khos); from *eune* (a bed) and #2192; a castrated person (such being employed in Oriental bedchambers); by extension an impotent or unmarried man; by implication, a chamberlain (state-officer).

For the most part, the word for eunuch is pretty much the same in Hebrew and Greek. One meaning is a castrated male, as we would assume in English. But that's not all it means. It can be a courtier, or a valet. In Greek it is made up of two words; *bed* and *to hold*. In Oriental bedchambers, it often meant anyone who could be trusted to hold the bedchamber of a wife or harem of a monarch. This man had to be someone the king could trust to protect and watch over his wives, and yet be trusted not to molest the women in their bedchamber. This person would be trusted to hold or guard the female bedchamber. This was a lot of responsibility. The person oversaw the princesses or the concubines of the king of the land, and as such often had influence in the kingdom. If they were promoted, even to a general in the army, or any other position of authority, they still maintained that designation of *cariyc*, or eunuch.

Often they were someone who had been conquered from another land, castrated, and then given a position of authority, such as watching the bedchamber. In this case they could be heterosexual by orientation, but they did not have to be. They could also be a gay man, because a gay man could be trusted to oversee the bedchamber of the women.

A eunuch can be an impotent male, an unmarried man, or one who voluntarily abstains from marriage with someone of the opposite sex.

According to Thayer[1] it also means "one naturally incapacitated, either for marriage or for begetting children." In other words it is someone who for whatever reason is not going to have sex with, or beget children with, someone of the opposite sex. It is one thing to be incapacitated for begetting children, as in male or female infertility, but a completely different thing to be incapacitated for marriage with the opposite sex. For some this is obviously because they are gay. There are many gay people who could not fathom sex with the opposite gender. It just will not happen! Though the sexual orientation of a eunuch is not specified, since they could be in that life situation through a variety of avenues, clearly gay people are not excluded but wholly embraced by the term eunuch.

Thayer further includes in the definition of eunuch "one who abstains from marriage."[2] It is anyone trusted to hold/guard a woman's bed. It also means to live unmarried.

By no means did the term eunuch have to be merely a castrated male. It was a broad term, and since a chamberlain for a harem could be promoted, and was a person trusted with the king's intimate things, the term often got generalized to mean an official in the court. Ancient Judah's king Hezekiah was told his sons would be eunuchs in Babylon. He didn't think that was bad news.[3] He thinks this is good news. He apparently is not worried that the royal line will be ended. Eunuch here, in king Hezekiah's estimate, probably means his children will be officials in the court of the Babylonians.

In the New Testament, Jesus uses the term eunuch. And it is obvious from what He says that the term eunuch includes a lot more people than castrated male humans.

Matt. 19:10–12
10   The disciples said to him, "If this is the situation between a husband and wife, it is better not to marry."
11   Jesus replied, "Not everyone can accept this word, but only those to whom it has been given.
12   *For some are eunuchs because they were born that way; others were made that way by men; and others have renounced marriage because of the kingdom of heaven.* The one who can accept this should accept it."

In this situation, Jesus and His disciples are discussing marriage and divorce, and the conditions under which it is permissible to divorce. Recall that divorce was easily accomplished for almost any reason in Christ's time among the Jewish people. Jesus is saying that unless your spouse has cheated on you, you don't have a good reason for divorce. The disciples think that is a tough saying. But then Jesus goes on to say not everyone can receive His teaching on divorce and marriage, because not everyone can get married.

His reasons for this are lumped under the category of being a eunuch. From the ensuing description it is obvious more people are eunuchs than castrated males. In the King James Version, Jesus says *and there be eunuchs, which have made themselves eunuchs for the kingdom of heaven's sake.* No one was ever required to castrate themselves for the sake of getting into Heaven. Getting into Heaven and/or serving God does not have requirements like this. God does not ask anyone to mutilate themselves to get favor in the kingdom. Jesus was bruised for our iniquities. We don't need to be bruised for ours also. We need to trust Jesus as our Savior.

The apostle Paul was someone who was single and celibate. (1 Corinthians 7:7). He did this for the sake of the kingdom. By the definition of the word eunuch, Paul could be considered a eunuch. Paul was not physically castrated. But he wanted to fulfill the call on his life, which required traveling. Being in danger was common for Paul in his travels. He didn't need a wife and small children tagging along for the trip. Paul recorded his lifestyle as full of hardship.

> I have worked much harder, been in prison more frequently, been flogged more severely, and been exposed to death again and again. Five times I received from the Jews the forty lashes minus one. Three times I was beaten with rods, once I was stoned, three times I was shipwrecked, I spent a night and a day in the open sea, I have been constantly on the move. I have been in danger from rivers, in danger from bandits, in danger from my own countrymen, in danger from gentiles; in danger in the city, in danger in the country, in danger at sea; and in danger from false brothers. I have labored and toiled and have often gone without sleep; I have known hunger and thirst and have often gone without food; I have been cold and naked.[4]

As we see from Paul's life, the term *eunuch* has much broader implications than castration. There are many reasons people can't get married to an opposite sex partner. Jesus said not everyone could.

So the Lord Himself has expanded the meaning of *eunuch* to include the unmarried for a variety of situations. Some were made this way by others. Some are born this way. They are unable to get married because they have no natural inclination to have sexual relations with the opposite sex. They are born that way. Others were made unable to have a sexual relationship with a mate of the opposite sex because of sexual traumas (abuse, etc.) in their past.

For some it is not an anticipated option. For others it is not an option at all. The hurts and scars are too deep. For whatever reason, and there are many, *eunuch* means anyone not likely to get heterosexually involved. At any rate, this list expanded by Jesus certainly includes gay people and others of either sex.

The Lord makes it clear that not everyone can get married, not everyone should get married. But when they do, Jesus made it clear God's plan was for us to stay with our mate for a lifetime.

Another *cariyc*, eunuch, shows up in the book of Daniel.

In chapter one, young Daniel is taken captive as a Hebrew slave to the land of Babylon where Nebuchadnezzar is king. The king requests his prince of the eunuchs to find the fittest and most handsome young men among the Hebrew captives from the royal lines to be put into the king's service in Babylon. They had a diet in Babylon to feed these beautiful young men, but it was contrary to the dietary laws of Israel. Daniel asks the eunuch in authority over him for help to keep from eating the foods that would defile his conscience. Reading from the King James Version we find:

Dan. 1:3-9
3   And the king spoke unto Ashpenaz the master of his *eunuchs*, that he should bring certain of the children of Israel, and of the king's seed, and of the princes;
4   Children in whom was no blemish, but well favoured, and skillful in all wisdom, and cunning in knowledge, and understanding science, and such as had ability in them to stand in the king's palace, and whom they might teach the learning and the tongue of the Chaldeans.
5   And the king appointed them a daily provision of the king's meat, and of the wine which he drank: so nourishing them three years, that at the end thereof they might stand before the king.
6   Now among these were of the children of Judah, *Daniel*, Hananiah, Mishael, and Azariah:
7   Unto whom the prince of the eunuchs gave names: for he gave unto Daniel the name of Belteshazzar; and to Hananiah, of Shadrach; and to Mishael, of Meshach; and to Azariah, of Abednego.

8   But Daniel purposed in his heart that he would not defile himself with the portion of the king's meat, nor with the
wine which he drank: therefore he requested of the prince of
the eunuchs that he might not defile himself.
9   Now God had brought *Daniel* into *favour and tender
love* with the prince of the eunuchs. (KJV)

God personally took responsibility for causing this *eunuch*, this
chief eunuch, to fall in love with Daniel, so that the *eunuch* would
be willing to grant Daniel's request to follow the dietary laws of
Israel, not Babylon. God caused this *cariyc*, this *eunuch*, to have
a strong attachment toward this handsome young Hebrew. Some
were born this way, Jesus said. This love and affection the *cariyc*,
eunuch, felt for Daniel brought about God's purpose for Daniel,
and kept him from being tried for insurrection.

Nebuchadnezzar was a demanding, arrogant king with an iron
will. No one crossed him. Nations and kings were subservient to
him. The *cariyc*, chief eunuch, defied the king's orders for one reason, and one reason alone: his God-given feelings of love for
Daniel. He felt that pleasing Daniel by granting his illegal request
was worth risking his life for. The *cariyc*, the prince of the eunuchs, was fearful. But the reassuring words from the object of
his tender love, Daniel, caused him to defy the ruthless king's
orders and risk it all. Since God was behind it all, it worked out
well for Daniel and Ashpenaz the *cariyc*, eunuch.

A closer look at the passage in Daniel 1:9 reveals these facts:

Daniel 1:9
Now God had brought Daniel into *favour* and tender love
with the prince of the eunuchs. (KJV)

The word *favor* in Hebrew is #2617 *checed* (kheh´ -sed). Some
of its meanings are: *love, everlasting love, an attitude of love
which contains mercy, unfailing love, beauty,*[5] and another meaning is *lovely appearance.*[6]

The richness of the Hebrew word *favour* means God not only
brought Daniel into love with the eunuch, but also caused Daniel
to have a lovely appearance of beauty. Verse 4 of the NIV shows

how they could be considered men of great beauty in the eyes of the eunuch.

Dan. 1:4
[they were] *young men without any physical defect, handsome,*

Daniel was a 100% pure male hunk, with no defects!

Here is this eunuch, someone unable to get married and trustworthy with the harem of the king, who is a high official in Babylon, under a ruthless king, who suddenly sees a handsome slave boy without any defects. The eunuch is overcome with love, and the charms of the Hebrew youth; his lovely appearance causes him to risk his life just to change the diet of the slave. He has lost his senses. But he is overcome with a tender, sensitive love. It seems God gave the eunuch a good dose of "I just can't live without you" kind of love. And when he looks at Daniel, the eunuch thinks he's hot! He's beautiful! He's perfect! He is in love with Daniel, and this love is worth dying for. He sticks his neck out for Daniel when it could easily cost his life. Remember, his boss is the ruthless King Nebuchadnezzar! Who cares! He's in *love*!

Daniel 1:4 further tells us Daniel was handsome and skillful in all wisdom, and cunning in knowledge.

Daniel was wise. He knew the score. He could tell how the prince of the eunuchs felt about him. This is what gave Daniel the boldness to even ask the question that could cost his life.

How could a slave in captivity ask such an insolent question as "Allow me to eat something different than what the king has commanded. Let me break the Law!" Just asking the question could cost a slave his life! But Daniel had wisdom. He knew the score. He knew how the eunuch felt! He could risk asking "a little favor" from the master over him. The Lord revealed to Daniel the very feelings He placed in the eunuch for Daniel. Daniel was wise. He knew.

Daniel 1:9
Now God had brought Daniel into favour and *tender love* with the prince of the eunuchs. (KJV)

The Hebrew word for *tender love* is #7356 *racham* (rakh′-am), which comes from its root word, #7355, which means *to fondle*. In the plural, by extension: the womb (as cherishing the fetus): by implication, a maiden. Translated in KJV as compassion, damsel, tender love, (great, tender) mercy, pity, womb.

This all says that God caused the chief eunuch to fall deeply into a tender love with Daniel.

If you use a lexicon to discover every time the word #7356 *racham* (rakh′-am), *tender love* is used, you see it is often translated as the word *womb*. When the word *womb* is needed in the text, the word #7356 *racham* (rakh′-am) is used. This may mean there is a motherly feeling. But the word also gets translated as compassion or love.

This is the word that is used in *Lamentations 3:22* where it says God's compassions never fail, and are new every morning. *So how deep is that compassion*? In talking about God and His compassion, here is this word *womb* to describe it, a very intimate concept. This is a deep kind of love. It is also translated as *sensitive love* and it's from the word *to fondle*. This is a very intimate word.

Amazingly, the text still says that God brought Daniel into this intimate love, this womb-like relationship of compassion and sensitive love, stemming from the word "to fondle." God did this. God takes credit for this. God caused the eunuch to have a deep compassionate womb-like love for Daniel. It was this prince of the eunuchs who was to look among the exiles and find the ones who were lovely, without blemish. That would have been by the eunuch's observation, choice and taste in esthetics. Ashpenaz the eunuch thought Daniel was good-looking, one in whom there was no blemish, or Daniel would never have been chosen.

THE PROMISE TO EUNUCHS AND STRANGERS

There are still other scriptures that deal with eunuchs. Isaiah 56 has several prophetic promises for the eunuch.

Isa. 56:3-8

3   Let no foreigner who has bound himself to the LORD say, "The LORD will surely exclude me from his people." And let not any eunuch complain, "I am only a dry tree."

4   For this is what the LORD says: "To the eunuchs who keep my Sabbaths, who choose what pleases men and hold fast to my covenant—

5   to them I will give within my temple and its walls a memorial and a name better than sons and daughters; I will give them an everlasting name that will not be cut off.

6   And foreigners who bind themselves to the LORD to serve him, to love the name of the LORD, and to worship him, all who keep the Sabbath without desecrating it and who hold fast to my covenant—

7   these I will bring to my holy mountain and give them joy in my house of prayer. Their burnt offerings and sacrifices will be accepted on my altar; for my house will be called a house of prayer for all nations."

8   The Sovereign LORD declares—he who gathers the exiles of Israel: "I will gather still others to them besides those already gathered."

To understand this scripture more clearly, we remember what the law had said. It had told us that any person who had any mutilation or defect or injury in the reproductive organs was not to be allowed in the congregation. Then that person, or the eunuch, feels like "What hope is there for me?" They were not allowed in the temple, they could not worship God in the temple. The eunuch ends up feeling like he has no hope, there is no place for him.

Then without hope, and without a place in the worshipping congregation, the eunuch feels he is like a dry tree. Yet the Word tells the eunuch not to say, "Behold I am a dry tree," spiritually, physically or emotionally. Still, the promise is not to every gay, lesbian, or bisexual person, but only to those who will take hold of God's covenant.

Acts 4:12
12   Salvation is found in no one else, for there is no other name under heaven given to men by which we must be saved.

Acts 16:30-31
30   He [the jailer] then brought them out and asked, "Sirs, what must I do to be saved?"
31   They replied, "Believe in the Lord Jesus, and you will be saved—you and your household."

Rom. 10:9
9   . . . if you confess with your mouth, "Jesus is Lord," and believe in your heart that God raised him from the dead, you will be saved.

Eph. 2:8-9
8   For it is by grace you have been saved, through faith—and this not from yourselves, it is the gift of God—
9   not by works, so that no one can boast.

John 3:16-17
16   For God so loved the world that he gave his one and only Son, that *whoever* believes in him shall not perish but have eternal life.
17   For God did not send his Son into the world to condemn the world, but to save the world through him.

These promises all point to the one covenant God made with whoever in the human race that chooses. There are no conditions of sexual orientation, marital status, age, gender, race, gender identification, national origin, or color of eyes, hair or lack thereof, health status or mobility, ability to see, hear or reproduce. The promise in Isaiah 56:4 [For this is what the LORD says: "To the *eunuchs* who keep my Sabbaths, who choose what pleases me and *hold fast to my covenant*—] is available to any eunuch who takes hold of God's covenantal relationship to Himself through Jesus Christ.
    The eunuch who will take hold of Jesus Christ will enter into

a very special relationship with the Father within His house. The prodigal son who returned home to his father's house was given great honor and a celebration at his return.[7] So it is with the eunuch who comes home to God. God's promise to them is this:

> . . . to them I will give within my temple and its walls a memorial and *a name better than sons and daughters*; I will give them an everlasting name that will not be cut off. (Isaiah 56:5)

Who then are sons and daughters? All the other folks who when following their own natural orientation are able to reproduce and have children. Some gay people have had children. Some through former heterosexual unions before they came to a full realization of their orientation, and some through other means like artificial insemination. But as they follow their orientation, a gay person mated with a same sex partner will not reproduce from that same sex partner. That goes without saying. Remember, some are born this way, Jesus said. Not everyone could marry an opposite sex partner.

The church often acts as though such eunuchs have no place in the house of God. Many churches act as though such eunuchs do not and cannot belong to God. Yet God says for the eunuch to grab hold of the covenant. God tells the eunuch to grab hold of the fact that Jesus Christ died for their sins as well as the sins of the whole world. If they will put their trust in Jesus, as any other son or daughter would, that eunuch will get a name that is better than any other of God's children.

THE PROMISE FULFILLED

When God promises to bring restoration to the Church, all the things we see in the early Church can be expected to be restored. She will be restored to her power and glory. Another early Church phenomenon was the entry of the eunuch into the household of faith.

Historically, it is obvious that the events recorded in Acts chapter eight occurred before the events recorded in Acts chapter ten. Acts chapter ten was a watershed moment in the history of the Church. Up until that moment the church was considered to be a Jewish phenomenon. When the events recorded in Acts chapter ten took place, suddenly the Church was no longer a Jewish phenomenon, but at that point got opened to the gentile world. The tent got enlarged and God expanded the circle. Cornelius, a Roman gentile is converted to Christianity, with his household. He is filled with the Holy Spirit and no longer is the Church exclusively a Jewish thing.

Prior to the doors ever opening to the gentile world through Cornelius, Acts chapter eight occurs. In that chapter a eunuch was added to the Christian faith.

Acts 8:26–31

26   Now an angel of the Lord said to Philip, "Go south to the road—the desert road—that goes down from Jerusalem to Gaza."

27   So he started out, and on his way he met an Ethiopian *eunuch*, an important official in charge of all the treasury of Candace, queen of the Ethiopians. This man had gone to Jerusalem to worship,

28   and on his way home was sitting in his chariot reading the book of Isaiah the prophet.

29   The Spirit told Philip, "Go to that chariot and stay near it."

30   Then Philip ran up to the chariot and heard the man reading Isaiah the prophet. "Do you understand what you are reading?" Philip asked.

31   "How can I," he said, "unless someone explains it to me?" So he invited Philip to come up and sit with him.

Here is a eunuch, who as an Ethiopian would also be a man of color. Remember, a eunuch could often be a gay person. He was reading the prophet Isaiah. He was not reading Micah, or Jeremiah, or another Old Testament prophet. In Isaiah 56 was the promise to the eunuch.

At the point of the text in Acts 8, the eunuch probably would have read Isaiah 56 about eunuchs who kept the covenant. He'd want to determine what that covenant was. He was studying Isaiah 53 when Philip joined his chariot.

Philip was joining the chariot of a gentile eunuch man of color. For many reasons, according to Jewish law, Philip could not associate with the eunuch, but he was obeying the leading of the Holy Spirit when he caught up with the chariot of the Ethiopian. It may well have surprised Philip to hear a foreigner reading the Word of God. But there it was, happening right before his eyes.

Acts 8:34-36
34   The eunuch asked Philip, "Tell me, please, who is the prophet talking about, himself or someone else?"
35   Then Philip began with that very passage of Scripture and told him the good news about Jesus.
36   As they traveled along the road, they came to some water and the eunuch said, "Look, here is water. Why shouldn't I be baptized?"

After Philip preaches about Jesus, the eunuch believes. The eunuch notices the water nearby and then asks, "Why shouldn't I be baptized?"

Philip could have said, "Well, you are a *eunuch*! Eunuchs can't get in the church! What's the matter with you!"

Philip could have answered, "Well, you're not a *Jew*!" or "Have you followed the law of Moses since the day you were born?"

Here is a very important question being asked by the eunuch. It is a life changing, life and death, question being asked by the Ethiopian eunuch. A man of several minorities wrapped into one, asking the all important question: "Tell me Philip, is there *anything* that hinders me? Anything at all that keeps me from having Jesus?"

"What hinders me, tell me if there is anything at all that stops me from being baptized, tell me so I can make it right!"

Philip said, "If you believe in your heart, you may." Believe what? The covenant. What covenant? That Jesus Christ of Nazareth died for the sins of the human race. That includes the eunuch of Ethiopia. That includes us all.

Jesus relates to the eunuch the same as anyone else in the rest of the Body, and says, "If you'll believe on Me, come."

The eunuch answered Philip: "I believe that Jesus Christ is the Son of God."[8]

He didn't say, "I believe I better stop being a eunuch." He simply said: "I believe that Jesus Christ is the Son of God."

Philip could have said, "Well, that's not good enough. You need to be circumcised, you need to stop eating pork, you can't have milk with your meals any more. When you dress you can't wear two kinds of fabric together. You can't grow two kinds of crops together any more. I know you have only the scroll of Isaiah, but I'll get you a copy of Leviticus, so you can follow it to the letter."

He said none of those things. Instead, Philip's answer was simply to make sure the eunuch believed in Jesus.

Acts 8:37-38

37   Philip said, "If you believe with all your heart, you may." The official answered, "I believe that Jesus Christ is the Son of God."

38   And he ordered the chariot to stop. Then both Philip and the eunuch went down into the water and Philip baptized him.

Philip, as a good Jew of the first century who would never have associated with a foreigner such as an Ethiopian, much less a eunuch, went down into the water with him, and baptized him. What could hinder him? The only thing that mattered was his belief in Christ. If a person will believe that Jesus is the Son of God, Who died for our sins, there is nothing that hinders them from being baptized.

CONCLUSION

We can see that God really offers a word to the gay/lesbian community and all other alienated peoples. God speaks to eunuchs;

those who couldn't get married to the opposite sex, realizing it just wasn't for them to be heterosexually coupled. They were just born that way. But if they will do what the Ethiopian eunuch did, believe that Jesus Christ is the Son of God, then they can be baptized and come into the covenant of Isaiah 56. God is doing it today just as in the day of the Ethiopian eunuch. God is drawing in the outcasts and making His house a house of prayer for *all* people.

DON'T QUOTE JESUS WHEN YOU CALL US NAMES!

Professor Paul Halsall at Fordham University, New York, has noted that Matthew 5:22 appears to be a gay friendly scripture.[9] Traditionally it is translated as:

> But I say unto you, That whosoever is angry with his brother without a cause shall be in danger of the judgment: and whosoever shall say to his brother, *Raca*, shall be in danger of the council: but whosoever shall say, *Thou fool*, shall be in danger of hell fire. Therefore if thou bring thy gift to the altar, and there rememberest that thy brother hath ought against thee; (Matt. 5:22–23 KJV)

Here Jesus condemns anyone who calls his brother certain names, and may be in danger of judgment for doing so.

In consulting the Greek text, according to Halsall the important words are *Raca/Rhaka*, and *fool/moros*. Professor Halsall comments,

> *Rhaka* is not a Greek word. This seems to be its only occurrence in a Greek text, and LSJ merely states that it is Hebrew. Most translations either ignore the word, or note it as a general term of abuse. Greenberg, relying on the work of Warren Johannssen, points out that its roots in a variety of Semitic languages mean *soft* [Hebrew *rakha*] and carries a connotation of effeminacy or weakness. The Akkadian word *raq* is used to denote a woman's name or occupation, and its

graphic representation in Akkadian derives from a Sumerian symbol for woman. In other words it can be argued that *Raca* [applied here to a *brother*] is an accusation of *sissy*, or perhaps *catamite*.[10]

Halsall further states "This argument works better if the word *moros* is considered. The word can mean *fool*, but it also has the amply used connotation of sexual aggressor, or even *homosexual aggressor*. LSJ9 confirms this, although Johannssen makes much more of it. It could reasonably be argued then that Jesus's words here condemn those who abuse others about their homosexuality."[11]

In other words it could be translated as:

But I say to you, whoever is angry with his brother will be liable to judgment, and whoever says to his brother *sissy* will be answerable to the Sanhedrin, and whoever says *You bugger* will be liable to fiery Gehenna.[12]

If this were the intent Jesus had when stating these words, then those who verbally abuse gays are themselves to be strongly criticized for calling gays unkind and cruel names.

NOTES

[1]*New Thayer's Greek-English Lexicon* (Peabody, MA: Hendrickson Publishers, 1981), 260.
[2]Ibid.
[3]2 Kings 20:16–19.
[4]2 Cor. 11:23–27.
[5]Zodhiates, *The Hebrew-Greek Key Study Bible*, 1593, #2617.
[6]Brown, Francis, *The New Brown-Driver-Briggs-Gesenius Hebrew-English Lexicon* (Peabody, MA: Hendrickson Publishers, 1979), 338, #2617.
[7]Luke 15:21–25.
[8]Acts 8:37.
[9]http://www.bway.net/~halsall/lgbh/lgbh-matt5.html
[10]Ibid.
[11]Ibid.
[12]Ibid.

SAME SEX LOVE STORIES

Now we begin to look at some very special people in the Bible. It is clear from scripture that these people all loved each other deeply and truly. It is not clear that this love was consummated with a physical sexual expression but they *were* in love with a member of the same sex. As we study these Old Testament people, we see that their lives reveal a great deal about the attitude of same sex love affairs in scripture. We will look at the loves of both King David and Ruth. However, before we look at their stories in the Old Testament, we will first turn to the New Testament to see what is revealed about them.

RUTH AND NAOMI

Matt. 1:1-6
1   A record of the genealogy of Jesus Christ the son of David, . . .
5   Salmon the father of Boaz, whose mother was *Rahab*, Boaz the father of Obed, whose mother was *Ruth*, Obed the father of Jesse,
6   and Jesse the father of *King David*. David was the father of Solomon, whose mother had been Uriah's wife,

Included among those listed in the lineage of Jesus are Rahab the prostitute, Ruth who loved a woman, and King David. When David is mentioned in the Bible, reference is frequently made to the fact that he committed adultery with Bathsheba, the wife of Uriah. After their affair, David had her husband killed and for this he was convicted in his heart. But David had many other sexual encounters. He had many women as wives, and he clearly also loved another man. None of these other sexual encounters and/or love affairs are worthy of comment or condemnation in the Bible except the one with Bathsheba, because she was already married, and her husband was murdered as a result.

We see God uses an interesting weave of people in the lineage

104

fabric of His Son, Jesus. Ruth was a Moabitess, who was not a Jew, but an alien to the covenant people; and David's love for another man was well documented.

As we look at their stories in the Old Testament, we first read of Ruth and Naomi. There is really very little said in scripture about Ruth and Naomi's relationship. We find their story recorded solely in the small book of Ruth. The four chapters tell the story of the life of Naomi. In chapter one, Naomi is a married Jewish woman whose husband is named Elimelech. Her husband took Naomi and their two sons Mahlon and Chilion to the land of Moab because of a famine in their homeland, Israel.[1]

Moab was not where Elimelech was supposed to be living. Moab was not part of the promised land or his inheritance from God. Calamity befalls them after leaving the promised land.

Naomi's husband dies, and later her two sons die. Prior to their death, each of the sons had married a foreign wife from among the Moabites. This was a legally prohibited practice for the Jews.

Jewish associations with Moabites and other heathen nations were forbidden by the covenant law God made with Israel.[2]

Therefore Naomi's family was under a curse according to the laws established by God for His covenant people. They were not to intermarry foreigners. They did. They were not to leave the promised land. They did. Calamity befell them.

Naomi was left without her husband and without her two sons. She arose to go home, back to the promised land. The story continues: she had heard in the country of Moab how the LORD had visited His people in giving them bread (Ruth 1:6).

The provision resides in the promised land, where God said it would be.

Ruth 1:7-15

7   With her two daughters-in-law she [Naomi] left the place where she had been living and set out on the road that would take them back to the land of Judah. . . .

12   [Naomi said to her daughters-in-law] Return home, my daughters; I am too old to have another husband. Even if I thought there was still hope for me—even if I had a husband tonight and then gave birth to sons—

13   would you wait until they grew up? Would you remain
unmarried for them? No, my daughters . . .
14   At this they wept again. Then Orpah kissed her moth-
er-in-law good-by, but Ruth clung to her.
15   "Look," said Naomi, "your sister-in-law is going back
to her people and her gods. Go back with her."

At this point Naomi feels it would be better for her daughters-
in-law to go back home and start their lives over. She says this
since she feels the hand of the Lord had gone out against her,
though it was not the Lord who brought her the calamity. Naomi
urges her daughters-in-law to go back home. Orpah kisses Naomi
good-bye, and plans to get on with her life. Orpah feels Naomi
gave good solid advice, and she plans to go back to her people and
find a husband.

Ruth, however, clings to Naomi, and won't let her go. Forget
the husband hunting. She wants to stay with Naomi. Naomi still
advises the young daughter-in-law to head back home and find a
new husband, as Orpah will do. In essence she says don't hang on
to me. There's no future in it.

Ruth was determined, however; she would far rather have
Naomi's companionship than any new husband. She wants to
spend the rest of her life living with Naomi. No man nor hope of
one can exceed her love for her female friend. She replies to her
dear one, unlike the other daughter-in-law, that nothing can make
her leave her side.

Ruth 1:16–17
16   But Ruth replied, "Don't urge me to leave you or to
turn back from you. Where you go I will go, and where you
stay I will stay. Your people will be my people and your God
my God.
17   Where you die I will die, and there I will be buried.
May the LORD deal with me, be it ever so severely, if anything
but death separates you and me."

These words of love that Ruth speaks as she is clinging to Naomi
are such intimate, tender, beautiful words of love, that for cen-

turies heterosexual couples have repeated them to each other at marriage altars: "Where you die I will die, and there I will be buried." We will be together until death do us part, Ruth says. Naomi agreed, and stopped trying to get Ruth to go home to her parents. Ruth was home as long as she was with Naomi. As far as Ruth was concerned, they belonged together.

Naomi could have said, "This is out of the question, woman!" But instead she agrees, and stops trying to push Ruth away. She is agreeing to Ruth's terms. They will be together forever. Nothing but death will separate them.

Ruth and Naomi go back to Israel to start a new life together. God blesses them, and God honors this covenant that these two women have made to each other. And Ruth becomes an ancestor of Jesus.

DAVID AND JONATHAN

To find the biblical account of David's life story, we turn to the book of 1 Samuel, the next book after Ruth.

To recap the story of Israel's history at this point, the Israelites asked God and the prophet Samuel for a king, a monarchy to rule their nation, rather than live under the theocracy of God's rule. A king is granted in Saul, but he proves to not follow God wholeheartedly. God is therefore determined to give the nation a different king: David, someone whose heart followed after God. David is a shepherd boy, watching his father's flocks, when the prophet Samuel comes to town and anoints David to be the next king of Israel. Years pass before that ever comes about. However, God begins to exalt David in the kingdom of Israel. David's name becomes known and from being a shepherd boy on the back forty he enters the household of the king, Saul. David shows up in the palace, and more than one person falls in love with him. One of them is the king's daughter, Michal.

1 Sam. 18:20–21
20   Now Saul's daughter Michal was in *love* with David, and when they told Saul about it, he was pleased.

21   "I will give her to him," he thought, "so that she may be a snare to him and so that the hand of the Philistines may be against him." So Saul said to David, "Now you have a second opportunity to become my son-in-law."

Saul was jealous of David, and he thought if he let David marry his daughter it could be a way to maneuver him into dangerous situations with the enemy Philistines, and get him killed. David was being exalted by the hand of God in the kingdom, and Saul could see it. By asking for a dowry of Philistine foreskins, David could be forced into mortal combat, and perhaps get killed. Therefore Saul thought it was good that his daughter loved David.

The Hebrew word for *loved* is #157 in *Strong's Concordance* #157 *'ahab* (aw-hab'); to have affection for (sexually or otherwise).
"This word covers the scope that the English word does for love."[3] It means to "be a passionate lover or paramour, it implies an ardent and vehement inclination of the mind and a tenderness of affection at the same time. . . . It denotes a strong emotional attachment for and a desire to possess or be in the presence of the object of love. . . . ."[4]

It means what we would mean when we say someone is in love, whether that feeling is actually a mature love, infatuation, or lustful desire to possess. Michal was in love. We have no problem understanding that. She saw David, and she wanted to be his wife. She wanted him. She desired him. She was in love.

However, the same word #157 *'ahab* (aw-hab'); or *'aheb* is used a few verses earlier in 1 Samuel 18:1–7.

1 Sam. 18:1–3
1   After David had finished talking with Saul, Jonathan became one in spirit with David, and he *loved* him as himself.
2   From that day Saul kept David with him and did not let him return to his father's house.
3   And Jonathan made a covenant with David because he *loved* him as himself.

Jonathan became one in spirit with David, and he *loved* him as himself.

Jonathan is Michal's brother. He is a prince in the kingdom of Israel, next in line for the throne, whenever his father King Saul dies.

The King James Version states that Jonathan's soul was knit to the soul of David. What is our soul? It is our mind, our feelings, our intellect, our personality. It is the sum of who we are on the inside, apart from our physical visible body. Jonathan's heart, his whole being, was knit to the personality, heart and sum internal makeup of David. Jonathan *loved* him, every bit as much as his sister did, and she became David's wife.

When David showed up in the court of the king, not only did the daughter of the king fall in love with David, but so did the son of the king, Jonathan.

And Saul took him that day, and would let him go no more home to his father's house. Then Jonathan and David made a covenant, because he loved him as his own soul.

Jonathan makes a covenant with David long before verse 20 where it becomes known that Michal, the sister, also is in love with David. Before it is ever known that the daughter loves David, the son hones in on David and makes a covenant with him. What is this covenant? It is a covenant of love. Let's look at this ceremony of love closely.

1 Sam. 18:3-4
3   And Jonathan made a covenant with David because he *loved* him as himself.
4   Jonathan took off the robe he was wearing and gave it to David, along with his tunic, and even his sword, his bow and his belt.

Jonathan, next in line for the throne, stands next to the young, handsome, ruddy shepherd, takes off his royal robe and puts it upon David. In a marriage ceremony there is the strong symbolism of coming under another's covering. Jonathan is giving this shepherd all the access to his royalty. Jonathan not only removes his royal cloak, but the rest of his garments as well, and even his sword. He totally surrenders to David. There was no battle, except of the heart. Jonathan is giving himself totally to David as if he were a prisoner of war. He was. A prisoner of love!

It is as if Jonathan says to the object of his love, this rugged young shepherd, "Here is my coat, my robe, my clothes, my position, my sword, my defenses are down. I'm yours!" Even later in the story, Jonathan makes David promise to raise Jonathan's children, if anything ever happens to him. Jonathan freely gives David his name, his identity and position in the kingdom (his royal robes), his protection, and all that keeps him safe (his clothing and his sword). He surrenders, because he loves David. So does his sister, using the same word for love, and she marries David also. Additionally, Jonathan gives David his bow, the way to provide food. He lets David be the provider, the breadwinner. He takes off his belt and gives it to David. We see the tunic surrendered as well.

Because of love, the prince offers up everything he has to his beloved, including even the throne, and all that symbolizes the royal position.

Saul is still very jealous and hates David. By 1 Samuel 19, Saul wants David killed. But Jonathan couldn't let that happen to the one he loved so much! Here is what the scripture says:

1 Sam. 19:1-2
1   Saul told his son Jonathan and all the attendants to kill David. But Jonathan was *very fond* of David
2   and warned him, "My father Saul is looking for a chance to kill you. Be on your guard tomorrow morning; go into hiding and stay there.

Jonathan, Saul's son, was *very fond* of David. He *delighted* in David. Delighted much in fact.

The Old Testament Hebrew word for *delighted* or be *very fond* of in *Strong's Concordance* is #2654 *chaphets* (khaw-fates'). This word means "to take delight in, to be pleased with, to have an affection for, to desire, to choose . . . the main meaning is to feel a *strong positive attraction* for something . . . this word involves subjective involvement . . . it means to like someone . . . very, very much.''⁵

Jonathan is obviously enamoured of David! That's why he is risking his own neck to go tell David to watch out and defy his own father, the very king! He loves him enough to risk his own life to save him.

The story between Jonathan and David continues:

1 Sam. 20:1-3
1   Then David fled from Naioth at Ramah and went to Jonathan and asked, "What have I done? What is my crime? How have I wronged your father, that he is trying to take my life?"
2   "Never!" Jonathan replied. "You are not going to die! Look, my father doesn't do anything, great or small, without confiding in me. Why would he hide this from me? It's not so!"
3   But David took an oath and said, "Your father knows very well that I have found *favor* in your eyes, and he has said to himself, 'Jonathan must not know this or he will be grieved.' Yet as surely as the LORD lives and as you live, there is only a step between me and death."

The word here for *favor* is *Strong's* O.T. #2580. It means preciousness, loveliness, favor, and charm. David is saying to Jonathan, "You find me charming, and your father knows you find me charming."

Jonathan declares he would do whatever David wants. But David is nonetheless concerned that since Saul knows of their relationship, he would not share the plots he has against David with his son.

The two of them concoct a plan to find out Saul's intentions of harm toward David, and how that will be made known to David once Jonathan finds it out. Continuing on, we find Jonathan speaking to David.

1 Sam. 20:14-17
14   But show me unfailing kindness like that of the LORD

as long as I live, so that I may not be killed,
15   and do not ever cut off your kindness from my family
—not even when the LORD has cut off every one of David's
enemies from the face of the earth.''
16   So Jonathan made a covenant with the house of David,
saying, ''May the LORD call David's enemies to account.''
17   *And Jonathan had David reaffirm his oath out of love
for him, because he loved him as he loved himself.*

Jonathan made a covenant of protection with David earlier that
resembles a marriage ceremony. Now Jonathan is making a second
covenant with David, and he asks for something special. Basically
the request follows this line of thinking: ''I not only want you to
promise me that you'll be good to me, but I want you to promise
that if anything happens to me you'll raise my children.''

This is very unusual, since David is a threat to the throne. Jonathan should have asked his sisters. He should have asked someone else in his family to promise to raise his children if anything
happens to him as prince. Under most circumstances, to continue
the family's royal line you would not ask the enemy of that throne,
who then would find it politically expedient to destroy the royal
lineage and eliminate all contenders for the throne. David should
be the last person with access to the children of the royal family.
Someone trustworthy to carry on the royal lineage, with no hidden agenda, should have those children in safe keeping to assure
they properly become the next monarchs of the lineage of Saul and
Jonathan.

But David is entrusted with the care of these royal heirs. Jonathan trusts David with his life, his future, and the care of his
descendants all because he loves him. And, because of this love,
David agrees.

As the story continues, David has residence in the royal palace.
He is hiding out for safety's sake since he knows his head is on
the line. He has not shown up for a few days already, and Jonathan wants to know if his father is really all that serious about his
beloved David's demise.

As they are sitting at dinner, Saul finally asks the question,
''Where is David?'' Saul does not ask the servants. He does not

ask the generals, or the captains who were under David militarily. He does not ask even David's wife, his daughter Michal. He asks Jonathan.

When Jonathan gives his father the agreed upon excuse for David's absence from the palace and the king's dinner table, Saul gets livid!

1 Sam. 20:25-31

25   He sat in his customary place by the wall, opposite Jonathan, and Abner sat next to Saul, but David's place was empty.

26   Saul said nothing that day, for he thought, "Something must have happened to David to make him ceremonially unclean—surely he is unclean."

27   But the next day, the second day of the month, David's place was empty again. Then Saul said to his son Jonathan, "Why hasn't the son of Jesse come to the meal, either yesterday or today?"

28   Jonathan answered, "David earnestly asked me for permission to go to Bethlehem.

29   He said, 'Let me go, because our family is observing a sacrifice in the town and my brother has ordered me to be there. If I have found favor in your eyes, let me get away to see my brothers.' That is why he has not come to the king's table."

30   Saul's anger flared up at Jonathan and he said to him, "You son of a *perverse* and *rebellious* woman! Don't I know that you have sided with the son of Jesse to your own shame and to the shame of the mother who bore you?

31   As long as the son of Jesse lives on this earth, neither you nor your kingdom will be established. Now send and bring him to me, for he must die!"

In verse 30, above, Saul is so angry he explodes and says everything he thinks and is angry about. There is no holding these emotions back. So out comes the truth!

Here Saul is calling Jonathan a pervert, blaming his mother. He's the "son of a *perverse* and *rebellious* woman." "You pervert!'' Saul is saying, "which, by the way, is your mother's fault, you are her son!'' (Calling him a momma's boy.) He is no son of Saul's!

"Don't I know that you have *sided with* [KJV: *chosen*] the son of Jesse to your own shame and to the shame of the mother who bore you?'' The father is saying, "Did you think I haven't noticed! Don't you think I noticed how you hang around David! Don't I know that you have *sided with*, or *chosen* the son of Jesse; I know you have *chosen* David!''

Chosen or *sided with* here is: (#977) *bachar* (baw-khar'); it means to love, to be especially chosen, and considered the best. Properly: to try, i.e. (by implication) select. Something is selected and judged to be the best after it has been tried.[6]

Saul acknowledges in anger what he already believes. He acknowledges that Jonathan is in love with David and he says so.

Furthermore in the King James Version he calls this affair confusion, saying it was "to thine own *confusion*, and unto the *confusion* of thy mother's nakedness.''

Confusion here [#1322 *bosheth* (bo'-sheth)]; speaks of shame (the feeling and the condition, as well as its cause); ashamed, confusion, greatly, (put to) shame (-ful thing).

Saul's outcry is condemning the relationship between the two men. He is yelling angrily. "This whole perverted affair of choosing and selecting David after trying him out and choosing him as the best, is shameful, you rebellious boy! You're no son of mine. You're a disgrace, a shame to the family!''

Regrettably in our own days, this certainly is an all too common emotional reaction in dealing with the disclosure of homosexual orientation among a family member.

Saul's solution is to kill David.

1 Sam. 20:31-33

31 As long as the son of Jesse lives on this earth, neither you nor your kingdom will be established. Now send and bring him to me, for he must die!''

32 "Why should he be put to death? What has he done?'' Jonathan asked his father.

33   But Saul hurled his spear at him to kill him. Then
Jonathan knew that his father intended to kill David.

Jonathan demands, "Why!? Tell me why! What has he done
that's all that bad?" Saul throws a javelin at his son, to kill him!

Jonathan grieves because his father treated David so badly. He
can't eat, he has no appetite. Not that he himself had been in-
sulted, but because his beloved David has been banished, and now
has a death warrant out for him.

They had a prearranged agreement to see each other once Jonathan got an assessment of the situation in the palace with Saul.
So David and Jonathan secretly meet.

1 Sam. 20:41
41   After the boy had gone, David got up from the south
side and bowed down before Jonathan three times, with his
face to the ground. Then they kissed each other and wept
together—but David wept the most.

They now realize they have to be separated, and David will have
to go into hiding from the king. This distressing interruption to
their relationship, and to life in general as it once was, causes them
to weep in each other's arms, kissing each other all the while.

After much crying and kissing, Jonathan is eventually able
to let go of David and separate from his beloved for a time
". . . since both of us have sworn in the name of the LORD . . ."
It is because of the covenant they have made in the name of the
Lord toward each other that they trust God to work it out. They
are still promising to watch over each other's children.

Time passes. David has a band of six hundred followers. Saul
is still trying to track David down to kill him. David is staying in
the wilderness.

1 Sam. 23:14–18
14   David stayed in the desert strongholds and in the hills
of the Desert of Ziph. Day after day Saul searched for him,
but God did not give David into his hands.
15   While David was at Horesh in the Desert of Ziph, he

learned that Saul had come out to take his life.

16   And Saul's son Jonathan went to David at Horesh and helped him find strength in God.

17   "Don't be afraid," he said. "My father Saul will not lay a hand on you. *You will be king over Israel, and I will be second to you.* Even my father Saul knows this."

18   The two of them made a covenant before the LORD. Then Jonathan went home, but David remained at Horesh.

Jonathan couldn't stay away. He went looking for and found the very David whom he loved, but that his father couldn't find. Interesting that God would not let Saul find David, but He let Jonathan find him. Jonathan went to strengthen David's hand in the Lord.

It was a very dangerous thing for Jonathan to go looking for David. It could easily have cost him his life. Also, the text does not say he had to search for David. He merely arose and went to him. He knew where David was hiding.

It is interesting to note that when Jonathan goes to strengthen David, he tells him that Saul will never find him, and that David will be the king over Israel. That's strange, because by heritage, Prince Jonathan should be the king, not David. God had declared this to David as a shepherd boy, but it was said secretly before only his family by the prophet Samuel. Saul was never told that David had this destiny. Yet Jonathan freely gives up his right to the throne to the man he loves as his own soul.

In verse 17, Jonathan says "*You will be king over Israel, and I will be second to you.*"

If a kingdom has two thrones set up, and the king sits on one, who sits right next to the king? The queen? Or perhaps the king's spouse? Jonathan was in line to be king, yet he says, David, you will be king, but that's fine with me. I'll be right *next to you.* That's what Jonathan thought. Jonathan was supposed to be king. He gave it up to sit next to a handsome shepherd who came to play a few songs in the court for his father. He fell in love with David as soon as he saw him, as did his sister.

At the risk of his own life, Jonathan sneaks into the woods and recommits his vows to David before the Lord, and clearly states he will submit to David as king if he can sit next to him. Yet, that is not what developed in their lives. While David was still a fugitive from Saul, Israel went to war with the Philistines, and King Saul and his son Jonathan both die in the battle.

In 2 Samuel chapter 1, David gets the news that Jonathan is dead. What David says when he hears that Jonathan is dead is remarkable:

2 Sam. 1:26
I grieve for you, Jonathan my brother; you were very dear to me. *Your love for me was wonderful, more wonderful than that of women.*

David declares the love Jonathan had for him was wonderful, it passed the love of women. David would know; he had also had a lot of women. If David had to choose one source of human love, he'd choose Jonathan's over a woman's embrace, because Jonathan's love was better.

He preferred Jonathan's love, the love that said "You can be King, I'll just sit next to you." This was the love that made a covenant with provision to be guardian over and have custody of each other's children. Jonathan loved David as he loved his own soul.

Once David became king, the household of Saul went to war against David for seven years. Saul's heirs lost eventually, and David's throne was consolidated. It is later in 2 Samuel chapter 9 that David then is able to do anything about the covenant he made with Jonathan.

2 Sam. 9:3–8
3   The king asked, "Is there no one still left of the house of Saul to whom I can show God's kindness?" Ziba answered the king, "There is still a son of Jonathan; he is crippled in both feet." . . .
5   So King David had him brought from Lo Debar, from the house of Makir son of Ammiel.
6   When Mephibosheth son of Jonathan, the son of Saul, came to David, he bowed down to pay him honor. David said,

"Mephibosheth!" "Your servant," he replied.

7   "Don't be afraid," David said to him, "for I will surely show you kindness for the sake of your father Jonathan. I will restore to you all the land that belonged to your grandfather Saul, and you will always eat at my table."

8   Mephibosheth bowed down and said, "What is your servant, that you should notice a dead dog like me?"

King David restores to Mephibosheth all the land his grandfather had owned, and commands that from now on Mephibosheth will eat at the king's table. He does this to the enemy's family because he made a covenant of love with Jonathan, and this was his son. David kept the covenant and took Mephibosheth under his care. The promises were kept, even after death.

CONCLUSION

David, who shows up in Matthew chapter 1 among the lineage list of Jesus, was never rebuked for his love for Jonathan, nor for thinking his love with Jonathan was better than the love of women. David was never rebuked for any of his relationships except the inappropriate one with Bathsheba.

The Bible never clearly states whether Jonathan and David had a sexual consummation of their relationship, but the Bible never denies it either. It does clearly state the feelings involved, and that it is not wrong for a man to be in love with another man. There is nothing needing "deliverance." There is no "homosexual lust" demon to cast out. There is an acknowledgment of love, deep and pure and intimate in its expressed emotions. The Bible does not rebuke those feelings, nor does it denigrate those feelings. It *does* show David's honor in keeping his vows to his very special loved one.

HISTORICAL SAME SEX COMMITMENT CEREMONIES
WITHIN THE CHURCH

The commitment Ruth made to Naomi was so rich in its stated love that couples have repeated those words at marriage altars ever since. The commitment ceremony that David and Jonathan experienced was a life long pledging of love for one another. Down through the ages there have been many other same sex ceremonies, even within the Church, in which same sex couples pledge love, commitment to one another, and to live and die for one another. Over time the ceremonies were formalized with the aid of clergy, with witnesses present observing the same sex couple exchanging vows, and then celebrating the ceremony with a banquet feast.

John Boswell documented with extensive detail the various ceremonies of committed life-long love relationships held within Christendom by same sex couples.[7] Often these ceremonies, when among male couples, were translated roughly as "making a brother."

Christians were already brothers and sisters in Christ, so there was no need to have a ceremony to make a person your brother unless the meaning was deeper than that of siblings. The rite in ancient Rome allowed a person to adopt another unilaterally with equal reciprocal rights. This was a legitimate way non-biologically related individuals could leave their worldly goods in their will to this person, superseding the rights of biological families. Under the early Roman empire, men began to adopt each other as brothers (rather than as sons). This made the relationship one of equals, and heirs, but not as children of each other.[8]

"Adopt a brother" was a specific term for establishing a legal relationship with a homosexual lover. Such adoptions were understood to establish in law a same-sex union.[9] The terms sister and brother even in scripture could have very real sexual and erotic overtones as in the *Song of Solomon*, as Boswell points out.[10] In the *Song of Solomon* the Hebrew scriptures consistently refer to one's spouse and lover as a brother or sister, and clearly are not referring to a biological sibling. (*Song of Solomon* 4:10,12)

Though the name of these ceremonies occasionally historically gets translated as *spiritual brotherhood*, Boswell points out that *soul-mates* would be a better definition.[11]

These same-sex couples would be ceremonially united because of affection, passion, or desire,[12] and were prominent through ancient history. They constituted the same sex equivalent of a marriage.

Boswell documented many examples of these. For example, in Plato's work, *Symposium*, he characterized same-sex unions very pointedly as permanent, exclusive unions of coevals. He describes the love of Archilles for Patroclus with his willingness to join his beloved in death as a wife would die for her husband.[13]

Aristotle describes as admirable but not bizarre a pair of male lovers who spent their lives together maintaining a single household, and arranged to be buried together.[14]

Harmodius and Aristogiton were a pair of lovers believed to have founded the Athenian democracy.[15]

Hadrian and Antinoüs, the former, one of the most effective commanders of the Roman army, and one of the five good emperors, were among one of the best known and romantically idealized couples of antiquity.[16] They were both free men, united by love, and when Antinoüs died tragically, Hadrian wept openly for him as he would have for a wife.

The poet Martial describes at the opening of the second century how "the bearded Callistratus married the rugged Afer under the same law by which a woman takes a husband."[17]

Among the early saints and martyrs of the church, the most influential set of paired same-sex saints was Serge and Bacchus. They were Roman soldiers of high standing in the late third, early fourth centuries A.D. They were noted in their love as being the same as a heterosexually married couple.[18] For their faith in Christ, Bacchus was the first to die, flogged to death, leaving his executioners exhausted from the effort. Serge was returned to jail, depressed and heartsick. Serge wept, and cried out in his cell, "No longer brother and fellow soldier will we chant together. Behold how good and pleasant it is for brothers to abide in oneness. You have been unyoked from me, leaving me alone on earth, now single, without comfort."[19]

Serge had a vision of Bacchus that night encouraging him to join Bacchus, and through a perfect confession to *obtain Bacchus* when he finished the course.[20] Bacchus promised that if Serge followed the Lord, he'd get as his reward, not the joy of paradise itself, nor the crown of martyrdom, but Bacchus himself. This was remarkable by early church standards.

Boswell comments that Serge and Bacchus came to represent to subsequent generations of Christians the quintessential "paired" military saints; and they became the preeminent "couple" invoked in later ceremonies of same-sex unions (see text below). In the church-approved story of their lives by the Byzantine Metaphrastes, Serge is referred to as the "sweet companion and lover" of Bacchus. They also apparently lived together in the same household.

Boswell's additional comments about Serge and Bacchus are worth reproducing in full:[21]

The various words used for "bond" and "union" in the account are striking. For example, σύνδεσμος is not only the strongest of the possible words for "union," or "uniting," but combines a fascinating range of associations, all certainly familiar to the author of the Greek life of Serge and Bacchus. The most direct of these would be New Testament phrases, many quoted or echoed in the text, especially Col. 3:14 ("love, which is the bond of perfection" [ἀγάπην, ὅ ἐστιν σύνδεσμος τῆς τελειότητος]) and Eph. 4:3 ("to keep the unity of the spirit in the bond of peace"). Less clear but even more startling is the use of the same word in [LXX] 1 Kings 14:24, where it has been taken since the time of Jerome to refer to homosexuality ("And there were also sodomites in the land: and they did according to all the abominations of the nations . . ."). This is likely a misprision of the Hebrew, but could hardly have been unknown to or missed by the author of the life, if it seemed obvious to Jerome. Its homosexual implication was, moreover, strengthened under Christian influence by the New Testament phrase "bonds of iniquity," which employed the same Greek word for "bond." Following classical usage, late antique and patristic writers used σύνδεσμος to describe particularly intimate unions of many sorts, ranging from the union of the Trinity to the marriage of husband and wife.

Another set of paired saints were the women martyrs Perpetua and Felicitas. They were a Christian noblewoman and a female slave martyred for their beliefs by the Romans at Carthage about 203 A.D. Though part of a group that was slain, these two were paired in Christian literature. They were called the "most manly of soldiers." Neither had a reference to a husband; even when Perpetua's father tried to dissuade her by appealing to the fact that her nursing son would have to live without her and what pain it would cause her brothers, no husband is mentioned.[22]

Other saints who chose death to be with one another include Polyeuct and Nearchos. Both were Roman soldiers who were martyred for professed faith in Christ in Armenia of the mid-third century. Roman authorities used the wife of Polyeuct to plead with him after his beloved Nearchos's death to avoid martyrdom himself. Polyeuct would not heed the pleas of his wife, and was specifically said to have embraced death for the love of Nearchos. Their fourth century biographer says that Polyeuct "never forgot his love for Nearchos because they were one soul and disposition in two bodies. And as Polyeuct gazed on Nearchos he said 'Brother Nearchos, remember our secret pledge.' " John Boswell comments that "the love between Polyeuct and Nearchos is the driving force behind the tale as well as its most moving component, even though at the outset it involved a pagan and a Christian. Moreover, this aspect of the story overrides considerations of orthodoxy. Polyeuct dies convinced that he will enter heaven and there be perpetually joined to Nearchos (but apparently not to his wife). . . . The story may have evoked particular enjoyment from those sensitive to romantic relationships with a party of the same gender, particularly since both men were soldiers, and there was a widespread and ancient Hellenistic connection between homoeroticism and the military."[23]

It is interesting to note, too, that all three of the above pairs (Perpetua and Felicitas, Nearchos and Polyeuct, Serge and Bacchus) were commemorated each year in the liturgical cycles of the church. And, as Boswell points out, in all three cases there was some social inequality that might have been essential to same-sex pairings: Felicitas was a slave while Perpetua was a Roman aristocrat; Polyeuct was of higher social standing than Nearchos; Serge was of higher military rank than Bacchus. Two of the three stories involve gender cross-dressing, even if involuntary.

Ceremonies and commitments of love among same-sex couples were known all over the early Christian world.[24] Initially these ceremonies were a set of prayers, but by the twelfth century they had become a full service, involving the burning of candles, joining the two parties' right hands, placing their hands on the Bible, saying the Lord's prayer, and a kiss.[25] It was closely related in ceremony to a heterosexual marriage.

The following liturgical office of same-sex union dates from the eleventh century in the Greek church of Grottaferrata in southern Italy (another version is also seen two centuries earlier):[26]

Office for Same-Sex Union

i.
The priest shall place the holy Gospel on the Gospel stand and they that are to be joined together place their [right] hands on it, holding lighted candles in their left hands. Then shall the priest cense them and say the following:

ii.
In peace we beseech Thee, O Lord.

For heavenly peace, we beseech Thee, O Lord.

For the peace of the entire world, we beseech Thee, O Lord.

For this holy place, we beseech Thee, O Lord.

That these thy servants, N. and N., be sanctified with thy spiritual benediction, we beseech Thee, O Lord.

That their love abide without offense or scandal all the days of their lives, we beseech Thee, O Lord.

That they be granted all things needed for salvation and godly enjoyment of life everlasting, we beseech Thee, O Lord.

That the Lord God grant unto them unashamed faithfulness, [and] sincere love, we beseech Thee, O Lord.

That we be saved, we beseech Thee, O Lord.
Have mercy on us, O God.
"Lord, have mercy," shall be said three times.

iii.

The priest [*shall say*]:

Forasmuch as Thou, O Lord and Ruler, art merciful and loving, who didst establish humankind after thine image and likeness, who didst deem it meet that thy holy apostles Philip and Bartholomew be united, bound one unto the other not by nature but by faith and the spirit. As Thou didst find thy holy martyrs Serge and Bacchus worthy to be united together, bless also these thy servants, N. and N., joined together not by the bond of nature but by faith and in the mode of the spirit, granting unto them peace and love and oneness of mind. Cleanse from their hearts every stain and impurity, and vouchsafe unto them to love one another without hatred and without scandal all the days of their lives, with the aid of the Mother of God and all thy saints, forasmuch as all glory is thine. [*See Boswell, op. cit., for scholarly research footnotes to this text.*]

As late as 1578 there was a gay marriage ceremony held in Rome in the church of St. John of the Latin Gate between a group of men. Roman theologians said that "since sex between male and female could be legitimate only within marriage, it had seemed equally fair to them to authorize these ceremonies and mysteries of the Church."[27] But this was already the time of the Inquisition, and capital punishment was meted out to some of the men by homophobic civil authorities, doubtless with ecclesiastic tacit consent. However, in other areas (Greece, Dalmatia) same-sex church ceremonies continued on into the 17th and 18th centuries.

NOTES

[1] Ruth 1:1-2.
[2] Deut. 7:3-4; 23:3.
[3] Zodhiates, *The Hebrew-Greek Key Study Bible*, 1575.
[4] Ibid.
[5] Ibid., 1593.

[6]Ibid., 1581.

[7]John Boswell, *Same-Sex Unions in Premodern Europe* (New York: Villard Books, 1994).

[8]Ibid., 98. [9]Ibid., 99. [10]Ibid., 24. [11]Ibid., 27. [12]Ibid., 56. [13]Ibid., 58–59. [14]Ibid., 60. [15]Ibid., 61. [16]Ibid., 64. [17]Ibid., 80. [18]Ibid., 147. [19]Ibid., 149. [20]Ibid., 150. [21]Ibid., 152–53. [22]Ibid., 140–41. [23]Ibid., 145. [24]Ibid., 184. [25]Ibid., 185. [26]Ibid., 294–95. [27]Ibid., 265.

TRADITIONS AND THE TABERNACLE OF DAVID

As we have studied scripture up to this point we have looked at the passages that people have traditionally thought dealt with homosexuality. But now we need to look at what the Lord is really saying to the Church universal, to the gay community, to the non-gay community and to others for such a time as this. No longer having to debate whether Leviticus chapter 20 means this or that, we can now lay all that aside to see what point the Lord is trying to get across to the Church. We begin by looking at Ephesians chapter 2. We will not be looking at homosexuality per se, since we have already looked at the scriptures that supposedly deal with that topic.

It becomes apparent that there is a parallel between what God was trying to say to the first century Jewish Church regarding the many gentile converts, and what the Lord is saying to the church regarding the many gay believers coming to Christ:

Eph. 2:11-22
11   Therefore, remember that formerly you who are *Gentiles* by birth and called "uncircumcised" by those who call themselves "the circumcision" (that done in the body by the hands of men)—
12   remember that at that time you were separate from Christ, excluded from citizenship in Israel and foreigners to the covenants of the promise, without hope and without God in the world.
13   But now in Christ Jesus you who once were far away have been brought near through the blood of Christ.
14   For he himself is our peace, who has made the two one and has destroyed the barrier, the dividing wall of hostility,
15   by abolishing in his flesh the law with its commandments and regulations. His purpose was to create in himself one new man out of the two, thus making peace,
16   and in this one body to reconcile both of them to God through the cross, by which he put to death their hostility.
17   He came and preached peace to you who were far away

126

and peace to those who were near.

18   For through him we both have access to the Father by one Spirit.

19   Consequently, you are no longer foreigners and aliens, but fellow citizens with God's people and members of God's household,

20   built on the foundation of the apostles and prophets, with Christ Jesus himself as the chief cornerstone.

21   In him the whole building is joined together and rises to become a holy temple in the Lord.

22   And in him you too are being built together to become a dwelling in which God lives by his Spirit.

This is a true word of prophecy to the gay community. When you read the passage and read the word *gentile* read in its place *gay community*. The passage in verses 11–12 could just as easily read:

Therefore, remember that formerly you being the *gay community* by birth and called "uncircumcised" [or those who were outside the covenant people of God] by those who call themselves "the circumcision" [or those who considered themselves to be the exclusive covenant people of God], remember that at that time you gay folks were separate from Christ, you were excluded from citizenship in Israel, and membership in the Church, and foreigners, outsiders to the covenants of the promise, without hope and without God in the world. [You gay folks were outside the walls of the Church, you simply were not knowingly admitted in]. You were excluded, were never introduced or thought acceptable for the promise. Therefore you were strangers to the promise, and without hope, because the Church thought you were in the world without God.

The majority of the *gay community* has been thought of as without hope by the Church. Because of what they have been taught, gays also thought they were without hope. However, the scripture goes on to declare:

13   But now in Christ Jesus you who once were far away
have been brought near through the blood of Christ.

The blood of Jesus is an established historical fact. No one considered to be outside the covenant has to wait for somebody to give
a stamp of approval. No board of elders has to approve whether
gay people can be Christians. No denomination has to have an affirming vote before gays can be placed in the Body of Christ. All
that brings gays or anyone into the Body is the shed blood of
Jesus. Those who were once far away from God have been
brought near to God by the blood of Christ. Not by a majority
vote. Not by a Congressional act, or a new law, or a decision in
a human court of law. The historical fact of the cross of Jesus
makes the way wide open to whomsoever.

Whosoever believes on Jesus shall be saved. Not just Jews, gentiles, heterosexuals. *Whosoever* has been brought near. They *have
been*, past tense, they don't have to hope to be or wait to be, because they *have been brought near*, two thousand years ago.

Some years back, several of our church members were visiting
another church in our city. The message we heard from Genesis
49:22 was how Joseph was a climbing vine.

We were told that a climbing vine has within its nature the ability
to keep on climbing. No matter how many times it gets ripped
down, torn down and stomped on, its very nature is to keep climbing again. Eventually a climbing vine will rip apart the mortar in
the bricks and the wall will come tumbling down. Many gay people
in the Church are like that. They are climbing vines. No matter
how many times they try to get in the house and presence of God,
they find a wall between them and non-gay believers. Gay believers
try to climb over the wall. To keep them out, they are torn down,
ripped down, thrown out, stomped on and told never to return by
non-gay believers. But their nature is to return, and start climbing over that wall again. That's the nature of a vine. The wall gets
worn down with each attempt of the vine to climb over. A little
more mortar gets knocked out with every encounter, and the wall
weakens.

Eph. 2:14

14   For he himself is our peace, who has made the two one
and has destroyed the barrier, the dividing wall of hostility

According to this passage in *Ephesians 2:14*, God has already
broken down the middle wall of partition between us. It is a sovereign work of the Almighty. As far as God is concerned, gays and
whosoever else will, are added into the Kingdom roll call and
placed in the Lamb's book of life whenever their trust is in Christ.
Votes among denominational delegates don't amount to anything
to the believer already brought near by the Blood of Christ.

Years ago I had a dream. I dreamt I was going to lead a worship service for a group of gay Christians. Our location, however,
was in a large college auditorium, and we were not scheduled to
have the entire auditorium, but a section of it. In this dream, a
Christian leader notorious for being against gay people was to have
a service in the other part of the auditorium. But it was no problem
because the large auditorium could be partitioned off by its dividing walls. As we each were about to start, no one could be found
to close the walls in order to separate the two groups. We looked
frantically to locate a janitor or maintenance person. None could
be found. It was a frantic attempt to get the wall to divide the
groups, but to no avail.

I became desperate in my attempt to get that partition closed,
and when no answer was to be found, I resigned myself to just forgetting about our meeting and sitting through the other, much
larger one. There was no point in trying to have competing micro-
phones and speakers in the same large auditorium. At this point
I awoke. Then ever so quietly this scripture came bubbling up into
my heart:

Eph. 2:14

14   For he himself is our peace, who has made the two one
and has destroyed the barrier, the dividing wall of hostility

It was suddenly one of those divine moments when you get a
glimpse into the heart and purpose of God. The book of Ephesians continues:

Eph. 2:15-16

15   by abolishing in his flesh the law with its commandments and regulations. His purpose was to create in himself
one new man out of the two, thus making peace,

16   and in this one body to reconcile both of them to God
through the cross, by which he put to death their hostility.

It is the cross of Jesus that destroys the enmity, and He makes
peace. We look backward into history and we see that both the
cross and blood of Jesus are historical facts. Therefore His cross
has already knocked down the dividing wall, giving gays and lesbians freedom to walk in liberty with the rest of the Body of
Christ. This is so in Christ whether the rest of the Body receives
this revelation about gays or not.

If the eye says to the hand, "I have no need of you," it does not
negate the hand still being part of the body, nor does it mean the
hand does not exist. The hand does exist, and God made all parts
into one body. Whether others receive gays and lesbians gladly or
not, if they are Christians, they are part of that Body. It doesn't
matter if non-gays say they have no need for gays; the gay person, by belief in Jesus, is still a part of the Body of Christ.

In the early Church, the same questions were being raised about
gentile believers by Jewish Christians that are being asked today
by heterosexual believers about gay Christians.

According to Acts chapter 10, Cornelius was an Italian, not a
Jew. He was a God-fearing man who prayed, and gave alms to
the poor. Cornelius was not a Christian, however, because he had
not yet believed in Jesus. Before Cornelius can ever be told the
good news about salvation for *whosoever will*, God had to first
prepare Peter for the radical idea that the Lord just might love
someone besides Peter's own little group. The box humans try to
force God into is too small for God. God could work with gentiles in ways that were not yet prescribed by scripture. God can
also work with gay people in ways that heterosexuals might not
suspect. Preconceived ideas about how God has to work do not
limit God, except in our own mind.

According to the Jewish religious understanding of the scriptures, it was illegal [read: *sin*] for a good Jew to even *go* to the

house of a gentile. Peter had to receive a vision from the Lord in which a sheet was lowered before him three times from heaven. On it were all the things a good Jew knew he could not eat, everything forbidden by the Laws of the Old Testament.

In Acts 10:9-15 we see Peter in a trance, on the rooftop while lunch is being prepared. God shows Peter a sheet, lowered before him from Heaven. On it is everything forbidden to eat under the old Jewish dietary laws. God tells Peter to eat this stuff anyway. It is truly abhorrent to Peter, and he says, "No, I can't!" He has always been a good Jew, and is not about to defile himself now! Three times God lowers this sheet and commands Peter to eat. Each time Peter says no. Then God says what He has cleansed is not to be called unclean, or unholy.

Now Peter has to ponder this, because he thinks God is speaking about food. But the reality is, God is not talking about food, He is talking about people. The very people, in fact, that God is going to require Peter to visit. Yes, *those* people! Those *unclean* people! They are Italians!

That meant quite a bit to a Jew of the first century, since Rome had the Jewish nation in submission to them. Romans persecuted Jews. God wanted Peter to go to *those* people!

"Do not call anything impure that God has made clean."[1]

It was a hard lesson.

By verse 34 in Acts 10, Peter finally discovered God was talking about people, not food. He shares this truth with the gentiles he was called to minister to:

Acts 10:34-35

34   Then Peter began to speak: "I now realize how true it is that God does not show favoritism

35   but accepts men from every nation who fear him and do what is right."

God is in the business of cleaning people up. What God has cleansed, no one can then call unclean. He did not say He was going to make gays become heterosexuals. He did not say to Peter He was going to make gentiles into Jews. Peter was not to try to get these gentiles to become good Jews, following all the laws prescribed in the Old Testament. God was not going to make the gentiles become followers of Moses, going back under the bondage of the law, which Paul and Peter both admitted no one could follow. But they were instead going to be under the liberty of the Spirit. That means their conscience would guide them as believers. God said, "What I have cleansed don't call unclean." My life, like any Christian's life, has changed since I met Jesus. It continues to change. My sexual orientation has not changed, it just gets lived out more responsibly.

Picking up again with the account in Acts 10, at verse 44 we read:

Acts 10:44-47

44 While Peter was still speaking these words, the Holy Spirit came on all who heard the message.

45 The circumcised believers who had come with Peter were astonished that the gift of the Holy Spirit had been poured out even on the Gentiles.

46 For they heard them speaking in tongues and praising God. Then Peter said,

47 "Can anyone keep these people from being baptized with water? They have received the Holy Spirit just as we have."

Though the Jews with Peter were amazed, they quickly concluded that these gentiles truly were added to the kingdom of God the same as they were. They understood that God had accepted these gentiles because they had been filled with the Holy Spirit, just as they had been on the day of Pentecost, years before. There was no other conclusion.

Peter responded by saying, "Can anyone forbid water, that these should not be baptized, which have received the Holy Ghost as well as we?"

The fact that these Gentiles had been filled with the Holy Spirit, just as they had been, was proof positive that these non-Jews were accepted by God.

There is nothing in the revelation Peter received that would make Cornelius have to first convert to Judaism before he could receive the Jewish Messiah. He heard the good news. He believed. He was saved and filled. He heard God was no respecter of persons. He heard how God anointed Jesus to heal all who were oppressed. This same revelation is currently appropriated by the gay, lesbian, and all other sexual minority believers. They do not first have to become like someone else—become heterosexuals and join the majority establishment. They only have to do as Cornelius: hear the news, and believe the news. Cornelius was still every bit as much an Italian after he got filled as before. He was still what he had been born.

The criterion to know whether someone had been accepted of God was to have had a life changing encounter with the Holy Spirit. Pentecostals in the early days of the 20th century were often known to say if you got cleaned up, you might get the Holy Spirit. But the truth is, the Holy Spirit comes first, then He cleans people up. Cornelius didn't get cleaned up in his own power and then get the Holy Spirit. He got the Holy Spirit, then God did the cleansing of the heart.

According to a prophecy on TBN, God said He was going to prove to the world and to the church that He [God] could clean up the gay community. Cleansing is an issue of the heart, not of orientation. The prophecy did not say the gay community was going to clean themselves up, but it would be a sovereign move of God. As God began to move upon the hearts of the gay community over the last several years, God has been doing a work. The standards have been raised. This was not imposed upon them from without, but a transformation of the heart from within has occurred. The standard was raised to become the standard found in scripture, which we have already seen is not anti-gay. Gay folks began to understand that the standard of commitment in relationship for heterosexual couples was the same standard of commitment in relationship for gay and lesbian couples. With no external prompting, with no seminars or political movement, I have seen the standard raised in home after home in the hearts of the gay Christian community. Today, as God does this work in the hearts of His gay and lesbian children, they perceive it is possible to have a lifelong commitment and desire to do so. As a result, many gay couples now want the same legal permanence for their relationships as do their heterosexual counterparts.

Internally, as the Holy Spirit moves upon lives, people begin to desire to be in monogamous lifetime relationships, and to be willing to work at that commitment with their partner. They begin to accept no less than God's best for their domestic spousal relationship. God is no respecter of persons and is not one to show partiality. What He provides for one family unit He provides for any other. His promises work for any Christian home, heterosexual, or otherwise. There are not two Bodies of Christ. There are not two Holy Spirits or two Kingdoms of God. There is one.

The Kingdom principles of salvation, and righteousness and standards for home life all operate for people fairly and equitably, whether one's mate is a male or a female. In Christ gender distinctions are no distinctions. In Him there is neither male nor female. But there are right ways to love and respect your mate, whatever their sex. There are right ways to tell the truth and be honest, open, caring, communicative, with your mate. There are right ways to honor your spouse above even your own self. Commands to be selfless and forgiving and charitable toward your mate apply regardless of their gender.

The behavior that God's love requires is unchanging for either sex. According to the Living Bible:

1 Cor. 13:4-7
4   Love is very patient and kind, never jealous or envious, never boastful or proud,
5   never haughty or selfish or rude. Love does not demand its own way. It is not irritable or touchy. It does not hold grudges and will hardly even notice when others do it wrong.
6   It is never glad about injustice, but rejoices whenever truth wins out.
7   If you love someone, you will be loyal to him no matter what the cost. You will always believe in him, always expect the best of him, and always stand your ground in defending him. (TLB)

These ground rules for love are true whether you are male or female and whether your recipient of love is the same sex or the opposite. And no matter who is receiving or giving this love, it never fails.

In Acts chapter 10, however, just because everyone in Cornelius's household became Christian believers, it did not mean everyone in the Church was ready to receive them into fellowship with open arms. As soon as Peter got back to Jerusalem (Acts 11:2), the circumcised Jews took issue with him. Immediately a debate ensued. They essentially said, "What did you think you were doing, Peter? You went to uncircumcised gentiles! That's unacceptable behavior for a good Jewish follower!" Peter was rebuked for even talking to the gentiles, much less for eating with them.

In the ensuing verses Peter explains why he felt justified to even go to the home of gentiles. He recaps the vision of the lowered sheet, and of the angelic visit to Cornelius. He has to recall how before he could finish speaking, God poured out the Holy Spirit.

Peter concludes his defense before the Jews saying:

Acts 11:15-17
15   "As I began to speak, the Holy Spirit came on them as he had come on us at the beginning. . . .
17   So if God gave them the same gift as he gave us, who believed in the Lord Jesus Christ, who was I to think that I could oppose God?"

Peter asked who was he to stand in God's way. When they heard this, then they finally concurred with Peter.

The same set of facts is true about the gay community. The Lord has had His Word preached in the gay community, and has provided this Good News for gays for several decades. God gives the gay community the same gift of eternal life as He gives to the non-gay community when they receive the Lord Jesus Christ. Who is it who can stand in God's way? The late Sylvia Pennington, who wrote the book *Good News for Modern Gays* and *But Lord, They're Gay*[2] was an Assemblies of God evangelist who went to San Francisco years ago to convert gays. But soon after attending some worship services within the gay Christian community *she* was converted. God got her heart, and said, "What I have cleansed, don't call unclean."

She spent the rest of her life traveling North America to find downtrodden gay people and give them the good news of God's love. She let untold numbers of people know that God was no respecter of persons.

In the case of Peter's defense the Church quieted down. Many heterosexual Christians who have come into the gatherings of gay Christians and their friends, begin also to quiet down and experience God's peace. Evelyn Schave is one such Christian who saw first hand what God was and is doing among the gay Christian community.

Evelyn Schave has been an evangelist for more than forty years. She and her husband Dennis have ministered and pastored for many years. Prior to her marriage, Evelyn traveled the country holding revivals in churches throughout America, and often with another woman, Naomi Harvey. After their traveling days were over and Evelyn got married, it became known that Naomi was a lesbian. Evelyn, in her fundamentalist mindset felt Naomi was now lost forever with a "reprobate mind."

As she says in her book, ". . . when I received word that my faithful co-worker and dear friend of sixteen years had come out as a lesbian, I naturally experienced great shock. . . . My early religious training delivered an instant judgment . . . there is no need to pray for her; she is beyond hope!"[3]

But through the Lord's dealing with Evelyn and her husband Dennis, they discovered it was not Naomi who had the problem with God, but them. Evelyn says, "We discovered ourselves to be under bondage through prideful considerations."[4]

Little by little through grace and mercy, God led the couple to start a church in their hometown that would minister to *whomever* was hurting. God laid this as a heavy burden on their hearts. One day after years of silence and separation, Naomi walked through the doors of their church bringing her same sex mate along. Once it was known that Pastor Dennis and Evelyn had opened the doors of their church to known lesbians and gays, a great persecution arose. Their building and parking lot were targets of hate crimes. Leaders and members alike fled the church, and eventually Dennis and Evelyn were left with no congregation at all.

Yet doors to the couple's understanding were being opened. Evelyn was asked then by Pastor Naomi to visit and minister in the Christian and predominantly gay churches she pastored in Seattle and Portland. Eventually an invitation was extended by Rev. Thomas Hirsch for Evelyn not only to attend, but even to minister at one of the national conferences annually held in the Christian gay community, at that time called the Advance Conference, sponsored by Advance Christian Ministries.[5]

Evelyn said she went as a "looky-loo," not sure what to think of all this business of gay people and Christianity. She said she had lots of questions! But she had been in worship services most of her life, and she knew the presence of God. God was clearly present at that conference. The lives of the Christians present bore witness that they loved God, and God loved them too. She was changed. Evelyn cried through much of the conference because of the awesome presence of God and the witness born in her heart. She and Dennis now joke that when she called long distance from Houston to let Dennis hear the tremendous worship taking place by holding out the telephone toward the worshippers in the sanctuary, all she could do was cry.

Evelyn recalls in her book, "When I saw with my eyes and recognized in my spirit these people had the same Spirit of God that I had, a major change took place."[6]

From that momentous conference God began to open doors for Evelyn and Dennis both to begin ministering among the gay and lesbian Christian community. Theirs was no longer a ministry of judgment and alienation but one of reconciliation.

THE DEBATE ENSUES!

Years later, after Peter's defense for his encounter at Cornelius's house, the debate was still raging. Paul became an Apostle and went on evangelistic journeys. Churches were raised up among the gentile nations. Paul made his journey with Barnabas, and as churches were birthed they put new elders in place. By the time we get to Acts chapter 15, we see that Paul and Barnabas have ended their missionary tour and were back in their commissioning home church in Antioch.

Antioch was a mixed church of gentiles and Jews. In Acts 15, it is in this mixed Christian church that controversy stirred whether gentiles could be saved without also following the Jewish laws and customs.

Acts 15:1-2
1   Some men came down from Judea to Antioch and were teaching the brothers: "Unless you are circumcised, according to the custom taught by Moses, you cannot be saved."
2   This brought Paul and Barnabas into sharp dispute and debate with them. So Paul and Barnabas were appointed, along with some other believers, to go up to Jerusalem to see the apostles and elders about this question.

"Unless you are circumcised, according to the custom taught by Moses, you cannot be saved," they said. The debate was still raging, just like it is today. In many quarters of the Christian churches gays are told unless they become heterosexuals they cannot be Christian. Or unless they become celibate homosexuals on the way to being restored to heterosexuality they cannot be saved. It is the same issue. Unless gentiles get circumcised and follow the law of Moses, they were told, "you cannot be saved." They had to become something they were not, and do something God was not requiring of them, in order to please the tradition of men. There were Jews at that time who still equated salvation with works. They declared gentiles could only enter God's kingdom when they met certain criteria through works of their own: certain prescribed behaviors and actions. It was the old argument that says when we get our act together all by ourselves, and clean ourselves up, then God will reward our good works with His salvation and Holy Spirit. But that is not what God does!

"What I have cleansed," God said to Peter, "don't you call unholy!" God takes the responsibility and the credit for cleaning people up. God takes the responsibility and the credit for making people acceptable to Him, according to His standard, not according to what we think that standard is or should be for others. In so many places, therefore, the New Testament tells us not to judge others, unless we want to fall into condemnation. Matthew 7:1-2 is only one example of many.

We don't set up laws for others to follow for them to get saved. We point people to the Savior.

Continuing on with our scripture, we read in Acts 15:2 that Paul and Barnabas were embroiled in a great church debate. Neither side was budging. Finally others were called upon to give sound advice.

Acts 15:4-7

4   When they came to Jerusalem, they were welcomed by the church and the apostles and elders, to whom they reported everything God had done through them.

5   Then some of the believers who belonged to the party of the Pharisees stood up and said, "The Gentiles must be circumcised and required to obey the law of Moses."

6   The apostles and elders met to consider this question.

7   After much discussion, Peter got up and addressed them: "Brothers, you know that some time ago God made a choice among you that the Gentiles might hear from my lips the message of the gospel and believe.

From verse 4 we see Paul and Barnabas reported the things God had done. These acts of God were the same things Peter had seen in Cornelius's household. God kept raising up churches in new locations, and many gentiles were coming to God. Elders and pastors were being put in place. Signs, wonders and miracles were happening; all without the law of Moses, but through the grace of God. These were the things Paul was able to report.

Verse 5 continues to tell us, though, there rose up a certain sect of the believing Pharisees saying that it was necessary to circumcise them, and to command them to keep the law of Moses. Verse 7 shows us as a result there was much debate. This same debate started off in Jerusalem with Peter and Cornelius, goes out to Antioch, comes back to Jerusalem again for a council. This debate is not resolved.

Peter then gets into the debate reminding the council that God has been moving ever since the days of Cornelius among gentiles. He recalls how God is not asking anyone to walk by the same Old Testament laws. They should all know by now that no one has ever been able to fulfill their requirement. It was a yoke no one had been able to bear.

"God put no difference between us and them, purifying their hearts by faith." He continues, "But we believe that through the grace of the Lord Jesus Christ we shall be saved, even as they." (Acts 15:8-12)

Peter knows that there is only one way to become a Christian for everybody. It is not by becoming a Jew. It is not by the ritualistic obeying of the commands of Leviticus that people get saved. Peter knows no one can do it that way. It is by grace we are saved. It is by believing through the grace of the Lord Jesus Christ.

After Paul and Barnabas finished recounting the things God had done in the gentile community, then James began to speak. When James speaks everyone listens. He was the half brother of Jesus Christ. He was raised in the same household as Jesus, his older brother. They had the same mother. He and Jesus were raised by the same set of parents, and he spent all his growing up years in the presence of Christ, literally. James was also the one who became the senior pastor of the church in Jerusalem, the mother church of all Christianity. When James speaks, everyone wants to hear his wisdom. His words will wrap up the debate and bring closure to this council in Jerusalem. Yet, what James says is not what you expect:

Acts 15:13-17

13   And after they had stopped speaking, James answered, saying, "Brethren, listen to me.

14   "Simeon has related how God first concerned Himself about taking from among the Gentiles a people for His name.

15   "And with this the words of the Prophets agree, just as it is written,

16   'After these things I will return, and *I will rebuild the tabernacle of David* which has fallen, and I will rebuild its ruins, and I will restore it,

17   In order that the rest of mankind may seek the Lord, and all the Gentiles who are called by My name,' (NAS)

James reminds those assembled how it was God's concern to take a people from those who were not a people. God brought in gentiles, who were not a people and brought them in by the blood. That was God's concern. Then James concludes by seemingly catapulting us into a different topic. It is not a new topic, really. It is the concluding proof to what he is saying; but without historical understanding of the point James is making, it easily gets lost in obscurity. It would be hard to understand what God wants to do in this generation, without understanding what James is speaking here.

James draws on an obscure prophecy in Amos in the Old Testament about the Tabernacle of David:

Amos 9:11
11   In that day *will I raise up the tabernacle of David* that is fallen, and close up the breaches thereof; and I will raise up his ruins, and I will build it as in the days of old. (KJV)

An interesting concept is being presented. Many people will read that statement about the Tabernacle of David, and think, "I don't know what that is all about." They will shrug their shoulders and read past it without any idea of what God was saying through the prophets and James about the last days. James is prophetically speaking about the Church. He is saying that God will rebuild the Tabernacle of David which had fallen.

In this passage James is coupling the topics of the Tabernacle of David with bringing people into the flock who were never in the flock before. To understand this, we need to understand the concept of *the Tabernacle of David.*

Note what God does *not* say. He does not say He will rebuild the Tabernacle of Moses. Had He been saying He would rebuild the Tabernacle of Moses, then God would be saying He would reinstitute the Old Testament law. The Tabernacle of Moses was the first tabernacle God had built. The Tabernacle of Moses was a tent. It was stitched together, and dismantled to travel with Israel wherever they went. In the innermost court of the Tabernacle of Moses, nobody was allowed to approach God, except the high priest, once a year, in order to make atonement for the sins of the people. The ritual law was so exact, that if the high priest did not follow it exactly he would be struck dead upon entering within the veil of the Holy of Holies. It was the place where Israel met with God, but they could not approach God.

In the time of the Judges, the people of God were walking in disobedience to God. As a result, God caused one of their enemies, the Philistines, to war against Israel. Israel was losing the war, and rather than consult God, they went into the forbidden Holy of Holies, and pulled out the Ark of the covenant to take into battle with them. The ark, a gold covered wooden box, contained the two tablets of stone with the law, the jar of manna, and the rod of Aaron. God commanded Israel to leave this Ark in the Holy of Holies, the innermost court of the tabernacle. Israel took the Ark into battle as if it were a good luck charm, and it was captured by the Philistines.

The Philistines took the captured Ark of Yahweh, the God of Israel, to one of their cities, Ashdod. The Philistines assumed their god, Dagon, was responsible for this victory over the Hebrew God. They brought the Ark as an offering into Dagon's temple and set it next to the statue of Dagon. During the night when the Philistine priests slept, God knocked over Dagon's statue. Dagon was a helpless rock. Dagon was reset, but the next night God did it again, chopping off his head and hands. Dagon couldn't move, get up, or cry for help. Dagon was merely a carved idol.[7]

God began to pour out plagues upon the Philistines. The lords of the city would quickly move the Ark to another Philistine location, only to have plagues poured on those city residents as well. After many months of this torment, the Philistine lords decided to send the Ark back to Israel. When Israel saw the Ark returning on an oxcart, they rejoiced. They stored it in a farmer's barn, but never returned the Ark to the Tabernacle of Moses, which was still standing. The Holy of Holies was empty. Sacrifices were still being made in that tent, and the required rituals were performed; but the representation of God's presence was missing. The Ark remained stored away for decades.

After King David came to the throne of Israel, he remembered the Ark, and wanted to bring it to Jerusalem and place it on Mt. Zion. Jerusalem was where the seat of the government was located as the capital city, and Mount Zion was a high hill in that location, so no matter where you were in Jerusalem or its environs, you could see the Ark of the Covenant, situated under a large open tent erected to house it. The Tabernacle of Moses was still standing, with its empty Holy of Holies, being used for the burnt sacrifices. The tent erected to cover the Ark on Mt. Zion was large and expansive.

This was the *Tabernacle of David*. In that tent, David placed 120 priests as singers to offer worship to God, non-stop twenty-four hours a day, every day. In the Tabernacle of David, worship, not the smoke of burnt sacrifices, went up to God around the clock in songs, psalms, hymns and spiritual songs.

The *Tabernacle of David* instituted a brand new concept that David discovered as a shepherd boy playing his harp to the Lord. David was such an anointed musician that when King Saul was demon oppressed, the only relief he could obtain was to send for that young shepherd boy from the hills of Judea. David would play his harp, and sing praises to the Lord. Only then would the evil spirit flee, giving Saul peace.

David learned a concept in spiritual warfare that is a powerful weapon of the Church today. Psalm 22:3 reveals that God inhabits the praises of His people. Once David had his tabernacle erected praises to God were continually being offered. God was inhabiting those praises, and there would be continuous victories in the camp of Israel. The enemies of Israel were defeated. People would remember and declare God's wondrous works and praise Him for His majesty and power. They would sing back and forth to one another in the sung psalms to recall the great works of the Lord.

The Psalms declare that in God's presence is the fullness of joy. It is impossible to have fullness of joy and walk in terror or dread. Fear has no audience in the presence of the Lord. Mountains become molehills in God's presence. Crisis events tumble and do not impede the pathway of the worshipper. Mountainous problems in life are removed and cast into the sea of forgetfulness, as God's presence brings answers, strength, and wisdom to deal with the situation at hand.

Acts 15:16-17

16   After this I will return, and *will build again the taber-nacle of David*, which is fallen down; and I will build again the ruins thereof, and I will set it up:

17   That the residue of men might seek after the Lord, and all the Gentiles, upon whom my name is called, saith the Lord, who doeth all these things. (KJV)

God did not mean He was going to place a large tent on Mt. Zion in Jerusalem. God is not talking about fabric, just as He was not talking about food to Peter with his rooftop vision. When Peter saw a vision of food lowered on a sheet and God said, "Arise, Peter, kill and eat," He was not talking about food. The point God made was that what God had cleansed, don't call un-clean. God was talking about people, not food. Here God again is talking about people, not fabric. He's referring to the praises of His people being re-established in the earth, and all that those praises brought about. During David's reign, while the Tabernacle stood, Israel knew its greatest glory. That glory continued all through the reign of David's son, Solomon, who also kept the praises to God going up twenty-four hours a day, non-stop.

Had God only been interested in rebuilding a structure, why not the Temple of Solomon? It was the grandest, most beautiful struc-ture built to the glory of God with human hands. Many times in the history of Jerusalem there were wicked kings who forgot all about God, and the Temple just stood there. Nothing happened. But in the Tabernacle of David, the whole time it was standing, non-stop worship took place. That is what God is saying He wants. He wants His people to praise Him, non-stop for their benefit. Re-joice in the Lord always, the apostle Paul says.

The next portion of the Acts 15:17 passage says God will restore the Tabernacle of David, in order "that the residue of men might seek after the Lord." Why would the rest of the human race seek the Lord if the Tabernacle of David is restored?

If the Tabernacle of David is reinstituted, which means that non-stop worship occurs, then the presence of the Lord will inhabit the praises of those people. God in His glory will be powerfully free to inhabit the Church. The world, which is in dire straits, has no good news, no *gospel*. As God moves among His people, suddenly they will look to the light of the world and the salt of the Earth, and realize there are answers with God's people!

In Ephesians chapter 2 verse 19 to the end of the chapter we read:

Eph. 2:19–22
19   Consequently, *you* [gay Christians and other whoso-evers], *are* no longer foreigners and aliens, but *fellow citizens with God's people and members of God's household,*
20   built on the foundation of the apostles and prophets, with Christ Jesus himself as the chief cornerstone.
21   In him the whole building is joined together and rises to become a holy temple in the Lord.
22   And in him you too are being built together to become a dwelling in which God lives by his Spirit.

It clearly states that Jesus Christ himself is the chief cornerstone. The cornerstone of what? The temple, or the tabernacle? Don't you know, scripture asks, that *you* are the temple? All of us to-gether are the building being perfectly built together as we grow into a holy temple in the Lord. You also (here Paul is talking to the gentiles, who had formerly been excluded from the worship-ping community of faith), are built together for a habitation of God through the Spirit.

In these critical times, often people trust their problems more than the God who answers problems. God wants to bring success. God has answers and He wants to help us! A greater measure of His power needs to be released in the earth, and in the Church in particular. In our generation we have not always seen all that scrip-ture declares is available to the Church. Jesus had compassion on the multitudes and healed them all.

When can the Lord have compassion on the multitudes in our midst in the way He wants to? When the Tabernacle is reinstituted. When the Body of Christ starts acting like a Body instead of an eye saying to a hand I have no need of you. While the Body re-fuses to acknowledge it has other parts, then it can only operate with limited success. More and more restoration and reconciliation is taking place. But there is much more that needs to happen. Worldwide revival and outpouring takes place when the Body walks as a unified unit, making room for God to join with humanity as His temple is built together as His unified Church, His Bride.

The proof in the Bible that God has accepted a people as His own, was for Him to pour out His Holy Spirit among them and upon them. As soon as God was clearly present among them, there was no more argument, and nothing more that could be said about it or them.

It was not acceptable to the Lord for Jews to say to gentiles, "Okay, you have the Holy Spirit, but you have to follow all these laws and rituals to be acceptable to God." No, God said what He had cleansed no one could call unclean. The proof they were cleansed was that they were filled with the presence of His Holy Spirit.

No wonder the power of evil has been so diligent in its war against the gay community, because it is one of the last remnant groups to be accepted by the Body. The cross has brought gays into the Body of Christ. The cross has destroyed the enmity between them and the rest of the Body. The proof that God has cleaned them up is the same proof He used to show Peter that gentiles were God's flock and His concern as well.

Gay people and other sexual minorities are being empowered with the Holy Spirit, and living a Spirit-led life. God's purpose is to make both groups one. Evil works so hard to keep the Body severed and separated from each other. If the Body comes together, evil is undone. There will be no place for it to dwell. Evil cannot dwell with God. God inhabits the praises of His people. His people are everywhere. When the Tabernacle is rebuilt—nonstop praises covering the globe—then the Lord can return. He will remain in Heaven until all enemies are put under His feet. The Church as the Body is the feet of Christ; He is the head of His Body. The enemy of God has to be put under the feet of the Church, overcome by the Body of Christ. The Body must be a bride without spot or wrinkle. She cannot be a wounded warrior, amputating her own limbs because she decided they were not clean enough to suit her. What God has cleaned is not to be called unclean. God is saving, sanctifying and filling His gay children around the world, and He is sovereignly adding them to the Body of His Son.

God is making all groups within His Church one unified Body. As His Temple glorifies and magnifies His name throughout the earth, God becomes more present and is able to move upon the earth in His fullness.

If others refuse to walk in unity with gay, gentile, or other fellow believers, that does not let us off the hook. We still have to walk in love. We still have to obey the Lord. The promise to the believer who obeys God, found in Isaiah 1:19, still holds true for us whether others will walk along or not.

As long as we willingly are obedient to the commands of God, we can still personally feast on God's best. God will still prepare a banquet table for us in the presence of our enemies. Even if the rest of the Body is not in a cooperative mode, you still have the opportunity to eat God's best in your own life by being obedient to God's principles and commands. As long as we are willing to take responsibility to see our soul prosper, we shall prosper. The scriptures say to rejoice in the Lord always. It is time for the Church to take seriously what God has said.

Denominational barriers that were erected more than a century or two ago are being dismantled by God's Spirit. I once read a story about three men in prison in Siberia in the former communist Soviet Union. One was a Pentecostal minister, another a Baptist minister and the third a Russian Orthodox priest. All three were in prison for having shared their faith. Prior to incarceration, the Baptist was not interested in the Russian Orthodox, because they were too liturgical. He didn't like all the incense, the robes, the crosses, the icons, and the theology. The Pentecostal didn't like Baptists because they warred over theology about the Holy Spirit. When the three found themselves in prison together, they began to join together and pray for one another and with one another. Suddenly the love that flowed between them melted all those barriers.

How will the Church flow together in love and unity? It will not merely be because people fellowship with each other. It will happen because God will reinstitute the Tabernacle of David. It will be through praise and worship that the Body of Christ will come together.

When we really enter into worship, and set our hearts on touching the Father's heart, external concerns fall away. It no longer matters what someone else is wearing, or how they might worship next to us. The temporal things about the person sitting next to us become inconsequential when we have entered into worship and touched God. What difference does another person's economic status, race, gender, orientation, or social standing have to do with you arriving in God's presence? When we are set on touching God's heart, what our doctrinal beliefs might be, whether we believe in this point or that, are all subject to change as God moves on our heart. Yesterday's understanding changes as we grow.

NOTES

[1]Acts 10:15.

[2]Sylvia Pennington, *But Lord They're Gay* (Hawthorne, CA: Lambda Christian Fellowship, 1982).

[3]Evelyn Schave, *For Such a Time As This* (Phoenix: Cristo Press, 1996), 7.

[4]Ibid.

[5]Now annually sponsored by the Alliance of Christian Churches, P.O. Box 226925, Dallas, TX 75222-6925.

[6]Schave, 13.

[7]1 Sam. 5:2-4.

LEGALISTIC CHRISTIANITY VS.
SPIRITUAL CHRISTIANITY
A Gay Perspective

There is a difference between a religion which has rituals, strict adherence to rules, and one centered in a relationship with God. That is why Jesus upset the Pharisees, the religious fundamentalist zealots of his day. The Pharisees had a rigid legalistic religion. They knew the rules and strictly enforced them. They brought everyone else into compliance or expelled non-compliers from the worshipping community. The people of that time feared angering the Pharisees even at the expense of their own integrity. The system made people hypocrites. The Gospel of John, chapter nine, tells us there was a man born blind, and Jesus healed him on the sabbath. When his parents were questioned about the new sightedness of their son, they were afraid to answer, because of the repression and bondage of the legalistic system:

John 9:20-22
20   "We know he is our son," the parents answered, "and we know he was born blind.
21   But how he can see now, or who opened his eyes, we don't know. Ask him. He is of age; he will speak for himself."
22   His parents said this because they were afraid of the Jews, for already the Jews had decided that anyone who acknowledged that Jesus was the Christ would be put out of the synagogue.

Although they were themselves Jewish, their fear was of the rigid religious system that kept them in bondage; so much so that when they knew their son was released from his lifelong prison of darkness, they dared not upset the religious establishment by testifying to the miracle that occurred. Religion meant more to them than truth. Here was their own son, and they could not share the joyful report with their religious peers. Their son had a miracle! He was released from a lifetime of bondage. Suppose, as in our day, their son had been gay. The son had lived a lifetime of oppression thinking he was unloved by God and unlovable. Then he was touched by Jesus, and made to see. He realized God cared enough about him to come directly into his life. This encounter started a fresh relationship with God.

This happens to gay people daily. They are often kept in bondage by the rigid religious systems of their parents, until one day they get a revelation, a Divine spark that lets them know God really does know and understand, and loves them unconditionally. Though parents may be excited that their child is emancipated, they may still be too intimidated by the religious rigidity and oppression to be open about the truth. This perpetuates the myth and enables the religious abuse to continue.

This rigid religious system within Christianity operates to keep people in bondage rather than bring liberty. They tenaciously hold on to their rules, which demonize gay people, and in so doing act just as the Pharisees of Jesus's day. Their stiff rules replace God's Spirit and ability to move in their life in a fresh way, and become idolatry. They are found fighting against God. In these religious systems, no one is free to think for fear of their peers and being put out of their religious institution. So many people hold to this system of marginalizing and demonizing, merely because it is tradition, and they cannot see the damage they do to their own children. Jesus said the religious are therefore blind leaders of the blind. They all fall into a pit of legalism that prohibits the flow of God's love.

Gay people caught in this web of legalism have few options. They can remain in the church and stay silent, stifled, and pretend to be straight, for fear of being put out. They can join a religiously sanctioned 12-step program, that forever leaves them in the process of recovering from their sexual orientation. This option is particularly damaging. It is the one that mandates a gay person start calling themselves a heterosexual, and made to avoid all singular social contact with the same sex. Otherwise they fall into "temptation." This sexual "temptation" still occurs even when the now "ex-gay" claims a cure from their sexual orientation. A car can call itself a garage all it wants to, but that does not make it so. It seems the gay person's last option is to leave, period. Fortunately, however, there is yet another option. Go where you are appreciated as a whole person. There are many gay friendly and affirming worshipping communities available today.

In the story of the blind man, he was put out for telling the truth. What else is new? His parents stayed, but could not testify to the truth. The parents had the benefits of rigid religion. There is a high price to pay, and often one's integrity is in jeopardy.

Jesus said much about and to the religious systems of these Pharisees.

> *Luke 11:39* Then the Lord said, ". . . you Pharisees . . . are full of greed and wickedness . . ."
> *Matt. 23:26-28* Blind Pharisee! . . . on the outside you appear to people as righteous but on the inside you are full of hypocrisy and wickedness.

It is the same today. Some of these rigid religious folk appear righteous, but are full of greed. Many with large mailing lists know there is too much money to be made off homophobia to start telling the truth. Hypocrisy perpetuates itself. It would all seem hopeless, except that God is still moving!

A powerful example is Gil Alexander Moegerle. He was one of the seven documented founders of James Dobson's Focus on the Family religious empire. But after a number of loyal years in that organization, Gil got a revelation. He was first marginalized himself because of a divorce and remarriage. The rigid rules of religion no longer made a place for him at the table. Then, after a career change, he met Dan at work. Dan was the first openly gay person Gil knew. The concept of homosexuality suddenly now had a name and a face. Gil could no longer demonize gays because he could not demonize his friend Dan. A friendship was the final detonator to the explosive religious system Gil had trusted and ended the religious rigidity. As a result, Gil repented and flew to Colorado, the headquarters of Focus on the Family. He made a public apology for his own involvement in it and asked the organization to return to its original, more gentle purpose: to build up healthy families.

There was an immediate reaction in the press. But more importantly many parents of gays and gays themselves heard the news that they were not the demons the religious right said they were. Liberty rang.

I met Gil when he attended one of the Alliance of Christian Churches' international Advance conferences. He stood as an invited guest, as a white heterosexual Christian male, and apologized and repented to about two hundred gay Christians and their friends for the abuse and arrogance of his past. He asked our forgiveness. In Luke 18:9–14 Jesus told the parable about some who were confident of their own righteousness and looked down on everybody else. His final point was that everyone who exalts himself will be humbled, and all who humble themselves will be exalted.

Gil humbled himself. He came to apologize and do whatever it took to undo the damage religious systems had perpetrated on the gay community. Gil is not an isolated example. Many Christians, one at a time all over the globe, are getting a revelation.

There is something to having a relationship with God that does not allow a religious Pharisee heart to exist any more. That is the business of God, to change human hearts. God is hard at work. Over the last thirty years it would now be impossible to say how many hearts have changed, but entire churches are pulling out of religious institutions because these church members refuse to stay in bondage. The rigid religious system is crumbling. It is losing credibility. It is losing its grip of fear on people's hearts. People are willing to walk away from religious institutions that stifle the testimony of truth. They want to breathe the fresh wind of the Spirit that is blowing through our land.

The liberty among God's gay people and their supporters is as much a miracle in our day as the man born blind encountering Christ and beginning to see for the first time in his life. Once you have light, darkness is too high a price for rigid religious approval. Those still caught in the web of bondage tenaciously hold to their favorite version of the Bible and their tradition. But it never occurs to them to get out of their tradition. They don't study the Bible's original languages to find out what it really says. They might have to change their relationship to God, and love like God does, once they discover that the Bible really is gay friendly!

OVERVIEW AND CONCLUSION

For close to three decades there has been a definite identifiable move of the Spirit of God in the midst of the gay community. More and more churches are birthed and more and more gay people are coming to know Jesus for themselves. Jesus is the answer to every human need we have. People have a right to know that God loves them, and that Jesus died for their sins. But he died for sins, not for sexual orientation. As more and more gay Christians mature in their walk with the Lord, a set of ethics is developing, led by the Holy Spirit. This is especially so since the Church has not yet believed completely that gay people can even be Christians. No one has been teaching us what is right and moral and ethical in our homes, except the Holy Spirit. He guides us into all truth. Gay couples have come to understand their homes are a sacred place, ordained by God, and a place for Him to be honored.

Too many gay Christian couples exist to deny this reality. Among these couples are countless testimonies of the way God moved to bring them together. Those who try to tell these gay couples that their relationship is wrong, immoral, or an abomination have come too late, and with the wrong message.

The scriptures that are used to keep gay people in bondage do not have that intent or meaning within them. Nowhere does the Bible indicate that gay people are anything less than full partners in the Gospel. Nowhere does it say they must convert to heterosexuality, nor is such a thing happening. Too many gay people who love God can testify they tried all the answers the church demanded: they became celibate, they started dating the opposite sex, they quoted the Bible daily, they had hands laid on them, they had exorcisms, they went to counseling, they attended prayer session after prayer session, they fasted and sought God. When they were able to finally get quiet and listen, God's message of reconciliation restored them to their rightful place in the Body as an openly gay Christian. It is too late for such gay Christians to buy the party line that they are an abomination or any such thing. Their relationship with God is too deep to accept a lie when they know their Shepherd's voice.

Concluding that scripture does not condemn homosexuality, bisexuality, or any sexual orientation, but only admonishes us all to be faithful at home to our mate, it is no longer tenable to object to gay marriages. These marriages have already been blessed by the presence of God. Lifelong commitments have already been made and lived out until death do us part. The rights that go with such commitments need to be legally granted, such as the right to hospital visitation, the right to inherit property from your spouse, and the other benefits heterosexual couples take for granted. I believe God will see to it these things take place. Our relationships need to be acknowledged and honored, and not be reduced to a second rate uncommitted live-in status. Our spouses are not our roommates, just helping with the bills for the time being. They are our lifemates, whom we love and cherish and with whom we expect to grow old.

The battle rages on, though. In the recent book, *Straight and Narrow*, by Thomas E. Schmidt, the heterosexual author concludes that gays still cannot participate in church life if they have a lifemate. In his words:

> Churches face an awkward dilemma. The exclusion of practicing homosexuals from worship and ministry may push them away from Christianity, but inclusion in every aspect of Church life may send a message of approval of homosexual behavior. The morally ambiguous "don't ask, don't tell" policy, which satisfies neither side in the military, is downright cowardly in a church. The better course is for church leaders periodically to make it clear from the pulpit (and privately in specific cases of concern) that the Church represents forgiveness and power to change, and it also *exercises redemptive discipline* in cases of sexual disobedience, including homosexual acts. If this is done in a humble and inclusive manner along the lines suggested above, it should be received well by all.[1]

Too many gay Christians know otherwise. The version of church Schmidt proposes offers neither forgiveness nor power to change, when what is meant by change is becoming a heterosexual. Too many have tried the party line, done their best to be heterosexuals, and found it didn't work. Did they receive help or forgiveness from the Pharisees when they finally admitted the truth about themselves? Hardly. Redemptive discipline, as Schmidt calls it, means kick them out of church membership and fellowship if they won't stop loving their same-sex mate. Schmidt believes this treatment should be received well by gay Christians. Hitler had a similar, though harsher, idea for gays. Rather than just kick them out of the Church, he exterminated them in his death camps. Wars have been fought over similar versions of the final solution for many peoples being persecuted and discriminated against. Schmidt's proposal is not acceptable.

Fortunately, Schmidt came too late. God is moving in the gay community, bringing restoration and reconciliation. No matter how much others try to force us back into their tradition and theology so they can be comfortable, it is too late. Gay Christians can no more go back into old wineskins of bondage, believing they are unloved by God, an abomination, or unworthy, than a butterfly at liberty can go back into its cocoon. They have become new wineskins getting filled with new revelation from the unfolding of scripture.

Whether the Church is willing to acknowledge this or not, God already has, and is moving in our midst in this direction. The church who will walk in *tradition* and not *revelation* will be left behind as God moves forward in the concluding drama of human history.

Many are seeing the revelation.

In the early 1970's, the *United Church of Christ* began ordaining openly gay Christians into the clergy. The *Evangelical Lutheran Church in America* declined to include homosexual acts among a list of "Some Misuses of Sexuality" in a document adopted by the Church Council in 1996. The denomination has several ordained pastors who are openly gay Christians.

In the 2.4 million member *Episcopal Church* many Episcopal bishops have indicated their belief that homosexuality should be embraced by the Church. The dialog continues over two specific issues—the ordination of openly gay Christian clergy and the development of rites for blessing homosexual and lesbian unions. Within the 2.7 million members of the *Presbyterian Church (USA)* there has been an escalating movement within the denomination to normalize gay and lesbian relationships. Some Presbyterian congregations openly support the ordination of openly gay Christians.

Several *United Methodist Church* ministers and officials publicly released a letter in early 1997 titled "In All Things Charity," which claims, "The practice of homosexuality is not in itself incompatible with Christian teaching." The *Christian Church (Disciples of Christ)* has proposed "A Call for Reflection on the Participation of Gay and Lesbian Persons in the Life of the Church" to consider opening "positions of Church leadership" to openly gay Christians. Since 1976, the Brethren/Mennonite Council for Lesbian and Gay Concerns has been educating membership regarding the position of openly gay Christians within the *Mennonite Church*.

The gay Catholics group, *Dignity/USA* is actively causing dialog and a recognition of gay Christian ideology within the church, one heart at a time. Many priests and nuns sponsor or lead local chapters of Dignity.

In the United Kingdom, a discussion over the ordination of openly gay and lesbian clergy occurred within the *Anglican Church*. Recently, the church's General Synod agreed to "reconsider traditional teaching . . . on homosexuality," a move seen by some as another step toward ordaining openly gay Christians.

In addition, the gay Christian movement has found support among members of the "evangelical left." Author and Eastern College sociology professor Tony Campolo has offered support to gays and lesbians. Testifying before a presidential Commission on the Assignment of Women in the Armed Forces in 1993, he said that the military should open its ranks to open homosexuals. In a February 1994 article in *Prism* magazine, he criticized mainstream evangelicals as "being tempted into hysterical animosity against gays and lesbians." Last year, Campolo was a featured speaker at the National Summit on Ethics and Meaning, which, as part of its agenda, called for "supporting homosexual and other 'alternative' families." At the summit, Mr. Campolo spoke alongside such individuals as Danny Goldberg, President of the ACLU Foundation of Southern California, and Roberta Achtenberg, activist lesbian and former Clinton administration official. Mr. Campolo has issued compelling admonitions for Christians to demonstrate unconditional compassion towards gay individuals. His wife Peggy has been an open supporter of the gay Christian movement, saying, "The sexual identities and the committed relationships of our gay sisters and brothers are cause for celebration."[2]

Scripture clearly prophesied that in the last days knowledge would increase. We are in the midst of a knowledge explosion all around us. New discoveries in medicine, technology, communications, transportation, science, biology, engineering, genetics, and more are bursting forth around us continually. Scripture says God's house has to be a house of prayer for *all* people. It is no longer acceptable to exclude any segment of God's people from God's house. To do so is to risk "Ichabod" (the glory has departed) being written on those doors, as God moves on to the place where He is free to operate as He chooses, and among whom He chooses.

We are living in exciting times, and they are times of change. Though God changes not, we do. We are growing in our understanding of the Word of God and its importance to our lives. It brings new revelation to each generation, and moves us closer to the time of Christ's return. Luther's revelation of scripture was not the last; nor Calvin's, nor Wesley's, nor Finney's, nor Moody's, nor Spurgeon's. But there have also been Charles Fox Parham, William J. Seymour, Eva Roberts, John G. Lake, Smith Wigglesworth, Maria Woodworth-Etter, A. A. Allen, Kathryn Kuhlman, Troy D. Perry and Mel White to name a few. There have been the Holiness revivals, then the Pentecostal revival, the Latter-day Rain revival, the Healing revivals, the Jesus Movement, and the Charismatic Movement. With each new wave of the Holy Spirit, as a truth is restored to the Church, the former move of God has historically persecuted the current move of God. Each of those contemporary movements came under great criticism from its historical predecessor.

As the Holy Spirit is bringing revival to the gay community, it is particularly those in the former moves of God that bring the loudest protest. Eventually though, as in the past, people understand that God has been doing the restoration.

Acts 3:21 shows us that Jesus remains in Heaven until the times of restoration are fulfilled. In the last three centuries there has been more Biblical truth restored to the Church than in any centuries previously since the Church fell into the Dark Ages. And we have seen more spiritual progress catapult forward in this century than in the previous two.

In this generation we are seeing the promise to the eunuchs fulfilled. Isaiah 56 promised that to the eunuchs who choose what pleases Him, God would give a name in His house that was better than that of the sons and daughters. Interestingly, the footnote in the *Spirit-Filled Life Bible*, New King James Version,[3] states that "the eunuch symbolizes all those the law prohibited from worshiping with God's people."[4]

Gay people fit that bill. The promise was to every eunuch who chooses what pleases God. The only thing we are required to choose for ourselves is a deep spirituality, hopefully in the Lord Jesus. After that, everything else falls into place, as we grow by the grace of God, through the Word of God, and by the leading of the Holy Spirit.

It is no longer acceptable for non-gay Christians to keep gay Christian brothers and sisters at arm's length. What God has cleansed, no longer call unclean. Leave it up to the Spirit of God to do the cleansing, sanctifying, and filling of the new vessel in Christ. Each believer is admonished to work out their own salvation with fear and trembling. We gay Christians await that opportunity within the confines of the Church. Some churches are already starting to glimpse that vision. At the risk of being catapulted out of fellowship groups and denominations, they are still performing weddings for same-sex couples and accepting God's gay children into the fold with full participatory rights as full citizens of the kingdom. Everyone may just be surprised by how much God can do if we will cooperate with God and come together as one Body.

NOTES

[1]Thomas E. Schmidt, *Straight and Narrow* (Downers Grove, IL: Inter-Varsity Press, 1995), 173, #4.

[2]Family Research Council, "The Bible and Homosexuality," 2-3, http://www.frc.org/misc/bible/

[3]*Spirit-Filled Life Bible.*

[4]Ibid., 1036.

BOOKS FROM GAY SUNSHINE PRESS

- ☐ **OPENLY GAY OPENLY CHRISTIAN: How the Bible Really *is* Gay Friendly** by Rev. Samuel Kader. $17.95.
- ☐ **QUEER DHARMA: VOICES OF GAY BUDDHISTS** Volumes 1 & 2. Gay men write about integrating their sexuality & spirituality. Vol. 1: $21.95. Vol. 2: $18.95 (special discount price for 2 vols: $35.95).
- ☐ **PARTINGS AT DAWN: Anthology of Japanese Gay Literature** Brilliant collection covering 800 years of Japanese culture. Illus. $21.95.
- ☐ **OUT OF THE BLUE: Russia's Hidden Gay Literature** 400 page large collection of fiction, articles, photos—New Russia & earlier. $21.95.
- ☐ **MY DEAR BOY: GAY LOVE LETTERS THROUGH THE CENTURIES** From ancient Rome to the 20th century a brilliant, moving survey of male-male love. Illus. $17.95.
- ☐ **MEN LOVING MEN: A GAY SEX GUIDE & CONSCIOUSNESS BOOK** by Mitch Walker. Illustrated. The famous classic on gay sexuality. $17.95.
- ☐ **GAY ROOTS: GAY HISTORY, SEX, POLITICS & CULTURE** Vols. 1 & 2. Ed. by Winston Leyland. Work by more than 100 writers and over 1000 pages in these 2 acclaimed books. Illustrated. Vol. 1: $24.95; Vol. 2 $22.95 (special discount price of $38.00 for both; save $10).
- ☐ **CRYSTAL BOYS** First modern Chinese gay novel—Pai Hsien-yung. $17.95
- ☐ **CRUISING THE SOUTH SEAS** 19th century stories by Charles Warren Stoddard. $16.95.
- ☐ **STRAIGHT HEARTS' DELIGHT** The complete gay love poems & selected love letters of famous Beat writers Allen Ginsberg/Peter Orlovsky. $16.95.
- ☐ **CALAMUS LOVERS / DRUM BEATS:** Two marvelous books on the gay life & loves of America's national poet, Walt Whitman. Incl. many photos. $16.95 each.
- ☐ **TREASURES OF THE NIGHT** by Jean Genet. Bilingual ed. $16.95.
- ☐ **NAKED TO THE NIGHT** Novel by K. B. Raul. $12.00.
- ☐ **MY DEEP DARK PAIN IS LOVE** A Collection of Latin American Gay Fiction (Cuba, Brazil, Argentina, Chile, Mexico) incl. famous writers such as Manuel Puig, Mario de Andrade. $16.95.
- ☐ **A THIRSTY EVIL:** Seven Stories by famous author Gore Vidal. $10.00.
- ☐ **BLACK MEN / WHITE MEN:** Afro American Gay Life & Culture in fiction, photos, more... $17.95.
- ☐ **A SAND FORTRESS** by John Coriolan "The most perceptive novel of homosexuality ever published." $10.95.

TO ORDER: Check book(s) wanted (or list them on a separate sheet) and send check / money order to G.S. Press, PO Box 410690, San Francisco, CA 94141. **Postage included in prices quoted**. Calif. residents add 8½% sales tax. Mailed in unmarked book envelopes. Add $1 for complete catalogue.

For Mom and Dad

PROLOGUE

FEBRUARY 1, 1961

BOCHNIA, POLAND, PRESENT DAY

The winter wind reaches me from beyond the aging walls and chipping paint, its icy fingers caressing my skin the way they always have, the most constant companion there has ever been in my life. It is quiet in this small house—the silence a deafening void—and its weight is heavy in a way that suffocates the faint memory of hope that remains in my dead heart. Still, nothing has changed. I never allowed it. Haunted by the emptiness once filled with the patter of childish feet across the floor, the air devoid of the delicious scents of supper cooking, and with the absence of all that once made this place home, I know I am the only thing completely different. Even the old ragdoll my little sister called Alma is still sitting where she's always sat on the couch, her button eyes heavy with sorrow.

Melodic chimes signal seven o'clock, and the light of the dark evening's moon trickles in from the window. Religiously, after hiding my shoes under a pillow on the sofa, I take a piece of bread from the bowl on the table. Some habits are too deeply ingrained to ever be broken. A bowl of bread and fruit sit in every room of the house, bowls I have never allowed to dwindle empty, and a crust of bread remains always in one of my pockets.

Shivering, I curl up on the couch beneath a thin blanket and a green wool soldier's coat that's always been much too big for me, and nibble on the dry slice of bread.

To think there was once a time I would have killed for this kind of luxury, this comfort...

According to world leaders, the war ended nearly two decades ago with terms of surrender and celebrations. But the war never ended for me. Despite whatever treaties they signed and however many people they liberated, they were too late... millions of lives too late.

My eyes settle on a painting that hangs in a large sycamore frame, as they often do on days like this, when my mind recedes to the dark abyss of my past and there is no escape. It is one of my own works, the portrait of a scarred soldier I painted many years ago when I first returned to Bochnia. It remained hidden away in my room for years, away from any prying eyes, where no one could question who he was or inquire into matters better left undisturbed.

So many ghosts, so many memories that have never passed beyond the confines of my memory. If I die never having released them, does that mean they all die with me? Who is left to remember when I am gone? Is that not what the Nazis always wanted? To make us disappear?

I have never spoken of the hardships I endured, not so much as whispered them in a prayer to the God of my youth, the God who vanished from me in the ash-covered snow. I still don't know if the stories and people in my head will ever become words I can speak. Speaking would make everything real, everything I have smothered since the moment I stepped off that train, but to leave them locked away in my mind would be the final act that erases them eternally.

I retreat to my bedroom, collecting pencils, pens, and every blank journal or sheet of paper I can find before settling at the table. Before the trembling in my hands can grow too fierce, the protesting in my mind too loud, I begin a letter to the ghosts.

For those I love and lost,

I must begin this first by saying I am deeply sorry. Years have passed by so quickly and now it has been nearly twenty-three years since the day the Nazis came. Sometimes it feels like it was days ago. In all this time, I have tried so desperately to forget, to move on, but I have succeeded in neither, and I can only assume there must be a reason for my failing in this. Times have never been easy. Perhaps once they were happy, but now I can't remember that genuine happiness. I don't feel much anymore. When I try, everything just feels empty. Not a day goes by that I don't think of all that was, our lives before the war, before the camp. If given the chance, I still don't know if I would willingly forget everything, and maybe with age these memories will disappear after all. Often, I wish I were with you all, and some days I don't think I'll have the strength to go on. I have never spoken to anyone of you. The pain has always been too near, but I do not want you to be forgotten. This is my testimony to you, my loved ones, the proof of the love our family shared, the lengths I went to just to try to save Bayla, and the man who ensured I lived to remember you.

With all my love, Halina Nowak, or, by the name you knew me,

Hodaya Alperstein

1

SEPTEMBER 1, 1943

BOCHNIA GHETTO, POLAND

Something horrible is coming, I know it. Perhaps it is the way the bleak morning light is beginning to fill the streets, replacing the restless night. Perhaps it is simply the way my stomach has been heavy with dread for several long, miserable days. The unnerving edge has me beside the window, my eyes heavy with hours of elusive sleep.

Beyond the street and the barbed wire fence, the shadows are moving, ghosts flitting here and there. I might have thought them people beyond the confines of the ghetto we've been forced to live in for the last two and a half years, but even my daze-stricken mind recognizes the occasional flash of a neat uniform, of a gun, of stone-faced creatures without hearts who could not possibly be human.

I wish I could drift to sleep like everyone else, snore quietly on the floor like Papa, curl onto the tiny bed with Mama and my little sister Bayla, or share in Naomi's warmth as she rests beside me. We've taken to this sleeping arrangement since the other occupants of our dingy apartment were deported, since we ourselves avoided the first two roundups. Even before we were expelled to the ghetto and Naomi had not yet lost her husband, she and I often fell asleep on the sofa of her old home, like little schoolgirl best friends having a sleepover rather than young women with their own families to worry about. Shivering, I turn my gaze back across the street, rubbing the fatigue from my eyes as the soldiers gather at the fence.

Wait... those aren't soldiers, I think, straining to observe the differentiating details on their uniforms in the fading darkness. *Soldiers have different symbols on their collars... soldiers don't wear coats like those...*

The realization dawns on me with paralyzing horror. The SS only ever sully their boots in the ghetto for executions, deportation roundups, or both.

"Papa!" I gasp, falling away from the sill. "The SS! They're outside! They're surrounding the ghetto!"

Papa jerks awake just as heavy boots are thundering up the stairs, screamed commands echoing down the hall. Our locked door rattles violently, then explodes open, ripping from one of its hinges as wood chips from the frame.

Bayla wakes with a jolting scream and Mama's arms go protectively around her as two SS men step over the threshold.

"Get up! You're all to report to the Umschlagplatz on Kowalska Street! One bag each, you don't need much! Now! Hurry up, be outside in ten minutes," one of them orders, lips curled in an ugly sneer.

Deportation! That's the only thing this could mean... it's our turn now, and there's nowhere to hide this time.

Papa hastens for the only suitcase under the bed, swiftly packing as many of our clothes inside as he can fit. We possess nearly nothing as it is, and Mama is able to tie the rest of our clothes and utensils inside an aging coat.

Our pictures! I suddenly remember the few photographs propped up on the tiny dresser in the corner. Our family portrait and the photo of Naomi and me on my twentieth birthday last year are at the forefront of them all, dull, smiling reminders of when times were happier.

And there have been a few happy times here... The ghetto has been nothing but pain, but there were a few moments we found small joys. My twentieth birthday was a good day. In a place where simply finding food had become a struggle, Papa surprised us with squares of chocolate that must have come from the black market. We used what little film was left in our old camera, and the photo of Naomi and me grinning, clinking pieces of chocolate together like wine glasses, is a memory I treasure.

Carefully, I tuck the pictures between a pair of socks along with my mother's wedding jewelry and four extra złoty, then use one of the old laces from my shoe to tie my coat around them as a makeshift bag.

"Hodaya, what's happening?" Bayla asks, her wide eyes searching my face for assurance.

I want to assure her that everything will be alright, but even I can't be certain what is happening. Thousands of Jews like us have been deported over the last two years and there have been rumors of labor camps and horror tales of places of murder, but it's impossible to know what is true. "I don't know, Bayla," I whisper, pulling her into my chest. "But don't worry, I'm sure we'll find out soon. We're probably going for work."

She nods, but suddenly tenses and pulls away. "Wait! We need to get Asher!" She moves to reach for the scraggly cat, who is hiding under the bed, but I grab her wrist.

"No, Bayla, he can't come."

Her eyes grow wide with dismay. "What? Why not? Why can't he come with us?"

"The Germans won't let him come. Only we can go."

"But we have to bring him!" Bayla cries. "We can't leave

him here by himself! Please, Hodaya, please! Let me bring him!"

"Bayla," I begin softly, taking her tired, reddened face into my hands. "Do you remember how we found Asher? It was a rainy night and he showed up at the front door and you wrapped him up in your blanket. He wasn't little or skinny, he's a smart cat. He knew how to live on his own back then and he still knows how to do it now."

Tears cascade down her cheeks and she sniffs, wiping her face with the sleeve of her coat.

"And when we get back, he'll still be here," I assure her, smiling as genuinely as I can. "He'll be waiting for you, and we'll make him a big plate of beef and warm milk. Alright?"

I sound as though I am trying to convince myself as much as I am trying to convince her. There is no way of knowing when we'll be back—that is, if we'll ever come back. No one ever comes back once they disappear. How can thousands of people be marched from the ghetto to the train station and never be heard from again? Where have they all gone?

"Come on, let's go," Papa says, fixing his hat into place.

I hold Bayla's shaking hand firmly, linking my other arm with Naomi's as we descend the stairwell of the apartment. Several other Jewish families emerge from their doors to hurriedly follow us, mostly mothers with young children, elderly men and women relying on canes and the guidance of younger, stronger family members. We are some of the first to make it outside, flushed out of our room into the waiting circle of armed SS men like mice driven to the cats.

We're pushed to the middle of the street, where the other ghetto residents are gathering. Babies and young children are crying in fear, their mothers and grandmothers try to soothe them with gentle words and whispered lullabies, fathers and brothers place themselves defensively between their families and the Nazis. Papa's arms encircle our bodies like a shield, as if he alone could prevent a hailstorm of bullets from raining down on us. Perhaps it is naive given all I have witnessed and endured, but with Papa's strong, protective presence encasing me, even as a lamb I would feel safe in a field stalked by lions.

As the SS continue to shout orders, they drag men, women, and children from their homes for not moving quickly enough, knock them to the ground and strike them viciously with clubs, fire rounds of bullets into the air that have the women and children screaming and crying with terror.

With Bayla wrapped rigidly around my waist, whimpering into my coat, I draw Naomi closer to us. In a steady, quiet voice, I begin to whisper my mother's poem.

"Worry not my child, the clouds may be here, yet there is nothing to fear. Think not of the thunder that you hear, remember the water that falls swift and clear. Think not of the lightning that hits the ground, remember the rain and its soothing sounds. Let the rain wash away your tears..."

"Let it wash away your fears," Mama whispers, her glassy blue eyes finding mine, and she smiles.

"Worry not my child, as long as I am by your side, you shall have no reason to hide." We finish the poem together, our gazes held fast, and Mama reaches out to run her fingers gently through my dark hair. Softly, I smooth Bayla's blond hair away from her face, her cheeks still stained with dried tears, her breathing now calmed.

After nearly an hour, the entire street is filled with thousands of people, and a fierce order rises up above the noise. "Everybody up! Get in line!"

Nearby, a young girl struggles to help an old man to his feet, a mother kisses her crying baby's forehead, a boy pulls his little sisters into line. Papa urges us all forward, our arms tightly linked, and whispers a quick prayer.

"March forward! To Kowalska Street!"

The road to Kowalska, pressed against on all sides by those

who still remain after the *Aktions* and massacres, is long and miserable. All these tiny houses and empty apartments—I remember a time when people still lived in them, where parents raised their families and children played with their friends. The few businesses, long abandoned and with smashed windows, still bear signs that say JEWISH OWNED. Mrs. Ellen's boutique, the cozy place Bayla and I once visited just for the pleasure of gazing at all the fine dresses and jewelry, is just past a deserted bakery. The door was boarded shut long ago, the flowerbeds have been stomped to ruins, and now it is nothing more than a distant ghost of my past. I wonder what happened to her, the sweet, kind old woman who I haven't seen in the four years since the invasion.

When we make it to the designated street, we all come to a halt. I strain on my toes to see over the heads in front of me, catching a glimpse of SS-Hauptsturmführer Hasse with two other Nazi officers at his side. Steadily, everyone moves forward, a mass of thousands of people all shuffling down the road to pass before the Nazi captains. The closer we draw, the clearer Hasse's words become. "You, to the left, and you four, go to the right. You there, take your children, to the left. Stay in line! Stay together! You, to the right! All of you to the left!"

Sweat trickles down my temple even in the cool morning air and my heart thunders painfully in my chest. Soon, the people at my toes are directed to the left, an elderly couple and a woman with a baby and a little boy. Hasse observes us for no more than a few seconds before waving his hand dismissively. "To the left."

As we all pass by, Bayla's foot catches on a loose brick and she stumbles, causing one of the Germans to scoff cruelly. Like a vicious snake, he strikes, hitting the backs of Bayla's legs with a baton, making her cry out in pain. Papa whirls around as if to attack the man who dares hit his daughter, but Mama grasps him desperately, and we all hurry on. I lift Bayla into my arms, supporting her tiny body against my hip, and her nails bite into my skin as she muffles her whimpers against my neck. It seems like miles and hours have gone by as we are herded down the street but, when a long line of cattle cars at the station comes into view, the sun hasn't moved.

"Up! Load up! Keep moving! Keep moving!"

Men and women hastily pull themselves into the first wagon at the front of the line, straining to haul the elderly and children on after them. By the time Bayla and I are standing before the opening, Mama and Papa have already been pulled up, pressed so tightly against the others I can't imagine there's room for even a needle to fit. Even after Bayla and I struggle onto the bit of remaining wooden floor, four more people are crammed on behind us.

As the thousands of other men, women, and children on the platform are directed down toward the rest of the train, two soldiers appear before the cattle car's opening. The door slides shut, leaving us in nearly absolute darkness aside from the tiny bit of light trickling in from the barred window. Something heavy and metal slams and then clicks from outside, which I can only assume is the padlock.

The stifling air is thick with the stench of a hundred filthy, unwashed bodies sweating against one another, packed tightly together from all directions. The chilly wind that whispered promises of the approaching autumn weather just moments ago is promptly forgotten, smothered by a heavy, oppressive heat that feels too thick to even breathe. On the other side of the cattle car, someone shifts, and the movement ripples all throughout the minuscule space, making everyone shift uncomfortably in turn. The silence that once reigned in the presence of the German soldiers, police, and SS is shattered, filled with labored breathing, cries of pain and terror, babies screaming in discomfort, everyone jerking back and forth with every tiny movement, bodies, walls, air, and shadows all crushing down on us.

"Hodaya, I'm scared." Bayla's strangled voice reaches me through the darkness.

I reach for her hand. "It's alright, Bayla, don't be afraid. I'm right here."

The hours pass slowly, agonizingly. The sun rises, then sinks, hours and hours with nowhere to lean, nowhere to sit, no food nor water, and I desperately try to remember how many cattle cars I saw before we were locked inside.

My feet and stomach ache painfully, my legs are stiff and cramped from standing in one place for so long, and Bayla sags, exhausted, against me. The children are crying even louder now, their voices hoarse and pleading, the young ones begging their mothers for a little food or water, somewhere to sleep, the babies wailing wordlessly without consolation. I lean against the wall, my nose just reaching past the tip of the boarded window, my hair sticking to my face and neck beneath my head covering, my shirt and blouse hanging on me like soaking-wet rags.

"My feet hurt," Bayla mumbles, weak, sounding nearly delirious.

"I know. Mine do, too."

"I want to sit..."

There's no room to sit, no room to even turn around, but I feel myself pushing away from the wall, leaving just a tiny sliver of space before myself. Several voices rise in protest at my movement.

"Right here, Bayla, kneel down. Sit on your knees."

She collapses before me, her head slumped against my leg, and breathes out a sigh of relief.

"There's no room!" a man protests indignantly. He is nearby, but I cannot see him in the darkness. "Make her stand up!"

"Leave her alone!" I snap, straining to keep from being pushed back to the wall.

"We're all tired, not just you! Make her stand up, you selfish—"

"Shut up, you old fool!" Papa's voice bellows from somewhere in the wagon. "Leave my daughters alone!"

"She's sitting down! There's not enough room for us!"

"One more word to them and I'll sit you down just fine when that door opens!"

The man says nothing in response to this threat. And on the hours drag, all of us sweltering in our own sweat and grime, the air reeking of heat, vomit, and terror. Darkness returns again, an empty night visible from the cracks in the window. My eyes blearily search to discern something in the blackness, but my head is reeling, numbing along with my legs. A few stars seem to have slipped from the sky and now move shakily on the ground, speaking in relaxed voices. One of the stars rises to the window, painfully blinding me as it flickers across my face, and the padlock rattles outside.

"All secure. Let's get them moving."

Suddenly, our wagon shakes, sending startled cries throughout the others, and I jerk abruptly, pushed from several different directions where people have collapsed. Just as the voice said, we are moving. In what direction or to where, I have no clue, but my fatigued mind is relieved by the knowledge that we have not been locked away just to be left to die.

I try to breathe steadily, feeling for Bayla's face to make sure she has not suffocated, threading my fingers shakily through her matted hair. All other thoughts of where the Germans are sending us and the home we are leaving behind are futile, for my mind is consumed only with each intake and exhale, managing to balance on feelingless limbs, and the constant grind of the train tracks. The wind is cold, a welcome respite against my burning face. I close my eyes and am taken quickly by unconsciousness.

The next thing I know, I'm struggling to open them again, unsure of how much time has passed. The world is still dark, drowning in a starless midnight, but seemingly from nowhere, past the wooden bars of the window and the opaque night sky, there is a glow in the distance. For a while, I think it is just some illusion of my imagination, but the faint orange color that is like a single burning ember lost in a world of darkness is far too vivid to be some fabrication of delirium.

"I see a light," I mumble.

Those who still have the strength shift restlessly. "What is it? What do you see?"

"A light..."

The glow gradually begins to grow, perhaps an eternity passing in the span of several minutes. Beneath us, the wheels are grinding to a slower pace, preparing for a stop. Ahead, there is a sign, small and lit faintly by a lamp, which can only mean we are approaching a station.

"There's a sign."

"What does it say?" someone asks.

I squint, waiting patiently for the sign to come into view, and it passes slowly, giving me an opportunity to read the single word painted in bold black letters.

AUSCHWITZ

2

AUGUST 27, 1939

BOCHNIA, POLAND, A WEEK BEFORE INVASION

Restless, I shift in my bed to find a comfortable position, but I can't manage to shake away the thousands of butterflies fluttering in my chest. Side by side with me in the small room across from our parents' room, Bayla lies burrowed beneath the blankets, cocooned like a caterpillar with her ragdoll, Alma, while I huddle as close as I can without disturbing her. At our feet, her little orange cat, Asher, lies soundly asleep, purring contently.

The morning of Bayla's sixth birthday dawns clear and cool, and I excitedly wait for the signal tap on the door from Mama and Papa that means it's time to surprise her with decorations and the cake that Mama and I baked together.

The cake itself is simple, small with white frosting and sprinkled sugar, but it's a luxury we usually cannot afford. It's the first time in my seventeen years and Bayla's six that we'll have a cake for one of our birthdays. There's never been enough money for excess, sometimes not even for necessities. Still, Mama and Papa always find ways to make the days special;

taking us for picnics and to bird-watch in the park, building snowmen in the winter, then cozying up together inside to take turns reading the Tanakh to each other, teaching us how to paint and carve little figures out of wood. However scarce it is for us, money could never compare.

A tap on the door makes my heart lurch, and I quickly pat my pocket for the tenth time to make sure Bayla's gift hasn't vanished.

Papa helped me carve the wooden beads for the necklace and I painted them blue with careful designs, then carved *chai* —the symbol of life—onto a white pendant. Mama strung it all together with a bit of twine. It's a small gift, but I know Bayla will adore it. Even when she was a baby, she was fascinated by the large, sparkling jewels that dangled from the necks and ears of the wealthier women, and would reach out to touch them, always fruitless in her efforts.

"Bayla, Bayla, wake up," I say, shaking her a bit. "Happy birthday! Come on, it's time to get up."

Her soft blue eyes flutter open, still heavy with sleep and looking up at me puzzledly. She kicks the blankets off and sits up to reveal a wild, fuzzy head of hair, and I stifle a laugh as her hands drift up to pull the tangled mess down. When she's managed to get up and I've instructed her to cover her eyes, I guide her by the shoulders into the hall, where Mama and Papa are playfully shushing one another. Their smiles are comforting and I cannot help but grin back at them as we lead Bayla down the hall.

Mama hasn't been in good spirits for a while now, ever since we got word that Hitler had taken Czechoslovakia. Bochnia isn't far from the border Poland shares with Czechoslovakia, and the news unsettled many people in the city. "He's moving closer," I heard Mama telling Papa a few days after we saw the headlines, but they hushed their discussion when Bayla and I came around the corner.

The sitting room is decorated with dozens of flowers and scattered petals, pink and white ribbons, and colorful giftwrapping paper strewn across the hardwood floor. In the center of the table, six blue candles are already alight, glowing atop the little white cake.

"Can I look now?" Bayla pouts, her lip stuck out, and Mama, Papa, and I all share smiles of anticipation.

Bayla lowers her hands, her mouth falling agape, eyes comically wide as she tries to take everything in at once. She jumps, pouncing like a bunny, squealing with excitement and disbelief.

"Happy birthday!" we exclaim together, and Papa swings Bayla into his arms, twirling her in the air as her joyous laughter fills the room.

"Thank you, Mama! Thank you, Papa! I love you!" she giggles. When she's finally on the floor again, grinning and breathless, she throws her arms around my waist. "Thank you! Thank you, Hodaya!"

"Happy birthday, Bayla." I draw away, kneeling at her level. "And guess what? We made you something." From my pocket, I withdraw the *chai* necklace, and present it to her in the palm of my hand, and even her awestruck expression at having seen the cake on the table is incomparable to the smile now on her face.

Mama has been cooking borscht for the past two hours, filling the entire house with the delicious scents of pepper, garlic, beetroot, tomatoes, and cabbage. I try to eat as slowly as I can, savoring every bite of the red soup even though there's still an entire pot. Bayla, on the other hand, has no such reservations and eagerly spoons bite after bite into her mouth so quickly that I'm not sure if she is pausing to chew.

"Don't worry, Bayla, the soup isn't going to run away," Mama assures her, wiping the juice dripping down Bayla's chin.

Papa chuckles and adds, "Even if it did, your mother made enough to feed the whole city."

Mama shoots him a playful glare. "With your stomach, I'd say just half the city. You know, Bayla, Aunt Dalia is going to be here any minute now."

Bayla is delighted at the mention of Aunt Dalia and immediately begins to enthrall us with a tale of herself and Aunt Dalia's two little boys trying to catch doves after last week's communal prayer at the synagogue. Papa, however, frowns slightly, and he tenses when a knock at the door cuts Bayla off mid-sentence.

"Speaking of Dalia, that must be her." Mama sends Papa a warning glance before opening the door.

A thin woman with a large crescent moon birthmark on her temple, curly blond hair, and a plate in hand steps inside. She greets Mama, her lips turned up into a smile that doesn't reach her blue eyes, then turns to Bayla. "There's the birthday girl!"

"Aunt Dalia!" Bayla squeals, jumping to her feet and rushing over to hug her.

"Oh my, look how big you're getting! You'll be as tall as your sister soon! Look, I brought you a treat." Aunt Dalia forces a cheerful grin, patting Bayla's head and being careful not to muss up the intricate braid I've woven in her golden hair.

Bayla eagerly takes the offered plate. "Thank you, Aunt Dalia!" She smiles, before rushing back to the table with her chocolate babka. She pushes the plate halfway between us. "Do you want some?"

"Oh, no thank you, Bayla. You have it, it's your birthday. I've had enough cake."

She shrugs but eats a small piece of babka appreciatively, savoring every bite and licking the chocolate from her fingers.

Neither Mama nor Aunt Dalia have moved past the door. Papa has already joined them, his face stern as Aunt Dalia whispers something to Mama. I can't make out what she's saying, but it doesn't look like it's good news.

A few weeks ago, Aunt Dalia came to see Mama and Papa in tears in the middle of the night when Bayla and I were supposed to be in bed. She was certain the Nazis would soon be invading Poland and intended to take her family away. I listened from down the hall as they spoke in hushed voices, Mama trying to reassure her younger sister and Papa dismissing her as always. It took two hours for Mama to calm Dalia down enough to convince her to stay in Bochnia.

Mama catches my eye now, and draws away from Aunt Dalia immediately. "Hodaya, why don't you take Bayla around town for a while?"

I frown at her dismissal, but nod nonetheless and lead Bayla back to our room. As Bayla pulls on her coat and I slip on my shoes, the small box under the bed catches my eye. I don't have much, just the little bit of money I've saved for emergencies tucked away inside it. Nearly all my money from working at Mr. Abergel's diner and taking odd jobs around the city goes to Mama and Papa to help support us. They were both disappointed when I dropped out of school last year to provide for the family and take care of Bayla, but it was the best solution, and now my time is spent much more productively than it would have been studying mathematics and poetry.

Papa has worked in the salt mines all my life and Mama used to be a teacher when I was little, but, once Bayla was born, she stayed home to take care of us and gave private lessons in English, German, and Ukrainian. Even added to my income as a server at the diner, it doesn't amount to much, and monetary pleasures are not things we can overindulge in.

"Hodaya! Come on!" Bayla calls, waiting by the door with her hand on the knob. The sight of her excitement at the prospect of simply going around the city for her birthday makes my heart twist.

She should have something nice. For my sixth birthday, Papa took Mama and me to the cinema to see a silent comedy called The Little Eagle. *I need to make this day special and memorable for her like mine was.*

"I'm coming, Bayla. I'll race you outside!"

Bayla throws our door open and dashes down the hall, giggling, and I rush to shove the money into my pocket before chasing her outside. She dances out to the sidewalk, chanting, "I won!" with a gleeful smile. I follow close behind and take one of her gloved hands into mine.

"Where are we going?" she asks, swinging our arms back and forth as she skips at my side.

"That's up to you, you're the birthday girl."

"I want to go to Mrs. Ellen's shop! Can we?"

"Of course," I say with a smile. "The princess gets what the princess wants."

Mrs. Ellen has always been very kind to us, the grandmother we never had. She knew Mama and Aunt Dalia when they were my age, and now Bayla and I have taken their places as her most frequent visitors. She used to be a nanny of sorts when I was little, and I would sit at the shop counter painting pictures for her all day while my parents were working. I've helped her stock shelves and take inventory in her little women's boutique at least twice a month since I was ten. Even those less strenuous tasks have become difficult for her in her old age.

Tall buildings line either side of the street—family-run shops and apartments, bakeries, jewelers, and salons—and the rain has darkened the sandy-colored walls and wine-red roofs. We pass a few families and several girls my own age who I once went to school with, two little boys run by kicking a bright red ball, and a few horses with carriages in tow trot noisily down the road.

I breathe deeply, taking in the lovely scent of petrichor as we walk, reminded of the poem about the rain Mama used to recite when I was little. Quietly, I hum the poem's verses like the Mother Goose rhymes she also used to read to me back then, the ones Bayla adores, smiling to myself when she begins to sing along at my side.

> *Worry not my child,*
> *The clouds may be here,*
> *Yet there is nothing to fear.*
> *Think not of the thunder that you hear,*
> *Remember the water that falls swift and clear.*
> *Think not of the lightning that hits the ground,*
> *Remember the rain and its soothing sounds.*
> *Let the rain wash away your tears,*
> *Let it wash away your fears,*
> *Worry not my child,*
> *As long as I am by your side,*
> *You shall have no reason to hide.*

Mama used to recite it to me all the time before Bayla was born, when there were storms and I would hide under my blankets from the sound of the thunder. Bayla is the same way, terrified of the flashing lightning, and on rainy nights she buries herself into my side while I recite Mama's rhyme to her.

When we reach Mrs. Ellen's small boutique, Bayla races to the window, where several jackets are on display. Her eyes lock on a yellow winter coat with white fur and a simple butterfly embroidered over the heart with white thread.

"It's so pretty! Look how soft it is!" She grins with admiration. "Why is the fur white, Hodaya? How do they make it?"

"The animals make it. They have hair just like we do."

"Oh, so how do people get it? Do animals let us have it?"

I smile as she looks inquisitively up at me. "Of course, but we have to trade for it."

"So that's why Rabbi Amasai doesn't have hair? Did he trade it all away to get fur?" she asks seriously.

"He must have." I chuckle. "When you grow up, animals will give you their fur if you give them your hair, so no one gets cold in the winter."

She nods, her curiosity satisfied for the moment, and returns her undivided attention to the beautiful yellow coat that has been on display for nearly three years now.

I twiddle with the few coins in the pocket of my mother's old coat. I doubt it would be enough to buy even the thread that has embroidered the butterfly.

Maybe there's something else inside... three złotych would certainly buy something in here. A pair of socks? New mittens?

"Why don't we go inside and look around?"

"Really?" Bayla exclaims, bouncing on her feet. "Yes, yes! Let's go in! I promise I won't touch anything!" To prove her point, she hastily shoves her hands into her pockets—the pockets of a coat that used to be mine, sleeves and hem cut short and sewn to fit her.

The silver bell jingles merrily as we step through the door. Two paintings hang near the windows, a matching set of bright landscapes I made for Mrs. Ellen a few years ago on her eightieth birthday, and a few of the watercolors I did when I was Bayla's age are pinned to the walls. The scent of candles and floral perfume is overwhelming, but there is something comforting about the clashing smells, like visiting a grandmother's house for cookies and tea.

"Dzień dobry!" In a plush, antique armchair, the tiny Mrs. Ellen sits with a worn copy of the Tanakh on her lap, her large spectacles sliding down her nose, and curly white hair piled atop her head.

"Dzień dobry, Mrs. Ellen."

"Oh, Miss Hodaya, Bayla! What a lovely surprise!" Beaming, she sets aside the Tanakh and struggles to stand. I quickly offer her my arm, and she takes it gratefully. "Thank you, dear, my legs don't quite work like they used to. Shouldn't be sitting in one place for so long anyhow."

Our arms linked, we move to the counter and the register. "How have you been, Mrs. Ellen?"

"Oh, just fine. And you, my dear? How has your family been? You must have your mother and aunt come and visit me; it's been too long. She and your mother came to see me at least once a week when they were your age. My, my, how long ago was that? Must be almost thirty years by now! I do believe I'm getting old!"

I smile fondly as she rambles happily on. "We've all been well. Mama is still teaching English in her private lessons, and Papa still works in the mines, but he's picked up a weekend job too. Bayla's going to be starting *przedszkole* in a few weeks."

"Already? Dear me, how the time goes! I'm sure she'll do just wonderfully. Such an intelligent mother and hardworking father, there's no doubt she'll be just the same."

And I hope she never feels the need to quit school. I hope she never worries as Mama, Papa, and I do.

Bayla has wandered off to the other end of the shop, giddy and smiling as she fawns over all the beautiful clothing and jewelry. True to her word, she keeps her hands tucked away and doesn't touch anything.

"Of course, today is her birthday." Mrs. Ellen smiles, watching as Bayla admires the yellow coat in the window again. "I've seen you girls outside that window for her last two birthdays, and whenever you pass by. When my daughter was little, she had a coat just like it."

"It's beautiful, Bayla's in love with it." Glancing back at her as she strains and bounces on her tiptoes to look closer, I feel myself once again curling my fingers around the money in my pocket.

I can't afford it, not today. But maybe if I could sell a few more paintings, pick up some extra grosze helping the tailor or the grocer, maybe next year...

"How much does it cost, Mrs. Ellen?"

"How much do you have, dear?"

A knot twists my stomach and I shift, fidgeting with the broken strand of thread on my sleeve I never noticed before. "Well... I've got three złotych. I know that's not enough," I say quickly, feeling the flush creep across my face. "I just thought I could get her something little and maybe next year I could get her a coat. She doesn't have many nice things. It's just been—"

"I know, I know, Hodaya." She smiles sympathetically and takes my hand gently. "The world's been rough lately, more than usual. If Melech and I were a few decades younger, we'd have left Poland by now. Alas, a long trip wouldn't fare well with us."

It's no secret that the Germans draw closer to us every day. Everywhere, in the newspapers, on the staticky radio stations, and in the flustered talk of concerned people, Hitler is the most constant subject, and our community dwindles a little lower every day.

"But enough about that unpleasant business," Mrs. Ellen continues. "I've just decided to mark that coat down. One złoty will be fine."

"*One?* Mrs. Ellen, you can't! Surely that coat's worth ten, at least!" I gasp. Before the war one złoty might have bought dinner, but it's hardly enough for bread anymore, let alone something so lavish.

She waves dismissively and reaches for my arm. "Nonsense. Help me over there and take it down for me. That coat's worth whatever I say it is and I say it's worth one złoty."

"But—"

"Enough of that now!" she whispers, swatting my hand. "I've had it long enough, it's about time someone else enjoyed it.

Bayla, dearie! I heard it was your birthday today! How old are you? Ten?"

"I'm six years old!" Bayla grins happily, holding up six fingers. "I got a cake *and* babka! Look, Mrs. Ellen! Look what Hodaya made me!"

"How gorgeous," Mrs. Ellen says, admiring the necklace Bayla proudly presents from around her neck. "Did you paint these beads yourself, Hodaya? They're beautiful. I just know it, one day you'll be a famous artist, like Adolph Menzel or Caspar David Friedrich, and I'll get to say I watched you grow up painting. Well, go on, grab that down for me."

"What for?" Bayla wonders as I carefully slip the soft coat off the tiny mannequin.

"It's your birthday present, Bayla. Your sister just bought it for you."

Bayla whirls around, eyes wide and hopeful. "Really? Really, Hodaya? Is it mine?"

There's nothing I wouldn't do to see her always smile like that. I'll just have to pay the rest when I get it... somehow.

"Absolutely, Bayla. Happy birthday."

In an instant, she's thrown her old coat off her shoulders and eagerly grasped the new one, caressing the fur and then the butterfly before slipping it on. No clothing has ever fit so perfectly; it's as if the seamstress had Bayla in mind when she made it.

"I love it!" she squeals, hugging me for a moment before rushing to a mirror. "Thank you, Hodaya! Thank you! Thank you!" She practically sings her gratitude, twirling and dancing before the mirror like it's a ballgown she wears.

While Bayla is distracted, I slip all of my money into Mrs. Ellen's hand. "Thank you, Mrs. Ellen. I'll bring the rest of it to you when I can, I promise."

"Hodaya, I said one was enough," she coos, but I shove my

hands into my pockets when she tries to return the majority of the coins.

"I can't pay just one, that's not enough. I'll bring you whatever the difference is as soon as I make the money."

"You're just like your father. Very well, dear, but don't be in any hurry."

Suddenly at my side again, Bayla tugs my hand insistently. "Hodaya, let's go home! I want to show Mama and Papa!"

"Best be on your way, girls," Mrs. Ellen says. "Hurry along, you don't want to get caught in the rain. Be sure to tell your mother hello for me."

We wave goodbye and Bayla all but drags me home. When we step through the door, the silence is strained and thick, so much so that I doubt it was our entrance that halted any conversation. Mama and Aunt Dalia sit across from one another at the table, both looking somber and defeated, and Papa stands astride his own chair.

"Mama, look!" Bayla exclaims excitedly. "Look at what Hodaya got me! I'm a butterfly now, I look like a Danube! See, it even has a butterfly on it!"

For a moment, Mama attempts to smile, but she settles for shock when her eyes fall upon the little yellow butterfly fluttering excitedly before her. She hesitates for a long time, eyes wide and struggling for words, running her fingers delicately over the fabric.

"Where did you get the money to buy this?" Mama finally asks.

"It was a gift from Mrs. Ellen."

Aunt Dalia smiles weakly and moves to stand. "Please let me know if you change your minds. We're getting an early start tomorrow, right at dawn. I'll let you hold on to these. They'll only take us so far; the rest of the way is on foot."

Papa waves her away as she moves to offer him several slips of paper. "Thank you for your concern, Dalia, but we'll be fine.

We can look after our own family. We won't be needing your tickets."

Aunt Dalia sends a pleading glance back at Mama, but Mama seems to be purposely avoiding her eyes. With a heavy, despondent sigh, Aunt Dalia nods, slipping the pieces of paper into her purse with trembling hands.

"Goodbye for now, then. May God be with you. I'll be sure to write," Aunt Dalia says quietly, her voice thick as though she may cry. Without looking back, she disappears into the cool afternoon, leaving a mournful silence in the air.

"What's going on?" I finally ask.

Mama shakes her head, her face now impassive. "Dalia says she and her family are leaving tomorrow. She wants us to go to France with her."

"Why?"

"Because she's been listening to the radio too much and believing in too many rumors," Papa mumbles under his breath.

Mama reaches out to hold his hand. "She thinks the Germans will be invading soon."

"They're not going to," Papa grunts. "The Germans won't come this far, they don't want war with Britain. I won't have my family uprooted for nothing. I doubt she'll even leave. Tomorrow morning, she'll already have changed her mind and be wanting her money back."

But she bought us train tickets... and Mrs. Ellen said she would have left if she could. Hitler hasn't made any advances on Poland... but what if they're all right about leaving?

The concern must have shown on my face more than I realized because Mama steals a single glance in my direction and swiftly changes the subject.

"Well, I'm going to start on dinner. We're having your favorite, Bayla. Why don't you ask Hodaya to read you a book?" Mama gives a reassuring smile, a smile that says, *"nothing is wrong, absolutely nothing at all."*

Bayla darts to the bookshelf and selects a navy-blue volume that looks rather large in her tiny hands. Even with the cover worn down from all the years of use since it was first given to Mama when she was a little girl, I recognize the book of Mother Goose rhymes. By now I must have read it to Bayla a hundred times.

I settle next to Bayla on the couch and she eagerly snuggles up to me with her little ragdoll, Alma, her eyes wandering inquisitively over the English print and Mama's handwritten translations in German.

"Are you sleeping?" I begin weakly, and the cheerful rhyme weighs heavy on my heart.

3

AUGUST 28, 1939

BOCHNIA, POLAND

Early in the morning, the rain begins to let up, and the endless streams of water that were leaking through the ceiling have slowed at last. While Mama heats breakfast and Papa lays out his uniform to go to the salt mines after prayer, Bayla and I finish our rain routine. She mops up puddles of water while I empty the nine strategically placed buckets to catch the rainfall, and, as always, we make it a game to see who can finish their chore first, and, as always, I let her win.

We finish off what is left of the kugel from last night's dinner and I try to hide my delighted smile at Bayla still wearing her yellow coat. Mama scolded her at first for eating in something so nice and new, but they finally came to a compromise and Bayla agreed to tucking napkins into her shirt and laying one over her lap. Asher sits at her feet, hoping for a scrap that Bayla or I might "accidentally" drop for him. Alma—much to my distaste—has joined us for the meal as well, sitting in Bayla's lap.

The doll belonged first to my grandmother when she was a

girl, then to my mother, and it was mine once before I gave it to Bayla when she was born. I've always found it quite ugly; a lopsided head with button eyes and a wide smile, white yarn hair that has begun to fray and take on a gray tinge after so many years, and a mustard-yellow dress that must have been the style when she was made.

As Mama begins to clear our plates, she glances up at the clock. "I'm going to get a bowl of borscht and we can all take it to Aunt Dalia before we leave for prayer. Go and grab your coats, girls, it's still cold outside."

"I already have mine!" Bayla exclaims, jumping out of her chair, caressing the white fur of her hood. Around her neck she wears her necklace. She hasn't taken either of them off since yesterday.

Mama shares a nervous glance with Papa as we lace up our shoes, and I wonder if she too feels the anxious tug in her stomach that makes it difficult to concentrate on whatever story Bayla is telling, like I do as we start toward Aunt Dalia's house.

When we arrive, Bayla rushes through the unlatched white gate and up to the door. "Can I knock?" she calls back, her tiny hand already paused in the motion.

"Oh, no, Bayla! I better." Mama quickens her pace to the door, forcing a chuckle. However, she doesn't knock, simply slips quickly inside while I latch the gate in case Aunt Dalia's aging terrier tries to run out to the street, and Bayla steps to the side of the porch as Papa follows Mama.

"What's wrong, Hodaya? Can we go in?" Bayla tilts her head to the side in a close imitation of a curious puppy.

Mama's worried. I think back to their conversation with Aunt Dalia yesterday and my own with Mrs. Ellen, tightening my grip on the bowl of borscht.

"Just wait right here," I tell Bayla, leaving the door cracked open as I step inside.

The radio is off, the children aren't playing, the terrier isn't barking or trying to make his escape past my legs, and my voice seems to echo through the house like a cave as I call out, "Mama? Papa?"

Nothing looks to be out of place, but I can't help the feeling of overwhelming emptiness that settles over me.

My steps are deafening in the silence as I walk the length of the house, peering into the children's room, then into Uncle Nir's study. At last, I come to Aunt Dalia's and Uncle Nir's bedroom. I find Mama and Papa, Mama with her face buried in her hands while Papa holds her to his heart, gently swaying as if soothing a crying child. All the pictures have been taken off the walls, several books are gone from the shelves, clothes are missing from the open armoire, and—which I now feel with a sinking dread—my family is gone.

"Goodbye for now."

The walls are suddenly closing in on me at the memory of Aunt Dalia's words. I draw in an unsteady breath, fighting back my tears. Papa's gaze snaps to me out of the corner of his eye.

"Take Bayla home," he says quietly. "We'll have prayer in private today."

I retreat from the house, desperate to escape the silence and emptiness, and find Bayla distractedly hopping from stone to stone on the sidewalk.

"Come on, we're not going to the synagogue today." I reach for her hand, and lead her back through the gate toward home, not bothering to lock it again.

"What about Mama and Papa?" she asks, throwing a glance over her shoulder.

"They'll be along soon," I assure her, swinging our arms in the way she usually does when she skips.

"Where is Aunt Dalia?"

For a while, no words will come, but I eventually settle for a half-truth. "She isn't home."

"Hodaya?" Bayla ventures after a moment of silence, tugging on my sleeve. "What's wrong?"

"Nothing's wrong."

"But why do you look sad?"

Tears burn behind my eyes and I swallow thickly, hoping the tremor in my voice isn't evident. "I'm just sad we're not going to communal prayer with Aunt Dalia today."

"Oh. Why not? Where is she?"

Probably on a train, on her way to France and wishing we were with her... Oh, I wish we'd gone with her! We could have gone! She bought us all tickets, and we missed her by a few hours!

"She's gone on holiday to France." I bite back the true explanation. Bayla wouldn't understand anyway—why Aunt Dalia leaving makes me so sad, how final this all might turn out to be. How can a child—to whom a two-minute timeout seems an eternity—truly comprehend the gravity of forever?

And why couldn't we go with her? Hitler won't touch France! Why didn't Papa believe her when she said she was leaving? Why didn't we leave too?

These thoughts boil furiously in my mind even as I begin to feel ashamed for the indignation burning in my chest. Bayla hums the rest of the way home, then takes the borscht from my cold hands and scurries into the kitchen. I bow my head for a moment in a quick prayer as I close the door, touching my heart.

Loving HaShem, I beg Your forgiveness. I make no excuses for my anger; I know it is wrong, to You, and to my parents. You have a plan for us. I will follow the path You lead.

Though we won't be joining the rest of our community in the synagogue, Bayla has shed her day clothes and slipped into her white prayer dress that falls to her ankles with a yellow ribbon that ties around the waist. For a moment, she struggles to tie a bow behind her back, before puffing her lip out pleadingly. Smiling despite my troubled mood, I manage to loosen the knot she's created and fix it into a perfect bow. "There we go, beautiful as always," I murmur, running my fingers through the few tangles in her blond hair before tying a worn scarf over it.

"Danke!" Bayla grins.

"Bitte." I smile approvingly.

Mama taught me to speak German when I was young, and, when Bayla was old enough to realize we weren't speaking Yiddish or Polish, she was eager to learn too. Hopefully, there will be no pressing need either for her to learn, or for me to use it.

"Hodaya, do we have an angel?" Bayla suddenly asks as she twirls her dress.

"An angel? What do you mean?" I ask, confused by the randomness of her question.

"Rabbi Amasai says that God watches over us, and that we all have an angel watching us too. Do we have one?"

Rabbi Amasai led our communal prayer even before the synagogue was built a few years ago, and Bayla has grown up listening with fascination to his every word.

"Of course we do. God watches over all of us, so do His angels," I assure her.

"So, everyone has an angel? That's a lot. Does Aunt Dalia have one too?"

I nod again, blinking back my tears. "Yes, of course she does. Everyone in the world has an angel."

"So, Aunt Dalia's angel must have told her to go on holiday. Right?" she wonders, reaching up to fiddle with the scarf fastened beneath her chin.

"I suppose he must have."

"When do you think he will tell her to come back?"

I falter for a moment, biting my lip. "I don't know. You never know what an angel will do."

"How come our angel didn't tell us to leave too?"

"I'm not sure. All angels are different. Maybe our angel just wants us to stay here and wait for her."

Even as I say this, the fear, the sinking sadness has yet to release my mind and heart. I want to believe she's coming back, that everything is going to be alright, that I'll wake up in the morning and realize it was all just a bad dream. Desperate for an excuse to end our discussion, I encourage Bayla to sing the rhymes from the Mother Goose book, and while we wait for Mama and Papa to return I distract myself with cleaning while Bayla twirls and sings "Ring a Ring o' Roses" in Yiddish.

4

SEPTEMBER 3, 1939

BOCHNIA, POLAND, DAY OF INVASION

The morning has been wonderfully peaceful and plentiful; the sky is clear and the sweet, fresh scent of bread and pastries fills the air, and I have removed my headscarf to let the breeze sweep through my dark, wavy hair. Truly, it is the calmest day the city has seen since the constant rain and overcast clouds the day Aunt Dalia left a week ago.

I managed to salvage two canvases from the garbage behind a bank; they had few imperfections, and I was more than happy to have them. If I've been taught one thing at all, it is not to be wasteful.

I used to sell my artwork for a bit of extra change, but it doesn't garner much these days. With news of Hitler scaring more and more people away every day, few have the means for luxuries—not that many of us indulged before.

One canvas depicts a vivid mountain scene simply too beautiful to paint over, so I've decided to repaint the second one, an indoor gathering scene painted Caravaggio style. Though I can't deny the mastery in its creation, that is all I can appreciate, for I find the realism and dark hues quite ugly. Impressionism is my favorite style; the mundane, simplistic themes, and vibrant colors.

For hours now, I've sat in silence with my paints and brushes at the park picnic table, altering the dark, shadowed background to take the form of a clear blue sky.

I wonder what the weather is like in France.

My mind is drawn once again back to Aunt Dalia, as it often is on relaxing, sunny days like this. It feels like it's been so much longer than a week since she left. She was always a part of our lives, a cheerful constant... and her sudden vanishing has been heavy like the earth of shiva thrown over my body.

It all changed so fast... oh, please let it all go back to the way it used to be. Let everything be alright. Let Hitler's conquest end and let life be peaceful and easy again.

It's nearly midday by the time I've managed to cover a large portion of the black paint with a calm sky and a few tiny birds flitting in the distance. The grave, somber discussion between its original subjects still goes on beneath it, a rude contrast to my additions.

A distant buzzing reaches my ears as I jog through the sodden grass to the sidewalk, my purse of brushes and paints slung over my shoulder. Pausing for a moment, I glance up toward the sky where the noise seems to come from. It's low, quiet, and I'm not sure whether it's just my ears ringing. The sound is getting louder, no longer a barely existent vibration but a deep, mechanical drone.

On either side of the street, men and women alike twitter nervously, gazing upwards for the source of the ominous noise, workers poke their heads out of doors and windows, dogs bark and strain against their leashes.

A shadow darts overhead and a woman screams. A plane

has shot across the sky, three others following in its lead, and the ground rumbles. I stumble, catching myself against a wall as the ground jerks violently beneath my feet.

Screams and swarming planes flood my senses, a family sprints past me, a mother drags her crying children into a bookshop, someone knocks me to my knees. The shouts of a dozen languages fill my ears, Polish, German, Ukrainian, French, all of them indistinguishable from each other, and I can't pick out the words I know I understand.

Amid the pandemonium, I finally catch the Polish words of a banker, who is shouting, "*Bombowce!* Bombers! They're bombing us!"

Another plane darts overhead. Searing pain shoots through my ankle as someone stumbles over it. I scramble for my canvas, panting, blood rushing thunderously in my ears. A crushing grip snaps around my wrist and hauls me to my feet, but I can't hear the man's words as he urgently tries to yell over the noise of the panicked city. A tremor shakes the ground, ripping me from the hysteria.

"RUN!" the man shouts, and shoves me down the street. I stumble, falling into another woman as she runs to a bakery, am shoved by a man bolting to a little boy as I turn and sprint, spots clouding my vision in a blur of panic and planes.

The earth rattles, a flowerpot drops, narrowly missing my head, and shatters. Again, the world shakes, I stagger, another pair of hands steadies me then disappears. Sweat pours down my face, my erratic heart pounds against my tightened chest, I tear through the stampede of civilians frantically fleeing the streets.

Run! Hide!

By some miracle, my unspoken prayer is answered, and Aunt Dalia's empty house comes into view just a few yards away. The gate ricochets as I run through it, I trip over the steps and barely catch myself on the door, throw it open and stumble inside.

Another bomb shakes the house violently. The furniture rumbles, the radio tumbles to the floor, the windows vibrate like placid water disturbed by a falling rock. My heart skips several beats, an empty frame slips from the wall and shatters in jagged shards across the carpet, and I clamp my trembling hands over my ears.

"Lord Almighty, God of our forefathers, Eternal HaShem, please save us!" I cry, backing away from the door until my back hits a wall, digging my palms even deeper in my ears. The wall vibrates through my veins, icing my blood and numbing my legs until I slip to the floor.

God, please! Help! Save us!

The drone of monstrous machines from the sky and explosions assaulting the ground from every direction are all-consuming, swallowing my prayers beneath their destruction, and I can no longer hear myself begging God for deliverance. At my side, the paints and brushes have spilled from my purse, my canvas lies lifeless at my feet, and I hastily gather it into my arms. As I crush it against my chest, the damp paint coats my clothes and fingers, smears, distorts, and is devoured by the dark scene below.

"Worry not my child, the clouds may be here, yet there is nothing to fear. Think not of the thunder that you hear, remember the water that falls swift and clear," I whimper, eyes screwed shut, curling even deeper into the corner as war rains from above. "Think not of the lightning that hits the ground, remember the rain and its soothing sounds. Let the rain wash away your tears, let it wash away your fears. Worry not my child, as long as I am by your side, you shall have no reason to hide."

Bayla! Mama, Papa! Oh, God, please be safe! Please hide! Please, God, protect them, protect us all!

. . .

Several hours elapse before the bombs stop, before I dare to move from my corner. The silence is deafening in the aftermath of the air raid, and each creeping footstep I take toward the window echoes loudly like a drum. The sounds of vehicles and horses are not muffled by the closed door, nor are the voices that make my heart clench. All orders are being shouted in German, and for a moment I think I've never heard the language sound so sinister.

I risk a peek from behind the curtains, allowing myself only a crack to look through. Motorbikes speed by and several mounted soldiers trot proudly down the street. Among the blur of guns and solid green uniforms, I spot a few men wearing vivid crimson patches around their arms, black swastikas glaring straight through me.

Nazis...

The floor stings my knees before I register that I've collapsed, gasping and struggling for air; the wind has been knocked viciously from my body.

This is what Aunt Dalia was running from and we didn't go with her! Oh God, why have You let them come here? Why is this happening? I need to get home!

By the time the street just outside the house has cleared, the sky has begun to grow darker. The shouting has ceased, the sound of planes and motorbikes are only rumbles in the distance, and the world outside seems to have settled into a tense illusion of an ordinary evening.

Shaking, I open the door, greeted by a cold wind that is suffocating and thick with the scent of metal and gas. I bolt across the street, ducking into side streets when German soldiers pass me on their motorbikes, sticking to the shadowed areas of buildings and alleys. Eventually, after another mile, I reach the comforting sight of our plain brown door, wishing for nothing more than to wrap myself up in a blanket and sleep away this awful nightmare.

I softly whisper my thanks to God for keeping me out of sight and slip inside. "Mama—" I start, but stop abruptly when I find her at the table, serving bowls of soup to three German soldiers.

"There you are!" Papa exclaims loudly in German, emerging from the hall. He stalks straight up to me and wraps me in his arms. "I was about to go and look for you! Where were you, Hilda?" he demands as he pulls away, his quivering hands gripping my shoulders.

Trembling, I respond to him in German, stunned by his sudden use of the language. "I was taking a walk. I went to see Aunt Dalia."

"For the entire day? Your mother and I have been worried sick about you!"

"Hilda," Mama calls and I turn, assuming Hilda must be my new name. She too speaks only in German. "Bertha was wondering where you were. She is in your room."

I recognize her subtle dismissal and retreat down the hall. I suppose Bayla is Bertha, but do they mean for us to pretend to be an ordinary German family?

"Hodaya!" Bayla gasps and throws herself into my arms, almost knocking me onto the floor. She grips me tightly, nails digging through my coat as if to cement herself in place. "Hodaya, what's happening? Mama won't let me go outside. Mama said I couldn't talk to the people in green. Why can't I?"

I embrace her, carrying her to the bed. "You just can't, Bayla. Listen to what Mama tells you, alright?"

"It was storming so loud. How come it isn't raining?" Slipping from my arms, she bounces on the bed, restless as she twiddles with her necklace. "Who are those people?"

She'll believe whatever I say, but I can't lie to her... there will

be no hiding from this storm, not when it's flooding the streets
and leaking into our front room.

"They're German," I whisper gently, fighting back tears.
"They've come from Germany, and they'll be staying for a
while."

What alternative is there? An army must be fed and sheltered, why would the Nazis waste money and effort providing
such things when there are thousands of townsfolk to force
them onto? And what power have we to refuse them?

"Oh." Bayla shrugs and jumps down from the bed. Skipping
to our dresser, she busies herself rummaging through them,
messing up the clothes and discarding some on the floor. "Let's
play princesses," she says, pulling on her white prayer dress and
tying an awkward bow. "Mama said we can play but we have to
be quiet. I'm still the princess, you can be the knight again. Can
I have one of Mama's books too?"

Keep her distracted. Play princesses and knights and forget
about the trolls outside.

"I'll go get one. But remember, keep being quiet. We
wouldn't want any trolls to find your castle." I force a smile and
she returns it contentedly. Bricks weigh heavy in my stomach as
I head reluctantly for the front room.

Papa has seated himself on the sofa, legs crossed and newspaper open, the perfect picture of a relaxed man undisturbed by
fellow Germans. Mama hasn't moved from the kitchen, and is
nervously drying dishes while casting glances at the soldiers.
Only two remain at the table with their bowls of soup,
discussing their commands for the morning. The third has
wandered to the bookshelf.

I dig my nails into my palms to stop the shaking, hold my
breath, and make a cautious approach.

The soldier turns to assess me, a man with dark brown eyes
and a defined face. "Hallo, Fräulein," he says pleasantly.

"Hallo," I mumble, desperately fighting back the tremor in my voice.

"My name is Otto. My comrades are Friedrich and Emil."

"I am Hilda."

He pauses, catching my gaze, which is directed at the bookshelf, and steps to the side. "Ah, I apologize. Am I in the way?"

"No, not at all," I assure him, hurriedly turning my undivided attention to the books. "My sister wants a book."

"Looks like she might already have a few." Otto chuckles, tapping the wood where it is clear a book has been removed. His finger lies mere centimeters from the empty place where the Tanakh once rested.

My heart seizes in my chest, recognizing the sudden absence of every book printed in Yiddish, and a breathless chuckle escapes my lips. "Yes, I think so."

"Here, perhaps this one," Otto says, drawing a blue volume from the bottom shelf, flipping it open a few pages. His lips quirk approvingly as his eyes wander over the words, then he offers it to me. Thankfully, he looks upon my face and does not notice the fierce quivering of my hands.

We're Germans. We're Germans living within a Jewish community. We have no reason to fear soldiers. They are most welcome, I recite over and over in my head, hoping if I repeat it enough times that will make it true. Mama and Bayla certainly pass as Aryan with their blond hair and blue eyes, even if Father and I don't have the look with such dark hair and eyes.

"Danke. She loves this one." I smile weakly, gripping the Mother Goose book tightly to my chest, forcing myself to bid them all a pleasant goodnight and walk calmly back to my room. Closing the door softly, my lungs burning, I finally take a shaky breath.

"Look, Hodaya, you can use this," Bayla whispers enthusiastically, dragging the sheet off our bed and throwing it up and over my shoulders. "That can be your cape, Mrs. Knight. Hurry, you have to get the troll under the bed and save Princess Bayla!" Snatching the book from my nearly limp fingers, she dashes to the bed and bounces into a circle she's made of pillows and blankets, into all the safety a child shall ever need from the monsters under the bed.

"Fear not, Princess Bayla, I will rescue you. No troll stands a chance against Sir Hodaya!" I declare, flapping my cape dramatically, brandishing an invisible sword, taking some small comfort in her oblivious giggles.

It isn't until some hours later when Mama brings supper to our little room and orders that we lock our door that I realize blue paint still stains my coat and blouse, and I remember my ruined painting, forgotten and abandoned in Aunt Dalia's house.

5

SEPTEMBER 4–11, 1939

BOCHNIA, POLAND

Early the next morning, with my coat drawn tight and head low as I pass German patrols, the first thing I hear as I approach the diner for work is the owner shouting. Mr. Abergel's loud voice rises in protest: "You had no right! This is vandalism! I will go to the police!"

Mr. Abergel, a tall, burly man with a porcelain complexion, is red in the face as he confronts two men, each of whom hold buckets and paintbrushes that drip spatters of yellow and white to the sidewalk like blood. They stare back at him unafraid, and shout, "Go to the police, dirty yid! See who's in the right here!"

On the diner's beautiful oak door, a yellow Star of David is painted across the wood, and the white word *"Juden"* stains all the windows. Naomi Gurewitz, one of my fellow waitresses, a willowy woman with wavy brown hair and stunning green eyes, kneels with a bucket of soap and water as she tries to clean the marks from the face of the restaurant.

"I am a Catholic!" Mr. Abergel shouts indignantly at them. "And even if I were Jewish, you—"

One man steps forward threateningly. "Oh, shut up! We know who your mother is!"

"Your father can dirty his blood all he wants with her, but she's still a filthy Jew, even if she pretends she's Catholic now! Like mother, like son," the second barks, then dips his brush into the yellow paint and slings it to spatter Mr. Abergel's face and Naomi's back.

I know them! I recognize the men a moment later as they turn to leave; two brothers I attended school with who are the most talented violinists I've ever heard. They're just a year older than me.

"Here, let me do it, Naomi. Go get cleaned up," I say soothingly, taking the sponge out of her trembling hand. She is near tears as she tries to wipe the paint out of her hair, and she smiles weakly at me. We don't speak much, but she is Jewish like me, and right now we understand one another better than sisters.

"Thank you, Hodaya," she says, but she still sits beside me as I start to wash the paint away.

"Are you alright?"

She sighs. "Yes, I suppose. It's just... well, it was just so sudden. Like they've been waiting for a reason to do it."

Maybe they have, I think, frowning. *But no one has ever cared that we are Jewish before... well, not much.* Of course, there have been stray comments here and there, but nothing unbearable. Bochnia fell to the Germans not even a full day ago, and already there are townsfolk following in their lead, as if they've hated Jews all along and have been suppressing the resentment for so long that now it's exploding all at once.

But surely it can't get much worse than this. Insults, vandalism, the rare fights, we've seen these things before. What more can they do to us?

. . .

"I don't believe I have ever had such a delicious home-made meal, Mrs. Achen," Otto says. Of the three soldiers he's been the most pleasant, even going out of his way to help Mama and me with chores. The others, Friedrich and Emil, mostly leave us be, except when they want to draw Papa into conversation about Nazi policy over a game of cards and cigarettes.

"Thank you, Otto." Mama smiles, sitting down next to Papa on the sofa.

The table has all but become the men's. No one has actually said it, but it's an unspoken understanding that the soldiers get to sit in three of the four chairs. Mama and Papa have taken to the sofa, and Bayla and I usually sit together by the bookshelf, the fourth chair our makeshift table and a few pillows substituting for chairs. For the second night in a row, Mama has served us rouladen for dinner. Ever since the Nazis invaded, she's been making strictly German meals, even when the soldiers aren't here to eat it.

Bayla has swiftly grown accustomed to them, though remaining silent has proven a challenge. She doesn't speak German and cannot feign the accent, so Mama and Papa have told her never to speak in front of the soldiers, and explained away her silence as muteness. Now, at night when we should be sleeping, she babbles on and on for hours in hushed tones.

In the short time they've been here, all of them have been polite and neat, but I know better than to think them harmless. They don't know we're Jewish; it's evident they suspect nothing of us, constantly praising Hitler and making sneering comments about "filthy *Juden*". We've been extraordinarily careful about hiding our true identities; all the books written in Yiddish stashed away, our certificates and any documents tucked beneath the floorboards, any religious items—few though we possess—hidden in the attic. No language other than German is spoken even when the soldiers are gone, and our prayers have been restricted to silence behind locked doors.

"Hilda," Otto starts. "How is your school going?"

Be careful, I think, glancing at Mama and Papa to see that their eyes hold the same caution.

"I haven't been able to continue," I say. "I've needed to help with work."

"Yes, but hopefully not for long," Papa interjects as he catches sight of the soldiers' frowns. "I remember when the treaty was signed, an utter humiliation it was."

"So terribly unfair," Mama agrees grimly.

Papa shakes his head. "It's why we had to leave Germany. I'm ashamed my family has had to suffer the aftermath of it, but now that we're fighting back my girls will be able to go back to school and experience the life we had before the Great War."

Despite the men's disapproval at my answer about leaving school, Papa's fervent explanation has them agreeing whole-heartedly.

"I think it's good you work to help your parents," Friedrich says.

"Yes," Otto agrees. "Very noble. I started working when I was thirteen to help my mother. We all have to do our part to benefit the new Germany. It's very good of you, Hilda."

I force myself to smile at their approval, reminding myself that Hilda Achen would be glad for their praise, even if Hodaya Alperstein is terrified by the mere sight of them.

They are absorbed once more into a discussion of policy, which Mama and Papa both listen to with rapt attention. Seizing the moment of distraction, Mama nods for Bayla and me to go to our room. Bayla first grabs the English and German copy of the Mother Goose rhymes and I carry our plates to our chilly bedroom, locking the door.

I am almost relieved that I'll be working at the diner tomorrow evening and away from the soldiers, though I don't like the idea of being gone while Papa is in the mines and Mama and Bayla stay home alone. I usually work on Sundays like today, but this morning I pleaded illness to Mr. Abergel, not wanting to raise the soldiers' suspicion by being absent from home on a Catholic holy day nor reveal to them where I work.

The soldiers are Catholics, and so observe their day of rest on Sunday rather than my family, who honor Shabbat on Saturday. Today, the soldiers had no duties, and so remained here while Mama, Papa, Bayla, and I pretended to be attending mass at the church like God-fearing Catholics but instead strolled through the city for a few hours, pointing out birds and shapes in the clouds like when I was a child.

But how much longer can we keep up this act? Mr. Abergel will eventually become curious if I keep "falling ill" every Sunday, and surely the soldiers will eventually notice discrepancies in our religious practices—what will happen then?

Monday morning is spent like every other day since the invasion a week ago. We have a quiet breakfast with the three soldiers before they leave for military duties, kiss Papa goodbye on his way to the salt mines, and Mama shoos Bayla and I out the door after chores. She seems desperate to hold onto a tiny bit of normalcy, and urging me to take Bayla on long walks and to play in the park for a few hours while she minds the house or teaches her private lessons is one of her ways of doing so.

Already, Bayla and I have walked back and forth for several miles, admiring the clothing in display windows and pointing out the shapes of horses, flowers, and other objects in the clouds. She happily chatters away, no longer restricted to silence like she is around Otto, Friedrich, and Emil.

We stop at the window of a popular toy store, and Bayla longingly gazes at the beautiful porcelain dolls and music boxes. "I want a doll like that one day," she says with a grin, pointing to a rosy-cheeked babydoll with curly brown hair in an old-fashioned suit.

Normally, I'd be trying to come up with a plan to afford the doll before she outgrows the desire, but now all I can manage to say is, "Maybe one day."

The door of the toy store opens with a merry jingle of the bell, and Naomi steps outside, her arm linked with a tall, blond man, and several bags in her other hand. Her face lights up with a brilliant smile, and her green eyes seem to glow with happiness.

"Hello, Hodaya, it's good to see you," she says as if we didn't see one another at work a few days ago, but her joy is infectious, and I smile in return.

"It's good to see you too, Naomi."

"I'd like you to meet my husband. This is Adam," she says, and the gentle-faced man gives a small smile and nod. "Adam, this is Hodaya, she's a friend from the diner."

We exchange pleasantries and Naomi shifts our conversation far from the concern of our now occupied city. Bayla takes an instant liking to Naomi, babbling on about our walk today, but I've noticed Naomi tends to have that effect on people.

A week ago, we were little more than acquaintances, but the vandalism incident is an experience we share, and we've grown closer in the last few days in a way that is usually only achieved through time. She is endearing, the sort to give her heart fully to everyone, and I don't believe there is anyone in this world who couldn't be charmed by her disposition.

Somehow, the topic turns to Bayla's birthday, and she excitedly regales Naomi and Adam with all the details of the day. They don't seem bothered by her endless chattering, instead smiling at one another and gushing over "what a darling" she is.

"And see, look! Mama, Papa, and Hodaya all made me this!" Bayla proudly presents the blue *chai* necklace from around her neck.

"Oh, it's lovely, Bayla," Naomi coos, and Adam nods his agreement. Bayla begins to tell them about the doll in the window that's captured her attention, then her own little ragdoll Alma. They share a glance, seeming to communicate without words. Naomi's eyes appear to suggest something, Adam looks thoughtful, and eventually they nod to one another.

"You know, Bayla, I think we have something for you. A late birthday present." Naomi slips one of the several bags from her arm.

Bayla looks up at me as if awaiting permission, and after a quick glance at Naomi, whose joy glistens in her eyes as if *she* were the one receiving a gift, I nod. From the giftbag, Bayla draws a blond babydoll. She gasps, grinning with excitement as she begins to bounce. "Look, Hodaya! Look, look! I have a doll now! Thank you, Miss Naomi!"

The three of us share a smile, and I feel tears prick my eyes at their generosity. This simple gesture means more now than ever, when everything else seems to be going wrong.

Adam checks his silver watch, and, after regretfully declaring his lunch break is over, takes one of the smaller gift-bags, straightens his suit, and kisses Naomi goodbye.

"It's a beautiful day. May I join you for your walk?" Naomi asks, and Bayla agrees before I have the chance to.

"Thank you. I hope that doll wasn't too expensive," I whisper as we walk, suddenly feeling guilty for accepting the gift.

"Now, *that* is no concern." Naomi shrugs. "One of Adam's partners at his law firm, Mr. Chornovil, has a daughter. We've already gotten her a few presents for her birthday next week. I think Bayla appreciates it a lot more."

Bayla has skipped ahead of us, clutching her new doll like a baby and pointing out pretty flowerbeds and butterflies.

Such a kind, lovely woman, I think to myself. Naomi isn't poor like my family, she probably wouldn't have to work if she didn't want to, but the company of others and seeing them happy is something she enjoys, like I enjoy painting.

"When I have a daughter one day, I hope she's just as lively and happy as Bayla. She's such a darling," Naomi says with a smile, and the dreamy, longing tone of her voice is evident.

We spend the next few hours strolling through the city, talking, laughing, playing every guessing game Bayla suggests, and humming along with all the songs she sings. We part only when Naomi has to hurry home to get ready for her anniversary dinner with Adam, promising to see one another at work in the morning and for tea in the evening. The way home is infinitely brighter despite the sinking sun, and I could almost forget that our entire world has been turned upside down in a matter of days.

I could almost believe everything is going to turn out alright, I muse, feeling the weight over my heart lift, and as we arrive home Naomi's cheerful smiles and our easy conversation have nearly convinced me no more misfortune will ever befall us.

6

SEPTEMBER 1, 1943

AUSCHWITZ-BIRKENAU

"Auschwitz? What is Auschwitz?" a woman asks from somewhere in the cattle car, but no one has an answer for her.

The train continues past the sign into a station flooded with lights, where just beyond the cattle car there are ghostlike figures behind a barbed wire fence.

Wait... those are people! I realize in horror as we draw closer to them. *Oh, God, those are people!*

These creatures, that appear to once have been human, are staggering around behind the threatening barbed wire like animals, slipping and falling in the mud, wearing tattered clothes, their heads shaved, large eyes sinking into their hollowed faces. Each of them are screaming in different languages, being struck by SS men with clubs and guns. The noise and the stench of filth is overwhelming.

I shake Bayla awake, dragging her to her feet before she even opens her eyes. "Bayla, stand up! Stand up!"

"Where are we?" she gasps, disoriented.

The people pass out of view, but their screams, their pleas, and their fear still linger like some dark spirit. "I have no idea."

The train comes to a halt, a whistle announcing our arrival cuts through the air, and I am seized by a strangling, inexplicable terror.

I squeeze Bayla's hand. "Don't leave my side," I command.

The wagon door clatters open. Two men in prisoner uniforms lash out at us, snatching arms and legs, dragging people from the car. "Out! Everybody Out! Be quick! Leave everything inside! We'll take care of it!" the men shout, first in Polish, then German, and other languages I don't understand.

A prisoner reaches his arms upwards to me, "Jump down! Hurry!" Without a thought, I crouch, allowing him to take my waist and swing Bayla and me to the ground. A dog runs barreling toward us, teeth bared in a vicious snarl. Bayla screams and I jerk her back just as a German officer pulls on the dog's leash. I grasp Naomi's hand, pulling her closer as Bayla clutches my waist in terror. Uniformed officers watch the proceedings with scrutiny, their dogs barking, growling, trying to break free from their masters to maul us. Prisoner men direct thousands more people off the train, screaming at us, striking us with clubs, throwing our bags and bundles without aim or care.

"Hodaya! Bayla!" Mama and Papa rush staggering toward us.

"Mama, what's happening?" Bayla sobs.

Neither Mama nor I have the time to lie, for another order is shouted by one of the German officers. "Men to the left! Women and children to the right! Hurry up! Schnell! Men to the left! Women and children to the right!"

There is no time to think about anything. Papa kisses Mama, my cheek, then takes a knee to quickly embrace Bayla, and backs away. He gives a reassuring smile, the wrinkles in his face and around his brown eyes deeper than what is usual for a man of fifty-five, his dark hair streaked with gray. "I love you, girls. I'll see you soon," he promises, turns, and is swept away to the left by the swarm of men.

Mama, Naomi, Bayla, and I move to the right with the rest of the women and children, thousands of people hustling to obey the same order being repeated again and again. "Schnell! Men to the left! Women and children to the right! Schnell! Form rows of five!"

The lampposts, floodlights, and flashlights shine so brightly in my deprived eyes, glaring straight through and burning my skull. And somehow this place still feels so dark, like some shadow hangs above it, a waiting noose. A strange odor wafts throughout the area, and it grows stronger and fouler the further we walk.

Mama sniffs, her nose crinkling in disgust. "This is a strange place. It smells like burning meat. Do you suppose they're roasting cow at this time? It smells like a whole herd."

Naomi and I exchange a glance, her eyes holding the same confusion that my own must surely carry. The chefs in the diner used to cook all kinds of meat: chicken, cow, deer, duck; I even recall a Polish man roasting a pig on one occasion. But I don't recognize this scent at all, so vulgar and foreign I cannot describe it.

Soon, we come upon a crossroads. There is a dark-haired SS officer standing there, calm and stern, wearing white gloves, looking neat and almost elegant in his uniform. Efficiently, he waves people to the left and sometimes to the right, but more often to the left.

Within only a few minutes, Mama is standing in front of him. He doesn't speak to her, just frowns, looks her up and down, then directs her to the left. She steps forward and turns to look back, perhaps waiting for us to follow.

A blond SS guard pushes her. "Move along!"

Mama begins to walk reluctantly, never turning to look back

at us. Naomi's hand tightens in mine, gaze fixed on the man with white gloves.

"Your age?" he asks, his voice cold and hollow.

Naomi doesn't understand, and her eyes dart frantically around as she stutters for a response. I quickly lean to whisper in her ear in German, "Twenty-six."

"Twenty-six," Naomi tells him timidly.

"Are you in good health?"

I continue to whisper answers to her in German, so she can reply to him in his language.

"Yes."

"Occupation?"

Do we tell him we are servers? An artist and a housewife? "Tell him *seamstress*," I shakily whisper for her to repeat. Whatever this place is, it is best to be useful.

"Seamstress."

He points to the right and Naomi slips from my grasp. A young girl perhaps only twelve years old is directed to the left without being questioned, leaving only Bayla and me. He looks me up and down, smiling almost kindly.

"Your age?"

"Twenty-one."

"Are you in good health?"

"Yes."

"Occupation?"

"Seamstress." I repeat the same profession I told Naomi to give.

He indicates for me to go to the right as his eyes flicker down to Bayla. Not a second passes before he points to her, then to the left.

7

DECEMBER 1, 1939

BOCHNIA, POLAND

The blood red of the Nazi flag flashes dangerously, the pure white circle marred by a tilted black swastika replacing the simple red and white Polish flag.

Several hundred people stand nervously to attention in the market square. The shuffling of a thousand feet across the cobblestones rings much louder than any voice, all of which have restricted themselves to either silence or whispers. Even the children present, some still mere babies cradled in their mothers' arms, make no sound.

SS Leader Schneider, the Nazi officer bearing the same dismaying swastika on the band around his arm, has only just arrived, a picture of stone, expressionless and cold. It's hard to believe he's a man of flesh and blood, a man with a mother, maybe a wife and children, a man who eats, sleeps, and breathes the same as us. There is something distinctly inhuman about him.

At my side, Naomi shifts closer as he moves to the center of the square. Mr. Abergel closed the diner early and dismissed the staff for the rest of the day when we heard there was to be an important announcement. Naomi and I were among the first people to arrive to hear it first-hand, and for two hours we have waited anxiously, casting fearful, suspicious glances at the SS, German police, and—their mere presence turning the blood in my veins to ice—several Gestapo.

One of Schneider's men steps forward. "Silence! Schweigen!" he shouts. "SS Leader Schneider will address the citizens. This announcement will be transcribed and posted as well."

Whispering, I quickly translate the German words into Polish for Naomi, my breath catching in my throat for a moment when Schneider steps onto the platform. Naomi squeezes my hand reassuringly as Schneider's eyes flit, uninterested, over the crowd. I hadn't realized that I'd latched onto her, but she links our arms comfortingly.

He begins without preamble. "Effective beginning today, the first of December, 1939, the city of Bochnia shall be under curfew. All persons are to be indoors before seven o'clock in the evening and are not permitted to leave before six o'clock in the morning. All violators will be punished to the furthest extent of the law. Exceptions to this will be made for persons with valid work permits or with written permission from a recognized official, and no others.

"Furthermore, let it be known that effective as of today, the first of December, 1939, all Jewish persons are required to wear a white wristband bearing the blue Star of David, and will be allowed three days to comply. Those who fail to do so or present false documents denying themselves as a Jewish person will be punished to the furthest extent of the law, which is the death penalty. That is all."

The last few words die on my lips as I stare, wide-eyed and breathless, but Naomi doesn't need me to tell her the last bit. She's heard enough. We all have.

The effect of his words is immediate, and all at once the square erupts in shouted questions, confusion, and fear. Try as I might, I can't pull my eyes away from Schneider, not even when I feel Naomi pulling me insistently away from the ensuing commotion.

Obey, wear the marks, or be put to death. How could he give those terms so mundanely as if stating nothing more than the price of a jacket? A murderer or a rapist I might understand him passing this judgment on, but only the Jews? Would he really enforce it?

Yes, I think, shuddering. There is a darkness in his eyes, a dead stillness that leaves no room for doubt. He would kill us without a second thought, without remorse.

I feel myself being shaken gently. "Hodaya? Are you alright?"

"Hmm?"

"I've been talking to you for the past few minutes, and you haven't said a word," Naomi says, our arms still linked as she directs me down the street.

"I'm sorry, I was just thinking... did you see the way he was looking at us? It was like... like we..."

Naomi's eyes are sympathetic. "I know what you mean..."

"Like we were *vermin!*" I spit the word incredulously. "It's like we were rats, and he couldn't wait to stomp on us."

"I thought so too. And now with the marks and registration... it's all been so sudden. I never thought they'd really come, at least I hoped they wouldn't."

"I did too. My aunt left with her family right before the invasion. Papa thought she was being ridiculous for running, but now we're the ones trapped and she got out in time."

Longing and disappointment flash across her face as she smooths the fabric of her dress over her stomach. "Adam wanted to leave too, but there wasn't anywhere else to go and... we thought we might be expecting."

"You're pregnant?"

"We thought so. There were all the signs, but I wasn't. We've wanted a baby for so long, but... maybe it's better this way right now." She is silent for a moment in her thoughts, then smiles fondly. "Permilia and Wilhelm. I love those names so much. One day when it's safe again, I'd like to name my children that. Whenever the war is over."

She talks about the end of the war, this mystical *'one day'*, as if it's a certainty, like she's foreseen the Germans' defeat and is simply waiting for the days to play out accordingly.

Maybe she's right. With Germany at war with Britain now, maybe this nightmare will all be over soon. There won't be any curfews or marks, no more soldiers, no need for pretending, no—

"Oh, God!" I gasp, doubling over beneath the force of the sudden realization. "They think we're Germans! Now we'll have to wear the stars! When they find out, they'll kill us!"

"Hodaya! Calm down! Breathe, deep breaths. Tell me what's wrong," Naomi soothes, holding me steady. "When who finds out what?"

"The soldiers! Three of them have been living with us since they came! We've been pretending to be Germans!" I exclaim. "I have to go home! I have to get Mama and Bayla out!"

Her eyes widen with horror. "Let's hurry."

The cold air freezes the tears in my eyes, stings my cheeks as we run. I should be watching for other soldiers, being careful to stay out of their way, but I can't make myself care about them right now. Stumbling several times as I outrun my own legs, I am consumed by nothing but the thought of Mama and Bayla, lambs in that house while their time unknowingly ticks lower.

I am about to yank the front door open when Naomi grabs me.

"No, wait," she pants, gripping her chest. "You have to calm down, Hodaya. If you don't, they'll know something's wrong. Just wait a few moments."

A single minute has never felt so long, each second stretching into hours as I dread a sudden shout, a gunshot. My heart still pounds painfully, but my breathing is stable enough and I can't stand to wait idly for another moment. Naomi follows behind me as I step inside as calmly as I can manage.

Friedrich has thrown off his green coat and kicked off his boots, and he lounges on the sofa with a book. A cigarette hangs from Emil's lips as he shuffles a deck of cards at the table. In the kitchen with Mama, Otto has discarded his coat and rolled up the sleeves of his white shirt as he dries a dish.

"Oh, Hilda!" Mama startles. "What are you doing home so early? It's not even noon."

"We closed early today. We wanted to hear SS Leader Schneider's announcement."

"Ah, yes," Friedrich mutters absent-mindedly. "High time, too. Dirty Juden waltzing around everywhere like they've got all the right."

"They're not doing anything to get rid of 'em yet, but at least they can't hide anymore," Emil says around his cigarette. "Compliance won't be a problem. Anyone feels like they're above the law, we'll just have to—BAM!" Chuckling, he gestures like he's shooting a pistol.

"Oh?" Mama wrings a towel in her hands under the guise of drying them. "What's happened, exactly?"

Naomi inches closer nervously. She doesn't know a single word of German and the language shift has left her lost and uncomfortable.

"All the Jews have to register, Mrs. Achen," Otto says, finishing the dishes. "They'll all wear blue stars from now on, makes 'em easier to spot. Now you don't have to worry about getting too close to anything dirty."

"What a relief..." Mama sighs shakily, her panicked eyes seeking mine.

"And who might this be, Hilda?" Otto grins and takes Naomi's hand in greeting. "Ich bin Otto. Du bist?"

Naomi stutters, her eyes begging me for help.

"This is my friend... Nata," I interject.

"A pleasure to meet you."

She attempts a polite smile, probably hoping whatever he said to her doesn't require a response.

"Mama," I start, desperate to get away. "The bush outside is getting overgrown, would you and Bertha help me—"

Suddenly, Bayla bounds down the hallway with Alma and the blond babydoll Naomi gave her. "Hodaya, you're home!"

Three words.

Three words shouted in such oblivious excitement.

Three words spoken in Yiddish slam the room into a dead silence and my heart plummets to the floor.

All eyes have turned to Bayla, who now presses her lips together in remembrance of our instructions, as if silence now will erase her words. The soldiers stare, shocked, and the towel slips from Mama's hands in horror.

Emil crushes his cigarette on the table. "That wasn't German. Not even *Polish*."

"You said that girl was mute," Friedrich growls, slamming his book shut. He turns on Naomi and me. "And what about that one? Is she mute too?"

"She's—"

Friedrich snaps, "Shut up, Hilda! If that's even your name. Let her talk. Well? Do you speak?"

Naomi's eyes dart frantically to mine in obvious ignorance, and the longer she says nothing the more furious the men's faces become.

"They're fucking Jews!" Emil spits, rising to his full height.

Disbelievingly, Otto whirls to assess me, perhaps waiting for me to deny it, but all the air has fled my body and I cannot utter a sound. His eyes shift to the bookshelf, and something seems to snap within him, a dawning realization that brings his handsome face into a frightening scowl.

"The books..." Otto mutters to himself, then turns to the others. "They're hiding their books somewhere. The rest of it's probably stashed away too."

Friedrich jerks his head in an unspoken order and Emil disappears down the hall, shoving Bayla into the wall as he goes.

"We're not hiding anything," Mama pleads, pulling Bayla protectively to her side.

"Then there's no problem with us searching the house!"

Bayla's wide eyes turn to me, filled with confusion and fear, but when I try to move toward her Otto's arm rises to block me and pushes me back. "Stay!" he commands as if speaking to a disobedient dog.

Naomi grips my arm tightly at the sound of shattering glass down the hall, heavy thumps and cracks that can only be wood snapping, furniture overturning. Friedrich storms to the kitchen, jerking cabinets open, throwing dishes and silverware without care, wasting bowls of precious food on the floor in his search.

"Juden!" Emil roars. A large piece of copper flies down the hall, and Mama cries out in pain as it strikes her in the arm.

The menorah! Papa hid it in the attic! Everything is in the attic!

Emil goes on shouting, hurling the Tanakh, the Shabbat candles, and all other items into the front room, and the proof of our deceit piles up. Mama and Bayla shrink fearfully toward us. With a sharp kick, Friedrich sends the menorah flying, and his hands lock around Mama's throat.

"No!" Screaming, I shove past Otto and rip Bayla from Mama's side. I grab his arm, tugging with all my strength. "Please! Let her go! LET GO!"

A stunning force strikes my head, blurring my vision. Terrified sobs and screams ring hazily in my ears as I blink, registering my body on the floor, the dampness on my temple. Emil's enraged face appears before me, his iron grip seizes my hair and drags me across the floor, and I choke for air as his boot strikes my stomach.

Mama claws at the hand strangling her as she fights to breathe. Bayla sits crying by the bookshelf, clutching Asher, who's meowling in her arms. Naomi begs incoherently to Otto, who shouts in frustration, angrily gesturing, neither understanding the other.

God, please, don't let them kill us!

Sobbing, I try to crawl away, to Bayla, to Mama, to Naomi, to anywhere but beneath Emil's beastly hands, but I cannot move. Every breath is forced out of my lungs, every punch makes the world slip further away, and then everything begins to darken and numb.

BAM!

Through tears and ~~crimson blurring~~ my eyes, Mama has fallen to the floor, and two men fight for a pistol aimed at the ceiling.

Papa!

Punching Friedrich in the face, Papa tears the gun from his hand and hurls it out of the open door. Emil ceases his relentless beating, reaching instead for Papa. With a strength and fury nearly inhuman, Papa knocks Friedrich to the ground and whirls to meet Emil's attack.

It is all I can do to drag myself to Mama, who cradles her bruised neck, wheezing for air. Naomi is at my side a moment later, hastily pulling us to the door. Bayla hides just behind her skirt, gripping the fabric in terror. She drags Bayla outside and rushes back to help me to my feet, but my head spins and I collapse again.

Otto doesn't try to block our escape, just eyes us with disdain before returning his attention to the fight. Papa takes and lands multiple punches, his brow and lip busted and bleeding, fighting to keep either soldier from moving toward us. Mercifully, neither Friedrich nor Emil is armed, and any notion of finding a gun seems to have been forgotten. Emil grabs the menorah and raises it.

"Eldad!" Mama cries, lunging weakly for Papa.

Too late Papa shields himself, and the metal strikes him with a sickening crack. He crumples, upright for only a moment longer before they're upon him.

"No! Papa! Please, please! Stop!" I scream, crying helplessly, not knowing what else to do as Naomi struggles to haul Mama and me out of the house.

Papa's arms lie limp at his sides, his energy spent, and the soldiers do not relent in their savage assault.

"Alright, that's enough." Otto eventually steps forward and grabs Friedrich's arm, sounding more aggravated than anything. "You're getting blood everywhere."

"Who cares?" Emil hisses, striking Papa across the face again. "He's a filthy Jew! He attacked us!"

Otto shoves Emil's shoulder, causing him to stumble back. "I don't care what he is, he's still got blood. You can be the one to scrub it out, I'm not livin' anywhere that—"

"You don't care?" Friedrich bellows in rage. Swiftly rising to his feet, he glares murderously down at Otto. "Have you gone soft? Do you feel *sympathy* for these rats? You were there in the trenches like us! Remember the Great War and all the things they did to us?"

"I've got no love for Jews, no more than you," Otto snaps. "I've just got more respect for myself than to bother with them."

"What the hell do you know about respect, boy? They're Jews, they tricked us, and you haven't done a thing! You've got no respect! I'd say you've been deceived by them! That's what they do, and you've fallen for it!"

"Watch yourself, Friedrich. I still outrank you."

Friedrich scoffs. "Judenliebhab—"

In an instant, Otto's pistol is pressed to Friedrich's chest. "Finish that word," he growls warningly. "Go on, say it, then Emil can clean your blood off the floor too."

For several moments, the tense silence is broken only by Friedrich's furious, ragged breaths, and a sudden sputtering from Papa's motionless body that makes me whimper with relief.

"The Gestapo, then," Emil says, fists clenched.

"Gestapo have more important things to worry about than a couple of rats with nowhere to go," Otto says, holstering his gun. "Rats belong in the gutter. Let them flail for a while and they'll drown eventually."

"Let them go? What's wrong with you?"

"Scum is still scum whether it's in the gutter or not!"

Papa groans and rolls onto his side. Blood soaks his swollen face, his nose sits crooked, and pain laces his every move. I crawl forward and reach for his hand. His eyes find mine, reddened with something more than any physical pain or fear, and our joined hands seem to give him strength. He struggles to his knees and shields me protectively as we distance ourselves from the arguing men.

"Fine!" Friedrich exclaims. "But if I see 'em in the streets, I'm putting bullets in their heads!"

We've all scrambled dizzily from the door before another word can be said, stumbling, holding each other upright despite our aching bones, bruises, and blood. I never let go of Papa's hand as we run for the back streets, Mama supporting him on one side, Naomi carrying Bayla as she clutches her little orange cat.

For how long or how far we run, I have no idea, only realizing when Papa takes a knee in exhaustion, biting back a groan of pain, that I no longer recognize the empty street. Mama bursts into tears and hugs Papa tightly, Bayla carefully nuzzles against me, and Naomi embraces me, her hands rubbing soothingly over the aches in my arms.

We're alive! Oh, thank God! We're alive!

A sob chokes my throat and soon I am sobbing, overwhelmed by utter relief and fear still.

What if they change their minds and turn us over to the Gestapo anyway? Where do we go? Now what happens to us?

"Hodaya?" Bayla sniffles. "Can we go home? I'm sorry, I promise I won't talk to them anymore. I'll say sorry. Please? I forgot my coat, and my dolls."

"It's not your fault," I whisper, hugging her. "We just can't go back for a little while."

"Why not? I'm really, really sorry I talked to them. Won't it be alright if I tell them sorry?"

They'd sooner shoot us like dogs... but not for lying to them. No, it would be for the unforgivable crime of being Jews. What is so abhorrent about us that they think of us as less than rats? And if we are truly so horrible, so different, why do they need stars to know we're not like them? Monsters are supposed to look as such, not as humans.

"You're staying with me," Naomi says resolutely. "Adam and I have an extra room you can stay in. We haven't used it in a long time, it's been for storage lately."

Mama gasps. "Oh, dear, do you—we couldn't possibly—"

"You absolutely could, Mrs. Alperstein, I'll hear no arguments. My home is yours. We all need each other right now, more than ever. It's only a little farther from here, you'll never see those horrible men again."

Speechless, I stare at her in amazement. We've only become friends in the last few months, yet she's already the closest friend I've ever had, one of the most generous, genuinely kind people I've ever met. Here she stands, fussing over my cuts and giving Mama and Papa—whom she's never even met—her headscarf for the blood, offering an entire family a place in her home like she's known us all her life.

"Come on, we're not far. Let's get those wounds cleaned up and then you can all get some rest," Naomi says, helping me to my feet. "I'll make some warm soup and tea."

My heart fills with such gratitude and love I feel it may burst, and with a tearful smile I pull her into my arms. "Thank you, Naomi, thank you so much. You're the best friend anyone could have."

"Don't thank me, not for this. We'll all take care of each other. We'll be alright," she says quietly, and, for a moment, I think I could believe in anything she says.

8

DECEMBER 18, 1939

BOCHNIA, POLAND

The hideous bruises on my face have finally begun to fade, but the memory of the Germans' vicious beating a few weeks ago will always feel raw and painful. I've never been struck before. Papa never raised even a finger to us, and somehow it never occurred to me that a man could be capable of such violence, especially against women and children.

Although Papa tried to insist he was well enough to work, he could barely move the morning after the attack. His eyes were swollen shut, several of his fingers broken, and Mama sat at his side in Naomi's and Adam's spare bedroom, nursing him and making sure he didn't hurt himself by accident. Mama couldn't speak in more than a whisper for days, and tears pricked Papa's eyes each time he looked at the purple bruises on her neck. Suddenly finding myself the sole provider for my parents, there was no time to rest and heal. I covered what injuries I could with the makeup Naomi gave me and learned to ignore the dull ache that accompanied my every move. But even walking for too long was agonizing, and after I refused to go home, Mr. Abergel allowed me to remain in the kitchen helping the chefs so I didn't have to move as much until I felt better.

Now, Naomi has taken up a position by the kitchen door of the diner, peering through the tiny window every now and again at the Chornovils, the Ukrainian family Adam worked with in his law firm until it was recently seized from him by the authorities. She would probably like to serve them herself, but an unsavory customer is still sitting nearby, sipping coffee and unsuspecting that the Jewish staff haven't been fired.

Our wristbands make for quick and easy identification, and many of our customers no longer feel comfortable being served by Jews. Even those we have served before, the people who were friends and acquaintances, shun anyone wearing a blue star. Twiddling with the white wristband sewn into my coat in irritation, I wish I could rip it off as I lean idly against a counter in the diner's kitchen.

When I returned to work after registering as a Jew the day after the announcement and my bruises hadn't turned completely purple yet, a man and a young woman took a seat near the windows around three o'clock. I recognized the girl; she was an apprentice at the library and she'd helped me find books quite often. I'll never forget the way they both smiled pleasantly when I approached, the way those smiles fell into reproach and utter revulsion at the sight of the star on my arm. The man stood abruptly and spat on me. They refused to be served by a Jew, have a Jew touch their plates or speak to them, and left the diner muttering profanities about Jews working in places they might spread disease.

I was too stunned to do anything, too shocked to be angry or sad. I could only stand there, frozen, unsure what to make of the entire interaction. Mr. Abergel instructed that from then on the Jewish staff only leave the kitchen to serve customers we knew were safe to serve.

Facing the scorn of the Germans isn't easy, but it is

expected. Their sneers and violence have become almost normal, the kind of behavior that makes sense coming from them. Facing the people I used to know is very different. To be looked down upon and avoided by people who my parents were friends with, people I used to help in their shops, people who were once my teachers, doctors, classmates... the humiliation is beyond words.

Aunt Dalia was so lively and genuinely adored, good friends with everyone she knew. Somehow, I can't imagine her being here right now, wearing a wristband, being glared at and avoided like the plague by all the people she considered friends. It would break her heart.

How long has it been since she left? A few months now? Has it really only been a few months and not years?

"They're gone," Naomi sighs woefully, and I assume she means the Chornovil family has left. "They're such nice people. We all used to treat one another to dinner every week. Their daughter is such a darling, and very intelligent. She's learning English, so we gave her the newest print of a book called *The Hobbit* for her birthday this year. We're told it's very popular in England. And their son, oh, he's absolutely precious. He was just born a few months ago..."

No one could miss the longing and sadness in her voice, mournful as if she were speaking at a funeral, grieving the sudden loss of her good friends. I lay a comforting hand on her shoulder, but it is all that I can do. I never had close friends the way Naomi does, the way Aunt Dalia did. Even before I stopped going to school, I was never involved with many people. Naomi is the first friend I've ever had who I've been genuinely close with, who I've shared my secrets, fears, and interests with, who shares her own with me.

"I'm sure they miss you too," I assure her.

She smiles at my meager attempt to console her. "Things will change when the war is over. Maybe by then I'll have a little Wilhelm or Permilia their son can play with. We'll all have to have dinner together again to celebrate things getting back to normal. You should come with Adam and me when we do."

When the war is over... one day... hopefully it's soon.

From outside the diner, I hear the loud familiar click of a speaker turning on. The Nazis installed the speakers all throughout the city shortly after they invaded, and turn them on at random times of the day, spreading their hate and propaganda for hours on end. A voice comes over the speaker and announces the date the impending speech was given: *The thirtieth of January, 1939, Reichstag.* A recording follows the introduction, a voice I have come to recognize as Adolf Hitler, his wrathful spirit and grisly passion palpable even through the garbled sound.

"*On January 30, 1933, I entered Wilhelmstrasse, filled with deep concern for the future of my people. Today—six years later— I can speak to the first Reichstag in Greater Germany! Truly, perhaps more than another generation, we may be able to gauge the pious meaning of the saying: 'What a turn of God's providence!'*"

What a turn indeed...

Naomi shudders at the sound of his voice, ignorant to the meaning of his words, but understanding the tone with which he speaks. I usually translate what I can for her, but it's impossible to repeat every single word.

"How did you learn to speak German, Hodaya?" she asks, shuffling away from the door.

"My mother started teaching me when I was little, I think I was about six or seven."

"Really? You were that young and learning another language? That's incredible. Where did she learn?"

"She and my aunt grew up in Germany from the time she was three until she was sixteen, then they moved from Berlin to Poland in '05."

"Is she part German?"

Wouldn't that be ironic?

"No, they just lived there for a while after my grandparents passed away. Mama lived with her grandmother and she was a schoolteacher, so she taught them English, Ukrainian, and German."

"I imagine it's a wonderful skill to have right now," Naomi says, then jumps slightly as the kitchen door swings open and a Polish waitress hurries through.

"How come you never learned?"

In some Polish cities it's an uncommon thing to come across a German speaker, but a good number of Bochnia's population is fluent.

"There was no real need, I suppose. I know a cousin of mine studied German for a few years before he left for university, but I never presumed it would be very useful to me. I've never wanted to leave Poland, or Bochnia for that matter."

"Neither have I," I admit. "Not until now. France sounds like a wonderful place to be. Bright skies, open countryside—imagine all the museums they have. Claude Monet, Camille Pissarro..."

"Cellos, the Eiffel Tower, and all the lovely people and food," Naomi adds. "I hear the cities glow all night, candles, lamps, all of it reflecting off the water and glass. It must be beautiful."

"I'd like to be there now... Once my aunt writes to us, I'll ask her what it's like."

They'll be safe. Britain and France are on the same side. Germany wouldn't invade.

"Would you teach me German?" Naomi asks suddenly after a moment of silence. "I hate not knowing what they're saying. I feel stranded in my own city."

I chuckle. "I'm not a very good teacher, but I'll certainly try.

It's probably best if my mother helps too, she speaks it a lot better than—"

The calm atmosphere is shattered by a round of distant gunfire. The entire kitchen freezes, everyone holding their breaths, pots, pans, and kettles left to simmer and burn unattended. For nearly a minute there is only silence—apart from the voice on the speakers. Another six rapid shots. Naomi latches onto my arm, and I return her crushing, trembling grip. She squeezes her eyes shut, her mouth moving in a wordless prayer, and I follow suit, only for another round of shots to puncture every whispered plea.

The succession of gunfire repeats over and over until I have counted one hundred and four shots in total... fifty-two people... two shots per person, one to kill, one to make sure they're dead...

It isn't the first time I've heard gunshots echoing across the city. People have been dragged from their jobs and homes by Gestapo to be executed in the streets, unsuspecting Jews have been shot on the sidewalks when they failed to notice an SS and didn't step away. But there have never been this many. This was no execution. It was a massacre—revenge.

A group called the White Eagle was responsible for attacking a German police station on Rynek Street two days ago, and the Germans arrested a large number of random men from the city in retaliation, but I never thought they'd...

I have no desire to speak nor move, only the sudden urge to sink to the ground and remain lying there until the earth swallows me whole. In this moment, I would be content to never utter another sound so as to never break the spell of denial, to never disturb nightmare into reality.

Normality, safety. Are those such outlandish things to wish for?

Every time I try to forget, when it seems the illusion of one of them is within my reach, it shatters in my palms and slices them open; and in our silence, the speakers drone on and on...

"... *if international financial Jewry in and outside Europe should succeed in plunging the peoples once again into a world war, then the result will not be the Bolshevization of the earth and thus the victory of Judaism, but annihilation of the Jewish race in Europe!*"

The dead dug their own grave.

One of the men forced to bury them was Mr. Abergel's brother, and he came into the diner an hour ago, shaken and disturbed. Mr. Abergel brought him to the kitchen so he wouldn't be bothered in the dining area—for even as a Catholic, with a Jewish mother, he wore a blue star. He drained several glasses of alcohol before the details spilled unbidden, and he described the German firing squad marching the men to Uzbornia Hill, watching the Polish and Jewish men despair as they dug the mass grave, watching each of them crumple, dead, into the hole, then burying them.

Naomi cried silently as he spoke, and we held one another in prayer as he recounted the horrific event. With a sullen face and a fragile voice, Mr. Abergel ordered us to finish serving the present customers and close the diner, then took his brother home.

Naomi and I leave the diner through the back door a few hours before curfew, coats and scarves drawn tightly against the worsening winter air. The snow has yet to fall this year, but the coming storms are palpable in the low howling of the wind, the soft white clouds darkening to gray.

The third speech of the day begins blaring over the speakers as we head toward Naomi's home that we now share, *"The first of May, 1935, Berlin."* The adoring cheers and applause come first, as if the crowd welcomes some hero home, and Hitler's voice follows.

"... *only that which was old, decayed, and evil perishes; and let it die! But new life will spring up. Faith can be found, if the will is there. Our leadership has the will, and faith is with the people.*"

Wincing at his controlled, passionate tone, I link my arm with Naomi's, and feel the same uneasiness shudder through her. We've heard little of him, only what the Nazis think we should hear him say, but there is a disturbing madness in his voice, a fury that treads the line of sanity.

"*When was a leadership at any time faced with a heavier task than our German leadership? Consider, my comrades, what our Germany is, and compare it with other countries. What have we?*"

"I'm nearly done with your new skirts," Naomi says quietly. "I ran out of thread last night. I'll get some more in the morning."

Mama and I have been wearing her old clothes since we moved in. They're a bit ill-fitting, tight at the waist and a few inches too long, but we've had to make do with what we have until we can sew new ones from old sheets and patches of fabric.

"Here. My tables left it for me today," I say, setting six grosze from my pocket into her hand. It's not worth much anymore, but it's all I have, and it's the least I can do for her.

"*What have we? One thing only; we have our people. Either it is everything or it is nothing. On it alone can we count. On it alone can we build.*"

In the distance, a rumble of thunder rolls over the hills, a promise of the coming rain. Darkness has already begun to fall and the streetlamps cast unnatural dots of light across the ground. An SS man strides down the center of the sidewalk in our direction. Hastily, we step off the sidewalk, eyes turned away from him, praying he ignores us and our stars.

"Everything that we have created up to the present we owe solely to its goodness of heart, its capacity, its loyalty, its decency, its industry, its sense of order."

The SS man's shoulder passes inches from mine. He lunges and I flinch as he spits aggressively in my face, cursing, then continues on as if his walk were never interrupted. We turn down another deserted street near the market square, keeping a watchful eye out for any more SS who might not be so kind as to let us go.

"What we want lies clear before us: not war and strife."

The first trickle of rain lands on my cheek, a single raindrop that becomes three, then another and another until I must lower my gaze. Suddenly, there is a strange disturbance in the lamp-lights that have been consistent until now—a dark shadow standing in the ghostly light. Rain drips from my hair and coat like a cold sweat and slides down my spine with a freezing dread.

"Just as we have established peace within our own people..."

Mere feet from the obscured glare of the lamppost, I hesitate, gripping Naomi fearfully. A pair of shoes floats above our heads. Blinking through the rain obscuring my vision, I shield my eyes, curiosity turning my gaze upwards despite the voice in the back of my mind begging me to keep walking.

"... so we want nothing else than peace with the world."

A shrill scream of terror rips from my throat. Rain and tears burn down my skin, a downpour of blood from the blackness above, and Hitler's voice rings in my head like a hail of gunfire. Two bodies dangle from the lamppost by nooses, bullet holes between their dead, bulging eyes. Lightning flashes, illuminating their armbands, and the blue stars are blinding.

9

AUGUST 11, 1940

BOCHNIA, POLAND

"I'm having second thoughts, Hodaya. This is very dangerous. And unorthodox," Naomi whispers, all color drained from her face, as we crouch behind an untended shrub. Up until dawn started to break, she was on board with the idea, but it seems that last night's plans have become the morning's fears.

"It's not stealing, it's already ours," I respond. "They're the ones who've stolen it. You and I are the *least* unorthodox people in this situation."

Our target lies just across the street. Bathed in the tranquil gray light of a new day's approach, my old home sits dormant, lights flicked off, curtains drawn, and soldiers barricaded inside. We never tried to come back after they threw us out last year, not even when they were gone on duty. Facing the Gestapo if we were caught wasn't worth the risk, not for clothes and shoes.

"Yes, I know, but *soldiers?* I won't even stand in the same vicinity as one, let alone steal from three... especially *these* three."

"It's not stealing," I firmly repeat. "My family worked for

everything in that house, it *all* belongs to us. We need everything we can get."

A fine of three million złotych was imposed three months ago, to be paid only by the Jews in Bochnia. I've grown up without much money, going to bed and waking up hungry more often than not, sharing clothes and rooms and shoes, never having hot water, toys, sweets, or tiny luxuries. But three million being demanded from less than a quarter of the population has forced even the wealthiest Jewish people to the brink of poverty, and there is no way to make ends remotely meet anymore.

We fall into a tense silence, watching the door and windows like hawks. Despite the racing of my own heart and the throbbing in my head, I could almost laugh at the irony of the entire situation. *Rightful resident hides in the bushes and stalks her own house, waiting for the thieves to leave so she can rob it back.*

Naomi starts suddenly when a window lights up. "Hodaya, I don't know about this. They might just shoot us themselves instead of bothering with the Gestapo."

"We won't have to deal with either. We won't get caught." I cover her hand comfortingly. "Like I said last night, I'll find everything, you just need to watch the door for me. If we have to, we can escape out of the bedroom window."

"I just... is it really worth it?" She sighs.

We're going hungry every night, we aren't getting paid enough anymore, Mama can't find work, Papa and Adam are making barely anything laboring for the Nazis, Bayla will be seven soon, and our lives have been turned upside down. We are strangers in our own city and outcasts among our townsfolk, hiding in the shadows where we once walked freely. Maybe a few złotych and clothes wouldn't have even nearly outweighed the risks a year ago, but my entire world was very different a year ago.

I let out a heavy breath, trembling. "Do you have a better idea?" I ask genuinely.

She struggles for a response, but in the end she says nothing, her shoulders sagging and her head sinking.

It isn't long before the lamps in the windows have flicked off once more and the soldiers emerge and stride purposefully down the street.

For several minutes we wait, watching for anything out of the ordinary besides ourselves. Stillness and silence remain, disturbed occasionally by the cooing of doves. We carry our shoes to stop them from clicking against the ground and hasten inside. Naomi breathes a sigh of relief before rushing to the window, barely peeking out from below the sill.

"Alright, we're here, now please hurry, Hodaya," she whispers urgently.

My old room is utterly destroyed when I twist the broken knob and push the door open; blankets and mattress thrown to the opposite side of the room, drawers ripped out of the dresser, skirts, blouses, scarves, and coats strewn about, books scattered with broken spines and torn out pages. Any hope that the soldiers may not have found the little bit of money I saved is quickly crushed when I see that the tiny box is missing from under the bed.

A bit of yellow catches my attention among the piles of fabric, and I uncover Bayla's coat. Two of the buttons are missing and many seams have been torn open, probably in pursuit of hidden valuables, but hopefully I'll be able to mend it. I sling it over my arm, then gather up a few more clothes, before moving to Mama's and Papa's room. The state of it is no different than ours, and I gather up the discarded pile of clothes from under the window, relieved to find the floorboard still in place. I tamper with it for a moment, feeling for the cracks and digging my nails into the wood the way Mama showed me until I can tilt the board upwards. Inside is a small tin box. When I pry the lid off, my heart jumps at the sight of a small wad of złotych, a golden chain and matching set of earrings, and several photographs.

The first picture is of Mama and Papa on their wedding day, Mama dressed in her beautiful white wedding gown and the golden jewelry. The second is of our family, probably a month or two before the invasion, Bayla and me between Mama and Papa wearing our prayer dresses. The third is Bayla and me when she was a baby, she sleeping peacefully in my arms while I smile adoringly down at her as if I were the proud mother.

I quickly pocket everything and turn to the door, ready to leave, when Naomi appears, hyperventilating and ashen. "One of them is coming back!"

"Let's go then!" I reach for the latches on the window to open the shutters. They don't budge. I shake them, more and more frantically as the seconds tick by, but they only rattle. "They're boarded up!" I whisper urgently and grab her hand. "Come on, we have to go out the kitchen window!"

"He'll see us!" she gasps, pulling me from the door. "Let's just hide until they leave!"

"What if they search the rooms? Then they'll see us! If we get out the window, at least we can run. Come on!" I urge, dragging her down the hall.

The kitchen window faces the street, but the view from the door is obscured by the tall bush. If we're lucky, we might not be seen right away. I climb onto the counter, reaching to unlatch the window just as the door opens. Emil has stepped halfway inside when there is a sudden crack, an egg smashing against his head.

"OVER HERE!" a boy's voice shouts. "Look! Over here! Jews breaking curfew! Szkop!"

Another boy's voice joins the first. "Szwab! Take up arms, Niemiaszeks! You're under attack! The yids are here!"

This time, a rock flies through the air, hitting Emil directly in the eye as he reaches for his gun. He yelps and stumbles, infuriated, then storms from the door. Shots are fired, multiple, in angry succession, but the two boys continue to scream and yell, "Nazis! Niemiaszeks! Szwabs! Try and shoot us!"

Outside, I catch a glimpse of two blond boys hurling eggs and large rocks before they turn and sprint, fleeing the livid soldier who's close on their heels—drawing him away from us. Friedrich and Otto soon appear, guns already drawn as they pursue, and are instantly gone from sight around the corner.

Naomi, who stands frozen in terror, must be shaken from her stupor.

"Come on! Hurry! Before others come!" I hiss, pulling her to the door.

No doubt every household is awake now, including the other soldiers and officers still housed with them. We can't be anywhere near here when they come to investigate or, worse, call the Gestapo.

I send a vehement thanks to God for not allowing us to be discovered and pray for those boys' safe escape as we run in the opposite direction. The streets are still deserted this early in the morning, but we stay in the dark, gliding along buildings, under windows, behind bushes and trees, and through cluttered alleys. Still miles away from home, we are forced to stop to regain our breath. There is still at least an hour before curfew is lifted, and we can't make it all the way back home in the light.

We find a decent hiding place between the board fences between two houses. The grass is tall and untended enough to keep us out of sight from anyone who isn't looking for curfew-breakers. Nestled side by side in the withering grass, curled up as tiny as possible, we wait for the sun to rise over the rooftops.

For two hours neither of us move, neither of us speak, neither of us so much as breathe too loudly. It must be nearing seven o'clock when we risk peeking from our spot.

"Do you think it's safe?" Naomi whispers.

I can see no immediate danger from where we lie, not a German in sight. "As safe as it's going to be."

While we are no longer breaking curfew, our bright wristbands still restrict us to the back streets as we crawl out of our refuge and start the long walk home. We've barely gone a block down Floris Street when someone calls to us.

"I thought you'd have run all the way to Warsaw by now!"

Two boys jog up beside us, each carrying a burlap sack. The older boy looks about eighteen like me, tall with dusty blond hair and a charming smile. The other boy is younger with the same blond hair and hazel eyes, but freckles dust his nose and boyish cheeks, and he blushes brightly as he walks beside me. They both wear a blue star.

"Great heaven!" Naomi gasps. "Who are you two? Have you no manners, to be running up to complete strangers and frightening them!"

"No manners? I think breaking into a soldier's house takes precedence over our offense. Besides, we saved your lives." The eldest boy smiles mischievously. "I'm Gavriel. This is my brother, Noam. There, now we're not strangers anymore. And who might you lovely thieves be?"

"Are you the ones who attacked Emil?" I ask, having not gotten a clear look at them before.

"Emil?" Gavriel wonders, eyebrow quirked and eyes appraising our wristbands. "How do you know him?"

Naomi and I exchange a glance, and silently agree there's no danger in telling the truth.

"That was my house, they lived with us," I tell him, bitterness tinging my words. "We pretended to be German for a while, but they found out and we had to run. We're not thieves. We didn't take anything that wasn't ours."

This makes Gavriel smirk widely. "Juraj Jánošíks, then? I tip my hat to you. I've never met a lady Robin Hood. We fancy ourselves honest Jerzys these days too."

"How did you escape from them?" Naomi asks.

Gavriel laughs. "Escape? Hardly an escape. The cats can chase, but the rats can slip through more cracks, right, Noam?"

Noam fidgets shyly with his bag. "Right. We ran into the old cinema and they ran right past us. We've been hiding there for a few days. They're looking for men to round up to take to Pustków. For work."

"But you're just boys," Naomi says.

"I'll be fourteen soon," Noam says quickly, glancing at me before averting his gaze, blushing. "I'm old enough. They took our father for the transport yesterday. They're still looking for us."

Gavriel throws an arm around Noam's shoulder. "And they'll find us if you keep shooting your mouth off like that."

Naomi mutters under her breath, "More likely for throwing eggs and rocks at them."

"We saved you from getting caught, didn't we?" Gavriel smirks. "You two might be on your way to the station by now if we didn't distract them."

"Or the street..." Naomi trails off, shuddering.

I link my arm with hers as she says this, realizing that she is still trembling. "Thank you for saving us, Gavriel, Noam, but we need to get home."

Naomi and I begin to pick up our pace, but the boys are soon at our sides once again.

"Wait a minute!" This time it is Noam who speaks, rummaging in his bag for a moment until he produces a smaller package. He offers it to me, stammering slightly. "H-here. We've got a lot. We get them before the bakers can throw them out."

Inside the brown packaging is a long loaf of bread, still warm.

I smile gratefully. "Thank you, Noam, you're very kind. Stay safe."

Eyes twinkling, he grins kindly. "Stay safe."

We go our separate ways, Gavriel and Noam disappearing down the next street as stealthily as they came while Naomi and I hurry the last few miles home in silence. By the time we make it back, it is nearly eight o'clock, but no one has emerged from their rooms just yet.

Safe at last, we both collapse into the chairs at the table, finally able to breathe easily. I lay the contents of my arms and pockets on the table: my mother's jewelry, three photographs, nine złotych, Bayla's ruined coat, some clothes, and the extra loaf of bread. Our rewards for waging our lives against Nazis.

In silence, Naomi and I stare at one another until a snicker breaks our composure. Then, we are laughing hysterically until tears slide down our cheeks and our sides ache with every breath, until we sound like madwomen, until we've woken the entire house and left them wondering what could possibly be so amusing at a time like this.

10

JULY 18–19, 1941

BOCHNIA GHETTO, POLAND

After the day they saved us, Noam and Gavriel seemed to find us wherever we went. As Naomi and I walked home from work, they would appear seemingly from nowhere with potatoes and eggs; when we took walks along deserted roads away from the soldiers and SS, we'd glimpse one another and wave like old friends. They managed to avoid the small roundup of a few hundred men to Pustków last year and returned to living with their mother, Ahava, a kind woman who was very pleased when they invited Naomi and me inside for tea, and we visited them often over the next months.

Back in December, when Bochnia's Jewish Committee was stripped of their self-governing powers and became a Judenrat so the Nazi authorities could further enforce their laws and regulations, Gavriel and Noam brought us two burlap sacks of bread. News about the newly formed Judenrat displeased all of us, and they seemed to think that we should start hoarding everything of value, from food to thread.

The ghetto within the city was established in early April, and suddenly it made perfect sense why the authorities had forced every Jew to register as such. No one was able to hide when the SS came door by door with lists of names and ages ready to be accounted for and ordered everyone to pack a single suitcase and be ready to move within the hour. The ghetto's tightly guarded borders at Kraszewskiego, Solna Gora, and Leonarda streets are surrounded by a high fence, inhabited by thousands of Jews from Bochnia, Krakow, and Mielec who we don't have the resources to house or feed. We are prohibited from leaving the borders of the ghetto without a permit, and it has become punishable by death to do so.

Various mechanical factories and sewing workshops are situated on the eastern border of the ghetto at Trudna Street. The German military base is just west of Leonarda Street, directly in our line of sight from the new apartment we were forced into once Jews were segregated from the rest of the city. I imagine our little room was once intended for a single person, maybe two. Every room is overflowing, and Gavriel, Noam, and Ahava ended up being crammed inside along with us. Naomi and Adam face a similar situation in the apartment room directly across from ours, sharing the space with another husband and wife, their three daughters, and elderly grandmother.

Papa and Adam have gone to the military barracks for work while Naomi, Ahava, and I have been forced to find places in the sewing workshops making uniforms for the German military. The Nazis haven't explicitly ordered us to slave for them yet, but they have taken away all other possibilities for work inside the ghetto, we cannot do business with anyone outside the fence, and so their factories and shops are our last resort. Mama has few other obligations but to take care of Bayla and continue her education at home, as both she and Papa are unwilling to send her to school anymore. They pulled her out of Bochnia's primary school last year after she arrived home with a bloody nose and told us that an older boy, fifteen, had thrown a book at her face and called her a dirty yid. Gavriel and Noam were not forgiving, having taken Bayla under their wing as their honorary little sister, and the boy ended up with two black eyes, a few missing teeth, and a sprained wrist.

I'll never admit to it aloud, but it may have been me who pointed the boy out to Gavriel and Noam so they could "repay" the favor. Papa must have known it was me, though, because, after Gavriel and Noam informed everyone of the mysterious attack on the boy, Papa had glanced at me knowingly, but remained silent, and the approving quirk of his lips made me smile sheepishly.

There are twenty women in our room of the sewing workshop, each at her own desk in the long rows of Singers, fabric, thread, and finished products strewn about, busy sewing underwear, shoes, and uniforms. I find myself sitting in the corner of the room against the wall, Naomi at my side, and two twins a few years older than me in front of us who Naomi introduced as Levana and Chasha some weeks ago. They have the most beautiful hair I've ever seen, long silky raven strands that nearly brush their waists, worn in a traditional style they called taregami.

"We're a bit more liberal," Levana had told me when I asked. She and Chasha didn't strike me as just Poles. "Our grandfather is Japanese. He converted to Judaism so he could marry our grandmother."

I suck a sharp breath between my teeth, jerking my cramping hand away from the Singer, my finger dripping blood from where I've just pricked it on the needle. I wrap it with a discarded piece of cloth, then resume working.

Won't this soldier be disgusted to wear something made by a Jew, or does forced labor not count to them?

We have been working for hours without a break and I have lost all notion of time. There are no windows, just blank gray walls and lightbulbs dangling over our heads. It's tedious work and intolerable at times, repeating the same mind-numbing process: thread the needle, turn the handwheel, slide the fabric, turn the handwheel, slide the fabric.

The others try to fill the void of boredom with purposeless prattle, and for months I've listened to the contents of letters from distant relatives, the current fashions in England, criticism of the Judenrat, food recipes, and newspaper articles. Perhaps it is something to occupy their minds, a sweet distraction from the nightmare that is our lives, but their talk only reminds me of all that was, all that is now so uncertain.

I finish sewing the last edge of a green uniform jacket and consider cutting the inside seams. Its owner would have a fit if threads of his brand-new uniform fell to pieces the moment he slipped it on. The image brings a smirk to my face, my hands hovering over the scissors at my desk. Pausing, I glance at the door. Our supervisor has gone for the moment and the other women are preoccupied with their own work. I make quick work of the inside seams, snipping nearly every single one of them before folding it neatly and laying it in my box of finished products.

I'll take these small victories where I can.

Naomi snickers beside me in amusement. I catch her mischievous, knowing eyes for a second before she does the same, cutting the inner seams of a jacket that already lay finished at her side. We share a quiet chuckle, suppressing impish smiles before we move on. Measure and cut the fabric, thread the needle, turn the handwheel, slide the fabric.

For the rest of the day, we cast glances back and forth at one another, giggling like little schoolgirls, breaking the seams of one article of clothing for every ten we make.

Silence and small victories.

It is past seven o'clock by the time we make it back to the ghetto's entrance, where two German soldiers stand guard. We show them our work permits and hasten past them as soon as they verify them.

"Today was almost fun." Naomi titters. "I hope the seams hold long enough for them to get outside. Can you imagine their uniforms falling to pieces while they're addressing their troops? They photograph those kinds of events, right? We might get to see our handiwork on camera one day."

"I'd pay every złoty I have to see it!" I giggle, glancing around for any sign of people and lowering my voice. "What with those salutes they always do, it's likely to fall apart right then and there. They'll say, '*Heil Hitler,* and *damn* this blasted tailor!'" I gesture with my arm in mockery of the salute I've seen the Nazis greet one another with.

"Hodaya!" Naomi gasps, grabbing my arm and covering my mouth, but she's weak with laughter and we both stumble toward home like a pair of giddy drunks.

But the fragile illusion of normalcy is broken the moment we ascend the stairway and enter my apartment. Adam and Papa will not return for several more hours, and it is more of a comfort to be together and know the other is safe and not alone. The single flickering light hanging from the ceiling casts a dim, sickly light over the makeshift mattresses made up of dirty sheets, the few suitcases we all brought when they first sent us to the ghetto, and the wretched people all cramped together in the stale, airless space. None of us have bathed properly in days and the stench is growing stronger. There's not enough water for everyone in the building to wash every day, nor enough facilities to accommodate everyone. Our persons, clothes, and sheets are festering in their own filth, and our stomachs are just as empty as they were this morning.

Bayla lies asleep in an early-evening nap, curled into a ball with her head resting on Mama's leg while she mends a few worn holes in her skirt. Likewise, Ahava has tasked herself with repairing Gavriel's shoes, whose soles have nearly worn down. Noam sits cross-legged by the tiny window, Asher curled up at his side.

"Jerzy! Welcome home! So, what new mischief did you get up to today?" Noam exclaims, his eyes brightening, as I enter. He's become much more open and talkative since we've all been put together.

I return his cheerful smile. "Nothing compared to you, I'm sure."

"Nothing, actually," he says and sighs, shuffling a deck of cards. "The police have been patrolling a lot more than usual today. Not much to do. Bayla and I have been building card castles. She's trying to teach me German too."

Mama smiles fondly and clips a long thread. "Yes, Bayla is very insistent that Noam be her pupil instead of mine."

"She's getting good at it, but I think I better learn from a fluent speaker."

"You know I'm more than happy to teach you, Noam," Mama says, a knowing smirk on her lips.

Noam flushes, stuttering for a response. "Oh, uh, yes, Mrs. Alperstein. I was just thinking that... well, Hodaya speaks German very well too."

"I'm not a very good teacher, though." I settle down on a bunched-up white sheet and pull off my shoes. "Just ask Naomi, she'll tell you."

"I'm sure you're much better than you say!" he insists. "I learn easily, I wouldn't be any trouble. I've already learned a lot, so it wouldn't be like teaching a beginner."

"I guess not... alright, but I still say you're setting both of us up for headaches."

"You won't be disappointed!"

The door creaks open and a moment later Gavriel slips inside, barefoot, and carrying a little brown bag.

The tension in Ahava's shoulders lessens at the sight of him. "And where have you been all this time, Gavriel? I'm nearly done with your shoes now."

He plops down on the bed. "Just across the street, with Mr. and Mrs. Mandel. Their nephew brought them some grain and potatoes from the Aryan side." Reaching into his full bag, he produces a whole potato, then proceeds to toss one to everyone in the room.

"*Gavriel*, I've told you a hundred times to stay away from those people!" Ahava scolds. "We don't need to be getting involved with smugglers in this place! We don't need that kind of trouble!"

"They're not smugglers, Mother, they're Jews. Like us. They just want to eat, like us. And it's my job to take care of you and Noam until Father comes back. In the meantime, we have potatoes for dinner."

"*Cooked* potatoes!" Noam pipes excitedly.

On the bed, Bayla stirs from her slumber and rubs her bleary eyes, the delightful scent of baked potatoes having summoned her from sleep.

"Good morning, sleepy little butterfly," Gavriel teases, handing Bayla a large potato.

"Good morning," Bayla mumbles tiredly. "Thank you."

My stomach rumbles in complaint and longing. The last time I ate was yesterday morning, half of a beef sandwich that I split with Bayla, so I start hungrily on my potato, and am pleasantly surprised to taste a bit of melted butter.

Bayla crawls off the bed and comes to rest against my side, clothed in her nightgown and what's left of her yellow coat. I mended what I could, but the fur hood still sits askew, and long lines of stitches run along the fabric like scars. Asher, having been repeatedly shooed off the bed—though he always manages to sneak up to curl beside Bayla when everyone falls asleep—quickly bounds to her lap and curls up snugly, purring.

"Now that you're awake, shall we continue, little butterfly?" Noam asks, spreading his playing cards before him. "I bet I can make a taller tower this time."

Bayla smiles groggily. "Nu-uh. I'll make the tallest tower again. I always do."

"We'll see, we'll see. I bet I'll win this time." Carefully, one by one, Noam begins to stack the cards, easily building a tower two stories high. Bayla discards her food momentarily and rushes to start on her own paper tower. Disturbed by the sudden movement, Asher steps away, his tail flicking and knocking Noam's growing tower back to the floor. Bayla laughs gleefully and gives the cat a quick scratch behind his ears.

"Hodaya! You have to help me! She's been beating me all day, I can't lose again!"

"No!" Bayla gasps. "You can't have help, that's cheating!"

"I agree." I chuckle at Noam's feigned affronted expression. "Hurry up, before you're too far behind."

And back to their game they go, Noam purposely slowing his pace, letting Bayla snatch up more cards, and pretending his own card towers keep getting blown over by the wind. Bayla smiles, her dimples growing deeper and her giggles becoming more carefree by the minute. Both Mama and Ahava smile tenderly at the scene before them, pausing their work for a few moments just to watch, and I find myself doing the same.

The world is black when I open my eyes, sweat beading down my face even as I shiver. My throat is dry, but there is nothing I can do to soothe it. In the darkness, Papa snores lightly from nearby on the floor while Mama, Ahava, and Bayla sleep together on the bed, their breathing soft and consistent. I try to take comfort in that, in the gentle reassurance of their lives, in the hot, stuffy feel of the room, in the silence as my mind slowly confirms reality.

Midnight peeks in from the window, and a soft scuffling near the door draws my attention, followed by a pause and a quiet shushing. The floor creaks loudly the way everything does in absolute silence and I turn my head slightly to the door. It cracks open, the dim light from the hall faintly outlining two figures, who stealthily slip outside.

Gavriel? Noam? Where are they going?

For months, I've awoken to their arrival and departure in the hours before and after curfew. For months, I've said nothing about their absences when everyone has gone to sleep. For months, I've wondered what they could possibly be doing, what could possibly be so important and demanding. Tonight, I don't think I can simply wonder anymore.

Carefully, I slip on my shoes, quickly tie a cloth over my hair, creep around my father's slumbering form to the door, and hesitate. A great wave of dread washes over my body, shudders bolting like lightning across my skin, and my knees weaken beneath me. Something isn't right, something beyond my breaking curfew, something beyond Gavriel and Noam, and I'm taken by a sudden panic that grips my heart and lungs with iron hands.

What if they're in trouble? The thought makes me stop as I step away from the door. How could I let them go running headfirst into something like that? They would never, under any circumstance, knowingly let me run off to possibly be hurt—and they had no problem risking their own lives to save Naomi and I from Emil. If nothing else, I need to make sure they're safe.

I step out into the hall, wearing nothing but my shoes and long nightgown. Gavriel and Noam are gone by the time I reach the stairs, but I've heard no doors open, and there is only one exit from the building. I take the stairs two at a time, my heart jolting with every click my shoes make against the floor. The front door closes just as I reach the bottom floor.

Across the street already, clad in their hats and coats, Gavriel and Noam are turning the corner. The sidewalks are empty as far as I can tell in the moonlight, spotted every here and there by the unnatural illumination of lampposts, serene, disturbed only by the occasional whispers of a summer wind. I keep my eyes turned away from the lights, half expecting to find more bodies strung from them. After the first massacre, the bodies Naomi and I saw remained hanging there for four days.

Quickly, I cross the dampened street, hoping that if there are any Germans nearby they don't notice a ghostly woman dart through the abandoned city after the two shadows.

The ghetto is quiet in a forbidding, eerie sort of way, the kind of fearful silence that only falls where predators lurk. Through the curtains in windows, from beyond the dark, empty streets, I feel the eyes of silhouettes watching me as I follow Gavriel and Noam down Niecała Street. I have yet to lose sight of them, though they keep darting in and out of alleys, changing their course, and slipping through areas of the city that are dense with buildings and easy to get lost in if you don't know their layout. I stray further and further from our apartment, so far that the military base is now out of sight, so far that the rapid pounding of my heart grows more painful with every step I take away from the safety of our room. They turn down Kowalska Street, and even under the canopy of night, I can see the barbed wire fence that separates the ghetto from the Aryan side.

I count a group of fifteen men just ahead at the fence, men who Gavriel and Noam willingly approach. They are not Germans; I can see that much. They wear no uniforms, they carry no guns, and they take hardly any notice of the two young boys joining them. On the other side of the fence, there is another group of men with satchels and suitcases arranged about them. Two men on either side of the fence step down on the tightly wound barbed wire and pull up on another wire, leaving just enough space for the men on the Aryan side to slip the bags through to the men in the ghetto.

Citizens... Jews and Poles. Resistance men, perhaps, but not enemies.

Taking a steadying breath, I step toward them, calling out in a whisper. "Gavriel. Noam."

Every pair of eyes turns to me, startled, and all movement ceases.

Gavriel is the first to recover from the shock. He storms over and pulls me off the street and away from the fence. "Hodaya! What are you doing here?" he demands.

I jerk my arm away from him. "I saw you sneak out, I've seen you sneaking out for months. I wanted to know where you were going."

"Were you followed? Did you see anyone?" he asks, eyes darting frantically in every direction before he looks back at me. "Hodaya, were you followed?"

"No. If I was, I'd probably already be shot," I bite back. "What's going on?"

"You shouldn't be here, it's too dangerous for you. You need to go home right now!"

"What's too dangerous? What about for you and Noam? What are you doing?"

"Gavriel." A deep, scolding voice interrupts our argument. I don't recognize the curly-haired man who approaches us. "Who is this?"

"I'm sorry, Mr. Szymański. She's my sister, we didn't know she followed us," Gavriel apologizes, stepping in front of me.

"Well, get her out of here." Mr. Szymański waves to the men over his shoulder and they continue on as though nothing out of the ordinary has occurred. "Take her home; not all hands are necessary tonight. We don't have much." He shoves a small burlap bag into Gavriel's arms, then returns to the group and starts directing Noam and two others to start piling the bags against the building.

Gavriel moves to grab my arm again, but I swat him away. "No! I'm not leaving until you tell me what's going on!"

His lips purse, eyes narrowing as he throws a quick glance back at the men. "Fine," he grumbles. "Look, this is the only way we're not starving right now. The farmers are helping smuggle food into the ghetto, we just need to be here to get it from them and hand it out. Where do you think Noam and I get all our food?"

Of course... he said it was his job to take care of Noam and Ahava. The first time we ever met, Noam gave me bread they'd taken from a bakery.

"Someone needs to stand up to them. If this is the only way we can do it, then that's what we'll do. Now come on, you can't be here. It's too—"

A shot cuts him off, followed by a man's pained scream. Suddenly, the fence is aglow with the aim of flashlights, and voices shouting in German accompany another round of gunfire. Three men go down, blood spilling to the ground. The Aryan men abandon the fence and disappear back into the city, the Poles and Jews still in the ghetto scream as bullets hit them, bolt from the fence and away from the lines of fire.

An agonized cry rips the breath from my body, a familiar voice that I could never have fathomed doing anything but laughing. Noam crumples to his knees on the red stones. Another bullet strikes his arm and knocks his entire body to the ground.

"Noam!" I dart toward him, only for an arm to snap around my waist, holding me back.

Noam's eyes find mine, their once boyish, playful hazel depths darkened with fear. His cheeks, once rosy with a shy blush, are stark white, and on his face there is a horrible resignation, and the very memory of his joyful smile has vanished. Our gazes lock, tears dripping down his face, and he screams, "RUN!"

He's too far to reach. The soldiers are bearing down on us now and Gavriel hauls me away, ducking into the brush along a building before the flashlights can reveal us. His entire body trembles violently against mine, and blood trails down his lip where it's bitten between his teeth.

Satchels and bodies lie scattered across the street. Nine of the fifteen men are surely dead, lying motionless in pools of blood. I can only be certain that three are still alive, for they writhe and groan in agony. I can't tear my eyes away from Noam, a lamb among wolves, helpless and alone while the soldiers prowl around him.

Please, God! Save him! He is so young and sweet and innocent! He doesn't deserve this!

An officer strides through the carnage, a man I only recognize as SS Leader Schneider when he orders, "There's more! They ran down the street! Find them, now!" He looks down his nose in disgust at Mr. Szymański's motionless form and scoffs, giving the body a sharp kick. "Disgusting rats. We'll have to man this fence more closely from now on. Day and night. I don't want anything coming in or out of this ghetto. Understood?"

"Yes sir," comes the synchronized acknowledgment of the soldiers.

Two more shots abruptly silence two of the wounded men, leaving Noam alone. But, when a soldier aims at his head, Schneider waves him off. "Bring the truck and get a ditch going too. I want this scum off the streets by morning. Leave the blood, though. Let these filthy Jews see what's left of their heroes."

My heart stops as Schneider steps toward Noam and

crouches beside him. The world tilts in every direction and I grasp Gavriel, holding him so tightly I can feel every pulse of his wrist.

"How old are you, boy?" he asks.

Noam says nothing, just whimpers, and stares up at Schneider in terrified confusion.

"Stupid Pole!" Schneider mutters hatefully. "Fischer! Get over here and talk to this damn Pole!"

Another SS steps up to Schneider's side, gun at the ready.

"Ask him how old he is," Schneider orders, exasperated.

"Ile masz lat?"

Face twisted in agony, Noam groans, "Fourteen."

"Hmm, fourteen. Young and reckless. But still a man by these standards," Schneider jeers, indicating Noam's blue star. "Ask him if he knows who I am."

Noam's head jerks in a nod.

"Good." Schneider taps his chin, seeming to mockingly mull something over. "I think you could be useful to me. I'm sure there's more of you hiding around here, and I'm sure your family wants you back." Lazily, like it's the most natural thing in the world, he draws his pistol from his side and runs a gloved hand down the barrel. "Tell me who the rest are, and I'll let you live."

Before Fischer has the chance to finish translating the words to Polish, Noam cuts him off. Gripping his wounded arm, he throws himself a few inches off the ground and spits directly in Schneider's face. "Szwab!"

"He said—"

"He said enough." Unflinching, Schneider silences Fischer with a wave and rises to his feet. He steps over Noam, pistol trained on his head, and in the shadows that befall his face, twisted with pure hatred, his eyes are cold. He pulls the trigger.

Gavriel smothers my scream as Noam's body goes limp, head falling back to the ground with a sickening thud. I can feel his tears against my shoulder, seeping through my nightgown as tremors surge through him, fierce and uncontrollable.

"Stupid boy," Schneider sneers.

The world blurs in and out of focus, the massacre before me seeming nothing more than an indistinct, awful figment of my imagination. Yes, that's what this must be! A nightmare, a horrific scene my mind has created to terrify me. Why does my own mind torture me so? Why must it plague me with such cruel images?

Wake up, Hodaya! Wake up, wake up!

There is movement again, several voices reach me from beyond the fog, but I don't know who they belong to or where they're coming from. Something drags me through a bush and into the darkness. My body goes willingly, but my head is still reeling. Sweat beads down my face and neck and my eyes stare sightless into the night. Suddenly, a bright yellow light blinds me and I squint, slowly noticing the strange shift in atmosphere. We're moving upwards now, my feet catching several times before I finally see the set of stairs beneath me. A door slams shut, engulfing us in momentary blackness before the room illuminates.

My sister's tired, frightened face is the first thing I see. Mama and Papa slowly come into view, their mouths moving frantically, soundlessly. I notice Ahava next, panicked, eyes wide and chest heaving. She grasps Gavriel, whose entire face is swollen with grief, his eyes bloodshot, and his abused lip cracked with dried blood. I examine the room, searching for Noam and his mussy hair as he is abruptly awoken by our entrance, but he is nowhere to be found.

"Where is he?" I hear Ahava beg, shattering nightmare into the broken shards of reality.

Schneider's bullet knocks Noam's head to the ground in my mind's eye and I collapse, vaguely aware of Papa's arms around me. I cannot stop the image from replaying again and again, not even the tears clouding my vision can block it out. Just inches away, Gavriel is sobbing. Ahava rips the bag out of his hands, clutching the rough burlap, staring disbelievingly, incredulously at the offending object, and falls to the floor.

A mother's wail pierces the night as, instead of her son, she beholds a satchel of bread.

11

SEPTEMBER 1, 1943

AUSCHWITZ-BIRKENAU

Dazed and blinded by the floodlights like the night Noam was killed, I stand stiff at the crossroads before the SS officer. I draw Bayla closer to my side as his white glove indicates for us to separate—for Bayla to follow our mother to the left with the other older women and young children. I refuse to let go of her, no matter what direction we walk. I have lost too much I love to let her go anywhere but by my side.

"Bitte, sir! Let us stay together. Let her come with me, or let me go with her," I plead.

"Keep moving," the man with the white gloves says evenly. "You to the right and you to the left."

Mothers! All the women and children are on one side! Maybe they'll let her stay with me if I say she's my child!

"Please, she is my daughter!" I try in desperation, though it is clearly a lie. I've already given him my age, and Bayla looks far too old to be mine.

The blond SS man who shoved Mama steps past the man with white gloves, his eyes flashing murderously. "Move! Now!"

I can feel Bayla trying to loosen her fingers, pull her hand out of mine to comply with the order, but I hold her firmly in place. "No! I want to stay with my daughter! Let us stay together! Please!"

The blond SS man lunges out with his baton, striking me with all his might. I cry out and shield my head, crumpling to my knees as he bludgeons me again.

"That's enough, Ulrich! You'll cause a panic," the SS man with the white gloves commands in annoyance.

Ulrich steps away and I scramble to my feet, my back and arms stinging from the vicious blows. Bayla winds her arms tightly around my waist, her whimpers of fear muffled against my coat.

"Ah! Obergefreiter Engel," the SS with the white gloves exclaims, looking past us, grinning with a disturbing twist of comradery and malice. He points, curling his fingers as if beckoning a child forward. "Come. I see you've been assigned supervision tonight. I could use someone *level-headed.*" He casts a pointed glance at Ulrich, who dips his head in apology.

A tall man, perhaps in his late twenties, with neat brown hair and a scar that runs the length of his left cheek, appears. Strangely, his sharp green uniform decorated with multiple black and silver crosses is devoid of the SS insignia of Hitler's special forces, instead sporting the ordinary Wehrmacht army symbols.

The newcomer nods with respect. "Hauptsturmführer Mengele. How can I be of service?"

"This is quite a large transport, Obergefreiter. Three thousand, if I'm not mistaken," Mengele says by way of explanation, gesturing at the lines of deportees. "I assume all the necessary paperwork for now has been filed?"

"It has, Hauptsturmführer," Engel confirms. "I am at your disposal tonight."

"Good. At least I can trust you won't cause any disturbances." Mengele lightly chuckles at Ulrich's expense. His smile might have been charming if there wasn't something eerily threatening in it. "What do you think of these two, Alaric? This one can work, though she's being difficult, but the little one needs to go to the showers. Perhaps they should both go left."

"I think they should both go to the right. She's a little one"— Engel nods at Bayla—"but we need more young ones, they last longer."

"Hmm... she's very small. Couldn't be older than ten," Mengele says indulgently to Engel's answer, observing us skeptically as if inspecting cattle. "What would be done with her? Children have no place in a work camp."

"I'm sure they could find something to do with her," Engel says almost dismissively, and I wonder if he will be reprimanded for speaking so nonchalantly to an SS captain, but Mengele seems intrigued when Engel's voice takes on a lighter, nearly malicious tone. "And why not? She's just one girl, after all. What difference will it make in a few days?"

Mengele chuckles, a cruel, sinister sound that makes me tighten my hold on Bayla.

Engel glances at her. She still refuses to move her head from my waist. Something flickers in his eyes, something distant that makes me wonder what familiar memory he sees in her, something strained and shaken that contradicts his callous words.

"We shall see," Mengele relents, looking back at me. "I suppose I can make an exception. Go on, you may keep the child."

A white glove points to the right.

Relief washes over me like a storm and I pull Bayla with me to the right, unable to spare a glance or even a thought about the other women or the officers deciding our fates. I'm sure there should be a million questions and concerns swarming about my head, but I am consumed only by one goal: keep Bayla at my side. Just a few yards ahead of us, Naomi is walking down the path, her slumped shoulders shaking in the unmistakable movement of weeping.

"Naomi!" I call, struggling to stand upright in all the mud. It is the second thing I've noticed about this place after the stench; there are no paved paths, no grass, only thick, deep mud.

She whirls around, her mussed hair and pallid face giving her a ghostly, feral look. "Oh, my God!" she whispers, throwing her arms around my shoulders. "You're still alive!"

"Still alive? What are you talking about?" I mutter, an icy chill raking down my spine.

Her lips quiver against my ear as she speaks, so lowly I nearly cannot hear her. "They said it's a furnace, they said that's where they're all going! We'll all be burned! This is truly Hell!"

"Shh, Naomi, keep walking with us," I urge her, wrapping an arm securely around her waist. "Who told you this?"

"The prisoners. They told me we're all being sent to the crematorium to be burned. We're not supposed to know! We just passed through another *Aktion!*"

"That's not true," I force out, breathless. "They wouldn't bring us here just to kill us. They *wouldn't*. Why would they tell you such horrible lies?"

The Nazis are evil, they've never left any room for denial... but would they really do what the other prisoners told Naomi? Burn us? Men, women, and children?

In the distance, I see the same orange glow, and smoke obscures the sky even in the night.

Oh, God! There are so many children here! Babies and toddlers younger than Bayla! No! Even the Nazis wouldn't do that! Would they? No, I don't believe it. I can't. They murdered thousands in the ghetto, why would they bring us all this way just to kill us? No, it can't be true.

"Hodaya," Bayla whimpers, and, when I look down into her

face, I have never before seen such raw terror. "Are they going to kill us?"

"No, no, Bayla, they're not going to do that," I say quickly. "They're just trying to scare us. Everything is going to be alright."

She continues to peer tearfully at me through terrified, innocent eyes, her lip quivering.

"It's *not* true. I promise, everything is alright. They're taking care of our things at the train, remember?" I assure her, squeezing her hand. "We'll get settled and then go see Mama and Papa. They've just gone to have showers, like that officer said you should have."

12

APRIL 16–AUGUST 25, 1942

BOCHNIA GHETTO, POLAND

Minutes ago, the street below our apartment was empty. Now, in the heat of a glaring sun, just over two hundred people march by, kept in line by armed SS men. Deportees. The roundups of people for work began before the ghetto was established, but this is the first expulsion of Jews from the ghetto. We don't know where they're going. They don't know where they're going. But we all know this will not be the last transport, no matter what the Nazis tell us.

I stand by the window, leaning on the sill as I watch them pass by. The Germans herd them at a fast, steady pace, heel-to-toe, lugging suitcases and bundles, their white wristbands and blue stars like bright brands.

There was once a farmer Papa and I used to visit when I was younger, an older man we called Abba; his true name escapes me now. Abba used to let me ride with him while my father watched us herd the cattle inside the corral and his little black dog barked wildly. I remember very distinctly thinking how amusing it was that the cows all ran together whatever way we wanted, ears pricked to attention, eyes wide and fearful of the most harmless movement. Now, I wonder if the cattle in the other corrals watched us herding their fellow friends and family the way I now watch the Germans, flinching away from their taunts, guns, and dogs, dreading the time when it will be my turn.

Beside me, Bayla shifts, Asher meowing and then purring as she readjusts him in her arms. "Where are they going?"

A whisper is all I can manage. "They must be going somewhere to work."

A blond man walks by, head low, a single suitcase clutched at his side.

Naomi turns her tear-stained face toward the curtains, her shoulders shaking as she tries to muffle her sobs. I wrap her in my arms, blinking back my own tears, holding her as tightly as I can as we watch Adam pass by. He turns as if searching for his wife's face in the window, but is struck and forced to walk onwards.

God, if You are listening, please watch over him. Give him strength, let him come through this, let him return to Naomi.

We watch them as long as we can, dreading the moment they are out of sight. Then they are gone, all of them vanished into the distance toward the station, and I tug Naomi from the sill so she cannot look upon the unbearable emptiness of the street.

The Germans have taken everything from us: our country, our home, our synagogue, our safety and way of life, our freedom. They have invaded every aspect of our lives with terror, branded us with our religion as if it were a mark of shame, murdered our people whether they were innocent or not, locked us away in our corral with nothing but what we could carry. They have taken everything we had to offer without remorse, then taken more than we ever would have given. The Nazis know no morals, their cruelty has no bounds, and their hatred of us sinks deeper than the darkest trenches of the sea.

But why us? What have we done to them? What offenses can one commit that justify the murder of innocents, the dehumanization and obliteration of an entire people? What monstrosities in this world have numbed them, blinded them to their evil?

The streets are busy for a Sunday morning, bustling with men and women alike on their way to work, families with their children and pets, everyone eager to grasp some tiny bit of normalcy. Maybe by walking without fear of being beaten or shot—ignoring the filth regardless of the confines of guarded fences we're forced to call home—it's easier to pretend if only for a few minutes that nothing is wrong. The Jewish police still patrol within the ghetto, but they are far kinder than the alternative, even if they must answer to the Nazis.

The sun of late August glints down from a clear blue sky, its golden beams warming my face. Not so long ago, this was the kind of day my family would have spent at the park with a picnic, trying to name bird species by their songs. Instead, I sit on the steps of an old hotel that has been converted to a residential place for ghetto inhabitants, waiting for Papa with an open book in my lap, keeping an eye out for any undercover Gestapo.

I never really considered how Papa made spare money for our family once we were expelled to the ghetto, the lengths he might go to to provide us with a little extra food, a few more złotych, less worn clothes and shoes. I never imagined the honest man of God who raised me would do business with the same people he once would have warned against, but desperation does that to a man, a husband, a father. It is a willingness born from the depths of privation's womb. It is a stolen part from the German vehicles. It is a soldier's pistol gone missing from the military barracks. It is ammunition and copied letters sold to untrustworthy buyers. It is an honorable man's dabbling in a black market, a once virtuous disposition worn down by imprisonment and poverty.

Papa was reluctant to involve me in his business, and he might never have told me at all if I hadn't outright asked him. It never occurred to me his absences were abnormal with his work hours, or that his procured goods could be coming from unsavory sources. Then, I thought of Gavriel and Noam, and the similarities terrified me. But despite my misgivings, I knew I needed to do what I could to help him. Our devotion to our family is stronger than any laws we're breaking. In that, we are more alike than many. Like brothers, every firstborn daughter is her father's partner in crime. So, while Mama has taken a job attending the patients in the ghetto hospital and Bayla remains at home, Papa and I do what is necessary to provide for them, and for Gavriel and Ahava.

After Noam died, Ahava deteriorated into her grief-stricken mind, unable to do anything but trudge through the days like a ghost, and Gavriel turned to using his work permit in the factories. He hasn't spoken to me for the last year, since that awful night, and, although he's never said it outright, I know he blames me as much as himself. Perhaps he is justified in that. I've often wondered if I was indeed followed, if it was my blind stupidity that got all those men killed, if that's why I lost more than one brother that night.

Noam's face has never left me. His beautiful eyes burn in my mind, his spattering blood haunts me in my dreams. I never thought I'd wish for nightmares of air raids and firing squads, but in the dead of night, when I wake with tear-stained cheeks and the emptiness in the place he once slept is more crushing than I can bear, I cry myself to sleep thinking of all the ways I might have saved him.

My attention snaps away from my thoughts as the door behind me opens. Papa emerges, the little brown package gone from his hands, and offers a tense smile. The transaction must have gone well, but I still wonder what the box contained.

Together, we slip back onto the sidewalk, a bit less impoverished than when we arrived, and start up Niecała Street to where it meets Galasa. Already, German police and soldiers are on either side of the intersecting streets, armed and ready.

I thought the Aktion *was tomorrow? What are they doing here already?*

We were all informed that everyone without stamps on their worker permits—with the exception of hospital patients—were to report to the military barracks at eight o'clock sharp. Men and women are gathered around, permits in hand, as they wait to have their names removed from the summoning. Our entire household has already proven ourselves and Bayla is prepared to be hidden in the tunnel beneath the building. It's the only way to keep her from being taken tomorrow morning, the only place we're sure no Nazi knows of. No one knows where the ones rounded up during the *Aktion* will be taken, but no one wishes to find out. Even the people taken in the smaller roundups who we were told were bound for labor camps haven't been heard from since.

Papa immediately directs me away, but we don't make it more than a few steps in the opposite direction before a military lorry speeds through the ghetto's entrance at Leonarda, and skids to a stop just feet from where we stand.

A dark-haired Wehrmacht officer steps off the truck, his eyes narrowed hatefully at the crowd. He looks at a piece of paper in his hand and starts to scream in German, veins in his neck and head bulging furiously. "You! Get on the truck!" He reaches out and grabs a man by the arm, then shoves him toward the lorry. "You! And you! What's your name?"

Papa and I try to move out of his way, but it's too late to leave. If we try to escape among the men and women paralyzed with fright, we'll be noticed for sure. The officer looks at his paper again and shouts several names, rounding up men and young boys who step forward from the line timidly.

"Sergeant Kurzbach, what is the meaning of this?" Another officer has stepped forward from the crowd, scowling.

Sergeant Kurzbach straightens and glares in return. "Some of these Jews are my workers and I need them immediately. It's essential to the war effort."

"Can it not wait? You'll have new workers soon enough when the next transport arrives."

"I'm sure I will, but the work cannot be delayed. We're already behind."

I shrink away as Kurzbach's fierce eyes turn to lock on Papa and me. Without warning, he lunges out and grabs Papa's arm. "You see this Jew? Tell him your name, filth!"

"Alperstein," Papa says in a steady voice.

"He's the best mechanic in my shop. I've seen him assemble an entire engine in an hour! He's necessary to the Reich's cause," Kurzbach lies, and shoves Papa toward the truck. "We have vehicles that need repairing and I need all of my workers *now*. There's more work than we were expecting."

I feel myself sway for a moment, speechless, unable to take my eyes off Kurzbach.

Why did he lie about Papa?

The two officers stare one another down, each challenging the other to question their authority. The second officer eventually relents and returns to his own work. Kurzbach's attention moves back to the crowd and his eyes settle on my aghast face. He considers me for barely a second before he seizes my wrist in a painful grip. "You too!" he growls, all but throwing me into Papa's arms.

There is no chance to escape; the men on the truck are pulling Papa and me onto the back with them. Between the men and a few women scrambling into our wooden cage, I catch a glimpse of the officer, still shouting and demanding names, pushing more and more people in our direction.

"Papa, do you know him?" I gasp, the air hot and constricted between bodies on all sides.

Papa shakes his head. "I've never seen him before," he says, winding a protective arm around my shoulders.

The truck jerks and we all stumble, holding on to each other and the rails. Kurzbach puts the truck into reverse, swings around in the street, and then we are speeding back the way he came. The pitiful eyes of the men and women left behind follow us, silently lamenting whatever is to be our fate.

All around me, faces hold the same panic and uncertainty as myself; husbands and fathers terrified for their wives and children left behind, young boys lost without their families, women muttering fervent prayers to God for protection. The city passes by in moments, the air thick and suffocating with confusion, heat, and fear, and the countryside comes into view. My heart seizes suddenly in terror at the sight of the hills and trees, and I fear that we're really being taken to the woods or graveyard to be executed as the Nazis have done to hundreds of others. After nearly an hour with nowhere to sit and being jolted from every direction, I catch a brief glimpse of high fences and breathe a sigh of relief. The lorry slows to a halt, and I hear the clatter of a gate closing.

"Get off! Everyone off the truck!" Kurzbach shouts, and we all hurry to obey, some falling into the dirt in their rush. Again, he's holding his slip of paper, calling out the names of his workers. Out of all those who step forward, there are only twenty or so people who were not on the list at all, who do not belong here, including Papa and me. He crumples the list and sends the first group to the lines of military vehicles outside the shop before turning back to us. "Do any of you know how to repair vehicles?"

No one moves, no one would dare to lie, but I sense Papa

hesitating at my side. After a moment of tense silence, he steps forward.

"I work in the military barracks, sir," he says. "My daughter and I work with the trucks."

Kurzbach looks doubtful, but he nods stiffly, his glare intense under the blistering sun. "Good. You will work with the other mechanics inside. Go, now!"

The overwhelming scent of oil, metal, and sweat assaults my nose the moment we step into the vast, musky room of the workshop. Papa and I approach a lorry similar to the one we came on, which is being attended by a man struggling with the bolts on a tire.

"Do you want that tire on or off?" Papa asks.

"Off. They all need to come off," the man grunts shortly, face screwed up in frustration. "Damn thing's ready to break off the truck but these bolts won't budge."

"Let us help you, the sergeant says we're to help with repairs today."

The man mutters under his breath, giving up for a moment to wipe the sweat and grime from his brow. His dark-ringed eyes turn to stare at us unblinking, appraising me skeptically.

Papa crouches and takes up the man's tool. "She won't be any trouble, we'll finish the rest of this for you," he assures. "Hodaya, go find another wrench and start on the other tires."

A table nearby has an identical tool lying unused, so I grab it and retreat back to the truck, lingering a moment to watch Papa's strained movements before doing my best to discreetly mirror his moves. It takes much more effort than I would have thought, but I do manage to slowly loosen a bolt by the time Papa is moving on to another tire.

Sergeant Kurzbach enters the workshop just as Papa and I are pulling off the last tire. I hide around the opposite side of the truck to stay out of his sight and he passes us, not sparing us a glance.

"Why do you think he wanted us here?" I whisper, fumbling with a bolt.

Papa shrugs. "I don't know. Let's just stay quiet and keep our heads down. We'll be back home before we know it."

Home... nothing feels like home anymore.

It's been years since anything felt like home, since our family all went to the park together, since we attended prayer with Aunt Dalia and her family, since Bayla and I last visited Mrs. Ellen. The last time I remember truly feeling at home was before Aunt Dalia left. Will anything ever feel like home again, even if it all ends? When Noam is no longer here to laugh and live his life? When I have heard and witnessed the cruelties people are capable of?

Somehow, I don't believe that is possible. I doubt anything will ever truly feel normal again.

Multiple times Sergeant Kurzbach walks the length of the shop, barking orders and peering out of the windows as if expecting someone to come, but, despite the disdainful tone with which he speaks, there is something odd about him. Perhaps once or twice, when he is lost to his own mind for a few seconds, he appears almost strained, haunted, and there is no true resentment in his eyes when he looks at us. Something about him is different from the other Nazis I have encountered, something that is... human. I can think of no other way to describe it.

Papa and I pass the hours quietly, though every now and again we reminisce, sharing stories of when life was normal; the first time he took Mama and me to the cinema, on my sixth birthday, the painted wooden horse I made for him when I was little, the day we had a mud fight when Mama asked us to plant her seeds in the flower garden out back, when Bayla was born and I couldn't pass by her crib without kissing her forehead.

How I wish I could turn back time to those days, to keep

spinning the hands on the clock back to always live then when
life was happy and simple.

By the end of the day, my entire body is aching and slick with
sweat, and my hair sticks to my face and neck beneath my scarf.
The sun has already touched the distant hills, painting the sky
with vivid oranges and pinks, casting shadows over the land that
lies between us and the ghetto.

We'll be back soon, I tell myself hopefully as all the other
mechanics begin to gather the coats they discarded in the heat.

"What are you doing? Did I tell you that you could leave?"
a voice thunders from the opposite side of the shop. Kurzbach
storms through the line of trucks, his eyes narrowed and a deep
frown marring his features. "You think because the sun's gone
down, you're going home? Lazy dogs, the lot of you! You'll all
stay here for the night! There's still much work to be done!"

No one dares to question him, but we all know he's lying.
No vehicle in the entire shop has gone untouched—Kurzbach
cataloged the day's progress himself—and I cannot fathom why
he wants us to stay here. Tired, deflated, and afraid for our families, we return obediently to our finished work. We inspect
everything once, twice, three times, and three times again,
Krupp Protzes, Maultiers, armored cars, staff cars, and radio
carriers, until they're likely the finest-functioning vehicles in the
German military.

The sun sinks and disappears, a nearly full moon rises to
glint through the windows, and we are left in the dim glow of
the lightbulbs. Papa and I are some of the first to retire, curled
up on the floor of the shop along the walls with only our clothes
for blankets, and, when the rising sun is beginning to stream in
through the stained windows once again, everyone has taken to
the floor for sleep.

The *Aktion* will be happening soon, I know that even

through my muddied mind, blearily watching the warm rays of sun steadily creep up on my feet. Kurzbach should have taken us back by now, but he has, strangely, locked the gates, locked the doors, locked us all inside with the promise of returning us to the ghetto in a few hours, and I am too tired to bring myself to do anything but slump against my father and sleep.

Papa nudges me awake. Judging by the dark circles under his eyes and the deep lines in his face, he hasn't slept. The workshop is now bright with sunlight, and the intense heat of the day is already upon us, when Kurzbach reappears and orders us all outside and onto the back of another lorry.

The Aktion *is over.*

It is the only coherent thought I can form as the truck roars to life and pulls through the gates. Papa and I have been gone for over twenty-four hours, we've missed the *Aktion*, and I don't know if our family will still be there to know if we ever returned. They might have been selected for the transport, the Gestapo might have found Bayla, they might—

I stop that horrible scenario before it can complete itself, before Papa can see the terror reflected on my face. Looking upon him now, his gaze turned toward the city, despairing and yearning like it is both the only and last place he wants to be, I know he is thinking the same thing. I take his hand and give it a tight squeeze, a gesture of comfort that he immediately returns.

We pass through the ghetto gates at a slow, leisurely pace. Even over the rumble of the engine, the silence strikes me. The heavy summer wind carries no voices, the usual tapping of heels against the sidewalk is gone, even the melodic songs of birds have vanished. Everything feels so empty, like life has not walked these streets for many years. The memory of stepping over the threshold of my aunt's house resurfaces in my mind and my heart sinks, feeling the impending sense that

I've just crossed over to where something horrible has transpired.

We waste no time walking, and run the entire length of the ghetto the moment our feet touch the ground. There are no people outside, no police, no soldiers, but the evidence of the Gestapo still lingers even in their absence. Pools of dried blood mark places of execution, spattered high on the walls, glass windows have been shattered, bullet casings litter the ground beneath our feet, and the doors of our apartment building have been kicked inwards. Gestapo have been here.

"Lieba! Bayla!" Papa screams frantically, rushing through the doors and scrambling up the stairs. "Lieba! Where are you? Bayla!"

We run barreling into our apartment, terrified, dreading and denying the worst, begging God in Heaven for a shred of His mercy. Papa throws the door open, earning a startled scream in return. Inside, together on the bed with the curtains drawn, are Mama, Naomi, and Bayla. All alive. Bruises litter Mama's face, a dried cut runs the length of Naomi's temple, and the ghosts of tears streak down Bayla's dirt-stained cheeks.

We all cry out for joy. Papa sweeps Mama into his arms and collapses to the floor, sobbing. Bayla, Naomi, and I all rush to each other, falling back onto the bed in a tight embrace. Bayla cries into my neck and I feel Naomi's nails digging into my skin, but I cannot be bothered by the pain. They are alive, the proof of their beating hearts pound loudly in time with my own, and their cries against my skin are more of a relief than the first spring wind after a blizzard.

It isn't until a few hours later, when our tears have dried and I hear the first few whispered signs of life beyond our barricaded door, that I realize Gavriel and Ahava are missing.

13

NOVEMBER 9–10, 1942

BOCHNIA GHETTO, POLAND

The disturbed, tortured glaze in Mama's eyes has never quite gone.

In the days following the first *Aktion* three months ago, Naomi told me what had happened. The Nazis—though their deceit no longer surprises me—went back on all of the promises they made. Those with valid stamps were not exempt from the selection, nor were the hospital patients or staff. Naomi, Gavriel, Ahava, anyone else with work permits, Mama, and the other nurses were summoned to make the quota. As for the hospital patients, they were all marched to the forest and shot. The Gestapo conducted a search of the entire ghetto, tearing our entire community apart in search of hiding Jews, dragging hundreds of sick and elderly people from their homes and executing them in the streets.

Nearly everyone in our building was taken with the transport or killed. Even the couple who Naomi and Adam had lived with across the hall was taken. Their three young daughters and grandmother were all murdered by the Gestapo. Somehow, in their search of the building, they didn't find the trapdoor or the tunnel Bayla spent almost a day hiding in. Mama was able to insist she was still needed in the hospital and Naomi narrowly avoided being selected when Mama claimed she was one of her assistant nurses and still desperately needed. As for Papa and me, we only avoided the roundup because of Sergeant Gerhard Kurzbach. I thought his behavior that day was strange, but it wasn't until the Nazis arrested him a few weeks ago that I realized it was because he was hiding us under the guise of urgently needing workers. Why God saw fit to save our lives when so many hundreds of others were senselessly lost, I will never know.

But the terror is not past. Tomorrow, there will be another *Aktion*, and I don't know if God can save us all from a second. If the Nazis have taught me anything, it is that they hold more authority over our mortal fates than God.

The ghetto, recently divided into "A" and "B," has never been more dangerous. "A" for the workers and "B" for the elderly, ill, and children. We all would have gone to "A," but Bayla would have been forced to stay in "B." Rather than bear separation, Papa burned all of our work permits—which he was savagely beaten for doing—and we all remained in "B." Food is scarce, there is no money, no work, and the number of dead rises every day.

"We had a bit of this medicine left in the hospital," Mama says once we've all gathered around the window. "If taken with food and alcohol, it will make you very ill. Vomiting, headaches, diarrhea, fatigue, things of that nature. It will last for quite some time, hopefully no more than a few days, but long enough."

Night has fallen, and we are all prepared to take some manner of control over our fates, no matter how slight. In Mama's hands is a small bottle of griseofulvin. Spread out on the floor before us is a bottle of liquor and a loaf of sliced bread.

With a steady hand, Mama pours a large dose of the medication into a tin cup, and Papa drinks it down quickly.

If all goes well tonight, we will all appear to have dysentery tomorrow when the *Aktion* happens. We have no way of knowing the fates of the people taken with the trains, though some say they're going to labor camps. No matter the truth, we are all afraid to disappear—no one is ever seen again once they've disappeared. It is far better to face the danger we know than the danger of the unknown. Rather than chance the selection, we must blindly hope that the Nazis won't select anyone contagious, that they still see us as potentially useful bodies despite any temporary illness and won't execute us tomorrow.

Bayla will be the only one not participating. For now, she sits beside me with Asher curled in her lap, but later she will again be hidden in the dark, dirty confines beneath the building. Nine is far too young to be considered ready for work, and the Nazis would have no reservations about killing her. They had none when they killed the other poor little girls.

Men such as they must have no souls for God to save.

One by one, Mama gives us all a large dose of griseofulvin until the bottle is empty. Though my already queasy stomach is reeling with the sudden invasion of the drug, I eat two slices of bread. We all take drinks from the bottle, the liquor burning a blistering trail down my throat, until it is gone.

Silently, Papa takes Mama's hand and then Bayla's. I slip my hand into Naomi's and Bayla's, completing our circle. The light flickers above us, across Papa's composed face still dark and swollen with bruises, and he lowers his head.

In a deep, steady voice, he begins the Hashkiveinu prayer. "Grant, O Lord, that we lie down in peace, and raise us up again, our Guardian, to life renewed. Spread over us the shelter of Your peace and guide us with Your good counsel. For Your name's sake, save us, be our help. Shield us against enemies, illness, war, famine, and sorrow, shelter us in the shadow of

Your wings, distance us from wrongdoing. For You, God, our King, watch over us. For You, God, our King, are gracious and merciful. Guard our going and coming, grant us life and peace, now and evermore."

Already, the nausea is building, and an ache deep in my stomach has taken hold. From here, I know it can only get worse, and I pray our ruse will grant us some protection in the morning.

God save us, protect Bayla, I pray, hugging her tightly before we reluctantly part. Mama wraps a blanket around Bayla's shoulders, kissing her forehead with trembling lips, before she and Papa lead her from the room. In six or seven hours, the Nazis will come for us, maybe with their dogs, and Bayla must be well fortified before then.

Just across from me, leaning against the bed with her head drooping to the side, Naomi is watching me. "She'll be alright," she whispers gently. "I know you're scared. I am too. We all are. But everything is going to be alright, no matter what happens tomorrow. God will make sure of it."

"I know." I nod.

For a while, the silence stretches between us, and she hesitates, then says, "Hodaya... you've never talked about Noam."

"What is there to say?" I tense, drawing my knees up to my chest, trying to force the last image of him out of my mind.

"Anything. I know he and Gavriel were like brothers to you. It must have been so horrible. I just... I don't want you to keep everything locked up. You do that a lot."

I cannot bring myself to meet her eyes, but I know she is gazing at me sympathetically.

"Hodaya, you can talk to me. You know you can. I will always be here for you, you're my best friend, my sister, and I love you. If there's anything that you need to get out, anything at all..."

Her soft, woeful voice trails off, and tears prick my eyes as I glance up to see glistening in her own. She's never hidden from me as I have done from her. Her heart and soul are the sweetest, most genuine there could ever be, and she has always given them fully to the world. When Adam was taken, she wept for days, and many nights she fell asleep in my arms while she grieved for him as if he had died. And yet, the struggles and uncertainty of each new day only strengthened her hope, and dreams of reuniting with Adam and raising their children with love and peace made her smile in spite of everything. For years, she has always stood by my side, taken my entire family off the street, braved soldiers when I wanted to take our things back, embraced me, dried my tears, kept my hope alive through her own. She is far too good a soul for this world, a far better sister and friend than I could ever deserve.

Gavriel and Noam were too good for me. Such loving, selfless boys, and I destroyed their family. If only they had never met me, Noam would still be alive.

As her hand brushes soothingly against my shoulder, my resolve crumbles. "It's not fair," I cry. "What did he ever do? He was so sweet and innocent! He never hurt anyone in his life and Schneider shot him like a dog! And it's my fault! He didn't deserve it! I watched it happen! I just sat there and *watched!* He was all alone and so scared and I didn't do anything!"

Noam's eyes stare, terrified, beseechingly, back into mine, waiting for me to save him, begging me to do anything at all. A gunshot explodes in my ears and I recoil, sobbing as the light dies from the eyes that once looked upon me with such pure admiration, that brought my sister so much joy. He does not disappear when I open my eyes, when Naomi's voice slowly pierces the fog of my grief, when I become aware that I am cradled limply in her arms.

"I'm so sorry, Hodaya, I'm so sorry," she murmurs, running

her fingers through my hair as I did for her on those restless nights when her fear for Adam became too much to bear. "It wasn't your fault, it *wasn't*. There was nothing you could have done. You would be dead too, then Bayla and I wouldn't have a sister."

Bayla... Naomi... my sisters. But now Gavriel has no brother. If I could change the way things unfolded that night, if I could take his place, would I? Would I take myself away from Bayla and Naomi to give Noam to Gavriel?

The tears come with renewed fervor at the thought. My heart knows my answer and I am consumed by shame, loathing my own selfish soul, weeping for Noam, for everything I didn't and wouldn't have done, for not saving his life and for what I would have left behind if I tried.

"We all loved him so much, Hodaya, but it wasn't your fault. I swear I know that to be true, no one blames you. It was God calling His child back to Heaven. Noam is content now, watching over us. He wouldn't want you to feel responsible for this, I know it. It wasn't your fault. You can't blame yourself anymore."

As she always has, she nearly convinces me that it's true, but his eyes return to my mind, and I hate that I don't believe her. Still, I say nothing, the pain and regret I've smothered for so long assaulting me with the deadly force of a bomb. She's whispering to me again, words of love and comfort, but I can't bring myself to hear them. Instead I let her hold me, rocking me back and forth like a child, and I cry. The medication and alcohol are already taking over my system, and through my anguish and oncoming illness I can only whimper, "I'm sorry, I'm so sorry," over and over until I succumb to sleep.

Loud pounding on the door startles me awake and I groan. Knives are stabbing through my eyes and temples. The floor is solid and cold beneath me, and my bones ache from having rolled off the bed. The room reeks of vomit and sweat. Groggily, I force my burning eyes to open.

"Out! Raus! Everyone out!" a voice shouts.

I want to cover my ears, to ease the throbbing pain that stings more terribly with every order and demanding knock, but the very thought leaves me exhausted. The room is moving, tilting slowly like a boat swaying with the waves, and I squeeze my eyes shut, only for the dizziness to increase tenfold. It is as though even beyond my eyelids the shadows are spinning, twirling my head, until I slump back down to the hardwood. My stomach contracts painfully and I heave, my body desperately trying to drain the poisons within, but my stomach is empty, and I am left trembling with the strained efforts.

The door bursts open and several pairs of boots stomp heavily inside.

"Fucking hell," a man curses, gagging. "These disgusting pigs live in their own filth."

"Dysentery, sir," comes Papa's weak voice from somewhere in the room. "We've had dysentery for the last four days, but it's starting to pass."

The boots shuffle backwards.

"God, let's just leave them here. They'll probably be dead in a few days anyway. It'd be a waste of bullets."

"I'm not touching them, they smell like shit, fickende kühe!"

"Fine by me, make a note of it. We'll clear out the rest of the street."

And with that, the Germans are gone, slamming the door and moving on to other rooms. No dogs can be heard barking or growling, the shouting becomes fainter the longer time goes on, and the dozens of gunshots throughout the course of the morning are fired far away. By the end of the day silence has fallen, and I know in my heart that Bayla is safe.

We have been spared for another day, but we cannot hide forever. Our turn will come one day, I am dreadfully sure of it, and we'll disappear down the train tracks to whatever fate the Nazis have in store for us.

14

SEPTEMBER 1, 1943

AUSCHWITZ-BIRKENAU

The processing building at the end of the long, muddy road is called the Sauna. Naomi, Bayla, and I are all pushed inside along with other women SS-Hauptsturmführer Mengele sent to the right. There aren't many of us, perhaps a hundred, all around my own age. Bayla is by far the youngest at barely ten years old.

Marring the walls, phrases have been painted in German: *Work Brings Freedom. Respect Your Blockälteste! Follow All Orders. For the Glorious Reich!*

Another order comes. "Strip! Take everything off."

I freeze, staring in disbelief and horror at the other women, at Bayla, then at the SS. *Undress? In front of them?* Tears well up in my eyes and I begin to quake, hearing with uncanny clarity the filthy words the men sneer as the same horrific order comes once more.

"Strip! Take everything off and pile it up!"

Bayla presses firmly against me, visibly shaking in fear. I shield her as best I can, turning my back on the SS men as I begin to peel off my layers of clothing. With great hesitancy, Bayla follows my lead, tears leaking from her eyes. I've never been naked in this way before. I've never been bare before anyone, not even my mother, let alone a man, let alone dozens of enemy soldiers. I push Bayla further into the group of women, hoping their bodies will keep her from view.

Hot, furious tears stain my cheeks and I bite into my lip with such force I taste bitter, metallic blood, but I don't care. She's a child! She's still thin and undeveloped, she's never had a period in her life, and now here she stands, naked and shivering before grown men whose disgusting words I wish I couldn't understand. The rage burns deep within me much more intensely than the fear and humiliation, even as I can feel the eyes raking over my nude body.

Once everyone is completely naked, the only preservation of our dignity against the men's eyes piled in a corner of the room, we are all smeared with a green, foul-smelling disinfecting fluid. It is nearly impossible to swallow my bile as a stranger's hands run up and down my body, roughly rubbing the liquid into my skin, and I must look away to suppress my scream of rage as another stranger's hands violate Bayla in the same way. She sniffs away her tears, her entire body trembling, her eyes screwed shut. I block her from their view as much as I can, running my fingers comfortingly through her hair as she whimpers against me, her tears burning against my stomach.

What little solace she may find in my arms is short-lived as we are all pushed into a line. There are several Germans and clothed prisoners at its head, a woman with clippers, and piles of hair on the floor being swept away. When we draw close enough, the woman grabs me by the arm and yanks me over to her. She takes a hold of my hair, raises the clippers, and begins to shave with the methodic callousness of a machine.

I watch in disgust as locks of my soft hair fall to the ground, and feel tears leak from my eyes as she takes the clippers next to my legs and genitals. Once she is done, she pushes me away and again I follow the other women, slouched and disgraced.

Strands of my hair still cling to my shoulders, irritating the back of my neck, but I can't bring myself to swipe them away. I run my fingers over my head, feeling skin and rough patches where I once had my father's brown hair.

I don't know what to think anymore, what to feel, and I'm not sure I want to. The confusion, the shame in the pit of my stomach, the resentment deep in my heart have far surpassed intolerable, but everything has gone numb.

I find myself in another line in front of a young German woman, fully clothed with lovely, wavy golden hair. She takes the arm of each woman in line, jabbing furiously with some piece of equipment before moving on to the next girl.

Bayla comes up behind me, her tiny, fragile fingers brushing against my hand. My heart shatters at the sight of her, nude, her beautiful blond hair shaved away, the remains being swept and discarded on the growing mound in the corner.

What are they doing to us?

The German woman reaches out and grabs my arm, then takes her tool that looks something like a large needle and stabs it into my skin. It stings more in my heart than on my forearm even as it begins to bleed, and I cannot bring myself to watch what is happening. The woman pushes me away and another prisoner directs me to the other side of the room, where I am given a thin cotton shirt, skirt, and a pair of wooden clogs.

A soft, pained gasp draws my attention, and I turn back to see the German woman marking Bayla's arm. She shuts her eyes tightly and clenches her fist, tears streaming down her cheeks as she quietly whimpers.

For the first time I look at my own arm, where there is still a stinging sensation.

A—30972

It is a tattoo. A brand, still red and inflamed. Something inside me withers in this moment, looking upon the black marking seared into my skin, and I no longer feel like the same person anymore, maybe not a person at all. Cattle seems the better word, no longer Hodaya Alperstein, but A—30972. Does Hodaya even exist in Auschwitz? Is this who I am now?

But who did I used to be?

I could have answered this question with unwavering certainty mere minutes ago. And yet, now I'm not sure. Somehow, I never really thought the Nazis could take more than just my home and my family. When they invaded, threw us into the streets, killed without remorse or mercy, I always thought, *surely there's nothing more they can do to us.* But now, what have they done with my clothes, my pictures, and my mother's jewelry? Where are they sweeping my hair? What has my modesty and dignity been reduced to? Where are my documents, what is my true name? What have they done to Bayla and her pure, kind-hearted soul?

God, why are You letting this happen to us? Are You so uncertain of our faith that You see fit to test us with humiliation and torture?

I hurriedly dress Bayla before pulling on my own clothes. Carefully, I smear away the blood from her pale, pure skin, now blemished with the hideous black marking of the number A—30973. As I kiss her bare head, crying, I find myself questioning not the Germans or their motives, but God.

15

SEPTEMBER 2, 1943

"Inside!" a woman screams at us. "Schnell! Hurry up! Run!"

The chilly, early wind of approaching dawn nips at our skin through our thin clothes like the batons several prisoner women wield as they direct us toward a long wooden barrack. A hundred women all rush through the entrance at once, shoving each other down onto the mud floor in their haste to follow orders, in their desperate desire to hide from the Sauna, the officers, and their own shame. Bayla staggers, nearly knocked to the ground by another woman, and I clutch her to my side to make sure I don't lose her in the swarm of people.

Three-tier wooden bunks line either side of the barrack, hard, bare surfaces with only bodies occupying them. Despite my own sore muscles and trembling legs, I lift Bayla onto the center bunk, and only have time to lay down between her and a shivering woman before two other women are wedging themselves beside us. Bayla's breathing has already evened, the torment of the last two days having dragged her to sleep.

There are already several hundred women inside, who arrived before us, and there are still a few empty spaces in the bunks, but three more women pull themselves onto ours. No one is willing to be separated from the other, even if many of us are little more than strangers. Many have come from Bochnia with me, but I don't recognize any of them now. Even Bayla, one of the dearest people in my life, is almost unfamiliar, and I cannot find Naomi. We all lie side by side, pressed so tightly together that even the wind cannot slip through us.

In the pandemonium and confusion, screams of fear and misery ricochet off the walls, echoing the way I imagine a restless spirit's voice would haunt a grim, unending cave. Women cry out for their husbands and children, their parents and siblings, friends and relatives separated just an hour ago. The irritated voices of the earlier arrivals groan in exasperation, snap at them to shut up and stop crying so they can sleep.

I might have screamed for Mama and Papa, for Naomi, for anyone else who shared in our hellish journey to this wicked place, for any comforting, familiar face, but my heart is too heavy to allow me any words.

"Quiet! Den Mund Halten!" This time, it is a man's voice that slices through the algid air and silences everyone.

Standing in the entrance of the block is an imposing SS man, a lamp in his hand that casts fiendish, sinister shadows over his rigid features. At his right hand there stands a tall, broad woman in prisoner's clothing, eyes heavy and visibly displeased.

"This is your Blockälteste"—he indicates the large woman at his side—"and she is in charge of you for your time in quarantine. Roll call is to be at four o'clock, you will line up when you hear the whistle. We expect absolute obedience. Remember, you are in Auschwitz, and Auschwitz is a concentration camp. You will work or you will die. You have the honor of laboring for the glorious Reich and our righteous Führer or *that!*"

What *"that"* is, none of us know, but he jerks his head in a nod toward the place the ominous glow comes from.

"The choice is yours," he declares.

What a fantastic lie! The choice is ours? Oh, the nerve!

The officer takes his leave and the Blockälteste shuts the barrack door with a loud, commanding slam. "Everyone be quiet!" she shouts, brandishing a whip. "Roll call in a few hours, you greenhorns! I don't want to hear a sound from the lot of you!"

"Who is she?" I whisper to the woman beside me.

"Weren't you listening?" the woman hisses, shivering with fever. "Her name is Gerda, but don't call her that. Only call her Blockälteste."

"Can you tell me what's—"

"So many questions! If you want to live, don't ask questions."

Nearby, the Blockälteste's whip cracks down and someone screams. I quickly wrap an arm around Bayla and pull her closer, hesitating, waiting for the Blockälteste to move further away before I dare to whisper.

"How long have you been here?"

After a long silence, I think the woman is going to ignore me, but then she sighs woefully and mutters, "Four weeks, longer than all the others. Most don't live this long. You won't either, probably. That little one definitely won't. Children aren't supposed to be here."

"What are you talking about? What is this place?"

Her breathless chuckle is quiet and humorless. "Oh, sweet ignorance! This is Hell. We'll all die here; everyone goes through the chimney one way or the other."

The smoky air catches in my throat, suffocating like smoldering ashes. "What's the chimney? What's over there?"

"Fire, you pathetic woman, fire. Whenever they kill you, they'll burn you over there. Can't you smell it? All the ones who went left, they kill them with gas and then burn them. That's where the rest of your family is. That's where they'll take your little girl."

"Liar!" I gasp, stiffening at the audible approach of the Block-älteste. "You're horrible! Why would you say something like that?"

"We didn't believe it either," she whispers, her voice faint, "but it's true. There used to be more of us, but they're dead now. There is no God here, only the chimney."

"We're talkative tonight, aren't we!" the Blockälteste's voice booms, seeming to rumble the very wood we lie on. "Shut up, you stupid cows!"

The whizzing of air alerts me to the swift rising of her whip and I shield my head. It comes down with savage force, lashing repeatedly into the woman next to me... but she doesn't scream; she doesn't even twitch.

I don't dare to speak again even when the Blockälteste has left after spitting out several more abuses. After several minutes, straining to hear the woman beside me breathe, desperately waiting to feel her shiver or groan in pain, I can no longer deny it, and begin to tremble with more than the cold.

This woman who was just speaking to me, who is still lying pressed against me... she's dead. Then was it all true? A chimney where they're burning people? The foul odor consuming this place, it's human flesh? What the prisoners told Naomi... My heart seizes in terror.

Mama! Papa! Oh, God! No! It can't be true!

Mengele's face returns to my mind, his vacant, cold eyes as he looked Mama up and down with disapproval and pointed her to the left.

The glow... that's where he pointed her to...

The world crumbles and collapses into oblivion.

The loud scream of whistles tears me from a nightmare of flames, stripping, and horse barracks, and for the briefest of moments I think that's all it was. But then a large woman is stomping before me, swinging a whip over her head, battering the bunks with a club, and screaming, "Out! Raus! Schnell! Everybody out! Get up! Line up! Roll call! Zählappell!"

Bayla is shivering and curled against me like a newborn. Women stagger from the bunks, some falling in the mud, others too tired and weak to climb down on their own. I reach to shake the woman next to me, her face now clearly visible in the hazy morning light, and nearly scream as the memory of last night comes crashing back. Her eyes stare lifelessly into mine, her corpse-like face is hollow and bony as a skeleton, caked with dried blood where the whip has flayed her skin.

"She's dead!" I scream, scrambling down from the bunk to grab the arm of a woman who's likely been here longer than I. Her face, too, is hollow and bruised, as if she's been beaten and starved.

The woman regards me with disinterest and impassively says, "So drag her outside."

I gape at her in shock. She shrugs me off and walks away as if I'd just told her something so inconsequential as 'the sky is blue'.

"Hurry up you lazy dogs! Outside! Or you'll do Sport all day!" the Blockälteste shouts.

I hastily pull Bayla away from the dead woman just as another prisoner approaches. To my utter horror, she begins to strip the body. She tears the number and classification patch from the dead woman's shirt, a white triangle with the letter *P* marking her as a Pole, and slips the clothes on.

My own patch is a yellow triangle, like hundreds of others I have seen. The mark of a Jew.

Bayla and I follow the herd of women out of the barrack to where they are beginning to form rows of five. Ankle-deep in freezing mud, struggling not to slip and stumble in our wooden clogs, we trudge together to the lines. The Blockälteste is waiting for us with one hand on her hip, swinging her whip in the other.

As we near the front, a hand suddenly seizes my elbow. "Not the front, never the front," a woman hisses in my ear. "Do you want the little one dead? Why did they let a child in here anyway? This is no place for a girl that young!"

She insistently directs us to a row near the center of all the commotion, elbowing her way through, speaking in broken sentences of German and Polish. "She's much too young. The SS will take her over *there* soon. Best to stay unnoticed here, but they won't forget her. A child is too noticeable. Try not to be taken with the work parties, we're up for the taking during the quarantine period."

Out of the corner of my eye, I notice labored movement near the barrack, and swiftly block Bayla's view before she can fully glimpse the scene before us; women dragging bodies from the block, piling the corpses along the sides of our lines as if they were still living people waiting to be counted. It is surreal in the most horrific way; I cannot pull my gaze away, still partially convinced I'm inside some dreadful nightmare, that I'll wake up any moment in the ghetto, wondering why a sleeping mind conjures such gruesome images.

What kind of Godless wasteland have we been brought to?

For an hour we stand to attention, unable to move or sit, eyes lowered away from the Blockälteste and her prisoner subordinates. The Blockälteste prowls up and down the lines with a strut in her step, counting and tallying numbers as she goes. Another three hours elapse. Groups of women dispersed from different blocks beyond quarantine hours ago, marched away to the melodic sounds of a band, and yet we newcomers are forced to stand still. Several women have collapsed, too tired and feeble to stay upright. All of them are forced to their feet again and beaten with clubs and whips until they obey and stand to attention.

It must be nearing ten o'clock when two SS women appear, one holding a long, black stick, the other with a large, leashed dog. These women count us as well, verifying the Blockälteste's numbers. They stalk along the front rows, examining the prisoners, striking anyone who seems to move or raise their eyes. Suddenly, the dog is unleashed to savage a woman who has sunk to her knees in exhaustion, and her agonized screams are the only sounds in the silence of paralyzing terror. The SS woman calls her dog off, and, as the whimpering, bloody prisoner is forced back to her feet, I understand why I must avoid being caught in the front at all costs.

"Coffee! Line up!" the Blockälteste calls once the SS have gone, standing alongside her three other subordinate prisoners and a large pot.

The prospect of liquid to soothe my raw, dry throat is heavenly. I lead Bayla to the line beginning to form before the pot, the bowls we were issued after being given our clothes in hand. A single spoonful is slopped into my bowl, a brown fluid with a frightening blue tint, and I nearly gag at the nauseating smell. Bayla is next, holding her bowl out hopefully to the Blockälteste's helpers ladling the coffee.

One of the Blockälteste's subordinates exclaims, "What the hell? She's tiny!"

"Since when do they let children in here?" another barks, firmly lowering Bayla's serving back into the pot, and spits. "And look at her mark! A dirty little Jew! She won't last a day! A waste of rations! Go on, get, you little rat!"

Too young... too little...

I pull Bayla away from the line, her shoulders sagging and tears filling her eyes, and I switch our bowls. For the first time, I truly examine our fellow prisoners, the ones who came with us and the ones who arrived before, and I thread my fingers through Bayla's. She's the smallest, the youngest. There are no elderly here, no children. The frail bodies and haunted eyes of those stumbling to a place behind the block are young women, teen girls and adults no younger than fifteen and no older than forty.

But there were so many children when we arrived! Where are they now? Where are all the little boys and girls who came with us? Where are all the old men and women? Where are Mama and Papa? Where is everyone?

A hopeless, sullen voice echoes in my mind. *"There is no God here, only the chimney."* The chimney... a crematorium... if everything I've been told is true, then—

I bite harshly on the insides of my cheeks, choking back a scream, looking to the sky to drown my tears... but the sky is black, the smoke stings my eyes and burns my throat, the stench of burning flesh clouds my senses, and I double over, vomiting. The ground swirls and blurs beneath me, long buildings, a tall chimney spewing smoke in the distance, mud, watchtowers, and endless barbed wire flash before my eyes. There are voices screaming in my head; Mama and Papa, Naomi, Noam and Gavriel, everyone I've ever known and strangers whose eyes still stare into mine, empty and dead.

But I don't hear Bayla's voice in my head. I hear it beside me.

All at once, everything stills. The thick sludge where I've fallen soaks through my skirt to my knees, and Bayla kneels at my side. Her blue eyes gaze at me with helpless worry, filled with the unmistakable glow of life, and I brush a hand across her soft cheek. She is alive. By whatever grace of God or absurd chance last night, Bayla stayed with me. She lived. She lived when thousands did not, when Mama and Papa—

I bite my cheeks, clearing my throat hoarsely to drown the sobs and stomp the heartache down.

Mama, Papa... Bayla will live, I promise. I don't care if it's the last thing I do or if my life will never have any other purpose again. Bayla will live.

"I'm alright," I assure her, forcing away all other thought and rising shakily to my feet.

We join the other women in the open, marshy space behind the block referred to as the meadow. God, what wretched creatures we all look like! Shaved, beaten women have sunk to the ground, uncaring about the mud soaking their clothes, desperate for any relief to their exhaustion. My eyes are heavy, an ache throbs from deep within my bones, my legs quake in protest, and I have no idea what to do.

We are lost and vulnerable in a completely foreign place, a sea of unfamiliar faces, those who are obviously dangerous, and perils yet to tread. Are these women to be my allies in this place, or shall my yellow triangle be a target like the blue stars? There can be no pretending here; our heritage is sewn directly under our numbers, and, despite my ignorance as to the inner workings of this place, I know with dire certainty that a Jew is at the bottom of the trench.

There is much to learn if we are to survive here.

A face nearby catches my attention, a green-eyed woman sitting on the ground with two identical women leaning against one another. My heart jolts and I gasp, "Naomi! Levana, Chasha!"

Levana and Chasha nearly stop me dead in my tracks before I throw my arms around them. Their long, beautiful black hair they were once so proud of, that was always combed to silky perfection, is completely shaved.

"Hodaya, you're alright! And Bayla too!" Levana breathes.

Naomi embraces me tightly, tears dripping from her cheeks to my shoulder. "Thank God, I was so worried!"

"We're alright, all of us." I choke back my tears, settling myself into the mud at their sides and allowing Bayla to sit propped in my lap. She lifts my bowl to her lips, then her face twists in revulsion and she coughs up the sip she took.

"Don't drink that, Bayla!" Chasha warns. "I think it might be poisoned. Some girls were talking about washing with it."

"It's horrible," Bayla mutters, wiping the remnants from her mouth.

"It's all we're going to get. I'll find you some water later. Try to drink a little," I urge, patting her back.

"Surely they'll give us more," Chasha says, casting a fearful glance at the others. "Do you think they'd let us starve?"

"Of course not," I interject and tighten my hold on Bayla.

Naomi's eyes, ringed with dark circles, lift to mine, then flicker to Bayla. Wordlessly, she nods faintly, and attempts to drink from her own bowl.

Near midday, as we are sweating beneath the blistering sun with no protection and soaked with both mud and manure, a group of prisoners approach with large pots.

"Soup! Line up!" the Blockälteste yells.

"You see?" Chasha smiles with relief. "They're here to feed us!"

Levana and Chasha rush to line up with the others, and Naomi moves to follow, but I hold her back. Some of the other women look to be biding their time, their eyes calculating, purposely standing as slowly as possible as the line grows longer.

Observe and learn, that is the only way to live. These girls have been here longer, they know what's best.

When an older girl lagging behind finally places herself further back to the middle of the line, Bayla, Naomi, and I are at her heels. When we at last reach the front after what feels like hours, I am relieved to find different prisoners ladling out the soup.

The brown liquid—like the so-called coffee—smells and looks repugnant, and a few tiny slivers of what might be potatoes and swede float on top. The taste is far worse than the smell and bile rises in my throat at the mere thought of swallowing it, but I am too hungry to hand it off. Other new arrivals cannot bear the smell or taste and freely give their servings to women who beg and scramble over one another for it as if they've never eaten before.

The reward of our decision to remain further behind while the other new girls rushed to the front is evident in our bowls. In Bayla's, there is an entire chunk of potato, a tiny lump of what might be meat, and a few slices of carrot floating in an otherwise watery substance. My own holds less; only a single slip of potato bobs up and down. Still, it is more than the others near the front of the line got, all of the nourishment having sunk to the bottom of the pot, leaving them with only the fluid.

"You have so much!" a girl exclaims in whispered astonishment, peering into Bayla's bowl with ravenous eyes. Quickly, she unties the brown scarf from her shaved head and offers it. "Do you want a scarf, little one? Perfect to keep the sun off you! You can have it if you give me your ration."

"No, she's fine," I cut in, stepping to place myself between Bayla and the frail girl.

The girl's eyes narrow, cold and predatory. "She won't live long," she hisses. "She'll starve sooner than us, what's the point in her having so much food? A waste!"

I shove her back and she slips. "She's fine!" I snap.

And she'll make it longer than you if I can help it.

Evening falls and music once again rises from the camp band nearby, a cheerful parading song that escorts parties of laborer women back to camp. Functionary prisoners walk alongside the lines with clubs and whips, cruelly striking the women's battered bodies, ordering them to march and sing. Many of them cannot comply with the order to stride jovially. They struggle to stand, slip and fall in the mud, and try to drag objects from their work sites back with them.

I quickly look away, trembling, realizing with horror that they're dragging dead bodies.

"Roll call! Zählappell! Get in line, you pigs!"

I drag Bayla and Naomi along with me to line up, shoving and fighting my way to the middle, ensuring Bayla a place between two women on each side. The Blockälteste continues to scream orders, strolling up and down the lines, flourishing her whip and striking those who aren't fast enough.

Another few hours pass, a thousand women all standing together while the Blockälteste and her helpers prowl among us like wolves, counting, beating, screaming when the numbers don't add up, rampaging through the block until they've found everyone and whipped them into line. Another two hours. The sun is beginning to sink and whistles screech throughout the camp from within the barbed wire and whatever lies beyond.

A quiet whimper draws my attention down to Bayla, slightly swaying on sore feet. Sternly, I correct her posture, sending her a warning glance. We mustn't falter here, not with functionary prisoners loyal to our persecutors watching our every move, not where no reason is needed to beat or murder us.

The SS supervisor arrives on her bike with her baton in hand to verify the numbers from roll call, and, when she leaves again, we are allowed to return to the block. At the entrance, the Blockälteste's subordinates hand out small rations of bread. It is small enough to sit lightly in the palm of my hand with a bare smidgen of margarine. I cannot fathom how the bit of bread is supposed to suffice as a proper meal.

"This is all we get," says a woman in passing. She might be the one who pulled Bayla and me away from the front of the lines, but I'm not entirely sure. We all look the same here. "It's supper and tomorrow's breakfast. Make it last."

Make it last? How does one make a scrap last?

Newcomers in a block filled with women who've already been learning the ways of this place for weeks, we have precious little chance of finding places in the bunks, let alone the top, which seems to be favored. Rather than fight for a place we'll inevitably be pushed out of, Bayla, Naomi, and I squeeze into a center bunk, which doesn't have the luxury of a straw mat or a single decrepit blanket.

"Hodaya, I want to go home," Bayla sniffles, her bread crushed in her trembling hand.

I kiss her bare head, resolving to find her a scarf as soon as possible. "I know, Bayla."

"I want to see Mama and Papa," she cries. "I want Asher! I want Noam back!"

Her glistening eyes—flecked with spots of stormy gray and rivers of ocean blue exactly like our mother's—beseech me, fearful, drowning in youthful bewilderment and fear.

"... I know, I do too," I whisper, fighting back my own tears as Bayla sobs into my neck. "Everything's going to be alright. You'll be alright, *I promise*."

No matter what it may cost me. My sister... now my daughter, the beautiful, joyful ray of sun in my life, so carefree and kind, untouched by the true depths of human depravity... I will ensure she never loses that light. A mother will *do* anything, *endure* anything for her child. A child *needs* a mother. I am all Bayla has left, and I am more than willing to be whatever she needs, to sacrifice everything so long as she survives. No matter the level of iniquity circumstance demands I sink to, no matter how many *averas* spatter my conscience and soul, I will ensure she lives, even if I must coat my hands in the reddest of Moses' rivers to do so.

But will God forgive me those offenses?

If I surrender to *yetzer hara* not out of human flaw, but willingly, out of both greed and disregard for life, will I be cleansed of these sins in Hell? Will regret and shame outweigh the free will with which I shall rebel against God's wishes? And if they do not, if God decides my capacity for wrongdoing is too deep, does it matter? If I am barred from entering Heaven to join my loved ones, is that fate so unbearable if I've given Bayla the life she deserves?

No.

Within the span of this suffocating thought, I am overwhelmed by the feeling of nothing. My parents are dead. There is no escaping this place. I have nothing but the pitiful crust in my hand and the ragged clothes on my body. There is nothing left for me in this world beyond the tiny girl crying herself to sleep in my arms, beyond tomorrow and whatever lies outside the barrack. The realization should crush my heart, would have shattered it not so long ago, but I feel nothing, only resigned to whoever A—30972 must be as she takes Hodaya's place over the course of the bitter night.

16

SEPTEMBER 5–OCTOBER 12, 1943

QUARANTINE

Three days' worth of bread rations is what it took to buy a scarf. I hid my bread the first night, intending to give it to Bayla in the morning though my stomach was painfully empty, but a group of female prisoners from beyond quarantine approached our meadow on the second morning with offerings. One girl, who wore a long piece of fabric around her head, perhaps once yellow but now soiled beyond recognition, said she would sell it to me for three pieces of bread. I only had one, but she insisted she would wait, and this morning I traded each morsel with starving reluctance for the piece of cloth I then tied over Bayla's sunburnt head.

Hands trembling, weak with the heat of the afternoon and my attempts to survive only on the bit of soup and coffee for the past few days, I eagerly drink both without regard for the taste or for the illness they may bring. What we were told was coffee indeed contains some kind of poison, like Chasha thought, for girls have messed themselves and been denied permission to clean themselves or go to the lavatory, and all their pleas for changes of clothes have been refused. The older prisoners have confirmed that it is poisoned to stop us from having our monthly periods, but it's the closest thing to water we're given, so one must decide whether to drink it or wash with it. Dehydration is quickly becoming a more dire concern than starvation, and Bayla's lips are beginning to dry.

Long past caring about the mud, we all sit together in the meadow. Levana and Chasha still have their bowls of coffee from earlier and are carefully washing their faces and heads with one, forcing the other down parched throats. Naomi, whose eyes sink deeper with despair every passing day, leans against my shoulder, watchful of the Blockälteste and Kapos— the functionary prisoners who the SS select to keep order and who receive more food and privileges than any others. But prisoners or not, they are no better than the SS themselves; in fact some are worse, for the SS often choose the most sadistic, cruel prisoners or criminals to oversee us.

The beatings are frequent. Kapos eagerly seek out lesser, unwary prisoners to flog or abuse, and seem genuinely pleased with themselves when an SS nods approvingly. A Jewish girl who arrived with another transport a few days after us wasn't paying attention to her surroundings when one of our German Kapos, called Zlata, came raging to our block, and had to be carried away to the infirmary, looking more dead than alive when they took her away. She never came back.

Hundreds have died in the few days we've been here; starving to death, beaten by our fellow prisoners for food and clothes and favor, dying in the night and collapsing during roll call, suddenly dropping dead of shock and exhaustion. And there are always more to take their places. New arrivals enter quarantine every day, dozens, hundreds, and sometimes thousands, so many their faces all blur together in my mind, insignificant and similar as cattle in a field, differentiated only by their tattoos.

I sit ready on one knee, prepared to run at a second's notice, every sense on guard. I cannot afford to falter for even a moment. Danger can come from any direction, violently and without warning. If my years in the ghetto and the perils of living beneath the Nazis' boots taught me anything, it is to never be caught, to always be alert.

The women in quarantine are separate from the others in the women's camp. We will be segregated for the next few weeks as a precaution against disease outbreaks, then once that period ends we survivors will be placed with the rest of the camp. But until then, we have no work assignments like the others, and loiter all hours of the day in the mud and sun, watching for Kapos who might come to drag us off for slave labor where they don't have enough workers. We are up for the taking until quarantine ends.

Movement several blocks away catches my attention: a woman carrying a whip, running for the meadow. In an instant, I've jerked Bayla and Naomi to their feet. "RUN!"

My shout catches the attention of the others, who all in turn shriek at the sight of the German prisoner and sprint for cover. Twenty or so women crowd to hide behind the block. I pull Bayla and Naomi to the side of a neighboring barrack, far away from the cracking whip and the woman who wields it. Levana and Chasha are nowhere in sight, and I can only hope they've found places to hide. We cannot go back for them; I won't risk Bayla being taken or found.

Already dozens of newcomers are being rounded up, and the German woman is relentless in her screaming, whipping anyone too slow to get away. The women behind the block are caught and beaten, then shoved into the growing group of slave laborers. We make a daring dash to another quarantine block, barely avoiding the Kapo's sight.

Get away. Hide. Get away. Hide.

A trumpet rings out from God, His merciful offering for

safety in the form of a whistle signaling a Sunday afternoon roll call. All at once there is absolute chaos as women rush from the blocks beyond quarantine, and we use the disorder to hide until the German Kapo is leaving with a large group of nearly a hundred women.

"Levana, Chasha..." Naomi whispers helplessly as they go, and I catch a glimpse of them among the group, one of them with a bloody lash across her face.

Bayla is safe, I remind myself, loosening my grip when I look down and realize her face is pinched in discomfort and her fingers are becoming red.

The roundup has left everyone shaken and tense, and no one resumes their seated positions in the mud, despite their exhaustion. We rejoin the women in the meadow, vigilant for other Kapos or SS, but my attention is no longer focused on searching for that specific danger. With everyone now alert, I can survey our surroundings again, searching for direction from the older prisoners, hoping to discover whatever strategy has made them survive for so long.

Bayla tries to clear her throat soundlessly, but the dryness makes her voice thick and raspy, and her stomach grumbles loudly.

Water. Food can wait, I think, wiping the sweat from my brow, careful not to bump the sensitive burns on my exposed, peeling, throbbing head. *A scarf too, something to keep the sun off my head and protect from the rain and snow when it comes.*

I consider the hem of my skirt for a while. It's long, partially soaking with mud, but it would leave my feet and bits of my legs exposed if I cut it... After another hour of wandering the quarantine blocks, heat burning my face, I decide I don't care. I've seen women with extra clothes before, so hopefully I'll be able to find us some when winter arrives.

"Help me find a rock, a sharp one. I'm going to make a scarf with my skirt," I say, and Naomi kneels with me, digging down into the sludge in search of a stone. It takes nearly an hour, but my fingers at last nudge something solid. It turns out to be a rusty nail, probably lost during the barracks construction, and I use it to carefully slice a hole near the ankle of my skirt, then slowly tear. Naomi does the same with her skirt, and, though the wet fabric reeks of filth, it feels heavenly around my burning head.

Water, the word resurfaces again, and my thoughts shift back into an animalistic hunting mentality. I slip the nail beneath my breast, just in case it proves beneficial in the future. Nothing, not even this sharp, tiny piece of copper, must be dismissed as useless.

It isn't until evening approaches and we've avoided two more roundups that the opportunity for water presents itself. Or rather the risk of water. There are no opportunities, here where we are deprived of every means of survival, only calculated risks of our lives against the most meager necessities.

Some of the kitchen staff passed by our block some hours ago with wooden crates. Curiously, I followed, and watched with starving desire as they dumped bits of rotten tomatoes and other food into the long, deep trench that separates us from the watchtowers and electrified fence.

Tomatoes are mostly water. I remember Mama once told me that when she was teaching me to cook and plant the garden.

Hiding along the side of a barrack near the trench, I watch the armed guards across the fence, calculating just how far I'd have to run, how much time I'd have before being spotted, if my life is worth a few rotten tomatoes and beets.

Again, Bayla tries to clear her throat, longingly running her fingers over her empty bowl.

My life isn't worth it, but hers is. God, please don't let me be shot...

I turn to Naomi. "Please watch her. Don't let her look," I whisper, and she nods.

My heart throbs painfully as I step cautiously to the other side of the barrack, searching the ground for Kapos among the groups of prisoners, who are careful not to tread too close to the trench. I watch the guards gaze over the camp, then turn and talk to each other. With their attention momentarily diverted, I take a trembling step forward. As I draw a few feet closer to the trench, there is a gunshot. I startle, grasping my chest in search of a bullet wound, before I register the shouting, then a woman several meters away who is trying to run through the ditch to reach the electrified fence.

Seizing the distraction her suicide attempt affords me, I sprint forward, panting, slide down the muddy slope and desperately grab for anything the kitchen staff dumped. My hands tremble violently, snatching anything I touch without seeing what it is, stuffing it into my skirt like a sack, then I scramble back up the slippery grime.

"Oh, God, Hodaya! You idiot!" Naomi sobs as I reach the block, grabbing me forcefully and dragging me out of sight. My legs give out beneath the weight of relief and shock, and the contents of my skirt fall at our feet: five watery, rotten tomatoes and a lump of brown potato skins.

Naomi ignores the pitiful pile, instead hastily unwrapping my new scarf and shakily touching my neck. She cries, nearly wailing, but muffles the sound with a hand suddenly tinged with blood. My hand is weightless as I reach up and feel a slight burn and dampness just below my ear.

"You're alright, it just grazed you." Naomi shudders, clutching my hand.

The realization makes me slump against the wooden barrack, dazed and disbelieving. Terror, panic, and sheer adrenaline must have numbed and deafened me in those few seconds I was in the trench, and I didn't hear the gunshot from the guard towers, nor feel the bullet that was centimeters from entering my head.

"Eat," I whisper, a tremor in my weak voice.

We eagerly slurp the liquid from the tomatoes, devouring everything ravenously. Thankfully, there is no mold, and, though they are sour, nothing has ever tasted so delicious.

Our fourth day brings more of the same: slowly yet steadily declining autumn weather, hiding from the Kapos and their raids, alternating between standing and sitting, trying to learn from the seasoned prisoners.

Levana and Chasha were both taken to work on a railroad yesterday, but they've managed to avoid being taken for labor today even though their injuries make it difficult for them to run away from the Kapos. A raw lash has flayed Levana's cheek, and the gruesome bite on Chasha's leg where an SS guard let his dog maul her has made it nearly impossible for her to stand.

Just as the time for soup is approaching, the sight of a green uniform alerts me to danger. Before we can run, the Blockälteste screams for everyone to group up. The man at her side is a German with a leather satchel over his shoulder, the crosses on his jacket pocket gleaming as the sunlight catches them.

I recognize him immediately. He is the man who persuaded Mengele to let Bayla come with me, Obergefreiter Alaric Engel. Just as I realize I've been staring, his eyes turn and catch mine, and my heart drops to the ground. I quickly look away, my knees suddenly numb beneath me.

I'm dead, he's going to kill me! They think Jews are not worthy to even look *at those of the "master race"!*

However, seconds tick by and the corporal says nothing as the Blockälteste gathers everyone together, punching and irately berating us for keeping him waiting.

"Many apologies, Herr Obergefreiter!" the Blockälteste

implores in German. "Lazy, worthless pigs, this lot. They're all yours, sir."

Rather than acknowledge her, he steps forward and addresses us. "Who here speaks German?"

Two hands move timidly into the air, and the women who raised them are beckoned forward. I hear one of the girls give the corporal her number, A—30877, and her vivid blue eyes strike me even from a distance. I don't dare to volunteer myself, and pray he chooses to ignore my grave mistake. But luck is not with me today, I feel it deep in my bones even before the corporal stalks toward me.

"Number," he intones.

"A—30972," I recite, head dipped low.

"Number."

I open my mouth to give it again, but my heart stops short when beside me Bayla says, "A—30973."

"With me," he says, turning without looking to see if we're following. Obediently, Bayla and I fall into line behind him and the two other girls. As he leads us away from quarantine, I look helplessly back at Naomi, whose terrified, tear-filled eyes are begging for me to come back.

Where is he taking us? Why did he bring Bayla too? Would he kill both of us because I dared to look at him? Did he recognize us? Surely he remembers; Bayla is so recognizable. What does he want?

Further up the main road through the women's camp, the two women who claimed to speak German are passed off to another officer and taken away, leaving Bayla and me alone with Obergefreiter Engel. I cannot stop myself from slipping my hand into hers, drawing her thinning form protectively to my side, a move that does not go unnoticed by him when his gaze flickers to our intertwined hands.

We pass beneath the shadow of a watchtower and the

corporal steps inside another building and shouts, "Kapo! Get over here! I have your new küchenmädchen for you!"

The lingering scent of rotting vegetables and soup wafts out of the door, making my cramping, empty stomach rumble with longing. A short woman appears immediately at the corporal's demand.

"A—30973!" He gestures for Bayla to step forward and her hand slips hesitantly from mine, leaving a cold wind to fill its place. His next words are that of a language I find vaguely familiar—perhaps Ukrainian like the Chornovil family in Bochnia—but don't know. The woman nods her understanding and ushers Bayla into the building, casting me a reassuring glance. The exchange is brief, over before I can fully comprehend that Bayla is gone and the corporal is directing me away.

"She will be safe there. Yeva will watch her," he says simply.

My heart skips in confusion. *Safe?*

"What is your name?" he asks suddenly, the meaning of those words taking a few moments to register in my mind. Why would he want to know that? He glances backwards at me, and I realize he is waiting on an answer.

"Hodaya, Herr Obergefreiter," I mutter quietly, sounding uncertain even to my own ears. Is that truly my name? I feel so unsuited to that name and the girl it belonged to.

"My name is Alaric."

We enter another section of the camp not far off from our barracks. Though everything is identical, down from the grassless muck to the nails in the wooden blocks, it is foreign and unsettling to me, and I am desperate for the familiarity of my block, for Naomi and Bayla, for the women I'll never know longer than a few weeks. We come upon a barrack, where groans of pain emanate from a closed entrance and several gaunt bodies are piled in a heap outside. The number 12 is painted above the door.

"This is no place for a child," he says quietly, secretively. "Do not bring her here under *any* circumstances. You will remain in quarantine for now, but you are off the slave market."

He draws a wrap of cloth from his satchel and offers it to me. So startling are his words and demeanor that I raise my head, gauging his guarded expression with caution and confusion. With trembling hands, I reach out slowly, prepared for a flogging or a bullet, and am at a loss when he merely gives it to me.

"Hide it under your clothes, don't let the others see it. Report to the nurses inside, they're waiting for you."

Bewildered, I nod, slipping the object under my shirt without fully understanding what is happening. Heat radiates from within the cloth, something soft and warm I could never mistake for anything other than bread. He stares back down at me, impassive, but a strange flicker in his eyes reminds me of Gerhard Kurzbach, sets him apart from the men like Mengele and Schneider, men in whose eyes there was never any light to die.

"God be with you," he says with a subtle nod, then turns, leaving me before block twelve.

I cannot help but glare as I watch his back retreating. While a part of me wonders why he has fed me and what interest Bayla and I are to him, anger boils within my heart.

He knows what this place is, he is an active piece in this factory, he sent Bayla with me to the slaughterhouse. What could he possibly want from us? In what fantasy world does the wolf protect the sheep?

My stomach is clenched painfully to the point that my head spins and I think I might vomit, but I am not hungry enough to eat the bread a murderer has given me. I am about to throw his offering in the mud when I think of Bayla. She is the smallest of all the girls in the women's camp. She needs as much as I can get her.

I leave the bread tucked under my shirt and step inside the block. Row upon row of bunks line the inside of the barrack, packed tightly with women. Coughing and crying fill my ears, the heat of fever seeming to radiate from every direction, the usual stench of burning meat accompanied by those of sweat and feces.

At the entrance, I am greeted by a prisoner nurse. She examines me from head to toe before she finally says, "You're a lucky girl. Maybe you'll last a few months here. Come, Danuta is waiting for you."

Later, after I've returned to quarantine and suffered roll call, the nurse's words still echo hauntingly in my head. "*Lucky girl.*" The woman, Danuta, I was left with informed me I was to be a cleaner. I quickly learned that was just a euphemism for "diener" when she began instructing me to remove the dead bodies from the barrack. So many women, so many corpses to be carried or dragged to be disposed of outside for the lorries to then take to the furnace. "*Lucky girl...*"

There are those who say that death is peaceful; the books I used to read would describe one who had died as being at rest, their face a picture of relief, appearing to be asleep... but they *lie*. They all lie. Looking upon the grayish faces, I see only the same pain and distress in death that tortured them in life, and when discarding the remains of their starved, skeletal bodies like inanimate garbage, there is only hollow silence. Death is never peaceful. Those who die here, remnants of agony and dread are still frozen on their brutalized faces. Peace never found them, not even in death.

This is what Hell is truly like, I think, clutching my ration of crust. Bayla gratefully eats Obergefreiter Engel's bread and the few additional crusts I took from the infirmary... from the bodies

I threw outside. I ache and tremble with hunger, but for the first time in my life I have no appetite.

No matter what it may cost me, I remind myself. If keeping Bayla alive means taking from the dead, then that is what I must do. Clothing and food are no use to a corpse. The thought brings me a little solace. I shakily nibble my bread, resigning myself to the reality of what depravities survival will demand of me in this place.

"Miss? Miss, do you hear me?" I whisper to a woman lying motionless in an otherwise empty bunk.

Block twelve, which I have come to know as the typhus block, is eerily void of people. SS doctors came the day before yesterday, ordered the ill to line up, and took the majority of the women in addition to those who the cleaners had already removed. New patients have been admitted, but the empty spaces clouded by smoke and the wisps of fleeting memory where there used to be people will always be unsettling.

The woman's fluttering eyelids are the only movement that assures me she is still alive. Below her on the next wooden plank are three more women. One lies soundless and unmoving, and one coughs dryly, while the third weeps. These are the only differences in them I can see, for the sunken eyes, starved bodies, and sickly gray, corpse-like skin is the same in both the dead and the living.

Are they truly living, or just yet to die? Can one be dead and still breathing?

The crying woman shivers fiercely, grasping the sleeping woman beside her. "God, don't let them kill me," she mumbles over and over again.

Would God save us here? I wonder, moving on after I've found a weak pulse in the otherwise dead woman. Does the all-loving HaShem wish this upon us? As the Heavenly Father beyond the world and all human thought and reason, He is unequaled, unrivaled by any power. But does this all-loving, divine being incomparable to anything deny us our rescue? If so, and He is truly the creator and guardian of all in existence, does that mean He believes in and allows this mass murder? Has He the power to save and chooses not to, or has He not the power and wishes He could?

Either way, does it mean He is not all-loving as I've been raised to believe, or not the all-powerful, holy God whose word has ruled my life?

So much time to think in endless days and abominable work, and I wonder: where has God *ever* been? He's existed in my prayers, in the devotion of people who were once a part of my faith as much as God Himself. But now this seed of doubt that has been planted in my belief is beginning to sprout, roots slowly creeping deeper with every passing day they're nourished by this fertile, Godless land. Where does God exist anymore if not in my heart? Where is the angel that watches over all of us, the one Rabbi Amasai told us existed, the one I promised Bayla was real? Every whispered prayer to God has gone unanswered, and now, *here*, God has vanished.

A brush against my hand catches my attention, and I look down to find a woman reaching out for me. Her face is marked by irritated red spots, sores raw and open where she's scratched at flea bites. Now, it seems she's too weak to bother with scratching anymore, instead using every bit of strength in her malnourished body to touch my hand.

"Mazal? Mazal, my girl, is that you? Come to me, please, come to me," she gasps, her breaths labored, bony hands burning with fever against my skin. "I'm so happy you've come back. We're leaving now, you'll help me, won't you? It's all ended, have they told you yet?"

Sweet oblivion... may this reality live in her head until death takes her.

"Yes, yes they have told me," I whisper. "Where are we going?"

"Home, of course," she says dreamily, eyes misty with the faint glow of memories, lips parted in silent awe of some beautiful scene, and I find myself wishing I could see what she sees. "I'd like to go home now. Everyone's waiting... will you take me—"

Her last word—interrupted by a weak struggle for air—dies on her lips, and the woman who may have been Mazal's mother, aunt, sister, or friend falls limp beneath my hand and the dim light in her round eyes darkens to nothing.

God, please see her safely to Heaven, let her find her Mazal there. A quick prayer for this nameless woman's soul is all I can do for her as I quickly search her body for any rations of food, untie the bowl from the twine belt at her waist, then haul her starved form to the pile outside. I will keep the belt for myself, so I won't have to carry my bowl in my shirt, but I will sell her bowl to another prisoner. It's sure to buy me at least three days' worth of bread.

In the distance, the SS doctors are approaching on a lorry. A man sits in the passenger side, one arm rested out the window in relaxation. His white glove is a stark contrast to the desolate environment, and I wonder how often he must wash the blood from his hands to keep them so pure.

"I can't do this anymore..."

Ten days until the end of our six-week quarantine, and these are the first words I have heard Chasha speak in weeks. Naomi stills, hands cupped to raise another splash of coffee to wash her lice-ridden skin. Levana rears away as if she has been struck. I stare at the disquieting, bleary fog over Chasha's eyes, the hollowness of her cheeks and neck where skin clings raggedly to bone.

"How dare you say that!" Levana cries, dragging Chasha into her arms as if to pull her out of this awful stupor. "We're going to be alright, you hear me? We're going to live through this, someone has to. We'll be alright, Chasha! Have we come this far to give up now?"

"How much further?" Chasha whispers, her voice empty and distant, an entire ration of bread abandoned and ignored just inches from her fingertips. She hasn't eaten since the day before last.

"Until tomorrow," Levana says confidently. "And tomorrow, the day after that. Don't think of what's after it. We could be free by morning, or the morning after that. Will you want to have died then? If we survive today, we will be free tomorrow. *Tomorrow's winds will blow tomorrow.*"

She says this last phrase in Japanese, but she's repeated so many of these proverbs that even I have begun to recognize them. Chasha remains silent. I lean just slightly away from her, tightening my hold around Bayla's shoulders. So often have I seen that defeated, blank gaze from the women in the infirmary, and I know she is beyond saving. She is but a shadow, a *Muselmann* who has lost all hope and will, and her surrender is a disease. She's slipped quickly into despair over our days here, been abducted to slave over the dry earth digging trenches, carrying stones, and laying railroads, and she's stopped flinching when we try to nurse her wounds after being set upon by vicious dogs and bloodthirsty Kapos.

I glance down at Bayla as Levana whispers fervently in Chasha's ear. The thought of that same hopelessness flickering for just a brief moment in Bayla's eyes, imagining her slumped low, wandering without purpose, numb to the world and focused only on the electrified fence we're forbidden to go near...

"I can hide you," I offer quietly. "That's what we did for

Bayla in the ghetto. If you pretend to be ill, I can get you inside block twelve."

Chasha doesn't stir from her trance, but Levana's eyes light up hopefully.

"But it's dangerous," I warn. "SS doctors come almost every day for selections. As long as they think you look healthy, you'll be fine. You can get your strength back up and I'll bring you whatever I can."

"We can make it." Levana smiles with defiance. "We can make it, Chasha. We're strong enough. We'll rest for a while and be on our feet again before you know it."

The morning and evening pass and we line up for roll call, which is mercifully quick and only lasts for two hours, but we're not permitted to move for a while afterwards. Another functionary prisoner holding parcels stands at the Blockälteste's side, a frail man who's come all the way from the camp's mail block.

"It's not for Jews," I remember an older woman telling me the first time I saw this. *"Everyone can send and receive parcels, but not the Jews. Never for the Jews."*

I've never envied anyone more than the few women who gratefully accept the pitiful scraps that come in their parcels. They have someone beyond the fence—never from the men's camp, of course, that would get them killed, but there's someone in the outside world who thinks of them, someone who's alive and breathing, someone who loves them and sends all they can. Three women are called forward today.

Finally dismissed, we take our rations of bread and slip inside the barrack. There's only a few hundred of us, maybe half left of the thousand or so there used to be. Day by day they all become more unrecognizable, even my own friends are starting to look the same as the people I first saw from the train. It's horrifying how the human body can change, the astounding amount of abuse it can endure; shrivel like a flower deprived of water and sunlight into something neither dead nor living.

We huddle together atop the stone heating channel against the cold, trying to restrict ourselves to gnawing off only half of our crusty, solid rations. Levana insistently pushes pieces into Chasha's mouth, urging her to chew and swallow, which she does with a carelessness and foregone appetite I nearly envy. Bayla takes only a few bites of her own bread, then tucks more than half of it away under her shirt.

"Bayla, you need to eat more," I tell her.

"I ate yesterday," she whispers after glancing nervously around. "Yeva is the Kapo. She gives me carrots and potatoes, but she won't let me take them out of the kitchen. I can save this for tomorrow."

Truly examining her closely, feeling her ribs and back where she's grown awfully thin, I realize she isn't as malnourished as a child her age should have become by now. While her bones are still protruding and her skin is still sickly pale, there is a weak tinge of color to her cheeks, a little more solidity to her form.

"Yeva will watch her."

Did he know she would be fed there? Did he mean for them to take pity on her? Why would he?

The kitchen is such a desirable place to be. The work is indoors, out of the elements, safer from violence, and the opportunity for food is inconceivable. Only the bigger women with the strength to haul around the heavy pots of soup have even a prayer of getting into the kitchens. It's not the kind of place Bayla ever should have had the chance to get remotely close to. In reality, her presence in the camp at my side in this very moment is much like her position in the kitchens; Obergefreiter Engel is the only reason she's here.

She was never meant to see what lies beyond the train. She should have gone with our parents to the glow, where I would have followed... I wonder, did Mama and Papa find each other at the end? Did they share a smile, thinking we'd all see each other again? Were they together when they realized it wasn't water falling into the chambers? Did they despair in those final moments of terror, fear the same fate would soon befall their daughters? Or did they die alone?

Please, let them have been together—

"Hodaya?"

I could sob with relief as a stranger's voice tears me from these dark thoughts. In surprise, I look at the woman crouched beside the heating channel, cradling a parcel to her chest. I recognize her stunningly blue eyes, then the number beneath the white triangle on her shirt that reads A—30877. She was one of the two German-speakers Obergefreiter Engel collected, and she's been a messenger to the camp officials ever since.

How did she know my name?

Our gazes meet for a brief moment before she looks at Bayla. Seeming assured, she quickly draws a cloth-covered object from her parcel and pushes it into my hands before shuffling away with a pair of leather shoes.

The scent of meat and seasoning radiates from within the cloth. I shift further onto the heating channel, shielding it with my body as I peek inside. My mouth waters and I see rather than feel myself trembling. In my hands, there lies half a loaf of sliced bread dampened by butter and a handful of strips of chicken.

Bayla gasps and Naomi and Levana gawk at the feast so freely given to me. I immediately pull them closer, shushing them as I begin to pass around pieces of bread and chicken. We can hardly think to question where it has come from or why it was given to me as we huddle together, devouring everything before any of the others realize what we have and think to fight for it.

Soon everything is gone, the wonderful taste and warmth

still lingering on my tongue and fingers as I lick them clean, the pain in my stomach eased just slightly. As I am about to discard the empty cloth I notice a slip of paper, which was hidden beneath our banquet, damp and stained. Curiously, I unfold it. There are four words written neatly in black ink.

God be with you.

I freeze, the image of a man with a scarred cheek coming unbidden to my mind, and feel as though I may retch.

17

OCTOBER 13, 1943

LAST DAY OF QUARANTINE

Ten days and seven selections have gone since I managed to bring Levana and Chasha into block twelve. The two days the SS doctors didn't come to the infirmary were yesterday and the day before. Before that, they returned every day, sometimes Mengele with his white gloves and pleasant demeanor, other times Hans König or Werner Rohde. In ten days, they've sent over six hundred women to the gas chambers.

No one is supposed to know about it. Like lambs in the slaughterhouse, we're not supposed to know death is inevitable until the knife is coming down on us. But we all know. Prisoners talk, Kapos and block elders who aren't supposed to speak of it can sometimes be overheard whispering about the "gassing," hundreds of transports can be glimpsed walking to the crematoriums never to be seen again. We all know what the stench is. We all know what they're burning. Thousands of people don't just vanish into thin air. They are the true lambs, for how could they possibly fathom the truth even after the worst things they've been through, when they've just been told they're going to have showers? Some of us still can't.

Afternoon approaches with a palpable chill despite the humidity of the day. Three rations of dried bread are tucked under my arm as I shuffle to the back of the block, three pieces I've accumulated from the dead over the course of the morning. On the third tier of bunks, Levana and Chasha lie together.

A quick glance assures me none of the staff are paying me any attention. "Here, eat as much as you can," I whisper, dropping the bread into Levana's hands. "I'll try to find more."

"Thank you, Hodaya." Levana smiles gratefully and rouses Chasha from her sleep.

Chasha, though consistent rest and more food has lightened the rings under her eyes and brought the tinge of color back to her cheeks, still hasn't spoken. She's finally eating on her own again, after the first three days of Levana forcibly shoving food into her mouth, and she's even begun to look at me when I come to the bunk, recognition flickering in her eyes.

"Are they coming today?" Levana asks, looking nervously at the door.

Two days... I doubt they'll stay away for three. It isn't just in block twelve that the SS doctors have failed to appear. Not one of them has been seen in any of the sick blocks.

"They must be," I respond, flashing Chasha an anxious look.

"She can make it," Levana says sternly, more of an assurance to herself than me. "She's strong enough now, she can jump or run, whatever they want."

"Are you sure? We could try to hide her again."

The risk of Chasha being taken has been too great and remains still. Mengele has only come once so far, and didn't even enter the block. It fell upon the staff to herd all the women outside while the SS took down numbers and marked the bunks, so it was easier to "forget" Chasha inside while the others had to run in front of the doctors. König and Rohde have been the ones to conduct selection since then, often more disorganized than Mengele, and Chasha has evaded their notice, being hidden under straw mats and bodies while Levana participates.

Levana gazes at her dazed sister for a while, the weight of concern and determination heavy on her slumping shoulders. "You can make it, Chasha, you're strong. Remember, we'll be free tomorrow. Don't let them win. *Continuing on is power.*" Her last words, whispered in Japanese, bring a flicker to Chasha's eyes and she breathes deeply.

Each of Levana's proverbs seems to stir something within Chasha. Perhaps it is the memory of a happy life before this place that gives her strength more so than food and rest, but it makes me believe hope might not be lost for her after all.

"Do you really believe that?" I wonder, searching Levana's face for any sign of insincerity.

She regards me with all the patience and tenderness I'd expect from an older sister. "Of course I do—I must. What meaning does life have if we don't believe in anything?" Her smile, though carrying only a broken fragment of the joy it once held, is consoling. "I believe we're stronger than them, no matter what they do to us. I believe that one day God will have justice, and some of us must be here to see it."

Because many won't. Images that have long haunted my sleep surface in my mind: stepping off the train and into the fire, kissing Papa goodbye for what I didn't know would be the last time, watching Mama disappear toward the glow. All those people who came from Bochnia with us, the little boy and his sisters, the children and their grandparents, the mothers and fathers with their babies... they're all dead now. Try as I might to bar them from my thoughts, it is impossible to forget. Each new woman entering quarantine who cries for the murder of her parents or children, each brief glance at a person walking to the gas chambers, the stench of flesh and smoke that chokes my raw throat, is a cruel reminder. All of them, tortured and murdered by the heartless uniforms, cremated and discarded to remain only in the memory of ghosts and photographs... *If there is any justice, any love in God's heart, He'll punish these soulless killers for their sins.*

"I'd like to see it," I whisper, hardly recognizing the vengeful voice emanating from me.

"We will. Just remember, for now we only need to get to tomorrow."

Returning her reassuring smile, I nod, and am moving to climb back down when a voice hoarse with disuse stops me.

"And tomorrow we'll be free..." Chasha blinks wearily, her strangely steady hands reaching for a piece of bread.

"Yes, Chasha, that's right!" Levana cries, tears springing to her eyes. "Tomorrow we'll be free, we just have to make it there!"

For the first time in days, finally seeing the glimmer of life reignited in Chasha's eyes, the overwhelming hope in Levana's voice as she goes on reciting proverbs, I'm certain that they will.

An insistent hand suddenly tugs me down from the bunk. "What are you doing? They're coming soon, we must be ready. Mengele is coming today," Danuta mutters as she leads me back to the front of the block where the other staff are gathering, and his name alone sends cold terror coursing through my veins.

A group of SS doctors and guards enter the infirmary, Mengele in the lead, hair and uniform groomed to handsome perfection, white gloves clasped behind his back. Obergefreiter Engel brings up the rear of the group, his eyes quickly finding me among the other nurses and cleaners, betraying a look of remorse before looking away.

"Everyone up! Line up!" an SS guard shouts, he and his men striking and kicking the bunks as they walk the length of the block, cringing in revulsion from the women as they climb down. Levana and Chasha slip out of their bunk, stronger and healthier than the others, and I nearly cry with relief at the sight of Chasha standing solid and ready.

They can make it. They've survived nearly two weeks in block twelve, they're much stronger than they were. Mengele wouldn't take them; they're clearly recovering well, they're still useful, they'll be fine.

Patiently, we wait for the order to go outside and run, or for the women to line up to jump over the heating channel, but it never comes. Unusually, the women too sick to come down do not have their bunks marked for death with white chalk. Instead, they are forcibly pulled down and shoved into line. Obergefreiter Engel approaches the head nurse, jaw clenched, and she hands him a list of the seriously ill patients who will automatically be selected, but, strangely, the SS do not demand the list from the nurses as they usually do. Something is wrong. This selection isn't like the others.

None of the SS doctors have moved from the entrance, not even Mengele, who usually takes great pleasure in selection, who often walks up and down the lines, examining bodies, deciding how much longer they'll be useful for.

Obergefreiter Engel looks over the list, then approaches Mengele. "Perhaps it would be prudent to wait a little longer, Hauptsturmführer Mengele. Few of these women are—"

"Women?" Mengele chuckles as if he's just been told a ridiculous joke. He indicates the patients with a wave of his gloved hand. "Look at these ghastly creatures. You think *these* are women? Hardly. You've been away from home for too long. Perhaps you should pay the village a visit this weekend, find a girl to remind you what a woman is."

A few SS guards snicker at Mengele's jab, but Engel ignores it. "Prisoners is what I meant to say, Hauptsturmführer. Only fifty or so are listed as gravely ill," he says, indicating the list.

"Many others may still prove useful. Perhaps we should wait to empty this—"

Mengele's white glove rises, immediately cutting off Engel's words. "You're a military man, Obergefreiter. Tell me, what is the oath you swore when you joined the Wehrmacht?"

Engel stiffens almost imperceptibly. "I swear to the leader, Adolf Hitler, as the supreme commander of the German armed forces, loyalty, and bravery. I pledge the leader and those superiors appointed by him, obedience until death."

"Good." Mengele nods, all traces of amusement vanished from his stern face. "Then you understand that as a subordinate, when a superior desires your input, he'll *tell you* what it is."

"Yes, Hauptsturmführer. My apologies." Engel dips his head, lips pressed into a firm line.

Suddenly, something brings the smile back to Mengele's expression and a sickeningly excited glint to his eyes.

A shiver runs down my spine, each hair that remains on my body standing on end. I follow his gaze with trepidation, shifting anxiously when my sight settles on Levana and Chasha once again. Mengele starts down the block, each step a foreboding echo, the pleasant expression never once slipping from his face.

He's nothing like the wolves who terrorize this place, and yet he frightens me in a way the Kapos and SS could only ever dream of. The wolves are transparent as glass. If one approaches with its teeth bared, there is no mistaking its intentions, the savagery it will unleash, the satisfaction it will take from tearing you apart and drinking your blood. A fox is much smarter, so much so that, even if he stalks you and approaches with bared fangs, it is still possible to think he smiles, and mistake him for a friend.

Mengele stops in front of Levana and Chasha, smiling widely with excitement. "Twins, I see. Complete mirrors, I don't think I've ever seen a pair so similar. How could I have missed you? How wonderful you're still together! What are your names?"

A pin could be heard dropping two blocks over. Timidly, without raising her head, Levana answers. The fox smiles, raising a gloved hand to turn and inspect her features.

"Give me your numbers," Mengele says, and I notice even the SS men eyeing him uneasily. "I think you'd be most beneficial to my studies. There will be special treatment for you, of course, there is for all of my children. Obergefreiter! Document these two for my studies, and that will be all I require of you today."

They have no choice but to follow him back to the group of SS doctors, but there is no fear in their eyes... like lambs willingly following the fox to the cave. Levana catches my gaze, assured and relieved as she holds Chasha's hand, and nods subtly as they pass, as if to say, *don't worry, we're strong. We'll be alright.*

No! No, you won't be alright! He'll kill you! Run! Don't let him take you! I want to scream at her, run after them and hold them back, beg and plead this Angel of Death for mercy... but nothing comes. Rooted in place, I am too stunned, too horrified to move, my voice sticks in my throat, tears sting my eyes, and Levana and Chasha disappear through the doors just as Mengele shouts, "Today, we are emptying this block!"

Rushed outside in a blur of tears and confusion, the staff all link hands like a makeshift fence, surrounding the door and the German trucks, ensuring the patients herded out of the block cannot escape. I frantically search for Levana and Chasha, and find both of them with Mengele beside one of the trucks. As one might with a child, Mengele smiles at them, and from his pocket he draws and offers something. Hesitantly, with growing ease, they each take a sweet from his hand, and are then ushered to sit in the padded seats.

No numbers are taken. No one is ordered to run or jump. The prisoners showing signs of improving health and the prisoners too sick to move are all loaded into the trucks. Those who collapse into the mud must be thrown. A woman fallen to the ground grabs my ankle, screaming and crying, "Please! Please, don't!" The betrayal that glistens in her terrified, darkened eyes as I break her grip on my leg, then lift her up with the aid of another nurse, is forever seared into my memory. Danuta screams in pure misery as she loads up a young girl, and scrambles sobbing onto the truck right after her, fighting away the other cleaners and nurses who try to hold her back. There isn't a woman—patient or staff—who isn't weeping, begging for mercy or forgiveness, screaming in helpless anguish while the SS look on with indifference.

A truck roars to life, and through tears and drops of rain beginning to fall I catch a glimpse of Mengele's white glove resting contentedly out of the window.

"Levana! Chasha!" I scream, my voice drowned out by the wails of grief and rage, lost to the downpour of water from the black sky as the truck pulls away. I sprint after my friends, but make it only a few steps when an arm knocks the breath from my body and drags me back. Struggling to breathe, reaching in vain for Levana and Chasha as if that alone could pull them back to my arms, I grasp only the freezing air, and the world distorts to a blank haze.

A man's voice reaches me, again and again demanding the same thing: "What were you doing?" The familiarity of the voice slowly draws me back from inside my mind, first registering the inside of the block, then a green uniform blocking the gateway to the horror outside.

"What were you thinking? Were you going after them? Is that what you were doing?"

They're gone! He took them! They were well and healing and he took them!

My heart burns, aching deep at the core as I gasp for air. The world seems to spin, blurring here and there, and suddenly my legs are gone beneath me.

My fault! My fault! I brought them here! I knew how dangerous it was and I brought them anyway! They'll be killed and it's my fault! He took them, but I killed them, just like I killed Noam!

"I killed them!" I sob, the last glimpse of their ruined, beautiful faces, the lingering memory of his terrified, innocent eyes all haunting me. "Please, forgive me!"

But how can they forgive me if they are dead? God cannot forgive man's sins against man, only they can forgive each other. But if only the dead can forgive their murderer, how do they forgive? Are people worthy of heaven not bound to forgive even their murderer? If it is only who we do unto who can forgive us, then by what right does God decide who must still be cleansed in Hell? If all those Mengele has murdered forgive him, even if he doesn't repent, would God forgive him as well?

"Hodaya!"

Does God care at all? Why watch the genocide man inflicts knowing only they can forgive each other? Why give sentient beings the free will to do this kind of evil unto each other at all? If it is the almighty Creator who gives us the ability to commit evil, does that not mean He also has the ability to do evil?

"Hodaya!"

Obergefreiter Engel's arms as he kneels before me are a stiff prison around my limp body. I struggle from his grip, shuddering in disgust, the places his touch has burned me stinging like salt rubbed in an open wound.

"Did you really mean to follow them? To what end? What purpose would your death serve for you and your sister?" he asks, gently and not so accusingly as before.

Nails biting forcefully into my palms, I scramble to my feet, desperate not to be below him. He doesn't react to my reckless move, allowing me to look down on him, his face a fox's mask of regret and sadness.

"What does it matter to you? How many have *you* killed?" These words that will surely be my death sentence are spat before I can stop them, and my heart drops.

He stands with a bit of difficulty. "Many... but that was war, *this...* this is..." he rasps, a faraway glaze over his eyes. "There are none that I don't wish I could take back, but I have killed no prisoners here, no one innocent."

"What?" The word is less than a whisper, a stunned, doubtful breath.

What is a soldier in Auschwitz if not a murderer?

His lips have fallen into a pained, exhausted frown. "I was a soldier in the 9th Panzer Division before I was injured. Now, I work for the administration. I hardly leave my desk unless supervisors are in short supply. That is why I was at the train the night you arrived—but I have *never* chosen or sent anyone for death. And even if I wanted to, I don't have the power to decide. I am not SS, my war crosses only give me some honorary authority."

Perhaps it is the remorse in his voice, or the pain in his glossy eyes, but I find myself believing him, and speaking in spite of my fear. "But why?"

He swallows thickly, averting his gaze. "I was a good soldier, loyal, ruthless, blindly obedient... the only things Hitler needs a soldier to be good at. I wasn't a good man, and maybe I'm still not. A lot has happened between back then and now. A lot can change a man... a lot has changed me." He hesitates, then shakes his head. "It's a long story, and it's not a good one either. I will tell you one day if that is what you want, but you have to live. And you will if there's anything I can do about it."

"But *why?*" I nearly sob. "Why do you care what happens to

us? Why did you tell Mengele to let my little sister live? Why did you stop me now?"

His eyes hold a tragic understanding that makes me furious to see. *We are* not *the same, Obergefreiter. We will* never *be alike,* I think bitterly.

"I lost my own little brother to this war. I know what it's like to blame yourself... I wanted to die too, sometimes still, and I might have back then," he mutters, his anguished eyes beseeching me. "But there were better people who saved me, even though I didn't deserve it. I want to deserve it. I want to be the good man they thought I was. I don't want this to happen to you. You are not animals, you are human beings, but I can't help everyone, no matter how much I wish I could. No matter what I do, nothing ever seems to be enough..." He straightens suddenly, composing himself with such startling ease it is like he has donned a mask. He steps forward, placing his large hands on either side of my face so I have no choice but to look him directly in the eye. "Your sister needs you. Don't give in, you can't."

With these final words, he disappears as quickly as he came, leaving me alone and quivering in the middle of the infirmary. The faint rumble of retreating trucks, cries of agony, fear, and defeat ring deafeningly across the camp. I cover my ears, digging my palms deep and painful to block out the noise, the sound of the Obergefreiter's voice, and sink once again to the ground, sopping wet as the storm rages in time with my despair.

18

NOVEMBER 27, 1943

Days all bleed into one long, agonizing nightmare we cannot awake from, and yet it has only been a little over a month since our quarantine ended. Counting the days until each Sunday has been the only way to try to keep track of time. It is the only way I know that today—when the SS explode into the barrack in the darkness of the early morning, absolutely giddy with excitement —is Rosh Chodesh Kislev.

"Up! Get Up!" they shout and are soon joined by the Block-älteste and the Kapos in their delight. "A new month, a new day! Get up! Celebrate Kislev with us! It's a new moon today!"

I am jolted from the middle tier out of a disturbed sleep as a Kapo drags me by the wrist like a doll and drops me. I gasp, confused and weightless for a heartbeat until I land on a woman crawling out from the bottom bunk. Naomi and Bayla tumble down after me, crushed and trampled by the women scrambling blearily from the top. All the while, the SS continue to shout and smile.

"Quickly! Schnell! Everyone outside! Roll call!"

"It's Rosh Chodesh! Aren't you happy? Smile! Pray! It's a new month to celebrate!"

"Good month! Chodesh tov! We wish you all a chodesh tov!"

The approaching winter assaults me tenfold outside of the block. My thin clothes swiftly dampen and stick to my body, the freezing mud and sleet stab brutally to the bone, and each puff of white air that escapes my chattering teeth and sore nose chills my numbing face.

I pull Bayla and Naomi with me as I fight my way through the others, ruthlessly shoving, stepping over those who trip and fall, elbowing, pinching, and scratching a grueling path to the back of the lines. Six weeks in quarantine was mere child's play compared to the harsh wilderness of the camp. There, we were all on equal ground, all of us afraid and lost, desperately trying to learn the ways of survival. Here, it is every person for themselves. One must be hardened to survive, especially on a day like this.

The Germans celebrate the holidays of our Jewish religion more than we ourselves, they know the days, the prayers, and the traditions more than us. They love to rouse us before four o'clock, call us merrily outside for selections, demand that we recite our prayers while they carry out floggings and mark down numbers for the gas chambers. If there is anything the Nazis love more than killing and terrifying Jews, it is reminding us that they alone control our fate, not us, not God.

Beside me, Bayla shivers like a leaf in the wind, her lips tinged with blue as she stands stiff and waiting. Her hand slides timidly into mine and flexes fearfully. Naomi sways slightly with exhaustion, and I firmly correct her posture, grasping her hand. She doesn't acknowledge me, doesn't lower her head in prayer like she usually does. She only stares blindly ahead, numb to the world.

And truly, I cannot blame her. Every day, the world dies a little more, the awful ache in my bones numbs a little deeper, the obsessive hunger dulls a little further. Day by day, I understand the *Muselmanns*—the ones who have lost all hope, the ones who no longer live, who simply trudge aimlessly through the days waiting for death—a little more. Now, I cannot find it within myself to blame my friend for the way her mind and heart withered, for the way this place consumed and murdered her hope. Every day, I wonder if it was my friend who believed in tomorrow who may have been the truly foolish one. Now, I cannot bear to even think their names. It is far too painful, and I must smother anything that threatens the protective numbness I've built in my mind. It is the only way to keep from falling into despair.

Eager to begin, the SS conduct roll call themselves, and have all of the numbers tallied and matching in under two hours.

"Why so glum? It's a new month, Jews!" an SS woman calls out, bundled in a heavy gray coat and tall boots that keep her clean and warm. She strides before us, cheeks and nose rosy with the cold, curly blond hair done up nicely.

Resentment. Disgust. Each of these pricks at the bottom of my heart, demanding to be felt, the first powerful emotions that have penetrated the despondent fog in my mind since the day in the infirmary.

I wonder how cold she thinks she is, I'm sure that wool coat is just terribly heavy compared to our thin prisoner uniforms. Her poor feet must be so sore in those cramped boots. What we wouldn't give to trade our clogs for those. That beautiful hair is probably such a hassle in the mornings, she must have to sit in front of the mirror for an hour to tame those curls. I've forgotten what it's like to have hair.

"Come on now, say your prayers! Lord Almighty, God of our forefathers!" she begins mockingly, walking up and down the lines.

Like mindless machines who know nothing but obedience, every voice instinctively starts up to continue the prayer. Some weep as they do this and are picked out of the crowd by the SS to join the growing number of selected. Others pray fervently, even now never having forgotten their faith. Eventually, their voices, along with my own, all fade into nothing. It is an empty silence; not peaceful or tense, just... empty. Like there is nothing else that exists in the universe, nothing but my own acknowledgement of the gaping void.

Hodaya would have been shocked, appalled even, by A—30972's blatant neglect, but I think a part of her would be understanding. I wonder if God would be angry or sad for my depleting faith, or if He would understand?

Two girls a few rows ahead of me are selected by an SS man. Another frail woman nearby wavers in her footing and is dragged away. The woman directly behind me falters in her prayer, then vanishes. The SS are indiscriminate in their selection, carrying on completely at random. There is no difference between the strong or weak, the young and inexperienced girls or the older women who've survived the longest, those who follow orders or those who fail. Any can be taken. There is no system, no strategy. Life or death hinges upon the sharp double-edged sword of chance.

A hand covered by a warm black glove gestures in my peripheral vision. "You."

No! Not yet!

Heart surging to my throat, I dart out and snatch Naomi's hand as she makes to numbly follow the SS officer, then pull her back to my side. The SS who chose her for death has already moved on, never thinking a prisoner would dare to disobey, and doesn't notice that Naomi doesn't follow.

Maybe the Germans are the only ones who have any say in our lives now, and God has cruelly abandoned us to this horrific fate. Maybe we will all die here and no one will ever live to see vengeance exacted. Maybe they'll take us today or tomorrow, maybe not for a month or another year, maybe it will be by the hands of our peers and not the SS, and there will be no one left to remember us if this ever ends.

But not yet... Until that day comes, we're not dead yet.

Two hundred women are marched away to the death block to await gassing, and hundreds from neighboring barracks head straight for the gas chambers. Pushing their names, numbers, and faces out of mind, we all huddle, standing together like horses, desperate for warmth, hungrily awaiting our cold soup, and dreading the coming selections.

It is hours before the whistles blow and the SS decide we're allowed to be fed, hours in which the prisoners in the kitchen have had unsupervised access to the soup...

Worried, I pull Bayla and Naomi along with me closer to the front of the line. If we're too far back today, they might run out of food. However, our placement doesn't matter once the shouting starts.

At the front, the Kapos are screaming at each other, accusing the girls from the kitchens of eating the soup, fighting one another over rations for their blocks, claiming others are getting too much or they are getting too little. It isn't the first time a quarrel like this has broken out, and we all sag, deflated and starving, as we wait. The Kapos don't really care about ensuring we have enough food, they only want to prove who is more important, who has more authority.

My heart drops when the kitchen staff lift the cauldron and haul it away to another block.

We all linger for a while before we dejectedly disperse and trudge back to our small groups with our clogs stuck in the mud and early snow. Bayla's stomach growls loudly, and she whimpers, grasping her empty stomach in pain. It happens more and more frequently every passing day.

"He's gone..." Naomi mutters woefully, seeming to speak

more to herself than me, and her once-beautiful green eyes are glazed. She is much paler than she used to be, thin beyond health, the bones in her face and chest protruding rigidly from beneath her gray skin, and I can't help but remember that she used to be taller than me. "God... Adam... they're gone, I know it... I don't want to go on."

"Don't say that," I say sharply. "Don't you dare say things like that out loud."

"It's done, Hodaya... I don't know what, but we've done it. God has grown tired of us and our wrongdoings... we have turned away from Him."

"You would blame us for where we are today? That is wrong, Naomi, completely wrong! We are not at fault," I snap, taking her into my arms. "You are alive today! God allowed me to save you. Is that not proof that He wants you to live, that you can?"

"But I don't want to..." she whispers, and my heart shatters like glass.

We have turned away from God? What sins have the men, women, and children committed that God believes their bodies and souls must perish in gas and fire? What have those of us still living done that is so horrible God believes we must die slowly, in agony? How could a soul as good and kind as Naomi who has never done wrong by anything in this world stand *here* and say that we have turned away from God? We are the ones who have kept our faith in Him and He has left us to die.

With a fury I have never felt for anything, a disdain that I have not held so deeply even for the Germans, I mutter, "We have *not* turned away from God. It is God who has turned away from *us*."

Her voice is a mere broken whisper when she speaks. "Hodaya, I don't know how much longer I can go on—"

"Not yet! Not yet, do you hear me? I forbid you from despair, Naomi Gurewitz! One more day! We'll live, I swear," I insist firmly, almost angrily, cradling her brittle body to my chest the way she once did, a lifetime ago in Bochnia, but it is like hugging a corpse. "Adam is waiting for you! He is, I know it, and you're going to have a little Permilia and Wilhelm! When we get home and have dinner with the Chornovils, *I'll* buy all our food this time. And I still haven't taught you German. I'm a terrible teacher, the worst, but I'll teach you. I promise. Best friends, remember? You're the best friend I've ever had! I love you, I won't let them take you! We're going to live! Tomorrow, I promise!"

Wearily, she turns her gaze to meet mine, heavy with despondence and misery. Two empty holes fill the places where her loving eyes once were, and a knife pierces my heart as I realize the Naomi I once knew has already died. Life has lost all meaning for her. And what meaning does life have if we believe in nothing? What is there for her beyond tomorrow but me? And she might not even have *me* tomorrow.

A part of me sympathizes with her desire for death. If I could, if I had no one else to live for, perhaps I would join her in despair and fade from this world. The desire to live through this wretched existence was taken from me long ago, but my will to live through it remains unbroken, and my will is Bayla. She could never survive on her own in this place, she was never meant to. To die would be to condemn her as well.

And you've already condemned one sister, an accusatory voice whispers hatefully in my mind. How many days have I been so lost in grief for my friends, consumed only with surviving one minute at a time, that I have neglected her? How many days has Naomi tried to comfort me and I have not heard her? How long was it before my anguish became infectious? When did she look at me and realize—like the day I glimpsed that faraway, hopeless look in my friend's eyes—that we were beyond saving?

· · ·

"You dirty thieves! This block hasn't been fed yet!" a woman screams, drawing our attention. Zlata, a broad Kapo, is all but foaming at the mouth, lashing her whip at the staff from the kitchens.

The Russian woman who Bayla and the Obergefreiter called Yeva matches Zlata's ire despite the striking difference in size.

"Thieves? You dare call *me* a thief!" Yeva growls, never flinching from Zlata's whip. She rips an empty pot from a kitchen girl and swings it with all her body weight to knock Zlata to the ground. "We take nothing from you! I think you steal more than anyone! I think you eat as much as ten girls, pig! You eat last now!"

Again, for the second time in an hour, we watch with painful longing as the kitchen staff haul the cauldrons away to yet another block.

Zlata scrambles from the ground, shaking with fury, screeching incomprehensibly like a fiend after Yeva, cracking her whip viciously at the air. Everyone within fifty feet of the fuming woman has scattered in fear, desperate to never enter the line of her murderous sight. Zlata's eyes search greedily for something to unleash her rage upon, and snap sharply in our direction, locking on a target.

The entire world seems to fall from beneath my feet. At my side, Bayla leans helplessly against me, a vulnerable lamb oblivious to the danger swiftly approaching, her yellow patch blindingly bright against this bleak, colorless place. After such humiliation, such blatant undermining of her authority, there will be no mercy for the unfortunate soul who faces Zlata's wrath.

"Run and hide!" I hiss, shoving Bayla into Naomi's arms as Zlata starts toward us. The firm order appears to register in

Naomi's wretched face and she nods, stumbling away with Bayla.

God, if I am to die today, let my sisters be saved.

"Zlata!" I bellow, drowning in both relief and dread when she stops dead in her tracks, pursuit of Bayla and Naomi forgotten.

God, if I am to die today, let my death be swift.

I am breathless; the heat burns under my tingling skin like hot coals. The vivid image of Noam's kind, hazel eyes warms my wildly racing heart. "Szkop! Niemiaszek! Szwab!"

God, if I am to die today, let it not be for nothing.

I force my trembling legs to stand rigid, force my gaze to never lower from Zlata's stunned, furious face. If these are to be my last moments of life, I will not waste them running. If these labored breaths are the last taste of air I shall have, then I will spend them screaming all the rage I have long locked away.

"Fucking pig! Schwein! Look at you now, a prisoner with *Jews!* Not even the Reich wants you! Murderer!" I scream, hurling every insult I can remember the SS spitting at us. "Dreck! Mist! Blöde Hund! Schmutziger Wachhund! Damn your master race! Death to Hitler! Death to the Reich!"

The solid force of a truck slams into me. Stunned by the impact, I stumble, and a glimpse of Zlata's purple, enraged face is all I see before fists smash into my head. I crumple into the wet, freezing mud. The air is abruptly knocked from my lungs as Zlata throws her entire weight onto me, focused solely on beating every defiant breath from my body. My vision is gone, clouded by red, smothered by mud, and my nose is over-whelmed with a metallic stench. A brutal swing stings the side of my jaw. Searing pain tears through my mouth as several teeth are ripped from my gums, blood dribbling from my lips. The beating never seems to end. All sense of time has fled and all I can do is focus on breathing, crying out at the awful pain when I do. Seconds turn into minutes and minutes blur into hours, and life suddenly grinds to a black, bloody halt.

God... where are You?

Thud... thud... thud...

A drum beats somewhere, the wind whistles, the entire world throbs like a fading pulse, a dim stream of light trickles over my eyes. The desire to move is overpowered by numbness, a crushing weakness I never imagined existed. Is this death?

Thud... thud... thud...

The drum continues to beat, this time from within my chest, and a raw ache slowly begins to register in my ringing, clouded head. No, this isn't death, and that is no drum.

Thud... thud... thud...

My heart perseveres, clinging to life by a hair, forcing blood to pump through my veins, pushing my lungs to inhale. Choking, I sputter, and warm blood spatters across my bruising face.

Someone gasps in astonishment, "She's not dead!"

I struggle to open my sore eyes, and a wonderful if obscured vision graces me. Bayla kneels at my side, sobbing, her beautiful face untouched, and Naomi reaches out with a scarf, her eyes a little clearer than before. She begins to wipe my swollen face and I wince, trying to turn away, but she insistently continues. "Hodaya, you have to stand up, or they're going to take you to the infirmary."

A sob escapes my throat, stabbing my stomach and chest like a knife. *No, don't let them take me! I'm not dead! Not yet!*

Coughing, moaning at the awful discomfort with every movement, I struggle to raise my head. Naomi's hand quickly shoots up to smother my scream, accidentally ramming hard against my broken nose.

"Shh! Don't yell!" Naomi urges as I weep into her hand, each heaving breath intensifying the pain.

"Are you going to be alright?" Bayla cries, her tears dirt

streaks against her pale cheeks.

"Yes, Bayla, she'll be fine," Naomi answers for me. "Come on, Hodaya, stand up."

Closer to death than life, I whimper and struggle to regain my feet, longing for the sweet numbness of unconsciousness, trying to focus on anything but the pain.

Painting! I loved painting! Whatever happened to all my works, all the bright suns and clear skies? What else? Of course, books! We used to have a whole shelf of books! Alma too. Oh, I hated that hideous little doll! The blond babydoll Naomi gave to Bayla was so much prettier. I suppose Alma would think I look far uglier than she is right now. I wonder if she's still at home, wondering where her family went? Or did the Nazis throw her out too?

Naomi's hand remains firmly pressed against my lips and muffled cries. My legs buckle beneath me, and I slip back to the ground, sobbing as lightning stings my legs and a stampede crushes my chest. To move at all is to strengthen the pain, carve each lash and cut even deeper, break every cracked bone even further, and each breath burns through me like fire.

God, why have You brought us here? Why must my sisters' lives for today mean my near death? Am I meant to die here? Is that what You want?

I don't know how Naomi managed to support my weight against her for the rest of the day, how she kept me out of Zlata's sight, how I wasn't taken during another selection, how they hauled me into a bunk. The day is a dark, excruciating blur in my mind, a hazy recollection of icy rain, splotches of black and red, and I don't remember if any of us ate today.

How will I work now? How will I survive selections? We all look like living skeletons, but I must surely look like a walking corpse.

"Mama—I mean, Hodaya?" Bayla whispers hoarsely, and her hasty correction draws me slightly back from delirium. "When can we go see Mama and Papa?"

All this time, these endless, dreadful days since the moment we parted at the crossroads... all this time and never once has she asked about our parents, when we'll see them again like I promised her we would. Does she truly not know? After all this time, does she still not know where the smoke comes from? It takes several long minutes of scouring my fractured mind before I realize no one has ever told her the truth. And why would they? We all know, even if we're not supposed to, but who would dare to speak such things aloud?

"Not yet," I groan, sobbing. The words sting agonizingly in my heart and broken ribs, and I let the tears for our parents flow as I never have before, using my physical pain as an excuse to cry. And while everything aches, it is reassurance that I am still alive. "Not yet."

19

NOVEMBER 28, 1943

A new day breaks in darkness, and the promise of death hangs heavy over me like a noose. Zlata nearly killed me yesterday, and, though she left me for dead, her ire will not be forgotten when she realizes that I survived. The things I said are cause enough for the gas chambers. She has certainly told the SS about me by now and given them my number. They will come for me today.

This is the day I die. The thought washes over me with an eerie, calm acceptance. *At least now I can be with Mama and Papa...*

Naomi lies beside me, still asleep, but even now the pain is laced deep within her face. Sleep is supposed to be the time of comfort, the one time all traces of worry vanish from a face and you can see it settle into peace and youth for a while. Not anymore. Even as she breathes and shivers, she looks dead to me.

This is the day we all die.

Naomi will not survive when I am gone. She is far too good a soul to live much longer. All the decent, kind people who come here are the first to lose their faith, the first to die. How could people who believe the best of this world come to terms with such evil? It is people like Zlata—the ones who can detach themselves from all guilt and emotion—who live the longest. They are the only ones who *can* live.

Shivering, Bayla has wound herself around me like a blanket, her face buried in my neck against the cold.

Bayla... how will you survive when they kill me? Yeva will feed her, even if the Kapos say she is a waste of rations. But how will she fend for herself without any allies to protect her? No one can survive on their own, and a girl as small and vulnerable as she will be an easy target. Someone will steal her bowl and rations and clothes, someone will beat or flog her until she cannot walk, the SS will take her to the gas chambers.

Warmth trails down and dampens my cheeks as I try to make out the faint outline of her face, search for a shadow of the sweet, innocent little girl she's always been, and cradle her starving body against mine. With a heavy, sinking heart, I weep silently in the darkness, and when the whistles cut through the air I wish so desperately that I could have given her more than ten years.

"I'm sorry Mama, I'm sorry Papa. I tried. I *really* did," I cry.

"Raus! Raus! Schnell! Zählappell! Everyone outside!"

With as much haste as a person in my condition can manage, I crawl out of the bunk, slip my clogs off, and reluctantly step into the chilling, muddy mess that is the barrack floor, then fumble for a moment with my bowl. When I finally manage to untie it from my waist, I settle it and the detestable wooden shoes into Bayla's hands. Clogs and a bowl are no use to a dead woman.

"Do what you have to do with these. Use them, sell them, trade them, whatever you want."

Her bewildered eyes shoot to mine. "But *you* need them," she insists, trying to give them back.

I shake my head, then lean down to kiss her cheek. "If I come back tonight, I'll take them."

"Why wouldn't you?" she asks, frantic. "Where are you going?"

"... Over there."

So long as she hasn't yet learned what the place all the prisoners call *"over there"* is, hopefully it will be quite some time before she realizes that this is my goodbye to her, that these few pitiful items are the only and most valuable things I have to offer anymore. After today, she is alone in this world, and I pray that my death is the price for her life.

"I love you, Bayla, I love you so much," I whisper, kneeling to embrace her despite the stabbing pain, to hide the tears that have sprung to my eyes. "Remember, tomorrow we're free."

"Tomorrow we're free," she repeats, and we are swept outside for counting.

Roll call has never gone by so quickly, and I know my time is near when a tall male prisoner approaches our block. Normally, his presence anywhere near the women's camp would be enough to get him killed, but he is no ordinary prisoner. He carries himself with a confidence befitting only a Kapo, and there is something horribly predatory in his stride. There is no doubt in my mind that the SS sent him.

"I love you both," I mutter to Bayla and Naomi, releasing their hands so they do not feel me trembling.

The Blockälteste speaks to the Kapo for a few moments before she turns her attention to us. "Prisoner A—30972! Step forward!"

Feet numb beneath the icy mud, legs unsteady and feeble, I trudge forward with my head lowered, willing myself not to look back. The swift scratch of the Blockälteste's pencil across a sheet of paper grates on my ears like nails on a chalkboard, and the finality of my number being crossed out settles dreadfully within my heart.

A—30972 is dead.

In silence, the Kapo directs me away to walk in front of him. A sharp jab to my back rips down my spine and I yelp, nearly crumpling to the ground.

His dark, cruel voice emanates from behind me. "Death to Hitler?" Another vicious punch stuns the back of my head as we walk, and I stumble to my knees, only to be violently yanked back up and shoved along. "Death to the Reich?" Again he knocks me to the ground, with a kick to the backs of my legs, and I fall, crying into the mud, in far too much pain to try to stand anymore. "You must be suicidal, you stupid lunatic. Or are you just... resistant?" A hand curls forcefully around my neck, powerful fingers crushing as I whimper, and his breath is hot against my ear as he mutters menacingly, "I like that in a girl."

There is no escape, no rescue as the Kapo effortlessly drags me from the path to a barrack. Inside, the bunks are empty, the prisoner functionaries are gone, and we are alone.

"No!" I gasp, desperately trying to crawl back to the entrance, and a shoe brutally stings the side of my head. White-hot knives slice through my insides as my dazed body is roughly flipped onto my back and calloused fingers lock around my throat.

No! Not like this! Please, let the SS have me!

Fighting with all I have left, I try to shove his overwhelming weight off, but he is immovable, and his wicked laugh makes my blood run cold.

"Keep struggling, it's more fun that way." He grins, malice twisting the corners of his lips. "They can hear you, but no one's coming. No one!" Prying my legs apart, he wedges himself against me, tearing my shirt up and roughly grabbing my breast.

"No! Please!" I sob, kicking and hitting, but my pleas fall on a callous heart, and ears that rejoice in my pain and terror.

"You're dead anyway, the SS won't care if I've had my way with you first!" Grabbing my wrists and pinning them above my head, he attacks my neck, biting the flesh to draw blood, ripping my skirt down my legs, and I scream.

Not like this!

I am suddenly aware of a coolness under my breast, and realize I still have the rusty nail I once found to make my scarf. Adrenaline pumping, I strain and sink my teeth into his ear. He howls in pain, releasing my wrists to try to jerk away, but, like one of their guard dogs, I tear viciously at him even while he punches my face, numb to the pain.

NOT LIKE THIS!

I grab the nail, stab it into his side, and he screams. With a final, powerful wrenching of my neck, the Kapo falls away, shrieking in furious agony. Thick, metallic blood fills my mouth, and I spit the large chunk of flesh from between my teeth.

He is upon me seconds later, knees pinning my arms. "You fucking bitch! Whore!" he roars, and his hands lock around my throat. "You'll pay for this!"

"Yes, you will."

The third voice has barely registered in my fading senses when the Kapo's weight is abruptly torn off me. The metal barrel of a gun smashes into the Kapo's face, and the blood gushing from his mouth and crooked nose spatters across a green uniform.

Him! The world is ringing, spinning, fading in and out of focus, but I recognize the third presence in the block. The wood or the Kapo's bones crack as Obergefreiter Engel viciously hauls him into the air and slams his body against the bunks.

Sobbing in pain, relief, fear, and gratitude, I hastily straighten my clothes. When I've wiped the blood and tears from my vision, I find Obergefreiter Engel with his gun pressed against the Kapo's temple.

"I should kill you, you bloody scum! What were your orders? You were to retrieve a prisoner, nothing else! And what do you do?" Even through his gloves, I can see his grip tighten around the Kapo's neck. "You *touch* her! When were you permitted to even *look* at the women? You will pay severely for this, I promise you! I will kill you myself! I should put a bullet in your head right now and save myself the trouble of a formal execution!"

I crawl away to press myself against the bunks, trembling, wishing I could vanish from sight. I have always known a man such as he is dangerous, heartless, but to see the monster when all I have received from him is unfathomable kindness... it reminds me that, despite whatever gifts and words, whatever defiance of mine he has not punished, he is a killer.

But for a brief moment he falters, eyes flickering down to me, and drops the Kapo. "Get back to your block."

The Kapo limps from the block in a disoriented hurry, whimpering, cradling his nose and missing ear, grasping his side where the end of the nail still protrudes.

Obergefreiter Engel kneels slowly and moves his gun out of sight. I recoil from him, unable to bring myself to look up, afraid he will see my terror and revulsion.

"Are you alright?" he asks, but I don't answer. "I am not taking you to the SS. I will tell them you died of your injuries, say you were beaten to death on the way to them," he assures me, but still I don't speak. "I won't hurt you, Hodaya," he says softly, the way one might speak to an abused animal.

The use of my true name makes my eyes flicker to his face in surprise. So sincere are his words, so expressive his eyes, filled with sorrow and the desire for me to trust him, that for the briefest moment I nearly do.

He sighs, glancing at the yellow patch on my shirt, now stained with blood. "You can't keep wearing that, you or your sister. You're walking targets... I'm going to get you different ones."

The words knock the air from my lungs. "What?"

"You speak Polish, yes?"

My head jerks slightly in a nod.

"Good. I'll modify your documentation and you can pass yourself and your sister off as Poles. You'll be moved to a new barrack and your work will have to change. It will take me a few days. Your treatment won't be much better, but you're safer as anything but a Jew."

I am stunned into silence, overwhelmed by both uncertainty and gratitude, and, despite my better judgment, I want to believe him. Somehow, he looks honest, almost harmless the way he kneels at my level, even while clad in his uniform and crosses.

But he isn't harmless. Those are war decorations... what did he do to earn those?

It isn't until he speaks that I realize I've asked the question aloud, and I am surprised again that he answers.

"The Invasion of Poland, Second Class, for bravery," he begins hesitantly, indicating one cross engraved with the year 1939. He points to the one beside it, a similar cross with the year 1940. "For bravery, First Class, the Invasions of the Netherlands and Belgium." The last award, a Knight's Cross, which is pinned above the others, also reads 1940, and his finger trembles as he indicates it. "The Invasion of France, for bravery and extraordinary acts of *valor*. At least that's what the story is, the truth isn't so *noble*."

He spits these words like a curse, as if the very taste of them is abhorrent, and I cannot help but ask, "Then what is the truth?"

"It was spite... and maybe jealousy too." He frowns. "I had something to prove, to my father more than anyone. He fought in the Great War, always thought I was a pathetic excuse for a man. He was proud of my brothers, though. My older brother, Bruno, he's an SS-Oberführer for RuSHA, and my little brother joined my panzer division after we took Poland. I did everything to please him, to prove I was worth something. I believed in his ideals, I went to university so I could join Bruno in the government, I joined the Wehrmacht and participated in some of our greatest victories, but it was still never good enough for him. He made sure I knew that. He would send letters to my younger brother, but never to me... in the middle of a goddamned war, he couldn't even be bothered to ask if I was still alive!"

The loathing that fills his voice at the mention of his father is unfathomable to me. My papa was the most wonderful—

No! Don't think about them, I scream inwardly, cursing my aching heart and watering eyes that threaten to consume my soul. If I begin to grieve for all I have lost, I will never be able to stop, and a shattered woman cannot protect Bayla.

"So, what did you do?" I ask, desperate now for his words to drown out my thoughts.

"I went numb, or I tried to. The pervitin made everything go away for a while."

"Pervitin?

"It's a drug," he explains. "Everyone in the army was ordered to use it. It makes you... unstoppable. You don't have to eat much or sleep for days, you stop feeling. Some men like me became addicted to it, and that's when you start to lose control... God, it does *horrible* things to a person, makes you a mindless, psychotic machine that can't even *feel,* makes you see things, hear things. In France, before we took Paris..."

The City of Lights... Naomi and I once talked about going there, when I still thought we'd get a letter from Aunt Dalia, when I never thought Hitler would touch France...

For a while, Obergefreiter Engel has no words, and a

painfully familiar guilt haunts his eyes. God knows I saw that same expression in my own face after Noam died.

"My little brother—Heinz—he was just twenty-two, the best friend I ever had. He was the radio operator, I was the gunner... It was my fault. I should have insisted we switch positions, he was smaller than me, he would have fit in my spot better than I did. Our tank was hit and caught fire. Three of us made it out, two didn't... I didn't realize Heinz was dead until I dragged his body out. We'd split a few bottles of pervitin a few hours earlier while waiting for the command to attack—early celebration for the battle's victory ahead. We were only supposed to have two tablets. That much pervitin at once could have killed someone, but I was used to it. I'd been doing it to myself for years. After Heinz died... I only remember rage. I don't remember all of what I did. I wasn't in my own mind anymore, I was too far gone.

"My commander thought I'd gone mad. He told me I charged the French and never stopped, not even when I was getting shot, disabled four tanks, killed thrice as many men. When I somehow still didn't die, my superiors praised me for my valor in breaking the French line, named me a war hero. Only the men who made it out of our tank that day know the truth. I didn't care about winning France for Germany. I just wanted to kill and be dead."

Somehow, this doesn't repulse me as I know it should. I would kill for Bayla without a second thought, and if someone took her from me... I would want to kill and then be dead too.

Why must he look and sound so human? Why must I understand what he has just told me, sympathize *with it? How has the world twisted so that the lamb understands the lion?*

I flinch as he reaches out to me, but he is not deterred as he takes me gently into his hands and lifts me to my feet, his eyes lingering on my wounds. "Once you're not classified as a Jew, you'll be able to send letters and receive parcels."

Parcels. Food. The tantalizing words register before any of my doubts of his earlier offer. But why is he doing this? Perhaps it is his own conscience he is trying to clear. Maybe that is why he feels the need to tell me all of these things, feels obligated to answer me, to help me.

But why me? Why Bayla? What is so different about us that he thinks he must protect us?

"You will survive this," he mumbles, so quietly I wonder if he is speaking more to himself. Pensively, his thumb brushes lightly over the bite mark on my neck, smearing away the blood, and quickly withdraws when I cringe from his touch. "I'll take you back to your block now and give the Blockälteste an excuse. I just need a few days to get everything in order."

Naomi!

"My friend!" I gasp, latching onto the sleeve of his coat carelessly, emboldened by the lenience he has treated me with. "My sister, Naomi! I can't leave her! She will die without me! Her number is A—30981! Please, help her too!"

A strange flash of recognition passes over his eyes, and he nods without hesitation. "Of course. She will be transferred with you; I will make sure of it."

There is no choice but to believe him—though it is my own foolishness at having trusted the enemy, the naive hope that some bit of humanity lives in a monster's heart that could mean my death. But what is there left in this world? What meaning does life have if I believe in nothing, even if the alternative is faith in this man?

Wordlessly, I follow him back to where the women of my block stand idly in groups.

"Go to your sisters," he mutters, then approaches the Blockälteste.

I scurry away, weaving through the prisoners, and quickly find Bayla and Naomi. Bayla appears even smaller, and I am weakened by the sudden need to cry. Moments ago, I thought I would never see them again, but now I rush to take them into my arms, so overjoyed and overwhelmed at having escaped death once more that I begin to laugh through my tears.

Smiling in confusion at my bliss and in relief at my presence, Bayla lays my clogs and bowl into my trembling hands.

20

DECEMBER 1, 1943

Three days since the incident with the Kapo and there has been no word from Obergefreiter Engel. *A few days,* I remind myself once again. I've lost count of how many times I have recited this to myself, so often over the last two nights it's become a prayer. *A few days... surely he knows we might not last that long.*

Now, near the end of the workday, the sky has begun to darken, and the temperature has long been dropping. Shivering, I try to keep myself from standing still for too long, hardly daring to imagine the torture the prisoners digging ditches and building rails must be suffering. The infirmary is quieter than usual, more than half of the bunks empty, some of them marked for death with white chalk.

Some part of myself I hardly remember anymore cannot help but find some twisted irony in it. For some reason, I keep thinking of a story, but I'm not sure what it is. An angel of death... yes, there was a death angel, I'm sure there was, and... a lamb? No, I think it's a lamb's blood. Where did I hear it? Could it have been in the synagogue? I'm sure it's an important story... what am I forgetting?

Moses! Egypt!

Of course! How could I have forgotten his name? Let my people go, sacrifice a lamb and mark the doorposts with its blood, so that the death angel will pass by. I continue to steal glances at the white *x's* defacing the bunks where the women too sick to move have been marked for death.

The Angel of Death will not pass over the marked ones. He'll see them as a welcome sign, then take much more than a first-born... he'll take them all.

From the center of a bunk, a woman groans. I check the bunk from a safe distance first, approaching only when I've seen there's no marking. I can't help those who are already dead. The woman was brought in two days ago, and, though her symptoms are mild, she's only getting worse. She'll probably be gone after the next selection. My gaze flickers momentarily to the women crowded on either side of her.

They'll all be gone...

She groans again, louder than before, and I shuffle closer, shushing her. "Shh... it's okay. It's alright," I whisper.

Round, sunken eyes peer accusingly into mine. *How dare she lie to me,* they seem to say.

"It's okay, just a little longer," I assure her, but of which outcome I'm not sure. Just a little longer, you'll be dead soon, or just a little longer, you'll get better soon. The latter is unlikely, but what harm will one more lie do to her? My words might be the last comforting ones she ever hears. I lean closer, softly brushing a hand against her shaved head. "If you survive today, then you can be free tomorrow."

I always used to run my hands through Bayla's hair and braid it, Mama used to do it to mine. Maybe her mother or sister used to do the same thing.

"A—30972!"

I drop my hand and turn to stand to attention. One of the officers of the block approaches me. She's a broad woman, uniform straining against shoulders and arms I rather think I've seen on men, and her blond hair is tied back into a neat bun, revealing the masculine features of her face. Among ourselves, we nurses and cleaners have been referring to her as Bizon. She certainly has the build of a bison.

Bizon shoves a slip of paper into my hand. "You're being transferred today. There is a truck at the crossroads, north end. I'm sure I don't need to say you're to report *directly* there. No detours, or it'll be block twenty-five. But that would be a mercy. Get moving. You don't want me looking for you if the transport leaves without you."

The threat of block twenty-five, the death block where selected women are gathered until it is convenient to take them to the gas chambers, is enough to make me ignore any questions I have. Bizon shoves me down the block and all but throws me outside into the bleak cold. As I stumble, Bizon lifts her boot to catch my clog, and I gasp, falling into the snow. I grasp my ribs as pain shoots through every limb, and my toes curl as the snow stings my bloody blisters. Quickly, I scramble on the ground, groaning, desperately grabbing my clog and slipping it back onto my swelling foot.

"Filthy dog," Bizon jeers. "Look at you, no better than a stray in the gutter. It's a wonder they haven't just put you out of your misery yet."

A wonder indeed, I think, choking back a sob as I shiver and rise with difficulty.

Making it through selections has been more excruciating than usual because of my purple bruises and broken ribs, and how my feet are beginning to rub within my clogs. I can't appear too weak to work, and I can't go to the infirmary. No one goes to the infirmary to get better, and the doctors don't heal their patients. I've managed to survive so far, but just barely.

I start in the direction of the crossroads, but when the gateway comes into view I see no truck, no other prisoners, and the closer I draw the more the dread settles in my heart.

When I reach the crossroads, it is deserted. I stop just before the open gate, trembling at the thought of passing through it without permission and even more so at being caught standing idle.

"Hodaya."

Only three people here use my given name...

Obergefreiter Engel approaches me from just beyond the gate, a small package under one arm. My eyes widen, locked on the face I've both hoped and dreaded to see again. He is alone, and he stands before me, tense, with a strange look of unease and relief.

"I have your new marks."

The sound that escapes me at his words is something between a gasp and a sob. I believe him. I don't know why, but I do. There is something about the stiff set of his posture and the sincerity in his eyes that floods me with joy.

"How?" I whisper in disbelief, tears welling in my eyes.

"Filing is tedious work. The others would rather be off getting drunk than shuffling papers for hours," he explains. "I offered to pick up some of their slack so they could go merry-making, managed to rearrange a few files, and I had a favor to call in to have your uniforms put together discreetly."

A favor from who? I wonder. I am no stranger to the currency of the camp. Clothes, food, and, if you do something for someone, then you earn a favor to call in later. But who could an Obergefreiter do something for to earn a favor? *Do I now owe him a favor as well?*

He doesn't elaborate further and I don't question him. To be caught with a false identity would mean a death sentence for me, and surely a court martial for him if I implicated him. He breaks the seams on my bright yellow patch, takes the slip from my hand, and tucks both into a pocket out of sight.

"I am taking you to your new barrack. Yeva is taking your sister there as well. Your friend will arrive with the rest, I couldn't find a way to have her moved sooner, so watch for her. Walk behind me. I'll explain the rest."

I can feel the blisters on my feet splitting open again, but I try to push the pain out of my mind long enough to listen.

"As far as the records are concerned, prisoners A—30972 and A—30973 who arrived on September first are both dead now. However, the new prisoners A—30972 and A—30973 are Polish political prisoners who arrived in Birkenau on November twenty-ninth.

"Your new jobs are in the latrines, you'll both be working as cleaners in the Scheisskommando. It's not a good place. But you'll be inside, you won't be doing hard labor, and the SS come nowhere near it. It's the safest place for you."

Three SS men escorting several prisoners draw close to us, and I duck my head lower. Suddenly, a crushing grip is bruising around my wrist. Obergefreiter Engel whirls around, jerking me almost to my knees, towering over me and scowling with such hatred that genuine dread consumes my heart.

"Blöde Hund! Are you purposely dragging your feet? Do I need to get the dogs? Maybe that'll get you moving faster!"

"I am sorry, Herr Obergefreiter," I stutter in terror, trembling beneath his touch.

His grip loosens as soon as the SS pass, and the ease with which his expression shifts to one of regret and apology is unnerving. "I'm sorry. They would have seen you didn't have a patch," he says, brushing his fingers over the place he grabbed my wrist, which is sure to bruise, so gentle and featherlight that for a moment I think I've only imagined it. Could someone capable of such callousness also be able to touch so kindly?

"When you find your sister, take off her patch and get rid of it. In the latrines would be best but, if not, bury it as deep as you can. If you ever need something from me, write a letter. Prisoners are forbidden to talk about their situations—it must be something along the lines of 'I am doing well, and I am healthy.

Hope all is well with you.' Everything will be searched before it's delivered. Address it to Nuremberg, to the name Tomasz Nowak. That is how I will know they are for me. Can you remember that?"

"Yes," I breathe, my breath a fuzzy white cloud. *Nuremberg. Tomasz Nowak,* I repeat to myself.

"You can't plainly write what you need, it needs to be coded. Draw pictures to do this, they're not seen as threatening. I will use the first letter in the name of the objects you draw to spell out any words. A sun for an *s*, a cat for a *c*, do you understand what I mean?"

"Yes," I whisper again. My mind is spinning and my heart is racing, but I latch on to every last one of his words in my desperation, despite the grim voice in the back of my head that tells me he could be lying, toying with me for fun.

We arrive before a deserted barrack and just across from it is another with bold white letters painted outside the door: 25. I shudder, turning my gaze away from the forebodingly silent barred windows of the death block. He leads me inside the empty barrack and to the back, then sets the brown package in my hands, his calloused fingers ghosting over mine.

"These are your clothes. Stay hidden back here until you can blend in with the others when they return from work. From now on, speak nothing but Polish and German. Give no one any reason to suspect your true identity."

I nod, my eyes averted. "Thank you, Herr Obergefreiter."

"My name is Alaric," he says softly, but I cannot bring myself to use his first name.

Silence settles between us for a few moments before he speaks, his voice nearly pleading. "Tell me something good, Hodaya. Please, tell me something about you, something happy."

There is nothing happy, I think, biting my cheeks, forcing my tears away. There is nothing good left but Bayla. Should I answer him? He has been kind, honest, he has saved me, but I owe him nothing, certainly not my once-happy memories now tainted with blood and death.

"I made Bayla a necklace for her sixth birthday," I hear myself saying; I am astonished, but the words do not stop. "My papa helped me make the beads, he taught me to carve wood. I painted them blue. And I bought her a yellow coat. Her smile was so beautiful, she never took them off."

He smiles, and the soft upturn of his lips makes his hardened face seem years younger. "Maybe you will make her another one when this is over," he says, and the assurance in his voice reminds me of the way Naomi once spoke of the end of the war.

"Will *you* tell me something happy?" I ask, unsure why I want to know.

He frowns, brow furrowed as if this is something he hasn't considered in a long time. At last, a memory seems to overtake him, and he lets out a quiet, somber chuckle. "Heinz and I once caught a badger when we were boys. We were always getting up to no good. Mother made us let it go, threatened to dump all the dessert she made in the pig trough. My father was gone on business, so she was able to make us sweets. We ate twice as much chocolate that night."

I wish I could offer him the same comforting words in return, but they would be empty. His little brother is dead, there will never be another day to catch badgers or eat themselves sick with chocolate. Despite the sorrow that deepens the lines in his face, a flicker of happiness lights his eyes, and I find myself wondering once again how he can look so human.

He waits for me to crawl into a bunk on the top and tuck myself into the corner where I cannot be seen before quickly whispering, "God be with you," and disappearing from the block.

The peculiarity of his statement occurs to me for the first

time. Faith in God or any religion isn't something I imagined any SS or Wehrmacht men could feel. Can faith truly drive people such as they the same as it does the people they torture?

The question is an uncomfortable one, the implications too haunting, so I shake it away and focus instead on the package in my hands. Carefully, I unwrap the paper, finding an additional thin, gray piece of fabric. A blanket. I might have thought it dismal a year ago, but now no material has ever felt so soft. Two sets of women's prisoner uniforms are beneath it, skirts and shirts, one bearing my number and the other Bayla's, each of them stitched with red triangles bearing the black letter P.

We're at the top of the hierarchy now. The status of a criminal in a place like this is worthy of respect. They are the kind of people who find their way into positions of authority, the ones the Kapos are more likely to leave alone. We're not Jews, we're Polish criminals—no matter that our charges are imaginary— and that will buy our lives more time.

To have faith in a place like this is dangerous. I know deep in my soul that I shouldn't hope, but it's been so long since I have been filled with anything but emptiness or despair, and my traitorous heart refuses to sink from where it soars in my chest.

Several minutes later, Bayla arrives at the entrance with Yeva, her hand hiding and resting over her yellow patch in such a way that one might think she was nursing a sore muscle. After we've both slipped into our new identities, suffered roll call, and found Naomi, we hungrily nibble our bread rations. As we lie down to sleep, I wrap our new blanket tightly around Bayla's frail form, and for once I don't hear her teeth chattering quite as loudly.

DECEMBER 10, 1943

The cold is swiftly becoming unbearable. Temperatures have plummeted violently and rapidly this winter; snow buries the ground so deep that the mud no longer reaches our feet and the hellish white claws up to our knees. The snow never seems to end, continuing to fall long into the night and throughout the morning until there is no escape, burning like fire with an agonizing, numbing chill.

More and more people die in the night, freezing or starving to death in our living quarters. Skeletons give in to the sweet relief of death as we sleep, and their frigid bodies must be pushed out of the bunks until morning, so the precious, minuscule amount of body heat we find in the barely living is not wasted on the dead. Every night one can feel the flicker of heat within their core being smothered and must discard onto the ground the body of a stranger, a friend, a family member.

Most of the women who die here are the laborers, the ones who are sent to dig ditches, push boulders, and build rails while whips, dogs, and guns are brought down on them. They are the ones who have not the prayer to survive for long. While the latrines are foul, odious work, I've never been so thankful for any privilege in my life. Even being knee- and elbow-deep in human excrement, I'm never beaten by the SS, I'm never exposed to the harsh elements, and I'm not dying of exhaustion.

Even so, the question of our survival grows more and more dire. Death knows no status. Disease, starvation, and cold discriminate against none, and the patches Bayla and I bear will not save us from the harsh environment. We have nothing to keep us warm besides our thin prisoner uniforms and the blanket that was gifted to us with our second set of clothes; it is not enough. If the obsession that is hunger was not enough to drive one to the edge of sanity, the frigid nights are enough to push one over the cliff.

Enclose thousands of people in a single place, deny them sufficient food and water, kill them systematically day by day, work their bodies beyond human capability, force them to live in their own filth, degrade them brutally at every turn, and you will find that, once you have taken their civilization, human beings are, before anything else, animals. Throw a scrap at starving dogs, then all loyalty is reduced to ashes, and their common situation or bond means nothing.

Animals... that's what we are now, but an animal doesn't need much. First and foremost, it must get away from the predators, then all that is necessary is a bit of food, some water, a place to sleep, and somewhere to excrete.

Some women have procured extra sets of clothes by selling their only scraps of food and anything else they've managed to get their hands on for just one more shirt or pair of pants. I've managed to trade with the women in the latrines, allowing them inside before others for bits of bread or potatoes, ensuring them a few extra minutes to wash and have a hole to themselves in exchange for scarves, socks, and undergarments. The clothing allows us a bit more warmth and comfort, and the extra scraps of food only seem to make the hunger worse. It's not much, and certainly not enough.

In the dark of the approaching morning, Bayla lies motion-less against me, and I wind my arms tighter around her, hoping that my own trembling, skinny limbs bring her a bit of warmth. She's wearing four sets of clothing, two of which I managed to strip from the bodies of the dead before anyone else, but it's still not enough to keep the cold away.

We'll never make it through winter like this. Many already haven't.

Another thought interrupts the tunnel vision that has become my mind these days, and I wonder if the time I've spent here has undone what might have remained of my sanity.

Would Obergefreiter Engel help us?

He has helped us thus far, time and time again, without asking for anything in return. Even when I dared to ask him a favor for Naomi, he agreed without a second thought. He speaks to me not as a prisoner or a lesser, not as a Reich German to a Jew, but as one human to another, and somehow that terri-fies me more. It frightens, disturbs me to see that there is a man behind the uniform, a man who has brothers he loves, who feels pain and regret. It would be easier if he were like the other SS, whose cruelty and hatred allow us to see them only as monsters, to forget that they are humans like us...

And it could still be a trick, I think, drawing Bayla closer. Maybe he wishes to lure me into a false sense of security, like hunters who leave food for the deer. The SS like to do that, play with us and torture us like cats with a mouse.

Nuremberg, Tomasz Nowak.

I'd almost forgotten that I have the ability to write letters now. There is no one to write to, no one to write to me. It's perilous to rely too heavily on people, to expect anything from even a fellow prisoner. Of all the people to rely on, he is by far the most dangerous.

My eyes slip closed in exhaustion, but my mind continues to reel, restless and terrified. As the seconds stretch into hours, I've conjured a thousand different ways everything could go gravely wrong, and everything except his compassionate eyes morphing into Mengele's disappears. For that horrifying illusion, I am nearly grateful, because for once all other names and faces vanish from my mind; the bodies I've carried, the women I've sent to die, the friends who've been taken, the ones I loved, the ones I'm sure I should be grieving for...

Whistles cut through the air and I dart awake, shivering, and shake Bayla as the Blockälteste marches down the block. "Bayla," I mumble, shaking her shoulder more firmly. "Bayla, wake up."

The women beside us crawl out of the bunk to tidy our quarters, but Bayla doesn't stir. Through the darkness, her pale, ghostlike face is frozen in sleep, her lips are tinged blue, and she doesn't move. She isn't breathing.

Scrambling down from the bunk, dragging her along with me, I scream, shaking her with all of my strength, "Bayla! Bayla, wake up! Wake up!"

"Let her rest peacefully," a woman says in passing, her hand brushing my shoulder. "She's gone."

"She's not dead! SHE'S NOT DEAD!" I shriek, swatting the woman away, frantically shaking Bayla, and her limp body flails with my efforts like a ragdoll. "Bayla! Wake up! Do you hear me? Wake up! WAKE UP!"

A quiet, strangled breath escapes her lips, and blue eyes crack slightly open with life. I sob her name with relief, tightly cradling her to my chest, running my hands over her head.

"I'm cold," she whispers, her words a weak, freezing wisp of air against my ear.

Squeezing my eyes shut, biting back tears, I murmur, "I know you are. I will get you something. You're alright." But no matter how desperately I wish that to be true, the reality is a painful blow to my chest.

I can't save her...

The cold nearly ripped her straight from my arms and there was absolutely nothing I could have done about it. There is no begging or reasoning with winter. I've starved myself, traded, and risked bullets to feed her, been beaten almost to death to give her the chance at a few more days of life, kept her unnoticed during selections, but, when all is said and done, I cannot save her. I have no power, no influence, and all I can give her are chances. All it takes is a whim, being in the wrong place at the wrong time, the single wave of a gloved hand, and she's dead.

Not before me... If you are fated to die in this wretched place, if death takes you, my sister, my daughter, it will only be because I am no longer living to shield you.

Rubbing what little warmth I can into her arms, I look up to our bunk in search of the thin blanket that was Obergefreiter Engel's gift to us. Anger wells dangerously within me at the absence of it. Not a moment later, I catch a glimpse of the gray fabric as a woman tucks it under her straw mat.

"That's my daughter's blanket," I growl and rise to stalk toward her.

The woman might have been pretty once, with blond hair and charming hazel eyes, but now her eyes are lifeless and narrowed at me, her mouth drawn into a snarl.

"I don't care. It's mine now," she snaps.

Glaring, I refuse to back down from her, uncaring about our difference in both height and strength even as I have to crane my head to look up at her. "Give it back to me, or I'll take it."

She laughs humorlessly, revealing chipped teeth, and shoves me back. "Take it, then! I'm not freezing, and she won't last long anyway. Find another one."

"She won't live long."

"The SS will take her over there soon."

"She'll starve sooner than us."

"A waste of rations."

"She won't last long anyway."

The world bleeds away, leaving nothing but the memory of all their words. I begin to quake.

She will last longer than all of you, even if I must kill each and every one of you with my bare hands.

The next thing I know, I'm yanking the woman to the ground in a flurry of scratching nails, screams, and blind rage. Numb to the pain in my ribs as she rams her fists against them, I claw at her face like a wild animal. Her hands lock around my throat, but I am relentless as I pummel her into the ground, mud and blood splattering amid our struggle. When my lungs begin to burn, I grab her head, raking my broken nails as hard as I can down her face and eyes. She cries out in pain, bucking beneath me and throwing me off her. She snatches the metal bowl that's tied to her waist and lunges at me. Tearing both clogs from my feet, I hurl one at the center of her face, and her nose gives an audible snap. Once again I'm straddling her, smacking the bowl from her hand with my remaining clog and beating her over the head with it.

"LEAVE HER ALONE! OR I'LL KILL YOU! I'LL *KILL* YOU!" I scream, hysterical, too far gone to care if she's conscious enough to hear me, consumed only with rage and the warm blood coating my hands.

"Stop! Stop! PLEASE!" she cries, but only when she's barely moving do I stop.

I step over her body to snatch Bayla's blanket and the clog I threw. By some miracle, Bayla breathes evenly and her eyes remain shut. She is oblivious to the bloody scene before her. Naomi has crawled down as well, and sits at Bayla's side with her arm around her, eyes dull and emotionless.

The other women ignore us, moving about the block as if nothing out of the ordinary has occurred. I imagine that some of them might have thought to take advantage of the situation; perhaps steal my clog or the blanket while we were distracted. It's not an abnormal event for two or maybe even three or four women to be fighting for a blanket.

We were fighting for a blanket...

The realization is a haunting one and my eyes flicker back to the woman I left in the mud. Her nose is crooked, her entire face is swollen and bloody, and she whimpers pathetically like a beaten puppy. It could have been me or Bayla lying there. In that moment, we were animals, savages, what is left of a civilized person when they're stripped of their humanity, all other means of survival, and left to fight over the scraps thrown at them. In that moment, and maybe even still, that woman would have killed me if I let her.

And I would have killed her too.

I wasn't fighting for a blanket like she was. I was fighting for Bayla's sake, because someone dared to try and steal my child's chance at survival, and in that moment I knew nothing but rage and violence.

I wonder if this is how Obergefreiter Engel felt that day in France, when his own brother was killed in front of him, and he felt nothing but rage and emptiness...

I nearly don't hear Bayla's weak, tired voice as she whispers to me, "Hodaya..."

"Yes, Bayla? What is it?"

"My feet hurt..."

I'm reminded vaguely of our night in the cattle car. She said the very same thing that day, as we stood for hours on end before the train even started to move, and the tremor that goes down my spine at these three simple words has me pulling the clogs from her feet.

"They're too small," Naomi whispers as I struggle to remove the clogs gently.

Splotches of blood stain Bayla's dark socks, and when I peel them off her feet I see blisters have torn open along her heels and toes, and one toe is stiff and swelling up.

I draw in a sharp breath, trembling as I look upon her injured feet and then her pale face. Even Naomi's gaze is grave as she looks at Bayla's feet. If I don't find her some medicine or bandages soon, they'll get infected and there will be nothing I can do for her. But there is no medicine anywhere in the camp, not even in the sickbays.

Oh God, women have died from this! If she can't walk, she can't work, and they'll take her!

My eyes turn to the woman I beat. Her feet and clogs are much larger than Bayla's. The woman is barely conscious and is too weak to fight me anymore as I pull the clogs from her feet and push Bayla's old pair into her shaking hands.

It's not stealing, just a trade. She doesn't care about Bayla or me, why should I care about her? I wrap Bayla's feet in a piece of my skirt, then tie the oversized clogs onto them.

"Out! Raus! Everyone out!"

I carry Bayla as far as the door before I have to force her to stand and walk on her own to be counted, despite how she stumbles and whimpers.

When we're all accounted for, our coffee is distributed, but I eat and drink nothing this morning. Bayla eats both rations of bread and drinks both cups of coffee without resistance. After the morning meal, I am unable to carry her to our worksite without punishment by the Kapos, so I keep an arm around her shoulder, nearly dragging her through the snow as we head for the latrines.

Once we reach the long building, the Kapos leave us. Thousands of prisoners are already gathering outside. The functionary prisoner at the entrance lets us past into the dark brick and cement building, which has just a few windows to let minimal light inside. The toilets extend from the door to the opposite end of the building, nothing more than large holes barely a foot apart, lining the middle of the floor. The stench assaults me the moment we step inside and I hold my breath for a moment, trying to swallow the bile rising in my throat.

At my side, Bayla begins to gag and heave. I finally sweep her into my arms, clamping my hand down over her mouth and nose as I rush to the end of the latrines. I nestle her down against a square cement column. There are only a few holes between it and the wall and Bayla is so small, she'll hardly be noticed. I pull the clogs back off her feet and hand them to her.

She can't work, but they *can't know that.*

"Bayla, listen to me. Hold on to your clogs and don't let anyone take them. If anyone tries, scream for me. Don't talk to anyone. Just stay here and be quiet. Rest as much as you can."

Eyes now finally open, their once-blue depths appearing gray and dull, she nods.

For the next eleven hours, Bayla remains seated at the back of the latrines while I work removing feces from the holes with the other cleaners. If any of the thousands of prisoners notice her, they say nothing, either too focused on their own survival to see her huddled in the back or simply uncaring. Shaken by the events of the morning, I am more demanding than usual in my requirements from the women who want to trade. If a woman wants a hole to herself, it costs her ration of bread, or her cleanest scarf so I can make bandages for Bayla's feet.

By the end of the day, I know there is no choice for me anymore. I have to reach out to Obergefreiter Engel. With daily selections being carried out, and Bayla's youth and size already against her, she needs to be healing. If selection comes while she's hurt like this... there's no doubt in my mind that she'll be taken.

If she is, she won't go alone. That much is definite. In Auschwitz, I can be absolutely certain of only two things: selection, and that I will follow Bayla to whatever end.

. . .

We disperse after roll call, and, while some prisoners sneak away to see their remaining friends or family in other blocks, Naomi, Bayla, and I retire to the bunks. Bayla succumbs to sleep in seconds, holding her clogs, pieces of clothing from the women in the latrines wrapped around her feet, and the blanket tucked securely around her.

I once wrote lines and essays every day, but that was years ago, when I was seventeen and my biggest concern was making it from school to work on time. Now, if I am correct to assume that November tenth has passed, I am twenty-two, and I am terrified the SS will discover the code I am writing to Obergefreiter Engel with the tiny, stolen scrap of paper and piece of pencil. For a while, I consider the words I want to communicate, wondering if it will look suspicious if I draw too many pictures.

The word *cold* is my first choice. I ponder it for a moment, trying to conjure up the most common image for each letter in the German spelling of it, and draw each with as much detail as possible.

Shoes is the next word that comes to mind. I've seen women wearing leather shoes before, like A—30877, the woman with vivid blue eyes who gave me food from Obergefreiter Engel.

I glance down at Naomi as she shifts. She gazes dejectedly over the edge of the bunk at the mud, one arm dangling carelessly like a ragdoll. Once again, I can't help but think she looks dead. The only indication that's not the case is her subtle intake of breath. I've known for a long time that the Naomi I once knew is dead, withered into a shell I can no longer recognize, but it seems that every day she dies a little more. I've tried to convince her that Adam is strong and he'll be waiting for her at the end of this, run my hands comfortingly over her bare head the way I do with Bayla, but I'm not sure she hears me anymore.

"You're writing." Naomi's voice is brittle. She says nothing more, but there are unspoken questions in her statement. *What are you writing? Who are you writing to? Why are you allowed to write?* She never questioned why Bayla and I suddenly had new identification patches a little over a week ago, or why we were all suddenly transferred. She doesn't question much anymore, unable to find the will to care.

"We have someone," I whisper, hoping to see a spark of interest in her eyes, but there is nothing. I've never mentioned Obergefreiter Engel to her, out of fear, but maybe the prospect of help will bring her hope. "He is helping us. Do you remember the bread and chicken? He gave it to us. And these new clothes and marks, he got these for us too. He stopped the SS from taking me that day the Kapo came for me. Bayla is still with us because of him."

She hums, a soft rumble from her chest. "I knew you would go with her... I couldn't believe it when you both walked after me..."

"Of course we came to you." I press a kiss to her bare head. "I will always be here for you. You're my best friend, my sister, and I love you. Remember that, and believe me, I won't ever let you go. We will make it to tomorrow."

A faint light flickers in her eyes, perhaps the memory of the night in the ghetto when she spoke the same words to me, or maybe of our friends speaking of tomorrow. My heart jolts, for, even though it was only the ghost of movement across her lips, I could swear I saw her smile.

For a moment, I consider telling her everything, all Obergefreiter Engel has told me, all he has done, that he is the one I am writing to, but I cannot bring myself to do it. Instead, I hold her freezing hand and carefully draw the pictures for the German word *friend,* praying he knows who I mean.

22

DECEMBER 12–13, 1943

There are screams today, desperate pleas and cries that come from the broken, withering bodies trapped within the dark walls of block twenty-five. It's impossible to block out the sound of their wails, their begging for mercy and food, and my mind won't cease to believe that I can pick out a single voice in particular among them all—the woman I've killed.

She is an Italian. Bayla was too weak to stand, let alone run during selection two days ago, so when Bayla's number was called I nudged the Italian woman and she ran in Bayla's place. Then, when that woman's actual number was called, Bayla tried and failed to run, and that number was marked for death. The SS never noticed the switch I made. They rounded up the condemned women yesterday.

The cold has surrounded my entire body in its deathly grip and only the sight of Bayla asleep at my side in the bunk, shivering and pale but alive, offers some tiny amount of relief. I doubt that woman would have lived for much longer anyway; no one who doesn't understand the camp's combined Polish and German language lives long. But it is not guilt for the murder I've committed that dominates now. Fear is what clutches me tightly as my eyes flick down to my trembling hand, the hand that without a second thought I used to usher a woman to her death, and I wonder if I should wear a white glove like Mengele. I killed a woman, and I feel almost nothing.

Mama, Papa, would you be ashamed of the callous woman I've become? I've done everything I must to save our daughter, and I cannot be sorry for that.

I glance around the block, trying to tune out the screams of those who were taken from our block just hours ago. This barrack is no different than the others we've previously lived in; filled with sunken faces drained of all color and hope. In some eyes, determination and defiance can be found, but in others there is nothing, just pain and emptiness where there was once a soul, remnants of what was once a person and a life before Auschwitz.

A woman sits alone on the heating channel. She's new to this barrack, much like we are. Our last block held only a few hundred women even before the selected ones were taken, and the remaining hundred or so were divided among the other blocks, Bayla and I here, and Naomi in block thirteen directly behind ours. The woman on the heating channel—Roksana, I think is what I heard another woman calling her—wrings her hands anxiously.

We've never spoken before—I hardly ever speak to anyone but Bayla and Naomi. Roksana and I are similar in that way, but she has no one to talk to anymore. The only woman who talked to her was taken from this block yesterday. I've been able to learn that she works counterfeiting money, a far more desirable job than most prisoners have.

She's like Bayla, I think, watching the way she casts glances to the barrack doors every now and again, resigned to the death of her friend who was taken. I wonder what Bayla would do if she were in Roksana's place?

Die.

The answer is one I've always known, but it seizes me with an unimaginable, jolting fear no matter how often I acknowledge it. If Bayla *were* in Roksana's place, I'd want someone else to help her, I'd beg God in Heaven that another prisoner might take pity on her and protect her, I'd pray for the angel she believes in to watch over her.

"Roksana," I whisper, uncertain.

Round, brown eyes dart up to mine from above dark circles and her spiritless voice is apprehensive. "Yes?"

"Come lie with us. You'll be warmer," I say, motioning to the space at my side.

She stares at me for a while, and eyes the sad wooden bunks, before making a tentative approach. She climbs up beside me and relaxes when I take one of her freezing hands into my own. We all press tightly together, so close it's nearly suffocating, but I let Roksana curl against me.

"You work counterfeiting money, don't you?"

She nods wordlessly.

"I work in the latrines. If you could hide some paper money for us, I can get you access to them. We'll even get you a hole for yourself."

There's never any privacy in the toilets, two or three women must all share a hole at the same time, and we have nothing to clean ourselves with. The mere thought of having my hands on paper is heavenly.

Roksana is silent for a while before she peers up at me. "I can hide some from the SS."

"I have another friend, Naomi, she works with us. Could you bring some for her as well?"

Again, she nods. "And what is your name?"

It seems so long since I've been asked for my given name, and for someone else to want to use it. It feels strange, almost improper. Aren't we only supposed to be known by our tattoos?

Isn't that all we're supposed to be anymore, cattle without real names?

I lower my voice as if divulging some great secret. "My name is Hodaya."

"I work in the warehouses," comes a quiet, meek voice. A pair of soft hazel eyes are peeking at me from the muddy bottom bunk. The young girl's cheeks have yet to hollow and, though she is pale and shivering, the color of health has yet to drain completely from her complexion. She must be from one of the new transports. "I could bring things too, there's a lot of stuff. Whatever you want."

She's begging. Begging for a friend, begging for the tiny bit of security that comes in a group. Many new girls are rejected by senior prisoners, pushed aside like they're of a different class. I've only been here for three months, but I've survived longer than many. And after the incident with the woman I beat senseless for trying to steal from Bayla, I've garnered something of a reputation as one to be avoided. No one wants to provoke the violent prisoners, and my classification as a criminal lends me credibility. It all elevates my status, makes me a more dangerous, daunting ally to approach for a greenhorn like the young girl looking hopefully up at me.

No one can survive alone here. There's more safety in numbers. Five people would be incredible to have together.

"What's your name?" I ask, not failing to notice that she introduced her job.

"Orna."

"I'm Hodaya."

It's an unspoken understanding that passes between us and she gives a small, winsome smile before disappearing back beneath us.

The evening whistle sounds, but the block is never truly quiet. With a thousand women all shivering, coughing, groaning, snoring, and mumbling, it is impossible.

Block twenty-five is the only place that is ever silent, as it is now—there is only ever silence in death. Twenty-five is empty, no more cries or screams to grate on our ears, no more hands to be seen reaching through the window to beg for anything, the women all carted away to the gas chambers. Tomorrow, twenty-five will be full again, the rest of the prisoners from yesterday's selection rounded up for the slaughter.

I draw in a deep breath and close my eyes to sleep. The Italian woman is gone now, but her voice haunts me even louder in the quiet darkness.

The next day passes unusually slowly, the kind of dragging pace that makes every individual minute seem never-ending. It's only been three days and I've managed to keep Bayla hidden at the back of the latrines for now, but her feet show no signs of healing so far. It was only by sheer luck that I was able to save her from selection just three days ago, but the officers will notice if I keep trying to switch her with other prisoners. She needs something, and soon.

Once Bayla and I have returned to our block, we find Roksana and Orna standing together near the entrance as they wait for the whistles.

"I've brought some," Roksana whispers to me, fear evident in the tremor in her voice. Her eyes dart in every direction before she discreetly lifts the sleeve of her shirt to reveal a small wad of paper money.

I can't see the currency or even how many slips of paper she holds, but I know it's more than I've ever seen before. Months ago I would have gawked at the amount, marveled at the things I could possibly buy, wouldn't have known what to do with so much money. But money cannot be used here to buy anything, it is useless in that sense. Money is only valuable in a free society. For us, it will be used to wipe in the toilets.

The seven o'clock whistle sounds and we all line up for roll call, and are counted once and then twice. Before we are dismissed, a Kapo approaches our block elders, leading another male prisoner carrying small packages and a slip of paper.

Suddenly, my breath has caught in my throat and my chest tightens with anticipation. I'd nearly forgotten that yesterday was Sunday, and all the letters and parcels would have been searched. A woman's number is called and she hurriedly trudges through the snow. A tiny parcel is pushed into her arms, no larger than a shoe, but the relief and gratitude in her eyes would make one believe she was just given deliverance. The parcels dwindle lower. I clench my fists tightly in an attempt to stop the shaking, but, even as my nails pinch harder and harder into my palms, the tremors don't stop. *Was my letter thrown out? Did Obergefreiter Engel find it? Did he search at all?*

Two more numbers go and my jaw clenches so harshly my ears begin to ring. The painful resignation washes over me like a fierce storm as I watch the Blockälteste take the last parcel from the Kapo. The despair nearly rips a defeated scream from my throat and, for the first time in months, I think I may sink to my knees and cry.

The head of our block glances at the last remaining number on the slip of paper before crumpling it up. "A—30972!"

That's my number...

My knees weaken beneath me as I take a step forward, head pounding and tiny white spots floating about my vision. The Blockälteste lays the last parcel into my trembling hands and dismisses me. I draw in a sharp breath when my lungs begin to burn, still barely aware that I wasn't breathing.

The joy is so completely overwhelming that I think I might laugh, but my disbelief quells it for now. Even as I grab Bayla's arm and all but drag her back into the block after taking our daily bread, I'm almost certain the parcel is nothing more than a figment of my imagination and will soon dissolve into thin air.

Settled on the heating channel, I quickly tear open the packaging.

Inside are gifts beyond any dream I could ever conjure and a tear slips from my eye: three shirts and three pairs of pants of thick, heavy wool, three pairs of socks, undergarments, and three pairs of leather shoes.

Beside me, Bayla draws in a sharp breath, reaching out to run her fingers longingly over the leather the way she used to do with jewelry. "Where did these come from?"

Alaric... but no one else can ever know that. We'd all be killed if anyone ever found out.

"It was organized for us," I say, immediately moving to remove our wooden clogs. Organized is one of the only universal words of the camp. It doesn't matter how something was obtained, whether it was bought, stolen, found, or given, it is all one word. Organized.

We each slip on a pair of socks and a shudder of relief and pleasure rattles through my body. They aren't much, but they make all the world of difference in the freezing winter air. We pull on the slightly oversized shoes and I roll down our socks, so they're out of sight, and tie the laces tightly. Bayla visibly relaxes at the change in footwear, her sigh almost content. Our shirts and pants come next, an extra set of insulation.

And there's three sets. One for Bayla. One for Naomi. One for me.

My heart has not felt this light in so very long. I don't know why Alaric is protecting us, why he's giving us food and clothes, but he is. Whatever his reasons are, he is saving us, and I cannot question it. I must take whatever means of survival is offered no matter whose hands it is from.

Not everyone has come inside just yet despite the cold; some are still lingering outside, perhaps waiting to see if they might risk slipping off to another block. Just a few paces behind us is block thirteen. Just a few yards are all that separates me from Naomi's block, and yet those few feet have never felt so far.

Roksana and Orna step inside, eyes frantically darting about the barrack in search of me.

It has to be tonight. These won't last until morning. I tighten my grip on Naomi's clothes. If I don't go now before the chaos settles, they will surely be stolen from me as we sleep. I have to see her now, if only to catch a glimpse of her from afar and for her to see me around the side of the block.

I need to know she's alright. She needs to know I'm here for her.

"Bayla, I'm going to see Naomi. I'll be right back. Get some sleep." I wrap up the final set of clothes and shoes and tuck them under my arm. Once she's climbed up into the top tier and tucked the blanket around her, I make my way to the entrance. Outside, many blocks are still gathered together to attention, and the SS have arrived. But it is not just verification of tally marks that they're here for. Block twenty-five is empty, and they are here to reap the rest of the selected.

Hastily, I slip out and around the side of our block. The entrance of thirteen is in sight as I trudge shin-deep through the snow, dropping down to huddle on my knees when I realize a group of women are being surrounded by armed SS, willing myself not to be seen. Fate seems to be on my side this day, for none turn in my direction; they are focused instead on shouting orders at the group of selected prisoners. But, like a whispered command from something beyond my senses, the strange urge to lift my gaze to the women overwhelms me.

I look up.

Filthy, ragged clothes hang off skeletal bodies, tattered scarves are tied askew over shaved heads, large, sunken eyes are filled with terror and defeat. Lice-infested bodies bear bloodied, infected scabs oozing pus, graying skin more befitting of corpses clings to frail bones. The living, walking dead are marched away to the death block, where soon they will be taken to the gas chambers, and their bodies will burn as their souls did long ago. Among the many faces who've become nothing more than numbers, all nearly identical, I recognize one.

Time freezes like the burning snow soaking my legs and, if the entire universe could inhabit a single heart, it shatters in this moment, disintegrates from within my chest, falls away and is lost forever into an endless, dark abyss. Ripped mercilessly from the gaping hole where a beating heart once lived and hoped, the universe lies obliterated, scattered across the white earth in burning, ruined pieces of joy, anguish, memory, and regret.

No... I'm here! Please, look at me! Don't leave me! I haven't left you! Please...

The world withers and dies before me, and I can do nothing but watch from afar, silent, as Naomi is led away to her death. She does not see me.

If God is real, then he does not love us... Of all the people he's condemned to this torturous fate, if he could allow her *to die this way, then there was never any goodness in the world.*

The last image of Naomi is seared in my mind, a withered, half-dead creature I barely recognize as a woman, and I desperately search for a different memory of her. When she still had her clothes and hair, when she lovingly spoke of Adam and the children they wanted to have—always the same two names she loved the best, Permilia and Wilhelm—when she smiled and laughed through the worst of times like life was still a blessing.

Was that woman even real? All my life, was she truly a living woman, or an angel sent from above? Where has she gone?

Naomi disappears, her footsteps in the snow trampled by the mass of other dead women, ash trickling over the emptiness like snowflakes. I stagger to my feet, barely conscious of my own movement as the world numbs with every step. I realize I am back inside the block when the parcel slips from my fingers, and I barely register Orna's stunned, thankful gaze as she unravels what should have been Naomi's clothes. I climb into the bunk and curl up beside Bayla, all too aware that the woman lying on the other side of me is a stranger.

I hope Adam is dead.

I hope he isn't pushing himself to live every day, fueled by the thought of his wife waiting for him, the life they'll have together after the war, the children they'll love and raise.

I hope he never lives to know she is already dead.

23

FEBRUARY 25–26, 1944

Days, weeks, and months all seem to blur into nothing, one long, meaningless string of moments I cannot piece together or distinguish from each other.

I've decided I despise the color white. How ironic that the color of innocence and forgiveness is also that of an SS doctor's gloves, of the snow, of the faces of dead women who starve, freeze, or are taken by the doctors.

Naomi's face was white... deathly so. There was so much snow that day, it was so cold... The death block was full for days after the SS came... six days they starved and screamed, then her snowy footprints led to the chimneys, and the snow fell gray.

The cheerful tone of Mengele's whistled song draws me back from the memory, and I wonder if this was the sound she heard when she was sentenced to death. Naked, our skeletons, wounds, and illnesses on full display, we stand lined up before the SS doctors.

Selections have always been the greatest terror of the camp. They are the only certainty in Auschwitz, just as death is the only certainty in life.

Mengele walks slowly in front of us, smiling in spite of the cold while the other SS scowl and fidget in their heavy coats, gloved hands hooked in his pockets as he strolls, examining one woman at a time before moving on or waving dismissively. One might think he was taking a casual walk in the park, scrutinizing the sturdiness of the sidewalk or the health of the plants. After all this time, it is still surreal.

He looks a woman up and down, pondering her usefulness. "Turn."

She obeys without question, and Mengele disapprovingly eyes the long, raw lashes on her back, the red rashes and holes where fleas have burrowed and she's tried in vain to scratch them away. He waves. Such an inconsequential gesture, and yet the power it wields is godlike. Her number is marked down and she steps out of line, dead, and Mengele moves on.

I've seen him conduct selections a few times from afar, but this is the closest I've been to him since the day in the infirmary. Often, he is at the ramp, directing thousands of people to their deaths in the gas chambers, or holed up in his office in Auschwitz I outside Birkenau with whatever medical experiments he's so fond of. The other SS like to get selection done quickly, mark down as many feeble, ill people as possible and send them on their way to certain death, but Mengele... he enjoys his work.

Not a doctor, I think. *A bringer of death... the Angel of Death is what he is called.* Even his SS comrades seem wary of him, as if they too—ironically—sense something truly vicious and deranged in him.

Orna straightens as Mengele nears her, trying to appear larger in any way possible. It's been a little over two months since she came to the camp and it's a few weeks past her fifteenth birthday. She's thin and bruised, but she comes from a farming family, who lived in northern Poland before she and her family were deported, and she's managed to conserve some of that strength.

Mengele examines her for a few seconds before moving on. Her number is spared selection. Roksana and Judith are next.

Judith is the newest addition to our group and by far the weakest of us all, even in comparison to Bayla. Working on one of the labor kommandos, she isn't the kind of prisoner I would have associated myself with if not for the insistence of Roksana, who is the closest thing to a friend I have anymore. Perhaps it is cruel, but I have no faith in Judith, and she has become a burden to us. At least twice a month, I receive Alaric's parcels, marked as being from the Red Cross, filled with rations of bread, cheese, sometimes meat, and, on a few occasions, small squares of soap. Orna has been able to organize necessities from the warehouses, and Roksana trades some of our paper money for water. Judith is the only one who contributes nothing, and I cannot help the bitterness in my stomach when Orna and Roksana give her much of what we have, knowing it is all wasted on a dead woman. She is near that dangerous edge of hopelessness that all prisoners fear—and, by extension, the one who succumbs. If one is not careful, another's hopelessness could infect you just the same as typhus. Despair is a contagious disease.

I couldn't save my friends. Mengele and despair took them from me without remorse. Roksana, Orna, Judith... they are the only family one can have in a place like this. I'm sure if we were anywhere else, I would love them like my own sisters, just as Gavriel and Noam were my brothers. But I will not die for them, I will not kill for them, and, should it ever come down to a choice between one of them and Bayla, I may as well be a stranger to this family we have forged in hell on earth.

Roksana turns several times for Mengele before he deems her worthy to live a little longer and his attention moves on, to Judith. He barely spares her a glance as he waves her out of line, and I can only hope Judith's weakness makes Bayla—who stands beside her—look stronger in comparison.

"Hmm... a bit young to be with the women, are you not?" Mengele muses, almost teasingly. "Couldn't be one I let by, no, that would be cruel indeed. Must have been someone else on duty. Turn, little girl."

Bayla turns for him, ribs showing through her skin, cheeks hollowed, and red from the pinching—which we all do to give our pale faces more color and the illusion of life—shivering like a puppy dragged from an icy river.

"Yes, much too young. Who on earth would send you here?" He clicks his tongue disapprovingly, raising his gloved hand.

The movement is like an axe rising above our heads and I blurt the first word that comes to mind. "Engel!"

The entire world seems to hold its breath; wind freezes in icy tendrils around us, the ever-changing, ever-darkening smoke sits placid in the sky, snowflakes, dull and grim, hang motionless in space.

Mengele's voice manifests through the white fog of his breath: "What did you say?"

Death takes many forms, none so destructive as the barren night within the eyes of the rogue Angel of Death. I have seen death's eyes many times in the withered souls of this hell, in every fading footprint in the snow and mud, in the shadows and red stains that soak the streets of my memory, in the murdered face of a boy and darkened green eyes of a woman who were all of humanity's joy and hope, and I do not fear him anymore.

"Engel," I repeat, finding some strange satisfaction in the knowledge that the Angel of Death hears the name of the one who defies him from the lips of one he has protected.

Ironic, truly. Engel is the German word for angel...

Mengele examines me inquisitively, intrigued by my reckless nerve, and everyone else continues to watch our exchange with bated breath. "I'm curious," he decides, clasping his hands. "I know a man by that name. What makes you say it?"

*Thrown from a jagged cliff to the merciless sea below, do we
not strain for the only hand reaching for us?*

"Obergefreiter Engel is the one who sent her here, Herr
Hauptsturmführer," I say, pronouncing every word perfectly in
German.

He pauses for a long while and then chuckles lightly. "Ah,
of course he did," he says to seemingly no one in particular. "I
remember you now, the one who wouldn't let the child go."
Turning to one of the SS at his side, he gestures at Bayla.
"Engel said this one would last a while and look at her there!
Months and she's still going. Perhaps we're too kind to these
creatures."

The wind picks up again, the snow sinks heavily upon my
head and shoulders, and Mengele sweeps past us further down
the line. Breathless, I grab Bayla's hand and squeeze it tightly,
hardly daring to think about how close to selection she came
today.

The cries from block twenty-five echo well into the night,
broken, muffled sobs and prayers droning from behind the brick
walls. I wish they would all be quiet. They've been where we
are now, listening to the condemned women scream and beg in
vain, haunted in wakefulness and sleep by their wails. They
know how horrible it is to listen to, and yet they still cry. I
cannot bear the tears that soak Bayla's cheeks as she screws her
eyes shut and covers her ears. A lifetime ago, it was the sound of
rain and thunder she hid from, not the screams of those soon to
be murdered, and no soothing poem or reassuring words will
ever restore that innocence. I want to scream at them to be
quiet. She shouldn't be made to listen to them. She shouldn't
know what death looks and hears like. She shouldn't be here.
No one should be here.

This place should never have existed.

But why does it exist? Why us? Why has a civilized nation brought us to this hell like we are naught but inhuman monsters?

When the morning whistles sound, I haven't slept, my head pounds with a throbbing headache, and my eyes burn with the exhaustion of a disturbed night.

We wait for the women on the top tier to climb down before we in the center subject ourselves to the struggle of wriggling out from between the others' bodies.

All of a sudden, like a wolf stalking the unsuspecting sheep, an SS officer appears in the block, accompanied by three female Kapos. The blond officer wears several badges on his uniform, and a thin, angular face holds pale blue eyes beneath a permanent scowl that gives him an irate, unhinged appearance.

He shouts, "Blockälteste! Get over here! All of you be quiet and listen to me! Commandant Liebehenschel wishes me to inform you that the Kanada Kommando needs more workers. In Kanada, you will sort all possessions that arrive! Today, you have the choice to join or not. We will take your numbers now if you join."

Food, wealth, abundance. That is all we know of Kanada. The Kapos and girls on the kommando sometimes bring barrels of clothes to the saunas. Many of them hide bits of food and garments to give to the prisoners in the women's camp. Indeed, they are the envy of all, their faces fuller and healthier, wearing clean dresses and scarves, many with their hair grown down to their ears. I have no doubt that they too still endure the cruelty of their Kapos and the SS, but what a marvelous place to be!

But why offer this wonderful opportunity to us seemingly without ulterior motive? We are not ignorant to their brutality, their trickery, and we know that nothing is given in sincerity or without a price. Perhaps they mean to kill anyone who steps forward, pretend to take us to Kanada, then put us in the gas chambers... but what do we have to lose? If we go, we might die. If we stay, we might die.

"There'll be food there!" Roksana whispers urgently.

Orna nods in agreement. "And it won't be hard work, just sorting."

Even though they've made their desires clear, they both look to me for assurance, as if asking their mother for permission.

Both my heart and mind are wary of this odd concept called choice, something the Germans have never allowed me, but instinct tells me I would be right to agree. Giving Roksana and Orna a quick nod of approval, I take Bayla's hand, and lead our little group to the front. In all, only twelve women approach the officer and give their numbers.

The Blockälteste strikes our numbers from her list, and I wonder if perhaps we truly are going to be killed today. The officer and Kapos depart for a neighboring block while one of the Kapos stays behind with us.

"Follow me," she says in Polish, and leads us into the gelid morning. The band has already begun to play by the time we reach the gate inside the women's camp and emerge for the first time to the vast expanse of Birkenau. A dirt path separates two long trenches running the length of the fence, mere feet from a watchtower. The Kapo directs us up the narrower road of mud and gravel closest to the fence, another endless trench dividing us from a long railroad. With section B I to our left—the women's camp that's been our home for five months—we pass section B II on our right; the men's camp and quarantine camp, the Hungarian women's camp, the Theresienstadt family camp, the gypsy camp, a sea of barracks and ghostly figures as far as the eyes can see.

Ahead, the railroad leads between two brick buildings with tall chimneys rising above the trees. Black smoke spews from the top, bits of ash flit from the sky like snow and darken the treetops, the stench of burning flesh chokes and sickens me, and I nearly retch. We are walking directly between two crematoriums. The death factories that have been a nightmarish tale we've tried to pretend isn't real—they're undeniable now. But how could we not still deny it? Can the human mind truly come to terms with such a horrific reality, or is it so fragile that the ones who do either die or unravel?

Beside me, Bayla chokes and tries to smother her cough in her sleeve, and I turn her body halfway toward me, shielding her eyes with one hand, making sure her head is down.

Why would the SS let the Kapo take us this way? We're not supposed to know about this... unless they don't think we'll have the chance to tell anyone...

The Kapo takes us onto a road that leads through a patch of woods. Here, I have my first glimpse of grass since leaving Bochnia, and I'm terribly tempted to throw myself onto the ground and eat every blade I see. An open field lies in the distance, the promise of spring wildflowers ready to bloom even through the snow.

How could such a simply beautiful place be the opening to hell?

The trail through the trees is short and we soon approach a gate and barbed wire. Inside Kanada, thirty wooden barracks stand in three long rows. On the opposite side of the main road there lies another sauna. Further down the path, beyond more barbed wire, there are two more crematoriums. There are no trenches or guard towers to separate us from the electrified fence here. I've seen many women throw themselves on the fence or be shot trying to run through the trench to get to it, but here it's right within reach, almost like they're inviting us to touch it.

We enter one of the barracks and there are only fifty or so women inside rather than a thousand, some of them still lying asleep and others tidying the quarters. Shockingly, the three-tier bunks here are all made for a single person; there's a straw mat and multiple blankets for each occupant, and windows look over the grass and other buildings. The stench of unwashed bodies and filth is still powerful, but I am stunned by how neat —dare I say clean—they all look. While, like us, they used to be prisoners in the women's camp, they no longer wear the filthy, lice-ridden prisoner uniforms, and have exchanged them for blouses, skirts, and dresses that are new and unsoiled. What extravagance!

Our Kapo wears a white blouse and blue skirt, a soft blue scarf tied over her short hair. There is a small red cross painted on her back, indicating that she is an "old number" who's been here longer than the others.

She turns to us. "Some of you will work the days, some the nights. You'll have a daily function and quota to make. Don't be short of it. The SS will put you in your kommandos when the others come." With that, she leaves us alone and goes to gather her kommando.

Hide.

It's the only logical thing to do in unknown territory when the rules are still unclear. Stay out of sight and out of mind, observe from a distance, learn everything and learn it fast.

We slink away from the group, slipping in between two empty bunks to sit and wait. Nearly twenty minutes later, the second of the three female Kapos returns from the women's camp with thirty women in tow. Their Kapo seems a far nastier woman than ours; she abandons her newcomers without a word, leaving them to search anxiously for safety and direction.

"Look, Tzipporah, look outside the window!" a teenage girl exclaims and pulls another woman to the window beside us. "There're people coming! *Real* people!"

Real people?

Curiosity getting the better of me, I peer outside. Sure enough, lines of people are walking down the road across the fence in the misty morning. Men, women, and children dressed in their finest clothes pass by; mothers pushing strollers and carrying babies, elderly people with canes and graying hair, children holding their parents' hands, carrying small dolls and toys. They look to the Kanada kommandos gathering outside and some of the older children wave, pacified by the sight of others. One man's voice reaches us over the distance. He shouts, pointing at the chimney, "Do you work in these factories?" The kommandos don't respond to him; instead, they simply wave back.

A van marked with a red cross sits parked nearby. Transfixed, I find myself unable to tear my gaze from the unfolding scene despite the dread festering at my core.

Real people... there are no real people here.

Hundreds file into the brick buildings, calm and assured. Suddenly, the door to the van is flung open, and an SS man carrying a large tin can and mask jumps out. He quickly climbs a ladder up the side of the building, then takes a moment to fix the mask securely over his face. Only when he takes the metal can and tips some sort of powder into something on the roof do I realize what's happening. Moments later, even as he's still hastily scrambling back down the ladder, the screaming begins.

"What's happening to them?" Bayla gasps, perched on the center tier, watching in horrified fascination.

"Get down from there!" I hiss, dragging her roughly from the window to the other side of the block. "Don't look at that, Bayla! Do you hear me? Don't look at the people and don't look at those buildings!"

"But why? What's happening to them? Why are they screaming?" She tries to strain to look around my shoulder out the window.

"Bayla!" I snap sharply. "Listen to me! Don't talk about it, don't think about it, and don't *look* at it! Understand?"

Silently, tears stinging her eyes, she nods. And the screaming continues, loud, agonized, terrified screams that reach us from within the thick walls, unending for nearly twenty minutes until everything goes eerily silent. Bile rises in my throat when the screams finally end. I try to force away the thought of Mama's sweet voice repeating Mother Goose rhymes, Papa's loud, rumbling laugh, try to convince myself that they died quickly, that they never knew what was happening, that they didn't scream like that, for so long...

The barrack door opens a moment later and the final Kapo with sixteen women comes inside, followed by the tall, blond SS officer and two more SS men.

"You are now in Kanada!" the blond officer begins. "And because you are here, you will not be allowed back inside the main camp. What you see cannot be told to the other prisoners. That"—he points to the chimneys outside—"is the only way out."

"We'll all die here; everyone goes through the chimney one way or the other."

"You are not to make any contact with the arrivals; do so and you'll join them. Here, you will sort all the belongings that come into the camp: clothes, shoes, suitcases, and any other valuable items like glasses, jewelry, money, food. Everything is to be handed in. If you are caught hiding a single item, it's to the chimney."

"Thank you, Klaus," one of the SS men says to the blond officer, taking the list of our numbers.

The SS man called Klaus disappears, and the two others begin dividing us up into groups, complaining that such "filthy hags" had to be gathered from the camp's gutter. Judging by their muttering, there must have been a disease outbreak in this barrack, and I assume we are the replacements for the ones who were gassed before their illness could spread.

One SS eyes Bayla curiously. What with her being so young and her identification as a Polish criminal, he seems unsure what to make of her.

"How long have you been here?" he asks.

"Five months, sir," I answer in German for her. "My daughter and I."

This declaration appears to impress both of them; they are momentarily taken aback. The average lifespan of a prisoner is only a few weeks. How many people can say they've survived nearly half a year? How many still have a mother or daughter with them?

"You'll join Aldona's kommando. White shirts, blue skirts. Go on, get moving," an SS orders after taking our numbers.

Outside, we quickly find the group of women dressed as the SS described. The tension in my shoulders eases a bit when I see the Kapo who brought us here, who from what I can tell so far is a reasonable woman; she's yet to bully and beat her kommando, much unlike the other Kapos, who enjoy making everyone's lives around them miserable.

A woman in our kommando introduces herself as Leah. She is a Jewish girl not much older than me, her curly brown hair grown out several inches. "You'll have to find your own clothes like ours," she says, indicating her skirt and shirt as a large truck pulls into the camp. "It won't be too difficult. We're sorting women's dresses today, and the other sheds are still overflowing."

Prisoners immediately swarm the truck, two men climbing up to release the latches and let the back slip down. Like a rushing waterfall from behind a broken dam, the contents of the truck tumble to the ground in a massive heap: suitcases, clothes, shoes, prosthetic limbs, canes, toys, books, utensils, photographs, anything and everything one could imagine. The possessions of the dead, all that remains of those who've been gassed and burned.

For a while, before Leah nudges me forward and reminds me of our quota, I can do nothing but stare, equally mesmerized and horrified. A little girl's ragdoll has fallen at my feet, its blue button eyes staring lifelessly up at me, and beneath it is a photograph that's slipped from an opened suitcase. Two little girls in polka dot dresses sit between a young couple on a sofa in a cozy sitting room, a newborn cradled in his mother's arms. A prisoner sweeps the doll and picture away with her foot, never daring to look at them, and reaches for an identical pair of tiny blue and white polka dot dresses.

God is dead. Or at least he better be.

24

AUGUST 20, 1944

A girl from my kommando committed suicide last night. She recognized someone walking into the gas chambers and stood mute until we could hear the screams, then ran for the fence. And she is just one of the many. Dozens of men and women have thrown themselves on the fence, many of them members of the Sonderkommando, who are forced to work in the crematoriums, moving bodies from the gas chambers and into the ovens— sometimes even those of their own friends and family.

Perhaps I truly have no soul to have not gone mad. Or perhaps I have gone mad, and my broken mind simply will not allow me to believe that which has been before my eyes for the six months we've been in Kanada. Every day, the screaming echoes into camp, men, women, and children are slaughtered without remorse, and there is nowhere to escape it. Even now, with the murders happening just a short walk away, sorting through the possessions to package and ship to Germany for other uses while the smoke burns my throat, I don't believe it. The human mind will go to great lengths to protect itself, suppress anything too horrific to accept, deny everything up to the moment the gas is being tipped inside the "showers." There can be no emotion, no acceptance, or mind, heart, and soul will destroy themselves and be unable to go on.

I tuck all our blankets around Bayla, who lies beside me in the light of the coming afternoon. We've taken to sharing a bunk, though it is cramped with both of us, sleeping beneath four blankets and on two straw mats. Her cheeks have begun to fill out a bit more, daily, freezing showers have washed the layers of grime from her skin, the tinge of death has left her complexion, and, watching the gentle flutter of her eyelashes as she sleeps, I think she could almost look healthy.

Even in Kanada—though they number less as the year drags on and contain less food than before—Alaric's Red Cross parcels still find their way to us, sometimes discreetly delivered by our Kapo, Aldona. The food we find among the clothing is supposed to be taken to the Fressbarracke, but we all find ways to organize some of it for ourselves. Thankfully, our SS supervisor, a cruel, vindictive man called Heinrich, left on leave several days ago and cannot catch us stealing anything for the time being. Alaric must have requested or volunteered for the job, because he has taken the place as our supervisor in Kanada until Heinrich returns at the start of September, and he turns two blind eyes to our pockets filled with food and other necessities.

A strange buzz in the air sends a shiver down my spine, and I look around to see if anyone else felt it as well. The snippet of a memory surfaces in my head, a cool autumn day after the summer heat, a hazy sequence of images and sounds I try to piece together into a single coherent place. Flexing my fingers, I nearly expect to feel the smooth surface of a canvas, the thin handle of a paintbrush, but instead find only the coarse blanket and prickly straw.

The distant hum begins to grow, and the others start to wake, shifting nervously at the unfamiliar sound. Only it isn't unfamiliar to me; I recognize it from somewhere, that loud, thundering drone, the shadows from the sky, a park, painting... and running...

Airplanes!

A deafening, screeching siren blares over the loudspeakers where the officers' voices are usually calmly repeating directions to the new transports. The kommandos working the day shift rush into our barrack in a panic, fleeing from the SS men who bolt the doors behind them.

"Airplanes! We've seen airplanes!" they all shout in their languages, rushing to the windows, straining over one another to catch a glimpse of the sky. Faint though it is—nearly drowned by confusion and chaos—the excitement intensifies, the distant rumble of a mechanical giant thunders across the sky, and the earth quakes.

"Bombers!" a woman screams with glee. "They are bombing us! They are bombing Auschwitz!"

A cheer goes up among the women, euphoric and nearly crazed, and a chant takes form among their voices, all merging together in a multitude of languages to form one powerful cry. "Yes! Drop the bombs! Drop the bombs!"

The ground shakes again, bringing renewed joy and fervor to their screams, their tears, their pleas to the unknown pilots to unleash all their power and fury on us.

What sweet revenge! What sweet relief! Yes, drop the bombs! Kill us all! Let them all burn with us!

Death holds no place in my heart despite its constant plaguing of my every breath. I no longer fear what comes after this life, or if anything does at all. What a wonderful thing it would be to die and realize there is nothing afterwards. What a wonderful memory of the end to take to the void; watching hell burn in its own fire, knowing flames can devour the demons just the same as the tortured souls. In this, we are all united, all of us hand in hand beneath the single common desire to see the sinister, unjust world annihilated.

"Drop the bombs!" I join their cries, chanting with a burning rage and passion I've not felt in a long time. Where once I feared the bombs raining from the sky, I now beg for them to fall. Startled and afraid, Bayla latches on to me, and I cradle her against my chest.

"We are not alone!" a woman yells, tears of joy streaming down her cheeks.

For nearly an hour, we smile and shout, eagerly asking one another if they felt the ground move that time, filled with the strange, sweet sensation of hope that pours from our hearts and down our cheeks in burning rivers. Eventually, the tremors stop, the sky goes quiet, and so too do we. Silent, throats raw and inflamed, everyone settles into their bunks to wait. If we're still here to wait for something, then the bombs have not come close enough to kill us, and that must mean they haven't killed the others either.

"Are they coming back?" Bayla whimpers against my shoulder, her tears soaking through my clean blouse, and, as I run my fingers through the strands of blond hair beginning to grow, I know I've never wished for anything else so desperately.

"I hope so."

For the sake of the men, women, and children who arrive every day. The ones who die in the gas chambers and the ones who are tortured slowly to death in the camp. The ones I watch walk to the chimneys, who obliviously wait in the wooded meadow to be murdered. The ones who starve and freeze, the ghastly creatures who've been robbed of their humanity. Whoever in the world the Germans are fighting, whoever flew above hell today, they have to come back. And if not to liberate us, then to kill us, and we'll be saved one way or the other.

Still... I'm not sure which outcome I prefer... Can there be a life after this if we don't die?

. . .

Evening comes as if the airplanes and bombs never disturbed the morning, and Bayla and I arise with the rest of our kommando for the night shift of sorting and packaging.

Beneath the blinding artificial glare of floodlights and an endless veil of night and black smoke, the shadows of spirits both long and only minutes dead seem to haunt every corner of Kanada. I never used to be afraid of the dark, but it isn't the absence of light that terrifies me now. It is what may linger in the darkness, the ghosts of innocents across the wire fences, in the corners of the dimly lit warehouses, lying in the patches of woodland, following behind every one of us as if in search of the tiniest hint of life among so much death.

They must be disappointed with us, I think, getting Bayla started on her quota of skirts before starting my own. *None of us are truly alive. Should the restless dead seek out our warmth, our lives, they will find only hollow bodies, skeletons whose souls have long since departed.*

Several hours into the night, Bayla and I have feigned completing her quota. We all must present our completed bundles to our SS supervisor to have them tallied in the logbook, and many of us then return to the warehouses only to reopen them and re-count the same things again and again. We all know better than to work too efficiently. Workers aren't needed if there is no work to be done.

"Get some sleep," I whisper to Bayla as she yawns, covering her with a mound of clothing in the corner of the warehouse. I do this for her as often as I can, helping her finish her quota early so she may hide and rest among the mountains of clothing where she cannot be found.

As I resume work, I glance up toward the SS supervisor's office as Aldona emerges.

Since Alaric has temporarily taken charge as supervisor, he has always lingered somewhere in my sight, only ever entering the office to file paperwork and each shift's tallied quotas. He arrived in Kanada this morning as per usual, but since then he—strangely—hasn't left the office.

"Hodaya," Aldona says, suddenly at my side. "Herr Obergefreiter says there is a problem with your numbers. He says you're to report to him at once to straighten them out."

Hesitantly, curiously, I make my way to the office. I'm sure he knows that many of us fake our numbers, but he has never questioned us about it.

"Enter!" Alaric calls out when I knock, and I slip inside the dim, stuffy room.

He is seated behind a large oak desk, lanterns and candles casting somber shadows over his face, and he doesn't look up at me.

"There is a problem with my quota, Herr Obergefreiter?"

He shakes his head. "No, your numbers are fine, Hodaya," he mumbles, then indicates the chair across from him. "Will you sit?"

The question, the offer, the ability to choose is something that has never been given to me in this place, and he extends it so easily. Some of the SS like to play civil with us, then attack, others skip the false niceties and go straight for the kill. But I am certain that Alaric, if nothing else, is sincere.

I take the offered seat.

"You and your sister are eating well, I hope?" he asks.

"Yes, Herr Obergefreiter."

"Good... that's good. And you are staying strong? No illnesses? No... bad thoughts?"

Bad thoughts? Does... does he mean to ask if I've thought about committing suicide? It's probably best I don't answer that... sometimes the fence is more tempting than food.

"What is the problem, Herr Obergefreiter?" I ask. "I don't want to fall behind on my quota."

He is silent for a moment, drumming his fingers against the desk, then reaches for a pen and quickly scribbles something into the logbook. "There, your quota is done. It's not as if they'll notice anything missing with all those *mountains...*" His jaw tenses, face slipping into a mask devoid of emotion. Such an expression might have frightened me once—I have learned to fear the ones who feel nothing over those who feel only hatred—but I know his facade is not for lack of emotion.

You hide too, like me, I think, watching his hands clench to stop from trembling. *Because feeling is unbearable, because reality is a nightmare. But why are you hiding from me now?*

"Why did you call me here, Alaric?"

The use of his name for the first time aloud makes him visibly flinch, as if I had lashed out and struck him, and he finally lifts his gaze to my face.

"I needed to... I had to know—to *see* you," he rasps, suddenly rising, and pacing the room with uncertain, frenzied steps like a caged animal.

"You see me every day."

"Not today, I didn't," he mutters. "Everything can change so quickly. Who knows what might have happened to you? A few hours might as well be weeks! Nothing makes a difference, no matter what. It didn't matter to *him*. And it should have! Why didn't it..."

His voice trails away and his trembling body looks on the verge of collapse. Though I don't know what, something has very deeply disturbed him. My life is constantly in danger whether here in Kanada or back in the women's camp, but he seems to fear that, in this moment, I am in more immediate peril than usual.

I stand slowly, wary as I approach him. He's never hurt me before, but a man who isn't in his right mind is unpredictable, and I cannot fathom my sudden desire to comfort him. I owe him nothing, certainly not my sympathy. Perhaps it is because he is one of the few who treats me as a human... because, some-how, I consider him human as well.

But how could someone human be wearing this uniform? We all have our own stories that have led to this hell... how did he come to be here too? Surely, he isn't trapped like us... is he?

"What has happened?" I whisper, and he freezes as my shaking hand touches his arm.

For a long time, he gazes back at me with a look of utter helplessness, perhaps surprised that *I* was the one to reach out this time, and I allow him to carefully take my hand.

"I try to help who I can, but one man doesn't make much a difference against this entire system... Sometimes it doesn't matter what I do." His words are a mere broken whisper, and I tighten my fingers around his. "Sometimes they starve anyway, freeze in the nights, get killed by Kapos or SS, die of disease, sometimes they just disappear and I find their numbers on the lists of dead... Sometimes they live for a few days, maybe weeks, sometimes for months. Sometimes I think I might actually be making a difference to them... then I remember I'm not.

"I was transferred to Auschwitz when it was still just a prisoner of war camp. I was here before they built Birkenau, I've been forced to watch this place become the hell that it is... and so was Izaak. He was a Polish Jew, a prisoner before I was even assigned here. He became a good friend of mine. I did all I could for him. I told him about my life, and he told me about his life in Warsaw, his wife and two sons... and he was killed today."

He draws away from me abruptly, turns as if to hide the agony twisting his features, the dampness in his reddened eyes.

"He survived over three years... I thought he would live, he'd made it so long... and then Klaus shot him. One second he was standing by his block and the next he had a bullet in his head. There was no reason, no provocation. That SS scum just felt like shooting someone, and Izaak just happened to be nearby. Nothing I did made a difference in the end. It's never enough, in the end nothing is *ever* good enough!"

His shoulders sink and begin to shake, and I am gripped by the strange urge to hold him, like the day in the infirmary when he held me when I lost my friends. I step toward him again and he stiffens, moves as if to push me away, but then he draws me into his arms, cradles me delicately against his chest, which heaves with irrepressible sobs.

"I'm sorry, I'm so sorry," he nearly whimpers, though I'm not sure to who or for what exactly he is apologizing. Rather than speak, I let him hold me as tears roll down his cheeks.

"I wanted to die too, sometimes still," I remember he once said.

Is this why he wonders if I think about dying? We've both lost people we care about, people we blame ourselves for... and Izaak could have been me. Bayla and I have defied the odds since the moment Mengele pointed us both to the right, but, if a man who defied all odds for years could be killed on a whim, then what difference does anything truly make in the end? I couldn't make a difference to anyone either...

But how could a man who claimed to have once believed in Hitler—someone who fought for Hitler's Germany—be where he is now? Sobbing in the arms of a Jewish woman, contemplating death, grieving the death of a Jewish man he couldn't save... He promised he would tell me the story if I wanted to hear it.

As he slowly gains control again, I decide that I want to know. I *need* to know what has made him into the broken man before me, what has made him protect me, what has made him different from the others, what makes him stay.

25

AUGUST 27–31, 1944

The day of Bayla's eleventh birthday falls on a Sunday and we have the day off even though the transports are still arriving.

What kinds of things does an eleven-year-old girl even like? I wonder. The most luxurious thing I ever gave Bayla was a yellow coat while other little girls got numerous lovely, expensive presents. In celebration today, I managed to exchange her old undergarments for a new pair and her first bra, two carrots, and a sliver of chocolate I organized from the piles yesterday. What more do I have to give her but that which belonged to the dead?

Summer is nearing its end, but the heat still lingers pleasantly around us. No cloud can be seen for miles, birds chirp happily from the trees, and the sun strains to reach through the canopy of smoke that never stops coming from the chimney. Yet still, we ignore it, pretend smoke from a forest fire has drifted this way, ask each other whether we think the SS are cooking chicken or cow today.

Basking in the sun on a stretch of lawn between our barrack and the crematoriums, Bayla and I sit with Roksana, Orna, and Leah. What a lovely picture we must make, well fed girls in our clean clothing, relaxing lazily on this beautiful day surrounded by green grass and flowerbeds like we're on holiday and haven't a care in the world. What a calming ruse to the people who sit waiting in the woods, thinking nothing bad could possibly happen to them if we ourselves seem to be living so blissfully. Why should they think they'll soon be murdered if these girls are smiling and laughing together, joking, discussing recipes and family traditions?

The carefreeness we distract one another with as we pretend the world isn't crumbling around us draws me back to a stuffy workshop in the ghetto, to those long hours we spent doing the same thing we're doing now. I hate it now, just as I hated it then, and it still reminds me of all I've lost. If I try hard enough, if I don't look too closely at my new companions, I can almost imagine it's still my friends I'm sitting with...

"I used to cook for my husband and my boys every day. *Kotlet schabowy* is my husband's favorite. We raised our own pigs. He did all the butchering, and I spent hours baking potatoes and pork with seasonings his mother sent us from Italy." Roksana smiles. "Oh, and my boys have quite the appetites for such little things! Pork, potatoes, *szarlotka*, *zupa truskawkowa*, dumplings, *golabki*, casserole! Dear me, they ate everything!"

"My sister and I always made latkes for Hanukkah," Orna says. "My grandmother would make the most wonderful applesauce with lots of cinnamon and sugar and we'd drizzle the latkes with it and top it off with wild strawberries from the woods. Oh, and babka as well, my mother taught us to make it. We used to have it every Sunday after supper."

"I love babka!" Bayla smiles excitedly. "I had some for my birthday once a few years ago, our Aunt Dalia made it for us. It was my sixth birthday. She gave us the entire cake!"

"Sixth birthday?" Leah wonders aloud. "How old are you now?"

"Today's my eleventh birthday."

They all blanch at Bayla's answer, stunned momentarily into silence, their eyes wide with surprise and sorrow.

"... Eleven?" It's the only word Leah seems able to utter, and understandably so. Bayla is too young to have lived for so long in the camp... too young to have survived here at all.

"Happy birthday, Bayla," Roksana says softly, her smile forced and tears pricking her eyes. "I hope you have many more."

In the distance, the orchestra has begun to play, and Bayla smiles at the sound. "Music!" Jumping to her feet, she takes a hold of Orna's hands and pulls her insistently. "Dance with me!" Together, they spin and dance in circles, stepping to the rhythm of our clapping. Orna's hazel eyes twinkle amber and gold in the light, loving and protective as they dance, and for a moment it is Noam's face I see instead. Bayla's sweet, angelic voice rises up in song, and I freeze, listening to her merrily sing "Ring a Ring o' Roses" from Mama's Mother Goose book. As they both fall giggling back to the ground with the final verse, ash trickles over us like snow.

From the woods, the hundreds of Hungarian Jews smile and wave at us, then rise to walk to the chimney.

"What's happening to those people?" Bayla asks as she climbs into our shared bunk, but I ignore her question.

The red sun touches down on the distant hills. Against the empty canopy of a starless night, the glow still burns, and the chimney still spews flames and ash.

"Why won't you tell me? I can always hear them."

"Bayla," I begin sharply. "I told you not to talk about it. Go to sleep."

"But you know, and you never tell me," she protests. "I heard people saying they're being burn—"

"Bayla, go to sleep! Stop asking about it!" I snap angrily,

ripping our blankets from beneath the mat in frustration. "What did I tell you? Don't *talk* about it, don't *think* about it, and don't *look* at it!"

Shame consumes me when she flinches, eyes widening for a moment in fear. She watches me with trepidation as I try to slow the furious beating of my heart, force down the emotions her questions try to reignite.

When Bayla finally speaks again, her voice is little more than a whisper. "Why didn't Mama come to see me today? Why haven't we gone to see her?"

How can anyone answer a question like that given the truth?

"Hodaya... where are Mama and Papa?"

"I don't know."

"Yes, you do! Yes, you do!" she exclaims. "You said we'd see them again, but we haven't! We never see *anyone* again..." She turns hesitantly toward the window. In the span of a single breaking heartbeat, something changes in her glassy blue eyes. The faint twinkle of naivety shatters, replaced by a fiery glow that consumes her irises as she stares transfixed at the chimney.

She knows... Someone told her what happens over there, and, if Mama isn't with us, there's only one place she could have gone.

"Are they dead?"

I wish I could deny those few horrific words no child should ever ask. But there is nowhere to hide anymore, no monsters under the bed for me to scare away, no poems or lullabies to soothe the fear, nothing to run back to except the nightmares that were once the greatest terror to face and now our only relief.

Biting her quivering lip, she screws her eyes shut, hanging her head as her shoulders shake with sobs. I swiftly take her into my arms and she lies limp against me, weeping for our parents, for our friends, for all the people she's waved to just beyond the fence.

"They're not dead, Bayla... they're still here." Firmly

cupping both sides of her face, I press our foreheads together. "And here." Beneath my hand, her heart pounds frantically like a drum, and her chest heaves with every labored breath. "They'll always live right here, and nothing can take that away from you. Not this place, not the SS, not even Hitler. *No one* can ever take them from your heart, no matter what they do."

"But I want them back!" she wails unconsolably, clinging tight to me in desperation. "I want them back!"

"I know," I whisper, muffling her sobs against my chest, knowing there is nothing I can do to make anything better. "I want them back too..."

And I'll never have them back...

Immediately, I banish them from my mind, their faces, their voices, everything that tears at my soul, begging to be felt and remembered.

Our pictures! For the first time since our deportation, the thought of our photographs occurs to me, and my heart sinks. I've seen thousands of photographs in Kanada, taken from the people like my family when they arrived. This is the kind of place that our pictures will have been taken, the only proof beyond my memory that they ever existed, burned and destroyed, like every other aspect of our lives.

"Worry not my child... the clouds may be here," I begin quietly, fighting away my own tears, fighting to stay strong for Bayla as she cries in my arms. I whisper the poem to her over and over until my throat is sore and exhaustion quiets her grief and carries her to sleep.

Late into the night, when sleep refuses to take me, I find myself repeating the same poem again and again in my head. After several hours of scouring every corner of my mind in a panic, I begin to sob, still frantically struggling to remember the name of the woman who taught me the words.

. . .

The final day of August arrives with a palpable chill. Tomorrow, our SS supervisor will be returning from leave and Alaric will resume his usual work in the administration offices. The prospect fills me with more dread than I realized it would.

He calls me back to the supervisor's office often, seeming to need assurance that I haven't been killed during the hours he hasn't seen me, and there has been a feeling of ease since the day he told me about Izaak. We sit together at his desk, sometimes in a comfortable silence over a cup of coffee—real, rich coffee that I've not tasted in so long I cannot stomach it all—and other days he talks to me. He has tried to get me to talk about myself, but I would rather not relive all I have lost, so I am content to just listen to him, and he easily pours his heart and soul into my hands. Honesty, like anger, spills easily when it's been suppressed for too long.

He's told me about his farm in Nuremburg and the apple orchard, university, where he got the dueling scar on his face, his friends in the army, how his father seemed to despise him particularly growing up and abused his mother. He often talks of getting into mischief with Heinz, who had a wife, a son, Werner, and a newborn daughter, Gisela, who he never met. There are such details in his every word that often I feel I have known him my entire life, like I too threw eggs at his strictest primary school teachers, shared apples and cigarettes by the Pegnitz River, traded joking insults with the men of his panzer crew. However, he hasn't told me much about his time in Paris. After Heinz was killed and he was injured, he spent almost a year in the city recovering from his wounds and pervitin addiction before being determined unfit to re-enter active service. I am certain something must have happened in Paris, whatever he says changed him.

Alaric greets me now with a weak smile as I enter the office after I've hidden Bayla in the warehouse to sleep the rest of the night. His supper of beans, cheese, and bread sits untouched, his hands busy sketching in a leather journal, and he slides the food toward me as I take my usual seat.

I give a small smile of gratitude, which seems to make his face lighten more than words could manage. Tucking the bread and cheese into my pocket for Bayla, I inhale the wonderful scent of cooked beans and clean the plate quickly.

He sets the journal aside. "I'll be leaving tomorrow," he says, and my heart clenches. "I'll still send you everything I can. I know you can get a lot of food here, but I don't want you going hungry."

I nod, trying to swallow the lump that has risen to my throat, focusing instead on the table so I do not meet his eyes.

"What is that?" I nod to the journal, desperate for a distraction. It isn't the quota logbook, and I've never seen it before.

He reaches for it, a reflexive, nearly protective move. "It was a gift..." He hesitates for a moment, then offers it to me.

The cover is smooth and black, and to hold a book once again is a strange, almost uncomfortable feeling. I open the cover to read a small, neat inscription, and my eyes shoot up to him in surprise and fear.

For a man who has lost his way,

Be strong and of good courage, do not fear nor be afraid of them; for the Lord your God, He is the One who goes with you. He will not leave you nor forsake you.

Deuteronomy 31:6

Why does he have scripture from the Tanakh?

"Who gave this to you?" I whisper, snapping it shut as if merely reading the words will draw the SS and their wrath.

"A wonderful man I didn't appreciate. His name was Yigal... I knew him in Paris," Alaric says sadly, his eyes glassy with tears and the fog of memories seemingly now bitter and tainted with heartache. "He wrote that for me. Look through it."

Carefully, I begin to flip through the pages. Pencil and charcoal sketches fill the pages, stunning scenes of rivers, the Eiffel Tower, extravagantly dressed musicians, and luxurious cities. There are more disturbing images as well: jets diving toward the ground, tanks, firing squads, bloody battlefields, a sickly hospital, angry faces with such intense detail I find myself flinching from them. Every picture, whether children playing chase in a field or a soldier sobbing at a grave, is tragically beautiful...

"You are an artist."

"Not really." He shakes his head. "It's a way to cope. I've picked it up again."

"Again?"

"I used to draw in our apple orchard when I was little. That was my quiet place. Then, life happened, and I let it go for a while until a few years ago. Yigal gave me this journal and encouraged me to start drawing again while I was recovering."

"You're very good... I was never any use with pencil," I murmur, tracing the lines of his artwork wistfully.

"You are an artist too?"

An artist... yes, I was an artist, wasn't I? I used to paint every spare moment I got, and Mrs. Ellen always said my work would be famous one day, and Papa always promised one day he'd find the money to send me to art school...

"I used to paint," I whisper softly, glancing up to find Alaric smiling encouragingly. "Impressionism was my favorite style. I painted in the park. I did a lot of landscapes with watercolors and oils. I loved painting, but... life happened."

Life... Like war it forces us to grow up, to abandon the safety, dreams, and pleasures of childhood.

I continue turning through the story of his life, past images of smiling children, depictions of fire, bodies, and SS, and feel I am looking directly into the light and darkness of his soul. I flip quickly past the pictures of Auschwitz, and find two more pages consumed by an adorable white calf and apple trees.

"You like cows, I see."

"Millie. When I was nine, she was my pet. She followed me everywhere. I would pick apples and we'd share them while I drew." Alaric smiles distantly, but it is replaced almost immediately with a frown.

"What's wrong?"

He glances away. "Nothing... it's just... My father shot her. I couldn't do it myself, so he did, and made sure I watched. I stopped drawing after that. Even picking up a pencil was like seeing it happen again."

"No." My voice trembles, and I don't want to believe him. I hastily shake away a disturbing, intrusive image of Bayla and her little cat, Asher. What father would do such a thing to his child? What father beats his son, makes him feel unworthy in every aspect, refuses to even send him a letter when there's a chance he could be killed at any moment?

And what father would kill another man's child? What husband would kill another man's wife? And yet, many of the killers here are husbands and fathers...

"Will you draw something for me?" he asks, holding the pencil out to me. "There are still some blank pages. I would love to see your work."

His eyes are pleading, as if there is something good in my life that can join the tragedies in his journal to make them a little more bearable. I take the pencil from his hand, trembling. I am sure I have many happy memories of my family and friends, of Bochnia, even a few rare moments in the ghetto... but everything is blank. Try as I might, I cannot summon anything to the surface. The only image I can conjure is Bayla.

She is all that's left of me, all that's left of the love and family we once had, all that keeps me going.

I draw her as she was, as she *should* be, grinning from ear to ear with perfect teeth aside from one in the front missing. I long for paint, for color to bring to life the rosiness of her cheeks, the blue beads around her neck, the sunny shade of her coat as she dances. A tear glides down my cheek, dampening the page below her feet so it appears she is walking through a rain puddle, and I quickly slide the journal back to Alaric.

His smile is brittle and pained, and I wonder if he can recognize the joyous little girl on the page as the dull, starving girl who's always at my side. "Beautiful... it is my favorite of the whole book."

We sit in silence for a long while, and I am reminded once again that this is the last time we will ever sit together in such a way. He will be gone tomorrow. This is the last chance I will have to ask him...

"I want to know something about you, Alaric."

He tilts his head, encouraging me to continue.

A brief moment of hesitation passes over me, but I shake it away. "You once told me that, if I wanted to know the story, you would tell me... I want to hear it. Why are you protecting *any* of us?"

His face grows pale and haunted, eyes pleading for me to change my mind. "This... isn't a pleasant story, Hodaya..."

"I need to know," I say unwaveringly.

He heaves a shuddering sigh, suddenly looking decades older. "Alright... God, where do I even start?"

"Why did you come here?" I try instead. Perhaps that is something a soldier can do, answer to someone else.

"Do you remember what I told you about Heinz? How I... went rogue after he died, and I was awarded for breaking the French line?" he asks, and I nod. "My superiors and the higher-ups in Berlin started getting letters of recommendation about me, and my brother Bruno, the SS-Oberführer for RuSHA, talked me up to them. They thought I showed potential as an officer one day and, once I was fully recovered, I was transferred to Auschwitz in 1941."

He pauses, waiting for another question.

"Did you know what the SS would do to us? That they would build the gas chambers?"

"No. I wasn't privy to their plans. I knew Himmler had ordered an extension to the camp, but nothing else."

But you found out eventually... and you stayed. "Did you want us dead?"

The look in his eyes is one of utter shame, and his voice trembles as he speaks. "No... not by the time I came here—"

"But you did," I cut in shakily, accusingly.

His gaze lowers as if he is ashamed to meet my eye. "I was a horribly foolish, misguided man, and... yes. There was once a time when I thought Jews were beneath me... and I wouldn't have cared if they disappeared."

This confession shatters my heart more than I realized it could and I turn away, my eyes burning. I am no stranger to death, to living with the knowledge that there are many who would rather see me dead, who *would* kill me. But he is the one who has protected me as no one else has here. To hear from his own lips that he was one of the many is unbearable.

Alaric's chair scrapes the floor as he stands and suddenly he is on his knees before me, his trembling hands reaching desperately for mine. "It isn't like that anymore, Hodaya. I am so sorry that it ever was, but I cannot change who I was years ago," he says, his voice thick with guilt. "I am not that man anymore. I *don't* want you or anyone else dead, and I *don't* believe you are lesser. If anyone is inferior, it is me."

"But why did you believe it?" I force out, still refusing to meet his eyes.

"Like many, I fell for the Nazi propaganda. I grew up listening to my father and everyone I knew believed in German superiority, believed that all our troubles were caused by some

Jewish conspiracy. When you know nothing else all your life, then nothing else makes sense..." he says weakly.

"Then what changed your mind?"

"Heinz was killed... that's what forced me to change."

I glance down, but he isn't looking at me anymore. His head is bowed, brow drawn in anguish.

"I lost myself a long time before the war started. There was always... a void inside me that I didn't know how to fix. I hoped I could find fulfillment in the army, get away from my father, make something of myself, make my father proud of me like he was of my brothers. Deep down, that was the real reason I fought... all my life, I fought for his approval... but it wasn't enough.

"For a long time, I relied on hatred and spite to keep myself going, to... I don't know, maybe to forget how much I actually hated *myself*. Pervitin, whiskey, cigarettes, fighting... it became the only way I could cope. Heinz was the only good thing I had left and, after he died, I spiraled. I was guarded day and night in the hospital in Paris so I couldn't try to kill myself. I had to be tied down a few times while I was going through withdrawal and relapsing. I was a danger to myself and everyone around me, a grenade just waiting to explode. I would have died somehow, at my own hand or otherwise, but there were better people who saved me after I lost him."

"Who were they?" I ask when he doesn't continue.

"They were Jews," he murmurs, as if still disbelieving of the irony in that statement. "I had just been to Heinz's grave and two little French girls found me asleep on the ground. Their names were Soleil and Sunna. They lived with a group of sisters in a Catholic orphanage. They reminded me so much of Heinz, their eyes, their laughter, their mischievous personalities... such happy, kind girls. I don't think they realized I was German at first, they just thought I was a silly man who got lost outside... they saw *me*. Alaric, not a soldier or a killer, not a disappointment, not a useful chess piece.

"I didn't have military duties anymore, so I spent a lot of time with them. I took them to the cinema and parks, to see concerts, bought them desserts and toys. It was like they were the daughters I never had, and in a way it was like I had Heinz back. They made me realize that a father could love his children, *should* love them. They kept me sane, or really they brought me back from insanity. They gave me purpose, hope that there was still goodness in the world."

Again, he stops, the slight smile that formed on his face as he spoke of Soleil and Sunna suddenly morphing into a grimace as he rubs tears from his eyes.

"They liked to visit an elderly man they called Mr. Storyteller. He was actually a rabbi named Yigal. Looking back, I really should have realized they were Jewish, but I just never questioned it. I just assumed they liked to hear his stories... God, I was so angry the first time they introduced him to me. All I could think was that he was poisoning their minds with his degenerate ways and they were too innocent to realize it. I thought about turning him over to the authorities, but Soleil and Sunna loved him. They would have been devastated if he disappeared, and I didn't want to lose them. They were the only good things left in my life, I wouldn't throw it away because of a Jew."

His gaze focuses on me again, noticing my subtle flinch, eyes seeming to beg forgiveness for the follies of his younger self.

"I started going with the girls when they went to see Yigal, so I could supervise and make sure he wasn't trying to impress his beliefs on them. Then, he started talking to me... I was awful to him, I would spit at him, insult him, threaten him. Never in front of the girls, though. I would never let them see that side of me, and Yigal knew that. He was a *very* good talker. He knew how to make me question myself without even realizing it. He would compare our lives, cite the scriptures, insist that we weren't really that different...

"I'll never forget the day he brought up my father. I was arguing with him again, trying to justify myself, and he said to me, 'Your father must be a great man.' That made me furious. He pretended I'd never expressed how much I hated my father, because, if he was truly such a horrible man, then why was I trying so hard to make him proud?"

Alaric draws away to sit leaning against the desk, subconsciously reaching for the black journal that holds his life and Yigal's writing to a lost, confused man.

"I threatened to kill him that day," he mumbles. "I'm not proud to say it, but it's true. He was making me question all the lies I'd been telling myself for years, breaking down everything that had been the foundation of my entire *life,* my entire *identity,* and I hated him for it... because it was working. He saw something in me that I didn't. He didn't even think I *would* kill him when I threatened. 'You have a soul,' he told me—he was always so kind and patient, no matter how horribly I treated him. Sometimes, I think he was more a father to me in a year than my own was my entire life... I don't know why he thought I was worth saving. I wasn't, and I'm still not.

"But they did. He, Soleil, and Sunna saved me from myself when I was at my absolute worst. I began to find my faith in God again, I started to question my prejudices, started to think of what I wanted for *myself,* not what the Reich or my father wanted of me... I hoped I would be discharged and allowed to go back to Germany, then I could make my own purpose in life, perhaps get married so I could adopt Soleil and Sunna, and we could have a real family. Then I was transferred here and I've never left—"

"But why are you still here?" I interrupt, staring at him in disbelief. "If you changed your mind, if you don't believe in this... why not ask for a transfer?"

His head sinks wearily. "I did, believe me, I *did*. After the first experimental gassing after I arrived... God, I was horrified, and I wanted nothing to do with it. I asked for a transfer somewhere else, *anywhere* else, but it was denied. I wasn't fit to fight anymore, going back to the field wasn't something my superiors would even consider. Then, there was the complication that I knew too much. We're not allowed to tell anyone about what happens here. Photographs are forbidden, our letters are blacked out, or we could be prosecuted... and there are a few SS here who are suspicious of me. They won't let me leave now. They want to keep me close where they can watch me, and if I slip up... I still have my mother, and I can't risk Heinz's children. Werner and little Gisela—she's only four. I won't let the SS take them from me too, I won't fail Heinz again, not like that... They're all I have left now..."

The tears that streak down his pale cheeks come in rivers, and, no matter how his trembling hands try to wipe them away, they never seem to stop. "They're gone," he whispers helplessly, despairingly.

"Who's gone?" I ask carefully, as if my words alone could shatter his frail form.

"My girls," he mutters, pacing to the window. "In 1942, there was a roundup in Paris. Over thirteen thousand Jews were deported here. I was asked to supervise because of the large numbers arriving... and I saw them. Soleil and Sunna were on the back of a truck with dozens of other women and children. They saw me too... and they s*miled!* They smiled and waved at me because they thought they were safe, because even after everything they must have suffered, they knew I would protect them! They saw *me* and thought they were *safe!*" he chokes. "I ran after the truck... I don't even know what I would have done, they were too young to—I just ran after them... but I didn't make it. The gas had already been dropped inside and I could hear them screa—"

In an instant, I've thrown my arms around him, silencing the rest of his words, which I cannot bear to hear anymore. "Stop! Please, stop!" I beg him.

"I killed them with everything I once believed in, with this system I didn't even realize I was helping to build..." he whispers as if he hasn't heard me. "I don't want this, but if I even try to leave, then Werner, Gisela, and my mother will be dead too. I couldn't save them—Soleil, Sunna, Yigal, Heinz, Izaak... I am trying to be the man Yigal believed I was capable of being, save whoever God puts on my path, the way He sent them to save me, but—"

"Don't," I gasp desperately, trying to muffle his words, but it is too late. Their names and faces have already returned, the ones I loved, the ones I killed, the ones I couldn't save...

Noam, Mama, Papa, Levana, Chasha, Naomi.

I understand better than anyone the shame he feels, the self-loathing consuming his soul, the grief he is trying to force away, and I too wish I could simply die. But like him, I still have a fragile reason to live, and until that is broken I must force myself to endure whatever torment the world inflicts upon me. For now, that torment is their memory, my failings. I hold Alaric to my heart as we cry against one another, mourning all we have loved and lost for just a few stolen moments, enemies in the eyes of this world gone mad, and now just a man and a woman who understand one another's suffering all too well.

26

OCTOBER 7, 1944

The seams of over a hundred men's coats lie opened before me, all of which I have found from the mountains of clothes dumped in the sorting sheds and dissected. Sewn inside pockets and in between slips of fabric I've found jewelry, money and coins of varying denominations, and other small valuables. Photographs are a constant hinderance, carefully placed inside pockets and bags, and I blindly discard them without ever daring to look at the images of the people whose belongings I riffle through.

After completing another package, I start down from the long wooden bench to the end of the shed in search of more coats to make today's quota, flinching as my clothes rub against my back.

Aldona is a decent woman and Kapo, refraining from beating her girls without cause or tearing their packages open to force them to start over, but she is stern in her commands. Some days ago, another Kapo saw me trying to hide a bit of food from the piles and was upon me in seconds, beating me and threatening to bring me to our SS supervisor. Thankfully, Aldona intervened and, rather than face execution like the Kapo wanted, she insisted she would punish me until both of them were satisfied I had learned my lesson. Fifteen lashes and three days later, my back is still flayed and bleeds, but, like all pain, it reminds me that I am not yet dead.

Just as I reach the entrance, an SS woman steps inside. "I need a dozen girls!" she shouts, scanning the barrack for volunteers. In moments, eleven more women have stepped up to the front at my side and given their numbers. I've only been able to join these groups a few times before, taking handcarts of clothes and food back to the main camp.

"Come, we're going this way," the SS woman says, leading us away from the road between the electrified fences. She glares pointedly at each of us. "Now, you must not look around. When you walk, you keep your heads *down*. Understood?"

In response, we all nod then lower our heads. The path we take is the same one Aldona took us down when we first joined Kanada, past the sauna, through the woods and fields, and toward crematoriums two and three. The area is thick with smoke, and the same stench of burning human flesh I've smelt every day of my life for a year chokes my lungs and bile rises in my throat.

Don't look, my mind warns me, but my eyes fight to wander from the cart of clothing I haul down the road. The hazy memory of another life surfaces, of this same warning, of walking through the rain, an SS spitting, shoes floating in the lamplight...

I glance out to the fields by a crematorium, and what little faith in humanity there may have been left in my heart goes up in smoke. Littered at the feet of the Sonderkommando are countless dead bodies stripped of clothing and hair. The Sonderkommando throw them into the pit, men, women, and small children, and the flames greedily consume every bit of flesh they're fed without discrimination. The Nazis look on from a distance, indifferent, loath to sully their hands and instead forcing others to dispose of their crimes.

Prickling across my skin like millions of lice, the horror and disbelief ignite even the most minute senses, each strand of hair, each pulse, each shift in the wind a thousand needles piercing down my body. I've known for so long about what the Nazis are doing to these people, but I've never truly seen it. I've seen the smoke, smelt the stench, watched the Sonderkommando wheel the ashes away to dump—but I've never seen it.

If I had the chance, if I could push just one of those SS men into the furnace and listen to him scream, hear him plead for mercy while he burns alive, do to just one of them what they've done to those I loved... If I still believed in God, I wouldn't ask him for forgiveness.

Death has no preference, and Nazis will burn just the same as Jews.

Several hours past noon, the SS woman is finally leading us back to Kanada, empty handcarts in tow. Again, the SS woman takes us away from the main road through the fences, probably afraid she'll be electrocuted.

I wonder if I could push her into the fence... She's taller, stronger, but she'd never expect it. So confident are these killers in their abilities to murder us and break our spirits that they think none would ever dream of retaliating. An SS will boldly turn his back on prisoners carrying rocks and shovels, strut past thousands of prisoners resigned to their inevitable death and never once shudder in fear. How absolutely absurd that any of them might wonder if those inferior to them would ever lash out! When the wolf walks among the flock, why should it think the sheep will do anything but cower?

A shift in the wind carries a strange odor as we near crematoriums two and three, the familiar, burning stench of singed hair, but there's something else too... the scent of gunpowder. A shudder rakes down my spine, anticipation sinking its claws into my heart, and an exchange of glances with the other girls tells me they feel it too. The SS woman pauses warily and sniffs the air, hand moving to her pistol.

Shouting from crematorium three rises through the air, furious and legion, and an explosion shakes the ground. Fire spills from the chimney higher than it's ever reached before, and in moments the entire building is engulfed in flames. Frantic and bewildered, the SS swarm and scatter, sprinting in a frenzied fashion without any firm direction. From beyond the crematoriums, the men of the Sonderkommando emerge, brandishing hammers and knives, and one man gives a triumphant cry.

"Revolt!" screams a terrified woman at my side. We all throw ourselves onto the ground and crawl beneath our handcarts.

Another explosion rocks the earth beneath us. Amid the sirens, the hail of gunfire and mayhem, I watch transfixed in pure joy as a chimney crumbles beneath the power of a prisoner-made bomb and is swallowed by the inferno below. Swiftly regaining their wits, the Germans call for reinforcements, racing in on motorbikes with machine guns, firing on anything that moves. They chase after the prisoners making a daring run for the electrified fence by the woods that has been miraculously cut and, within minutes, they've massacred what looks to be hundreds.

A prisoner knocks an SS man to the ground with a brick from the collapsed building, and soon two other prisoners are upon the fallen murderer, plunging knives repeatedly into his body as he screams for help. By the time the three prisoners have been shot, it's too late. The SS man lies dead and bloody with them, and I feel a grin tug the corners of my lips.

Excitedly, the Polish woman sheltered beside me grabs my

hand, laughing gleefully. "They've killed him! They've killed him! Look there, on the ground! *Szkop!*"

There is another explosion from crematorium two, and soon it is burning and collapsing like the third. Smoke, ash, and falling embers choke the air, and rubble is blown mere feet from where we lie in the midst of the battle. I breathe deeply the scent of fire and destruction, reveling in the feel of my burning nose and throat, the painful sting in my eyes that brings joyful tears cascading down my cheeks.

Revenge! Sweet, glorious revenge! Burn the ovens! Burn the chambers! Burn the murderers! Burn everything!

When the gunshots are fewer and further in between, a group of men from the main camp arrive to extinguish the fires. Slowly, they tame and douse the flames, leaving nothing but smoldering ruins in their wake. The revolt is over, and, while the SS have killed or rounded up everyone who tried to rebel, this is no victory for them. This day can only be ours, no matter the death toll, no matter the failure. Several SS men are rushed away to the camp hospital with serious injuries and one of them lies dead. Those still walking among the corpses bear heavy shoulders, shaken to their cores by this impossible, unpredictable turn of events. How could they have allowed this to happen? How could the weapons and bombs have passed right under their noses? How could the prisoners have found the strength and will to rise up against them?

Our SS lady appears again, having abandoned us in the commotion, flushed and sweating. "What are you doing? Get up! Get up, you filthy rats! Back to Kanada! NOW!" she shouts, brandishing her gun at each of us, a visible tremor in her usually steady arm. "No! Leave the carts, you damned idiots! Roll call!"

Smoke billows from Kanada as we run barreling through the gate after the SS woman and back to our block, passing more lifeless bodies riddled with bullet holes. Crematorium four lies obliterated as though a bomb has been dropped on it, roof and chimney caved in, decimated beyond repair, and flames still lash out at the men trying to quell their burning wrath. The SS stand alert and ready with guns drawn.

Perhaps they'll shoot all of us here and now, I think, hurrying into line beside Bayla and our friends, and find myself straightening taller, staring ahead at the wonderful, smoldering sight of a realized dream.

"I believe we're stronger than them, no matter what they do to us." I remember my friend's words, some of her last words to me before Mengele took her, and for the first time, I believe it is true.

What I wouldn't give to have the strength the twelfth Sonderkommando has displayed today. They did not cower and accept their fates, they did not go as lambs to the slaughter, complacent and waiting for the butchers to slit their throats. Today, they were free men, choosing their own deaths, fighting our killers without fear or regret. By now their bodies will all be burning in the pits alongside the beautiful, blazing ruins of these killing machines; but, for just a few precious moments, they tasted vengeance and freedom.

27

NOVEMBER 10, 1944

"It won't be long now." The whispers and rumors have circulated around Kanada ever since the revolt. *"Just you wait, they're going to get rid of us all soon."* Every passing day, I must admit that I find myself believing them more and more. What use are we to the Germans now?

The transports of people and their belongings have stopped arriving. Instead, the trains are leaving Auschwitz, sometimes carrying prisoners. Now, rather than throwing bodies into the bonfires—though they have not ceased their killings—the SS dump thousands and thousands of files into the flames.

"They don't need witnesses," one woman muttered to Bayla when she asked me what the SS were doing. "We're next, mark my words. We're next."

Shivering in the early morning of roll call, I watch the Germans across the lawn from a distance. They work in the haze of the coming light, tearing up the foundations of the destroyed crematorium four in the still-smoldering smoke of explosives they themselves set off, beneath the shadow of the partially burnt crematorium five.

My heart once rejoiced at the prospect of seeing this place

burn, of going up in flames with it if that was what freedom meant. Now, the weight of despair is heavy over my sagging shoulders as I watch them dismantle their own machine of murder, destroy all the evidence of the atrocities they committed here.

And we're next; ashes don't speak after fire consumes their bodies.

"Prisoner A—30972! Prisoner A—30973!"

I nearly freeze stiff at the sound of our numbers, and for a heartbeat I try to convince myself that I must have misheard.

What's happening? We've done nothing wrong! Do they mean to kill us?

I can feel Roksana's and Orna's eyes on us as we step out of line, terrified and pleading, willing us to come back.

"You're being transferred back to the main camp," Aldona informs us, and her eyes gleam knowingly, as if some secret she holds is one we both share.

The main camp? We were told we could never go back... that the only way out is through the chimney...

Aldona nods in goodbye as she leaves, and I cast one last fleeting glance at my friends still in line as we follow an SS woman. For the first time in almost nine months, we're passing through the gates and down the main road, between the fences and away from Kanada.

Silently, I despair at the thought of returning to the cramped women's camp. After so many long months of sleeping in our own bunks with blankets and straw mats, wearing clean clothes and constantly exchanging our undergarments, being allowed to grow our hair, feasting on the food brought with the transports, and having our own holes in the lavatory, we've grown spoiled.

Why must we leave at all? Why would they let us leave if they don't want to leave any witnesses to their crimes alive? And why just us?

On either side, the fence hums calmly with electricity. Somehow, I think I can hear it buzzing in my ears like a bee, racing up and down the barbed wire, quiet and deadly. It's close, so very temptingly close, just an arm's reach away. I've considered touching the lethal wire on more than one occasion, taking Bayla's hand and leading her peacefully to our deaths, but I never dared to stray more than a few yards near it. Now, if death is my wish, there will never be a better chance.

Bayla walks leaning against me, trusting and oblivious of the haunting darkness in my mind that could kill even the light of the sun as I glance down at her young, tired face.

One touch, that's all it takes. One touch and we're both dead.

All this time, I've told myself that she'll survive, she'll make it through this and know a life beyond the fence. But who is there to say there will ever be an end to this hell at all? If the Germans win the war, we'll never be free again, and what will all the blood and tears we've shed have been spent on?

Maybe this is a kinder fate for us, we won't even feel it, I reason, slipping one of her freezing hands into mine, heart pounding. My arm has never felt so heavy as it does in this moment as I flex my fingers in preparation. I reach out several inches. Deadly, electrifying power tingles my fingertips, beckoning me closer.

"*Don't give in.*" His voice breaks through the haze of my misery, and I pause. "*You will survive this.*" Torn abruptly from my contemplation of death, a second's hesitation, the memory of his voice is all it takes to make my heart falter.

Soleil, Sunna, Yigal, Heinz, Izaak...

I don't know why I repeat the names, the ones he cared about, the ones he couldn't save. Who knows how many other names are on that long list that's all too similar to mine, names he hasn't told me, names that are now just ghosts...

I don't want to be another of his ghosts, I think, my mind eerily clear, and I drop my arm back to my side, trembling fiercely at the realization of what I nearly did. Dying now would end our suffering, but his would go on, strengthened by the thought that, despite all he did, he couldn't make a difference to us. And for some reason I find that thought unbearable.

Not yet. This must be his doing. He must know something and wants us out of Kanada.

Frost coats the thickened mud, white tinges the barracks and roofs, and the inhabitants of the women's camp all stand shivering and wretched as the block elders conduct morning roll call. The SS woman exchanges a few brief words with the Blockälteste before our numbers are marked and we're placed at the front of the lines.

Two hours later, the cheerful sound of the orchestra drifts across the camp, and the women of our block begin to disperse. Once again, lost in a place that used to be familiar, I'm at a loss for what to do and where to go.

When in doubt, hide.

The block door is cracked open just a hair, enough for only the freezing wind to slip through. There might still be a Kapo inside, checking to make sure no one is trying to get away from work to sleep, but it's the best and only place to go. We slink away to the back of the hundreds of women, through the barrack entrance, and I am relieved to find that we are alone. I rush to the back, climbing onto the heating channel to find a top bunk with a straw mattress to hide under.

"Bayla, up here," I whisper urgently. "Climb up."

"What are we doing? What if they catch us?" she whispers back, settling beneath the straw mat while casting a questioning look at the entrance.

"We're resting today. They won't find you, just lie still and don't make a sound."

Despite the food Alaric sends to us and the food we managed to swipe in Kanada, she's still terribly thin. No one will see her unless they climb up. Her heavy eyelids slip closed and her breathing evens, but the deep lines of concern around her eyes and lips remain. Gone is the peace and security a child should have in their dreams, and, among everything else they have taken from us, I loathe the Germans for robbing her of innocence.

How could we ever live again? If this does come to an end one day, what comes after? Where would we go? What would we do when we no longer have to guard ourselves against everything including our own emotions? How could we live as people and not as animals?

Don't think. Don't think. Like a switch, my mind shuts down, numb and walls raised against these thoughts that will send me spiraling down a dark hole if not kept silent.

JANUARY 9–10, 1945

Kanada is empty.

Black smoke still billows from the pits, but no new trains carrying people have arrived, and all the men and women who once worked separating their belongings have disappeared. The rumors vary. Some say they were all gassed, others that they were evacuated to another camp, but there's no way to know for sure, and sometimes I wonder if we would have been better off taking our chances in Kanada.

Probable death in the gas chambers, possible evacuation to some unknown danger, or this, crammed in the diseased, filth-ridden women's camp, faced with constant selections, hard labor, and starvation...

There has been no concrete reason for our transfer, and yet I am certain Alaric had something to do with it. He would have known what was happening in Kanada, he could have pulled a few strings, but, over the long months since then, I have agonized over what fate could have been so horrible as opposed to rejoining the rest of the camp.

The sound of the morning whistle cuts through the air like a knife, cutting off my train of thought before it can spiral into a dark abyss of uncertainty again.

Bayla's entire body jerks at the sound, and her shivering form is damp and unnaturally warm for the dead of winter. For a moment, I think she may have wet herself in the night—many do when they can't get to the bucket or the block leaders won't let us use it—but I smell no fresh urine. Thick beads of sweat coat her face, a scarlet flush tints her cheeks, and I realize she's sweated through her multiple layers of clothing.

"Bayla, are you alright? What's wrong?" I press my fingers gently to her forehead, and the heat nearly burns to the bone.

"I'm cold, Papa," she whimpers, half asleep, and weakly reaches for a blanket we don't have. "Why is it so cold?" Another whistle screams in the distance, and Bayla flinches, whining, "Is it storming? Tell it to stop, Papa, I don't like the thunder."

I pull her into my arms, hastily wiping the sweat from her face. "Bayla! Bayla, you need to wake up!" I urge, desperately swatting her cheeks and pulling her eyelids, which continue to slide shut.

Typhus... How many bodies ridden with this disease did I drag from the infirmary? How many women much older and stronger than my little girl who could not weigh more than thirty pounds have succumbed to death because of this?

A sob tears from my throat in a strained plea, and I pull her out of the bunk. "Stand up, stand up! Please, you can do it! You have to stand up! Bayla, get up!"

Her eyes crack open just slightly, and she moans in pain, legs buckling beneath her, when I try to make her stand.

"Everyone outside! Schnell! Raus! Zählappell!"

"Papa, why are the speakers on?" Bayla cries quietly as the other prisoners rush outside. "Please, I don't like it, I don't like them."

"Bayla, be quiet! Don't talk, just breathe!" I beg, holding her tightly. I must walk both of us into the winter morning while her feet drag limp through the snow like a ragdoll. Unable to fight for a place in the middle of the lines, we are forced to stand directly behind the first row, and I frantically try to conjure a plan, anything besides waiting for the SS to come and take Bayla away.

She can hardly stand, they'll never let her live like this. She can't work. I have to hide her! There has to be somewhere she can go. Maybe the latrines... no, we'll never make it inside. The block is out of the question, the Kapos will search them all day, but maybe... maybe...

Tears prick the backs of my eyes angrily as Bayla continues to quake and groan beside me. There's only one place for us to go, the worst place we could possibly be.

"This is no place for a child. Do not bring her here under any *circumstances."*

But Bayla will be dead today if we don't go; in the infirmary, at least, she will have ten days to recover before they select her.

The women in the front do not protest when I step past them and up to the Blockälteste. She's a German woman who's been here several years, and I know she recognizes me when I approach with the tiny girl clutched at my side. "Old numbers" have a higher status in her book.

"Blockälteste," I begin respectfully. "My daughter is sick, she has typhus. She must go to block twelve, or her lice may spread. I may soon be ill as well. Would you let me take her?"

She scrutinizes Bayla's ragged body, and eventually nods. "Give me your numbers."

"A—30972 and A—30973."

"Gertrude!" she calls to one of the Kapos. "Take these two to the typhus block."

I'm unable to recall the last time I carried Bayla properly, but now as I struggle to lift her into my arms I nearly crumple.

The familiar, foreboding sight of block twelve is like the tip of a knife trailing down my spine as we approach, and the pained moans and screams of women delirious with disease drown out the wind. Feces, vomit, sweat, urine, and blood all mingle together to create one single, vile, revolting stench, the unbearable odor of rot and death. Cramped together head to feet in the bunks, lying scattered across the ground, dead or dying, there is nowhere to go except for the earth hardened by ice beside the heating channel.

Bayla lies limp in my arms, head lolling heavily to the side. Already, her breathing is labored and raspy, but it's the only way I know for certain she's not dead.

"Not yet," I whisper, running my calloused, skeleton hands over her bald head. "Not yet..."

Evening falls swiftly along with the cold. The dead of winter pierces through my thin clothing and slices down to the bone, leaving me shivering against the bricks of the heating channel while I try to keep Bayla warm. She's not woken once since this morning, even when I try to shake her awake to eat, but her body still trembles and seizes every now and again, and her fever has worsened.

The bunks are still filled with women, some living and some dead, but the nurses and cleaners have retired for the night, and so all bodies will lie together until morning. Those still dying are too weak to throw out the dead ones.

Though my muscles ache and the blood seems to pump much slower through my veins, I manage to find the strength to pull myself to my knees. I've watched a woman in the center tier like a predator for hours, her ashen face and the slow rise of her chest, the way her hands curl protectively around a piece of cloth, waiting for her to stop moving. When the darkening barrack becomes nearly too dim to see properly and the lanterns have been extinguished, I can barely make out the outline of her motionless form.

Crawling forward, I reach up and tap her cheek, then, when she doesn't respond, hold my finger under her nose to see if she's still breathing. There is no sign of life. I take her under her arms and struggle to pull her from the bunk. The body lands with an echoing thud, but the constant, consuming sounds of suffering are not disturbed. Quickly, I strip her clothes and leather shoes, and snatch the ration of bread that tumbles from her hands. After I've slipped the new clothes onto Bayla, who still lies asleep, I wedge our bodies between the other women on the plank, ignoring their groans of protest.

There is little body heat to share in, and the frigid night digs deep like thousands of needles. Freezing, starving, lying in our own sickness, there is no escape, no relief. While Bayla's mind is taken by the sweet oblivion of delusion, sleep does not find me this night, and I lie awake until the first crack of dawn slips through the barrack door.

The nurses and cleaners rise in the morning, making their rounds, distributing rations and removing bodies. A girl drags away the body I threw out last night, but I don't dare to look at them.

With a groan, Bayla stirs beside me, and her face twists in discomfort.

"Bayla, wake up," I whisper. "You need to eat something."

"Don't want to," she mumbles, blinking blearily. "Not hungry."

I bring the crust of bread to her lips. "Yes, you are, you have to eat. Here, I have bread for you, it's all for you."

Again, she shakes her head. "Not hungry."

"Bayla, you have to eat!" I urge, trying to force her jaw open. After several minutes of coaxing and tearful, tired protests, she finally relents and nibbles on the bread. A tremor seizes her body and she heaves, turning her head away.

"No! Try to keep it down!" I gasp, clamping my hand over her mouth, but it does no good. She retches violently until what little liquid and food was in her body is gone, and she collapses against me, quivering and weak.

Water... food can come later. If I can't get any fluids into her, it won't matter whether or not she eats. I wait for one of the cleaners to pass by and reach out for the smallest of the women when she approaches our bunk. She still wears the wooden clogs that are agonizing to walk in, and the glint of desperation is prominent in her eyes.

"Fill up my bowl with snow and I'll give you leather shoes," I mutter, drawing her closer by the arm.

Her eyes narrow suspiciously, weighing the risks, and she shifts in painful discomfort in her clogs. "Show me," she finally says.

Not daring to let them within her grasp, I flash the leather shoes I took from the dead woman. She hesitates for a moment before taking my bowl and disappearing down the block. She returns several minutes later with it clutched close to her chest, and I hand over the leather shoes once she's returned it.

The snow is nearly frozen solid when I try to crush it, and I growl in frustration. It will never melt on its own, so I begin to breathe onto it. It seems to take hours before the first few trickles of water slide down the freezing white mounds, and my head spins like a feather in a storm. Time goes on like this for hours, melting the snow breath by precious breath until hammers are thrashing my temples and stars obscure my vision, shaking Bayla awake long enough to pour the few drops down her throat. Still, I force myself to stay awake, all too aware of the heaviness tugging at my stomach, the chill that creeps up my spine. Danger approaches from everywhere, but one who's lived within its shadow for so long can sense its presence like a hound can smell a fox.

From the entrance, a cleaner rushes down the block to a

nurse a few bunks away from us. "It's our block today! Mengele," she says urgently, and the sound of his name alone freezes my soul to the core.

Selection. She must have seen him coming. Death is close.

Time passes much more rapidly than is natural, minutes ticking by within seconds while my body seems to move as painfully slowly as in a nightmare. Ripping back the straw mat we lie on, I hide Bayla beneath it and cover her again, then drag the groaning body of a dying woman to cover her.

Not a heartbeat later, the block door opens, and a shadow darker than night fills the entrance, chasing away the light of the sun. The same sun that has risen upon this hell every day, unwaveringly stared down upon the atrocities the imposters of humanity commit, now refuses to touch something of such pure evil, dares not tread too close to the Angel of Death.

Monsters are supposed to look as such... and indeed they do.

"Get down and line up!" an SS shouts, storming down the block waving his baton.

Rather than bothering with the white chalk, the SS drag the women too weak to move from the bunks and mark their numbers before they even have the chance to try to stand. I climb down to line up with the others, sneaking a forbidden glance at Mengele. There is something grave and almost fearful about his face, a frown and drawn brow so deep the weight of distress must have hung heavy above him for many weeks.

We've all felt the shift in their attitudes over the last few months, the way their voices can no longer be heard singing drunkenly and merrily, the sense of impending defeat where there was once only the assurance of victory. Something is happening, something beyond the fence and the woods, perhaps a shift in the war that worries them.

Mengele's voice breaks just slightly when he shouts, "You will jump over the heating channel!"

A woman attempts to leap over the brick channel, but her

feet catch the edge and she falls atop it. One by one, the weakest of the ill try and fail to clear the small distance, and even the strongest can hardly make it over. Number by number, three hundred women are marked by the time it's nearly my turn, and the weight of my starved body is painful upon my legs.

Can I make it? Am I even strong enough?

I glance back to the bunk where Bayla is hidden. An SS man and doctor have stopped directly where she lies. The SS man grabs the arm of the woman atop her and the doctor marks the number before she's ripped down and kicked to the ground.

Not yet! Not yet!

Neither notice Bayla. They move on to another bunk.

A single gust of icy wind nearly knocks my knees out from under me and I choke back a sob of relief. Bayla will live for another day; now all that is left for me to do is survive. A surge of strength fills my heart and I ready myself in a crouch. Mengele took my friends, he took my parents, he's taken more from me than I ever would have given in a hundred lifetimes. If he wants to take me away from Bayla, he'll have to fight me tooth and nail with his own gloved hands, and I'll scream and savage him like the animal he believes I am. The only way I'll leave this block today is dead.

My turn arrives and I launch myself with all the power left in the muscles that have long died away from my flesh and frail bones. Stumbling just barely as I land on my feet, I look immediately to the doctors. None move to mark my number.

More than half of the entire infirmary is marched and dragged outside, their faces never to be seen again. Stretching out on the suddenly spacious bunk, I peek beneath the mat to check on Bayla. Mercifully, she lies silent and breathing, unnoticed by death, and I leave her to sleep hidden while I return to melting our bowl of snow.

29

JANUARY 18, 1945

I've not eaten in two days. Every ration of bread, each mouthful of soup, all the crumbs pried from frozen hands, I have given to Bayla. I cannot allow myself to starve much longer, but Bayla is far worse off than I. As she alternates between a dead sleep and a confused hysteria, her fever has only risen, any food I force down her throat comes up again, and she's constantly screaming in agony, begging for water and the plate of potatoes she sees in her delirium. The SS have conducted no selections in our block for the last few days, but we cannot go on like this anymore. It's already been nine days and, if Bayla does not miraculously recover by tomorrow morning, she'll be taken.

We only have one day left in block twelve... but maybe in one of the other sickbays we can last a little longer. But how could I get her out?

I look around the block, unsure what exactly I am searching for. Perhaps some wretched face, some empty bunk, some mess of blood or bodies will hold the answer to our survival. Nearby, a cleaner drags a body down from the top of a bunk, stumbling under the weight as it hits the ground. With eyes as dead as the corpse she carries, the cleaner drags it outside.

Of course! The answer hits me suddenly. *I was a cleaner once, I've done this a hundred times before!*

Looking down at Bayla, her hollow face and gray skin, the unbearable thinness of her tiny body, I surmise that she could pass for dead. The dysentery block is close to ours, just a few yards away, and if we can make it there she'll have another ten days to recover. The risk of contracting another grave illness seems almost inconsequential to me as I slip down from the bunk and drag Bayla along with me.

If we stay here, she'll be dead by morning. If I'm caught, we'll be killed right now. In another block, there will be a chance to live for a little longer.

No one, not even the Kapo, questions me as I drag Bayla by her hands to the door. Only the cleaners would dare bother disposing of bodies. Sometimes the best disguise is sheer boldness. Bayla remains silent, head lolling backwards in unconsciousness, thankfully not alerting anyone that she is still alive.

The dead of winter stabs deeply into my bones as I step backwards into the snow, and Bayla gives a quiet groan as the cold assaults her body. The evening is flooded with chaos and flashlights, the screams of whistles and prisoners, SS rushing to gather groups of prisoners. Even in sleep, Bayla cringes at the sounds of German voices screaming unintelligible demands. I haul her past the mound of women piled outside block twelve, hoping that I'll be overlooked rather than shot, and we make it to the entrance of the dysentery block just as a round of gunfire explodes somewhere in the distance.

The overwhelming stench of feces and vomit festers inside worse than I've ever smelt, and I gag, smothering my breath as I strain to step over women lying on the floor in pools of their own filth. I can only manage to pull Bayla as far as the third row of bunks before my strength fails me and I collapse beside a woman moaning in agony. Our presence seems to have gone unnoticed by the nurses and cleaners, and the Kapo of the block only casts me an exhausted look before turning away.

I've seen that look before, as I'm sure many have seen the same expression on my face, the deep frown and empty eyes that say, *They'll be dead soon. Why bother?*

"Noam," Bayla whimpers, straining to sit up on her elbows, her misty eyes staring dreamily at nothing.

Immediately, I produce a slightly nibbled ration of stale bread I swiped from a body back in block twelve. "Here, Bayla, you need to eat. Have this bread."

"But I want a potato," she groans, shaking her head, and tries to reach past me to some ghost. "Noam, please, let me have one! I promise I'll let you win this time! Papa, please! Just one! I'll save the rest for you!"

"Bayla, there are no potatoes, Noam isn't—"

"Yes, there are!" she screams, beginning to thrash, knocking the bread from my hand in a disoriented frenzy. "Look at all of them! Why can't I have one? I just want one! NOAM! PLEASE!"

Never before have her outbursts been this violent, and I must fight to gain control over her flailing limbs. She howls and writhes, scratches in an attempt to break free of my grasp, wails and begs for Noam to hand her a potato, cries inconsolably until her voice is hoarse and she falls back into my arms in exhaustion. Over the moans and screams of the other women, the chaos outside, I can hardly hear her feverish mumbling, and I lean closer to her.

"What is it, Bayla? What do you need?"

Again, she speaks the same few words. Strangely, whatever she utters is not in a language either of us know, but the foreign accent is so natural on her tongue it's as if she's mastered this single phrase by heart. It sounds like Russian... but one word sounds familiar, like something that is pronounced similarly even when spoken across different languages.

"Angel?" I guess, and Bayla slips back to unconsciousness.

Not an hour later, when the Kapo has finally approached to mark down our numbers, the block door explodes open. Three SS men storm inside, guns drawn, winter coats buttoned to their necks, and leather bags slung across their bodies. One of them shouts, "All staff! Cleaners and nurses, with us! Quickly! Schnell!"

No explanation is given as twenty cleaners, seven nurses, and the Kapo are rounded up and herded outside. The shouted commands continue, but no one comes back. The other patients are too consumed with their own misery to notice whatever peculiar, worrisome things are happening just beyond the walls, and those who are well enough to wonder are too weak to inquire.

Movement again at the block's entrance catches my attention, and a man shoves the door open and steps inside. Clad in a heavy winter coat, he carries a burlap bag slung over one shoulder, a gun and leather bag idle at his side. He turns quickly, panting and frantic.

Alaric!

My tightening chest strangles my gasp of shock, and my heart burns with such happiness at seeing his face that the intensity is both confusing and overwhelming. It is as though he can somehow sense my presence, for his eyes shift in my direction and lock with mine. He's rushed to where we lie in an instant, dropping to his knees with a deep sigh of relief. He reaches out, touching his cold, trembling hands to my face as if to assure himself that I am indeed real.

"Oh, thank God!" he rejoices, gazing heavenwards with watering eyes and a pained expression. "Thank God! When I didn't find you in block twelve, I—never mind. Quickly, come with me. I need to get you out of here."

I am far beyond questioning or disobeying any order given to me, but, through his relief and conviction, there is panic in his eyes, and anything that he fears is something I dread a hundred times over.

"Where?" I choke, drawing Bayla against my chest.

"Safety," he insists, his horrified gaze lingering on Bayla for what seems an eternity before he is able to look me in the eye again. "You must leave. *Now.*"

My face burns with shame as Bayla lies against me, resentment for my own failings in protecting her filling my heart. "She can't walk. I can't carry her."

"I will carry her," he says resolutely, and a bead of sweat slides down his temple. "But we have to go now! You must trust me!"

Trust... he's the only one I've ever truly relied on in this place. There is no one I trust completely anymore, but if I were to trust anyone...

He leaves me no time to agree or refuse, just pulls Bayla's bony, featherlight body from me to hold her gently in his arms. "Hurry now, we need to go!"

My head throbs like a pulse as I crawl to my feet unsteadily, fighting to stay standing, and it is all I can do not to collapse with hunger and fatigue. Following Alaric and Bayla, who resembles a pitiful ragdoll slumped over his shoulder, we step out into the frigid, dark evening.

Snowflakes and flecks of ash land on my cheeks, drifting down from an endless stretch of sinister black that I cannot discern between clouds or smoke. The world blurs with the vast night, blinding spotlights, the glow of multiple fires in the distance. We run away from the sickbays, and the chaos is like a roaring wave crashing against my ears and head. Hundreds of women shout and scream in fear and confusion, and move desperately like cattle trying to escape snarling dogs. In the distance, from beyond the women's camp and the mysterious void, the panicked voices of thousands of men echo over the ramp and the fence, gunshots explode, whips crack down on flesh, dogs bark wildly.

Alaric leads me away from all of it, though it seems to surround us on all sides, his grip bruising around my wrist as he drags me to keep pace. I sense my legs moving beneath me, stumbling and struggling to continue on, but even the short distance we've gone has numbed all feeling. My vision blurs as we run like the Angel of Death is on our heels and I peer up at Alaric. Bayla's head is hanging over his shoulder, her limbs dangling lifelessly, and for a moment I fear she may actually be dead.

Time seems to slip by in a matter of seconds, a haze of gunfire, shouts, and disarray, but when we've finally stopped running crematoriums two and three are just a short distance away. Now at the far end of the women's camp, we quickly enter one of the brick barracks and I collapse on the cement floor, legs and lungs burning as I fight to breathe.

"What are we doing—" The rest of my question dies as I reach for Bayla, who he still cradles in his arms. She is pale as a corpse, lips slightly parted, and her chest doesn't move.

"She's not breathing!" I shriek, lunging for her. "She's not breathing! No! Please! Not yet!"

Alaric shoves me back, dropping to his knees and hurriedly searching for a pulse in Bayla's wrist, then her neck. His face crumples.

"NO! No, please, please! She can't be dead!" I wail, my heart collapsing in my chest as I grasp her cold face. "Bayla! Wake up! Please! Wake up!"

"Get back!" Alaric demands, shoving me out of his way and laying Bayla flat on her stomach on the stone floor. He places his trembling hands on her back and begins to press forcefully.

"Stop it! Stop it! You're hurting her!" I cry, slapping him

and desperately trying to drag her into my arms, fearing he will break her tiny, frail body.

"Hodaya!" he shouts in distress, snatching my wrists. *"Get! Back!* I'm trying to help her!"

He resumes his compressions and I can only curl beside Bayla's body and sob, caressing her hollowed, lifeless face. "Please, wake up, Bayla. Tomorrow we're free, remember?" I whimper. "Tomorrow, we just have to make it there. *Please,* we've come so far. You'll be free, I promise, just not like this. Bayla... please wake up, *live... tomorrow...*"

Seconds blur into minutes and my body begins to weaken. I am unable to cry or beg any longer as Alaric continues applying pressure to Bayla's back. I hold her, limp, waiting for death to bring me back to her, to Mama and Papa, to Naomi and Noam, to Levana and Chasha...

A choked wisp of air is suddenly sucked through Bayla's lips. I feel her eyelashes flutter against my cheek and a fierce sob rips from my chest, as if all the air in my body is now her life source, filling her lungs as she begins to take small, ragged breaths.

Alaric turns her over, propping her head up against his leg.

Alive. Alive. Alive, I repeat to myself as I crawl to Bayla, unable to do anything but bow my head, my shaking fingers pressed over her pulse to feel the proof of her life. "Tomorrow you're free," I whisper, kissing her clammy forehead.

"You need to hide," Alaric whispers gently after a long silence, and I realize that tears of relief stain his own cheeks. "This block has already been evacuated and searched three times, they're not coming back to it. You need to stay hidden until it's all over."

"What's happening?" I venture, my voice barely a whisper.

Alaric regards me with troubled eyes. "The Soviets have broken our defenses. We're evacuating the able-bodied prisoners. If Commandant Höss gives the order to dispose of the prisoners unfit for work after I'm gone, I don't want you anywhere near the mass population. I wanted to stay behind longer to look out for you and the others, but I have no choice. I'm to leave tonight."

"Is... is the war over?" I ask, both hopeful and fearful, and see the same two conflicting emotions reflected within his eyes.

He nods reluctantly. "I think it will be soon."

And what does that mean for Bayla and me? For him? What comes after hell if not death?

Having regained his composure, he takes Bayla from me, and I let her go reluctantly as he settles her onto a blanket and straw mat on the top tier, then tosses the burlap bag into the corner of the bunk. He sweeps me into his arms without the slightest shift in expression, and I wonder how he doesn't cringe at the nauseating stench of filth that I myself have never grown completely accustomed to, how much like a corpse I must look and feel. When was it that I last saw my own face? Back in the ghetto?

"Stay against the walls and don't look out the window, you could be seen."

And I won't be here to save you. The words linger unsaid, but I nod in understanding.

"There's food and water in that bag, enough to last you at least two weeks. Conserve it. I know all you want to do is eat right now, but you're starving. If you eat too much, you'll kill yourself. Eat slowly and only a little at a time."

"Thank you, Alaric." My voice quakes in a whisper, and I blink away tears, knowing I could never express in a few moments all I am thanking him for.

He offers a mournful smile, and his eyes gleam with an emotion so deep his irises quiver with the anguish and devotion of it.

Blue, I realize, noticing for the first time the steel-blue shade of his eyes, the color of a vast blue sky after a storm, and I think I've never seen a color more beautiful.

"Will I ever see you again?"

He hesitates, lips pressed in a despairing frown. "I don't think so. Whichever way this war goes, perhaps it's for the best if we never do."

I cannot fathom why that answer pierces my heart the way it does, like the knife that has long resided there being slowly driven deeper. "Then would you answer something for me?"

"Of course. Anything."

"Why did you save us? There were thousands in our transport that day, and you chose *us*. You... you saved Bayla. Why?"

There is something in him that weakens in this moment. His face crumples to reveal the wistful, exhausted man in whose face the guilt is carved so deep he looks to have lived a thousand immoral lives. One of his hands rises to brush against my face, cradling my cheek, soothing me in a way I could no longer imagine anyone capable of, and I find myself leaning toward the warmth and gentleness that I've been deprived of.

"When I lost Heinz, and Soleil and Sunna, I almost lost myself again. I was ready to die, to let God pass judgment on me and all my sins and failings... but I remembered the things Yigal had taught me. Pikuach nefesh."

"Saving a life," I repeat quietly in Yiddish, and the words of my people are foreign on my tongue.

"Yes." Alaric nods. "Yigal believed that in saving one life we save the world. He saved me... and I couldn't save them, so I have tried to live by his words, to save whoever God gives me the chance to save. The night I saw you arguing with Mengele, you reminded me of myself, how much I wished I could have saved my brother and my girls. Your sister is the same age as Soleil was when... I believe God brought me to the train that night to find *you*, because we needed each other. God let me save you... and you have saved me too. *Every day*."

He leans forward, his breath ghosting against my face, and touches his lips to my cheek, near the corner of my own trembling lips. He lingers for several seconds, his fingers caressing the place where I once had beautiful brown hair, and the memory of his kiss is still warm against my cheek when he draws away. A tear slips from my eye, one that he quickly brushes away, then he presses another gentle kiss to my forehead. Swiftly, he shrugs off his green wool coat and slings it over my shoulders, engulfing me beneath the sheer size and warmth of it. "You'll be liberated soon. You're going to live through this. Please... promise me you will live, Hodaya."

"I promise I will live," I whisper.

Again, he takes my face into his hands, his watering gaze roaming my features as if committing them to memory, though I don't imagine I am very pleasant to look upon anymore. I let myself do the same, memorizing the color of his eyes, the length of the scar on his cheek, the arch of his nose, the tenderness in his face.

"Perhaps in another world... another life..." he murmurs, his voice trembling, and I reach out to softly trace the path a tear has taken down his scar. His expression twists as if in great agony, but he leans into my touch almost desperately, and places one more lingering kiss to my palm.

"Goodbye, Hodaya. God be with you," he whispers, and I wish I could find the words to beg him not to leave.

But, like yet another ghost, he slips from my grasp and disappears from the block, the door slamming shut behind him with an echoing, crushing finality. The emptiness is endless, stretching across the barrack and deep within my soul, and I question whether or not the man who saved me was indeed a living person or some creation of my broken mind. But he had to have been real, or else I would still be in the infirmary, perhaps awaiting a massacre, Bayla would be dead, there would be no coat covering my body, and I know I could never have imagined the wonderful warmth or the softness of his lips.

In her sleep, Bayla murmurs the strange words again, and I slide closer to shield both of us with the green winter coat and the blanket.

Angel...

Wearily, I rest my head heavily on my arm, blinking away the sleep that threatens to take over, and listen. Outside, the gunshots still fire, the screams still reach through the brick walls, and explosions like the day of the Sonderkommando's revolt shake the ground. Somehow, I cannot find it within myself to feel afraid, only resigned to keeping my promise to Alaric, and I softly press my lips to my palm where he did just moments ago.

30

JANUARY 27, 1945

The last of the remaining SS blew up the last gas chamber yesterday, then fled, and an eerie, empty silence has persisted since nightfall. The wind hums quietly today, carrying with it the whispered voices of a thousand wandering souls, lost and filled with sorrow. Yesterday, it howled with fury and rattled the windows, swept the scent of fire and ash to choke every creature still drawing breath, demanded to be heard and felt.

Somehow, Bayla has remained silent since we left the infirmary nine days ago, even when she wakes in a daze. Her fever, though still high, has come down slightly, and I've managed to get her to eat several rations of bread and half a canteen of potato soup. The urge to gorge myself on the precious bits of food I've been denied at every turn is torturous, and I now stow the bag beneath the bunks to keep the temptation out of sight and to work some of my strength back up by climbing the ladder.

I've risked a few peeks out the window, and even through the block door yesterday, and there have been no signs of life. The prisoners are gone, the SS are gone, and we can't stay here forever.

Maybe there are still others. Maybe they've been left behind too, I think as I wrap Bayla in the blanket, tucking it full of straw in hopes of it providing some extra insulation, wobbling when I carry her down from the bunk. She barely weighs anything at all, but I still struggle to hold her entire weight. The length of Alaric's coat brushes the ground on me, and the warm wool flaps are wide enough that I can button them around Bayla too.

The stillness outside the block has me hesitating for several seconds before I take a deep breath, reminding myself that it's now alright to leave without permission. Smoke rises in the distance from Kanada, the still-burning remains of the crematoriums. The late-afternoon sky is dark with approaching clouds that hang threateningly like a noose, and patches of ash coat the thick white snow, trampled into an ugly, black and filthy mess of thousands of footprints. The tracks are unavoidable, and I must pass through them toward the main gate, through the last remains of the people who've vanished.

This place, once crowded with thousands of people, now lies empty and waiting, the final resting place of a million murdered souls, the abandoned remnants of a manmade hell.

My foot slips atop a patch of ice and I stagger, nearly landing both of us on the wet ground. The snow is beginning to soak through all three pairs of socks, stinging like hot needles. White mist forms about my face, a tiny, single cloud of air alone among the smoke and suffocating silence. Grinding my teeth together, I force my feeble legs to continue on, to take one cautious step at a time.

Through the haze of every shuddering breath, shapes begin to take form in the distance, fragile, slender figures lingering near the barbed wire, but none make any move toward the gate. At the entrance of a brick barrack, a woman leans slumped against the door, staring out at the people by the fence. Faces of other prisoners lie in the windows, large, lifeless eyes staring intently into a meaningless void, others closed with the relief of escape, and I cannot tell whether or not any of them are alive.

We are all dead. No sane person could have survived this hell.

From the woods, a snowman moves, a strange furry animal atop its head. Squinting, befuddled by this odd illusion, I pace forward a few steps, wondering if perhaps my mind has come undone. What kind of sadistic beast would build a snowman here?

The flicker of a memory lights and quickly extinguishes in my mind, the image of a couple and two young daughters building snowmen outside a little house, of the girls placing their father's hat on it.

Was that real? I wonder almost dreamily. *Was there once a world where Bayla and I built a snowman?*

Another snowman suddenly appears behind the first, then a third and a fourth, more and more emerging from the woods until one has finally drawn close enough that I can discern that it is a person. Dressed in fur caps and white winter coats that camouflage them well in the snow, a group of men approach.

Are they soldiers? Soviets?

My heart quickens as they draw closer, tentative and apprehensive in their steps. Two men break the chains on the gate and shield their noses, cringing at the stench. Their wide eyes examine us with a terrified curiosity, and I wonder if this is how we looked to the other long-dead prisoners when we first arrived as new transports.

Poor, ignorant souls. They don't know what hell they've come to.

One by one, they enter warily, and the women back far away toward the blocks. Offering his bare palms as a show of goodwill, one soldier halts in his advance, and with a quick gesture orders the others to do the same. He makes a loud declaration, but the mere sound of a language I cannot understand makes me flinch, my stiff hold on Bayla tightens, and I am suddenly desperate to hide. All the ones who couldn't understand our killers' language never lived long. Again, the man calls out to us.

A woman wails in Polish, "Free! Jews, we're free!" She staggers to the soldier, throws her arms around him, and sobs. Momentarily stunned, the bewildered man glances at his comrades before gently patting her back, his attempts to speak to her drowned out by her cries of joy.

An entire battalion soon comes from the forest and dozens of half-dead prisoners emerge into the icy winter afternoon. Hundreds are still too weak to move and remain lying in their bunks, watching the unfolding scene from the barrack windows. Shouts of triumph, cries of relief and heartache echo hauntingly through the deserted camp. Distraught, ghostly faces dissolve into tears, bodies collapse with disbelief, hurl themselves into the confused, worried arms of our saviors, and kiss the flaps of their coats.

We're free...

The world beyond the gate is placid, a quiet scene like a canvas painting, snow coating the ground and barren branches. I always hated those kinds of paintings, the realistic ones, the dark, bleak images lacking lively colors. How often did I paint a sun over a moon, a blue sky over a storm, a family picnic over a funeral scene? How many of my works still exist somewhere in this colorless world, a dark reality beneath the pretty lie I wanted it to be?

I start toward the gate, and it seems to distort with every step, moving further and further away the closer I get.

"Do you speak German?"

A Russian soldier blocks my path, eyeing the green Wehrmacht coat I wear and the skeleton I cradle.

"Yes."

"Why are you here?" he asks, the words rolling strangely off his tongue.

"I am a Jew," I mutter, gazing longingly past him to the open gate. The pathway to freedom, the chains broken off, sitting wide open with no one to guard, no one to kill me if I try to pass through... why must it look so wrong, so out of place?

"How long have you been here?"

I... I don't know. How long have we been prisoners of the Reich? What day is it? What month is it? It's winter now, the second one I've seen in this place... "Over a year, I think."

A quiet gasp parts his lips and his eyes widen. "A year?" He slips the cap from his head and pulls it down over my ears. "Here, you're freezing. When did you last eat? What is this place?"

Hell.

If ever the human race wished to find the true depths of their ability for evil, they need look no further than what the Nazis can do to just a single person. Do so, and they'd be appalled to learn that man can justifiably do anything unto that which he doesn't consider human. If it's said to have no feelings, if it's said to not truly be human even if it looks to be, if it's said to have wronged you in some way, then to kill it is not murder. To kill a rat in the pantry is not murder, it is necessary to keep it from breeding and infesting the house, and this place is but a rat trap. This is where humanity comes to die. It is the physical proof of the hideous reality of a righteously gilded civilized world. Man is the only true evil on this earth, they are the only real monsters, and any god who could create or allow the existence of either is no being to have faith in.

I shield Bayla's head against the wind, holding my breath a moment to ensure I can still hear her breathing. "This is hell..."

"Hell?" He blanches, and he stops me again when I try to leave. "What's happened here?"

"Please, let me walk!" I protest, cringing away. "Let me go! I have to—I want... the gate..."

I have to touch the other side. I have to know it's all truly over.

He steps away in surrender, lips pressed into a concerned frown, eyes heavy with a compassion I've scarcely felt for a long time. Though he allows me past without any more questions, he stays close by, watching.

Of all the selections I've run, all the bodies I've dragged, and all the memories I've aided in destroying, no task has ever felt so strenuous, so unbearable as the last few feet between the camp and the unknown. At last, for the first time in over a year, I step over the boundaries.

I breathe deeply the bitter air, letting it fill my chest with piercing cold, my first breath of freedom... and it tastes of ash. I gasp; the thick sent of smoke strangles my throat, fire burns through my body, ruthlessly slaughtering any traces of hope or relief. Starvation, dehydration, and exhaustion still twist and writhe painfully against my bones from within, scars and open wounds still litter my skin and soul. Faintly, Bayla breathes, so close to death I wonder if her dreams are glimpses of the other side. The space surrounding what remains of us is a freezing, gaping void, a nothingness so heavy it crushes me to the ground, and there are no arms to make me feel safe, no voices to whisper my childhood poem, no hands to dry my tears.

Papa. Mama. Naomi. Levana. Chasha.

A broken sob tears from my throat, their faces and names now irrepressible in the face of liberation, and the hollowness in the places beside me where they never should have been taken from is excruciating. They're all dead. They're never coming back. We are still alone. Nothing is over...

My heart begs for mercy as the iron walls that have long surrounded it begin to heat and melt, burning it alive. It pounds against my ribs and pleads that I release it, save it from this torturous prison, curses the agony in the guise of freedom that I welcomed in, and I wish I could rip it from my chest. Fury rises from deep within the crack in my soul, a rage born of betrayal, misery, and indignation. A scream pierces the air, a blaring screech of anguish and defeat that fills the valley, and I realize it is my own.

God, forgive us our sins! I have lied and thought ill of my peers! I have felt envy and greed, stolen, hurt, and cheated! Punish me these unforgivable transgressions as you see fit, but what of yours? Mustn't you answer for your betrayal, the genocide you let your beloved creations inflict upon your others?

"Beg my forgiveness! BEG MY FORGIVENESS!" I scream, sobbing to the heavens, to the sky smothered by black smoke and the eternal stench of death, to the God I no longer believe in, and I despise how sour the taste of freedom is.

31

JANUARY 28, 1945–MARCH 30, 1946

AFTER

By the time Bayla was nearing recovery in the early days of February, typhus had taken a vicious hold of me. The Red Cross rushed in to treat the survivors, but, with only a few doctors and a dozen nurses for thousands of starving people suffering from typhus, tuberculosis, dysentery, and all other kinds of ailments, the situation was severe. Several hundred were dead within weeks. My own illness lasted well into April, during which at some point we were moved into the brick barracks of Auschwitz I, which had been converted into hospitals.

It was nearly June before Bayla and I were strong enough to leave the camp, and only a few hundred survivors remained behind, still too weak to do anything. With the continent still ravaged by war, I was reluctant to go anywhere, especially as a woman with a little girl. Halina, a volunteer from the Polish Red Cross who cared for both Bayla and me for the better part of four months, was the one to offer a solution. When I was coherent again, she told me about the displaced persons camps and suggested I take Bayla to a camp in Braunschweig, Germany, nearly five hundred miles away.

When she proposed the idea, I had rudely demanded if she wanted us to be raped by drunken Soviets before being killed by Nazis. She'd taken none too kindly to that accusation, but insisted she understood my mistrust. One of her uncles worked for the UNRRA, a British agency providing relief to victims of the war, and it was them operating the camp. Several members of her family uprooted by the war resided there, and so too did fourteen survivors her uncle had personally funded to make the journey. I refused at first, knowing well enough that no one would be willing to waste so much money and effort on two strangers without expecting anything in return.

For five days while I was too weak to escape her and Bayla slept at my side, she talked and talked of her uncle and Braunschweig until I would rather have torn my ears off than listen to her any longer. The subject faded for a month or so, and I assumed she'd given up. However, one morning she approached again, and I was prepared to suffer her persistence. Instead of stories she brought two identification cards, two tickets for a train station in a town nearby that was set to depart in two days, and a small purse holding folds of money. The blank cards were already stamped and signed, and asked all authorities to provide aid and excuse our lack of documents as we were prisoners in Auschwitz, where all our identification was destroyed. "You should go far away, far from this place and all the pain it holds for you. Fill in your names and birthdays, and you'll be in Germany in three days," she had said, sounding so hopeful I couldn't help but believe her.

In the end, I finally agreed, and she bade us a tearful goodbye two days later, wishing us all the luck and happiness in the world. It is the rare, genuinely kind people like Halina who bring some shimmer of light to the darkness. I never told her, but I changed our names on those documents and all the ones to come. The war killed everything of the woman I once was, and it felt wrong to pretend to be her now that she was gone, and so my documents bear the name Halina Nowak and Bayla's say Basia Nowak.

The train was horrendous. The grinding of the metal tracks, the scream of whistles, the horrid familiarity of it all made me sick, and I spent the entire time slumped against the window while Bayla chattered away with a little Polish boy across from us. The boy's mother had looked worriedly upon me when she asked if I was alright, then if it was my first time on a train. I had shaken my head but couldn't bring myself to speak. "Don't fret, dear, everything's going to be alright. Don't you know? Germany surrendered! Hitler is dead," she'd said with an encouraging smile.

I knew that, of course. Everyone did, but all I could think was, *too late.*

Braunschweig was a suitable enough place despite lacking some sanitary facilities, food shortages, and cramped living arrangements, but it was a dream compared to what we had grown accustomed to. While the Allies were still fighting Japan and people were fleeing to places like Britain and the United States, trying to piece their lives back together, we settled into a routine in Germany. I found work as a seamstress—though it took some time for my hands and mind to remember how to work the needle and thread—and farmed the vegetables from the small crops outside our living quarters. Bayla spent her days in the camp's school, quickly catching up on all the education she'd missed since the invasion and making friends with the other children.

I tried to find some level of normalcy, to forget, but the more time passed the harder it became to move on. My new reality was something I couldn't fully accept. That I could take my shoes off when I lay down to sleep and they wouldn't be stolen. That there would still be enough food tomorrow and it wasn't necessary to ration myself. That constantly looking over my shoulder for Kapos and SS was now just paranoia and not possible anymore. That I could come and go freely and be assured no one would stop me. How could I heal and conform to society again when I still felt more or less like an animal, a beaten dog dreading the moment its owner discovers it outside the fence?

Months passed and nothing ever changed. I worked and saved money, Bayla attended school and learned to be a normal twelve-year-old girl, we kept to ourselves and relied on no one else, as had become ordinary. Life went on, even if I often wished it didn't.

It was late September when I was once again confronted with the past I had so desperately been trying to forget. As I approached the pharmacy one day after work, a woman with vivid blue eyes was leaving, holding hands with a gentleman whose face was hardened much beyond his years.

"You were in Birkenau," I gasped, causing them to stop dead in their tracks.

I wished at that moment that I knew her name; it was far too wrong in my mind to speak the number tattooed on her arm, though it was all I knew her by. Instead, I could only recount the few times I'd seen her. "You gave me food from an Oberge-freiter, and you were a messenger. You told them you spoke German."

Recognition and disbelief suddenly shone in her eyes, and she embraced me like some long-lost friend. "He said your name was Hodaya. My name is Eliana. My husband is Toviel. We knew him too."

They were both survivors of the death marches. I spoke with them at great length, listening to them recounting their stories of the ghettos, labor camps, and Auschwitz, and telling them only fragments of mine.

I was reluctant to inquire about Alaric, but they both

graciously welcomed the subject. Toviel told me about how he had met a German soldier named Alaric Engel when he was working in a factory in Auschwitz, a corporal of the Wehrmacht who often slipped him and a few others extra rations of food. When Alaric realized that Eliana was registered within Birkenau, he offered to carry messages between the estranged couple, the only contact they could have, given the yellow triangle Toviel wore.

Eliana was terrified he'd turn them over to the camp officials for months, but Toviel insisted he'd never feared Alaric after he lied on behalf of a prisoner. Another man named Marek who Toviel worked with had stolen from one of the warehouses and was facing execution, but Alaric claimed the fault. He claimed that he had the missing items sent to the main camp and had just forgotten to document it, and saw no point in wasting workers. As far as Toviel knew, Marek was still alive, a survivor liberated with them in April after another death march from Buchenwald.

I wished then that I could talk to Alaric, tell him about the people he managed to save. After all, I knew better than anyone how he tormented himself for the lives he failed to protect, and I longed so desperately to hold him in my arms one more time and tell him that he made a difference to us.

Eliana and Toviel left Braunschweig shortly before winter, prepared to emigrate to America and never look back to the crumbling foundation of what was once their home. I loathed the idea of remaining in Germany, and the prospect of returning to Poland wasn't much more appealing, but I had no desire to leave Europe. Most chose to escape while they could, but for some reason I could not find it within myself to do the same, like some invisible chains still bound me to the ruins of my world.

Ultimately, the only choice for me was to return to Poland, to resettle in Bochnia and try to rebuild my and Bayla's lives.

We waited out the winter and I busied myself getting our documents in order. When the time finally came in the last days of March when we were set to leave, the uneasiness was a rock in my stomach, and I knew someday I would come to regret my decision.

At daybreak, with Alaric's coat stuffed away in a bag along with my life's savings, a bit of food, and the clothing I'd made for us, we boarded the last train leaving Germany. Bayla was quiet for the first hour, fiddling with the matching bracelet she and her friends had made together, morose and without appetite. I braided the silky blond strands of her growing hair, listened to her read aloud the book her teacher, Mrs. Weiss, gifted to her before we left, and wondered if she would resent me for being unable to let go.

APRIL 2, 1946

We have trekked at least two hundred miles on foot over the last few days, and now the third train we've boarded pulls into Bochnia station with just a few hours to sunset. For the first time in two and a half years, we're returning to the same tracks we once left by in cattle cars. How many of those thousands deported that day are still alive? How many of them will never see this place again?

Five of them reside hauntingly in my mind, and I fight away the tears that threaten to fall as I gaze out of the window at the familiar buildings.

There's no protection this time, no guidance, no one to stand between us and danger. I am the head of our family now.

"Come on, Basia," I mutter, nudging her awake from where she leans against my shoulder. "Wake up. We're home."

Are we really? Is this place still home, or the shadow of what is left of it? The broken remnants of a life that might have been and the reality of the nightmare it became. No... we're not home... this place can never be home again.

Blue eyes flutter open, soft with the peace of dreams of home and family. She wears the white-collared yellow dress embroidered with white butterflies that I made for her to wear for this occasion. Briefly, the image of a tiny girl clad in a yellow coat dancing excitedly down the pavement flashes before my eyes.

Bayla smooths the wrinkles from her dress and we slide out of our seat. As we pass down the aisle, I feel her slip her hand nervously into mine, and I squeeze it tightly in assurance. Part of me doesn't want to step down onto the platform, but I force myself not to hesitate, to be the perfect image of the confident leader I need to be.

To touch down again in the city of my birth and childhood, the place of all my fondest memories although I can barely remember them anymore... it is surreal, unnerving. I've seen all these buildings before, I've walked these roads and passed these gates and gardens, yet somehow, I recognize nothing. It's like this place is one I've only ever visited in my dreams.

"Halina?" Bayla mutters hesitantly, still unaccustomed to using our new names.

"Yes?"

She leans heavily against me as we walk, her eyes turned downwards. "What did you want to be when you grew up?"

What did Hodaya want to do with her life? She's so unfamiliar now I wonder if she was an entirely different person I grew up with, a long-lost friend I've not seen in so long we hardly know each other anymore. But if she had had the chance...

"I wanted to be a painter..."

And everyone thought I'd be a famous artist one day... Mrs. Ellen, Aunt Dalia, Mama and Papa...

"Do you still want to be?"

What I want in this life doesn't matter anymore. All that can matter is what I need to do.

"Not anymore. What about you? What do you want to be when you grow up?" I look down at her and try my best to smile, beyond grateful I am able to ask her that question.

She considers it for a while and eventually shrugs her shoulders. "I don't know. I liked all the books Mrs. Weiss read to us. She was really nice. Maybe I'll be a teacher like her."

Like Mama...

"I think you'd make a wonderful teacher."

Old doors sit cracked open, fraying curtains flap in the wind over broken windows, patches of dirt where there was once lawn and flowerbeds are empty, and some buildings—though fully intact—are dull and unkempt. The streets are empty in this part of the city, clearly avoided and untouched for quite some time. Perhaps it is now haunted by the spirits unable to escape it. There is something about the street we turn down that I recognize. Some sense of déjà vu has me searching my memory for an image of these quiet houses and apartments, the bakery and little abandoned shop, coming up short even though I'm certain this place holds more significance than most.

Bayla tugs me to a stop. "Do you think they'll come back now?"

Curiously, I follow her gaze to a little brown house, curtains drawn over the windows. The fence and gate must have been white at some point, but the paint is chipping, so worn down by rain and snow there's hardly any color left. The longer I stare at it, the more a forgotten memory nags at the back of my mind, inching its way forward until I suddenly realize what we're looking at.

Aunt Dalia's house! Is this really it?

Silent and somber, the house has evidently lived without inhabitants for many years. She never wrote to us like she promised she would. She's probably dead; she, her husband, and the children, just like everyone else we ever knew. I doubt they ever made it to France.

We are truly alone.

"Come on." I pull her along, holding her close to my side.

Never looking back, we wind our way down the street, toward a place I can only hope is empty like nearly everywhere else.

Gray rainclouds are beginning to gather overhead, and a rumble of thunder fills the air. Bayla gasps quietly and grabs my arm, her nails biting through my thin overcoat, and this simple reaction lifts my heart just slightly.

Like a dream fallen into reality, a house takes form before us, much smaller than I ever remember it being. A moment in time, preserved like a photograph; nothing looks any different. The bush beside the kitchen window is still tall and green, the curtains are still tied back to reveal darkness inside, the same few stones are missing from the sidewalk, and for a moment I could almost believe we never left.

Eagerly, Bayla releases my hand and runs up to the door, fist poised as if to knock, as if waiting for a kindly, beautiful woman in an apron with the same blue eyes to welcome her home.

When I turn the doorknob, I find it unlocked, and a cold, fusty draft sweeps outside as we step through the threshold. Dirt and leaves are tracked across the floor, dust floats in the fading light trickling in through the open windows, and the boards that were once nailed over them now sit abandoned below the sills. Layers of dust coat the furniture, flecks of paint are beginning to chip from the walls, and in the stillness there lies an uneasy silence, the suppressed whispers of memories long gone.

Two and a half years since they took us from Bochnia... six years since they threw us out of this house... and an eternity we've been gone.

Quietly, Bayla crosses the room to the sofa. Alma sits on the cushions, patient and watchful, and so too does the blond baby-doll a wonderful, generous woman once gifted to Bayla. Her bright green eyes, beautiful smile, and the last time I saw her pale, defeated face all flash before my eyes. I swallow thickly as Bayla takes the dolls up into her arms and hugs them tightly.

The babydoll stares at me over Bayla's shoulder, and I wonder how I never noticed its eyes are the most vivid green... I decide I will hide it later, somewhere I'll never have to see it again.

I glance up at the ceiling. The dark hole of an embedded bullet stares down at me. Men fighting for a gun, beaten, crying women, gentle hands trying to pull us away from soldiers...

"Do you want your own room?" I ask, desperate to fill the silence.

Bayla beams. "Really? I can have my own room?"

"Of course you can. You're almost thirteen now."

And there was once a time I wasn't sure you'd live to be that old...

Her eyes widen, as if she has suddenly remembered something important, and she turns swiftly to the bookshelf.

"What's wrong?"

"I put it back here when they made us leave," she says, pulling out several books at a time. "They weren't looking, so I hid it behind the books."

Brows raised at her anxious movements, I look over her shoulder. "Where you hid what?"

"This! I was so worried they'd found it!" Smiling as brightly as the day I gifted it to her, she slips a familiar string of blue beads over her head, adoringly running her fingers over the white pendant bearing the symbol of *chai*. Even though her coat is now gone and the necklace rises much higher on her chest, I cannot help but see the same little girl who once giggled at nothing and everything, smiled and sang and danced like no one was watching, loved everyone who came into her life and brightened their worlds with the gentlest touch.

And she's still there. In the now-dimmed irises of our mother's blue eyes that have seen the worst of humanity, there is a glimmer of hope, of happiness. In the arches and shapes of her young, experienced face, the memory of innocence is not so far away. In the kind heart of a girl that's survived what many could not, her soul remains pure and untainted. Somehow, the little girl who I thought died in the camp is still alive, still smiling and hopeful in the face of misery and uncertainty.

She is far stronger than me.

Down the hall, something rustles, and we both freeze. Soft, nearly soundless steps hurry toward us. Urgently, a cat meows, high-pitched and fervid, and, when the little animal emerges into the front room, Bayla cries out with joy. There, as surprised to see us as we are to see him, Asher stands, flicking his tail wildly.

"Asher!" Bayla scoops him up into her arms and he continues to meowl, purring contentedly and rubbing against Bayla's face, ecstatic to be back in the arms of the girl who brought him inside a lifetime ago from a stormy night. "Asher, you're alright! I'm so happy you made it!"

Smiling, I ruffle the scraggly orange cat's fur. "You see? I told you he would be fine."

"He's a smart cat," she echoes my words from the day we were deported. She looks up to me with glistening eyes. "Can we give him a plate of beef and warm milk now?"

I hope one day I'll be able to keep more than just that one promise to you.

"Bread will have to do right now. Maybe tomorrow we'll see. We can sleep out here tonight."

The rooms are still destroyed. I doubt the soldiers bothered with them. I'll need to clean them up tomorrow and find a job and get Bayla back into school. I can find essentials in the abandoned houses for now, blankets, clothes, maybe some food and medicine. We all left something behind, that which we couldn't carry with us, all the things we treasured and all the things we couldn't fit in one bag. There'll be more than enough for two girls, even if our former townsfolk looted them after we disappeared.

Content, Bayla bounces onto the couch as Asher squirms

desperately to burrow further into her arms. She murmurs quietly, stroking his coarse fur, cuddling him lovingly to her chest.

The wind whistles outside, gliding over the windows to howl throughout the house. It beckons me to listen, to follow, and I leave Bayla and Asher to reacquaint without noticing my departure. It brushes through my hair, finally beginning to grow past my ears, thicker with my improving health and the passage of time. The scent of approaching rain sends an uneasy shudder through my body and, to my dismay, my first instinctual thought is how we'll stay warm during roll call.

A drop of water lands on my cheek, another on my eyelid, another and another until a light mist showers me from above. It reminds me of the poem once again, of the words Mama and I once whispered to each other so long ago, the ones she soothed my fears with and I in turn soothed Bayla with, the ones with which, in a single moment before boarding a train, she passed responsibility to me. I have never forgotten those words, not even when survival was all that consumed me, and I couldn't remember the stories of my faith, the words of any prayer, or the names of people who were dear to my heart.

> *Worry not my child,*
> *The clouds may be here,*
> *Yet there is nothing to fear.*
> *Think not of the thunder that you hear,*
> *Remember the water that falls swift and clear.*
> *Think not of the lightning that hits the ground,*
> *Remember the rain and its soothing sounds.*
> *Let the rain wash away your tears,*
> *Let it wash away your fears,*
> *Worry not my child,*
> *As long as I am by your side,*
> *You shall have no reason to hide.*

I allow the rain to soak my face, gaze up at the gray clouds as lightning flashes, let my tears merge with the storm, and drop to my knees as what is left of my heart shatters. I am struck once again by the unbearable silence, the emptiness, and I sob, desperately trying to muffle my wails of misery, overwhelmed all at once with all the pain, guilt, and fury I've tried to smother.

The rain washes over me, but my fears and tears still remain. I am no one's child anymore. There is no one by my side, no one who can tell me everything will be alright... The only ones who could have are dead. For a few moments, I allow myself to remember their faces, to cry until I have nothing left, to grieve the world that might have been, the world that was butchered before my eyes. Then, I force myself to stand, to lock the pain away in the deepest, darkest corner of my heart, to remember the promise I made to Alaric, to return to Bayla and keep existing for her sake.

FEBRUARY 25, 1961

BOCHNIA, POLAND, PRESENT DAY

Her gaze lingers blindly on the final page of a third journal, the first two carefully stored at her side, and her hands tremble as she closes the cover.

"I don't even remember this much," Bayla whispers, as if afraid to speak too loudly, of disturbing all the ghosts of my memory now rekindled with new life. "Some of it, I do, but... there're a lot of blank spots in my mind."

Then I'm grateful for those small mercies.

"That's normal. You were young and the mind does what it must to protect itself," I say, and part of me wishes I too had these empty gaps in my memory.

"I remember Kanada the most, all the things we sorted there. And Orna. I can't really remember her face anymore. I just know I used to think she looked like Noam..."

Decades later, the mere thought of his name, his kind eyes and adoring smile, a knife sharpened by shame and sorrow still pierces deep in my heart. I only ever mourned him once; in the arms of a woman who was my family in everything but blood, a sister I have never been able to grieve for. So much guilt and regret... where does one begin to lament so many dead without shattering into a million pieces beyond repair?

And what of my friends in the camp? Whatever happened to Roksana, Orna, and Leah after we were separated, when we left Kanada and they stayed behind?

Bayla's soft ruminations draw me back from my head. "I think about Yeva a lot, too..." She shifts uncomfortably on the sofa, glancing up to gauge my expression.

Don't talk about it, don't think about it, and don't look at it. That was always our rule in the camp, and we honored it even after liberation. Nearly twenty years... now we sit together, no longer twenty-three and twelve but women of thirty-eight and twenty-seven, and still we've never spoken of it to one another.

"She stole food for me every day in the kitchens. She'd say the same thing every time." Delicately, like she's reciting a piece of solemn poetry, she forms the foreign words as she once did so long ago in her typhus delirium. "Angel khorosh. She always said that when she gave me food."

"Angel is good," I murmur. *Engel is good.*

Ever since liberation, I have poured my heart and soul into learning every language I could. It was an easy way to keep my mind distracted at all times. As I mastered Russian, I tried to recall what it was Bayla kept on repeating that night she nearly died, but "angel" was the only word I could pick out.

"I never actually saw his face. I was too scared to look at him back then, but I remember his voice. Up until now, I always thought Yeva meant God's angels were watching over me... but that wasn't it." Her eyes, as mine often do, turn to Alaric's portrait. "*Engel.* She wasn't saying angel. She was telling me his name."

"He saved us." I reach out to take her hand, subconsciously

brushing my fingers over her pulse to make sure she's alive. "We wouldn't have lived without him."

And I will never know why we lived. All these years, and I have still never been able to understand why it was us out of thousands who survived. We were no more important than the little boy and his sisters, no more than the old man and his granddaughter, and, truly, the mother and her infant had more reason to be saved than I did. Somehow, after he had lost, gained, and lost everything again, Alaric believed God had brought *me* to him. In the end, it is only what we believe that gives life meaning, what gives God and humanity virtue or vice.

"I wish I had known him." Bayla sighs wistfully. "Do you know what happened to him? Is he still alive? Did he die in the war?"

To contemplate that outcome brings tears to my eyes, and I wish I could put to rest this awful possibility. There are few who would mourn him. I would. I'm sure his mother would; so would little Werner and Gisela, if any of them are still alive. After the war, headlines started emerging about Allied bombardments in Germany, and Nuremberg was completely decimated—

I shake my head. "No. If he died, I hope it was quick and, if he is alive, I hope he has found peace."

She gives my hand a tight squeeze. "I think he would want the same for you, Halina. After all this time, I don't think you ever have."

There is no sense in denying it, not to her. No woman who's found some measure of happiness in the aftermath of so much death would live as I have, wasting away in the memories of a past long gone even when her only reason for living has made her own way into the world.

Outside, a little boy's joyous laughter is joined by a man's, and Bayla's face grows gentle at the sound of her husband and son. How strange it still is to think of her that way, a wife of five years and a mother for four. She's managed to find a purpose in her life, to move on from the dark, bloody past with a strength more resolute than mine.

"Please come back to England with us," Bayla murmurs, pleading again the same request. "Edward and I have talked about it a lot, you know that. We have more than enough room. I miss you so much, and you'll be able to see Eldad every day. It's time for you to leave this place behind. Please, Halina, I just want to see you happy."

"I know you do..."

I've had many chances to find happiness, but I was never able to take them. Over the years there have been six men who've courted me, but nothing ever lasted long. They were perfectly wonderful men, honest, loving, hardworking, and looking to build a family. It was something I wanted very much, but every time I tried to move forward something drew me back again. So many opportunities to escape Poland, this place I've come to think of with bitter loathing, yet I can never seem to let it go, and I've long resented myself for it.

"But I can't... I just can't, Basia. I'm not ready to leave."

Deflated, her shoulders sag and she sighs in resignation.

"But I *am* ready to start talking about it," I decide, and her entire body jerks in shock.

"You are?"

For so many years I have been silent, kept the horrors and tragedies of my life locked away in my head. But that is exactly what the Nazis would have wanted if my murder was no longer a possibility. They would rejoice in my silence, the anguish I've punished myself to fester in, wait for the day I die within the bounds of my own silenced prison where everything they ever did will fade with me. Only with my silence am I completely defeated.

"All this time, I've been trying to forget everything. Sometimes I still want to, but I know how wrong that is—Mama, Papa, Naomi... they never would have forgotten me, and I've killed them too, by trying to forget. They deserve to be remembered. All of them... everyone who died there."

"I think so too," Bayla whispers tearfully, wiping her cheeks before pulling me into her arms. "We can't forget. Never. I promise, we'll get through this together."

Suddenly, the aging door swings open and a small, dark-haired boy with caramel eyes runs giggling into the room, a perfect image of his grandfather. Edward follows close behind, his cheeks pink with the cold.

"Mama! Aunt Lina!" Eldad grins and bounds to the couch to land between us. "Papa said we could all go to the park if you said yes! Can we, Mama? Please, please, please!"

"Did he now?" Bayla smiles and pulls her son into her lap, ruffling the snowflakes from his mussy hair. "I don't know, it's awfully cold, don't you think?"

"No, I'm not cold!" Eldad shakes his head vehemently. "See, my lips are still pink!"

"I do see. Alright, as long as you don't take your gloves off this time, we can go. But only for a little while, it's getting late. We'll get our coats."

"Yay! Thank you, Mama!" Beaming, he jumps down and practically dances to the door with excitement. "Hurry, Aunt Lina! Before it gets dark!"

"We're coming, Eldad." I smile. "Give your poor old aunt a moment."

Life goes on... even when many are no longer here to see it through. Life always goes on.

Those of us left to carry on, all we can do is remember them, honor them. If we forget them, the millions of men, women, and children lost to the horrors of the worst of this world, we kill them a second time, we condemn them to an even more eternal death. Who is there to say they ever existed if not us? Who is there to say such terrible crimes were ever committed if not us? Entire families, homes, dreams, and lives were destroyed, and, though what happened can never be undone, we cannot forget.

For if we forget that this kind of evil can happen once, who is there to say that it could not happen again?

EPILOGUE

SEPTEMBER 14–15, 1961

SIX MONTHS LATER

"You want to go back?" I exclaim, shooting up from the table, and my cup of tea falls to the floor and shatters. "How could you ask this of me?"

Wincing, Bayla recoils from my outburst and looks up at me apologetically.

"Halina, please," Edward starts softly, a steady hand resting on Bayla's shoulder. "We're not doing this to be cruel. Try to be calm."

Bayla hastily shushes him and moves to embrace me.

"Calm?" I cry furiously, flinching from her touch. "How dare you ask me to be calm! You don't know what that place is to us! You've never seen the smoke coming from the chimneys, never smelt the burning flesh! Do you know anything of what they did to us? The Nazis took everything from us there! They murdered our family there!"

Their screams all echo in my head; terrified, ordinary people thrown from a train, condemned women from within the confines of a block we dared not tread too close to, withering souls crying and begging God for relief and he never answered, wails of the dying as they clung in desperation to the fortunate dead. So many bodies, hundreds and thousands a day, dragged from the infirmary, selected for death, beaten, shot where they stood, gassed and burned in open pits beneath a black sky.

"Halina! Halina, please, look at me! Look at me!" a voice begs, slowly reaching through the fog of horrific images, like an angelic hand breaking the surface of the water to grasp my drowning body. "Please, listen to my voice! We're alright, we're alive, we made it! Look at me!"

A face takes form in the blur of my tears; a young woman with delicate features, beautiful blue eyes framed by soft waves of blond hair. Her hands, grasping either side of my face, are smooth and warm, brushing away the tears streaming down my cheeks.

My heart skips a beat, and, for a moment before my mind begins to clear, I could have mistaken her for our mother.

Gently, Bayla guides me to the sofa, her hands clasped firmly around my own. "I know this is hard for you, unthinkable, and I am so sorry for asking it of you... but I have to go back."

My voice, weak to my own ears, is a mere broken whisper. "Why?"

"The war, Auschwitz... I've never been able to make sense of it, why it all happened to us. I've been trying to find someone who might have the answers we don't ever since I read your journals. A few months ago, I got into contact with a man who fought in the war. He's still living in Poland and he's willing to talk with me about it... and I've asked to meet him in the camp, at Birkenau."

"But why the camp?" I plead, my heart clenching painfully. "I won't try to stop you from asking about it anymore. Talk with anyone you want, but why do you have to go back there? Please, help me understand."

"The answers to the questions I have are in that camp. I know it's a horrible place, I know what they took from us, and I hate the thought of going back... but I have to. I have to see it just one more time. I need closure... and so do *you*. Sometimes, I don't think you ever really left..." She pauses, drawing a deep, trembling breath, and tries in vain to fight away her tears. In an instant Edward is by her side, rubbing her back soothingly and laying affectionate kisses on her head. "Edward will come with me," she continues, "but I can't be alone in that place. I need you with me... Please, I can't face it alone."

Because I'm the only one who understands... We survived it together. No matter how much Edward loves her, he can't understand like I can. Of all the things I have done for her, is this truly the most unbearable one? Go back once more...

"Who are you meeting?" I ask.

"His name is Hans Hoffmann."

Why it all happened... someone who would have the answers we wouldn't... a man who fought in the war... Hans Hoffmann.

"He's a German," I say stiffly.

Tense, eyes filled with worry and tears, she nods.

"He wasn't a prisoner."

Her silence is answer enough, and I draw my hands away.

"Basia, *who* are you meeting?"

"He was a guard," she finally admits. "We've written back and forth for a few months and he told me that himself."

A guard... if he's been on trial, a man like him will only have served a few years. What would be the point in meeting a former victim to discuss his people's crimes?

"And have you ever met this man? How do you know what he wants?" I demand.

She shakes her head. "No, we've never met before. Only letters. I know you're worried, I was too, but we'll be safe. Edward will be with us. I only want to speak with him. I need to understand how everything during the war was allowed to happen to us. Hoffmann fought with them, he was one of them, he's the only one who can truly explain it, and he is the first person *willing* to talk to me about it."

"Then let him tell you in a letter!" I protest weakly, but I know it will not change her mind.

Her voice is a strained whisper, and, in a rare moment of vulnerability, she uses my old name. "Hodaya, I *have* to go back... please come with me. I need you."

I survived that place a million times. With every breath, every moment my heart beat defiantly in the face of death, I survived again and again... I can do it one more time. For Bayla. It's always been for Bayla.

"When are we leaving?"

Edward and Bayla left Eldad with a sitter for the day first thing in the morning.

As I find myself climbing into the back of a blue Syrena, the sun is just beginning to rise over the trees, and there is not much time to truly comprehend what's happening.

Perhaps that's for the best.

The first time I came this way by train, there was no way to prepare for what was going to happen to us. We were exhausted, thirsty, sick, hungry, and consumed already by the drive for survival, and there was nothing else we could think of. If we had known, if we had had the time to mentally and physically prepare for the hell we would endure, I doubt any of us would have lived long enough to step out of that cattle car.

The city slips by in a few moments, a blur in my unfocused eyes until we are driving through the lush green countryside. As I lean against the window, the chilly autumn wind lashes numbingly against my face, sunlight glares through my closed eyes, and I strain to block out every sound and image, focus solely on each breath.

Yes... perhaps it's best to go like we did then, suddenly and unprepared...

I pull my coat tighter around my body, dreading the moment the engine shuts off, watching the view outside the window slowly morph until a patch of birch trees appears. Hours seem to have passed in seconds and, before I fully realize it, the car is slowing to a stop.

"Halina..." Bayla begins quietly. The rest of her words fail to come, but we both know what she means to say.

We're here... we've arrived again.

"I know," I whisper shakily, hands clenched inside my coat pockets, eyes trained on the tightly tied laces of my shoes.

"Hoffmann is already here," Edward says.

"Would you go and meet him? We'll be along in a moment."

Edward steps out of the driver's door and Bayla crawls into the back to sit beside me, slipping her arm through mine.

"I'm scared too," she mutters, and leans further against my side. "It's alright to be afraid, that's the only way we can be brave."

"You're much stronger than me, Basia, you've always been."

"You lived for both of us. You fought and survived for both of us. I never could have made it on my own." She gently wipes the tears from my cheeks and draws one of my hands from my coat to link our fingers together. "If I have any strength today, it was yours that made me so. We're alive because of *you*, of everything you did to save us. But you won't be alone this time, I swear, we'll have each other now."

Her freezing hands curl protectively around mine, her wedding ring glinting in the light, and I force myself to meet her watering gaze.

"Alright." I sigh heavily. "But you have to promise me something else too. Promise me this is the last time, promise me that we'll *never* come back after today."

She nods. "I promise."

She shifts toward her door, but I hold her steadfast. "I'll go first," I say when she looks worriedly at me, and swing the door open before I can change my mind, desperately wanting this day to be over with.

The ground is wet and overgrown beneath my feet, unkempt with years of abandonment. A thin, nearly clear fog has settled, slowly vanishing as the sun rises higher into an empty, bleak sky. Barbed wire disturbs the placid scene, lines and lines stretching further than I dare to look, rusted metal tracks lie hidden beneath the vegetation; and towering before us as a wicked monument to the hell it holds is the gate of death.

The guards in the towers are long gone, the roads are deserted, and the dreadful emptiness of a place that was once so full of people is unnerving. There are no screams, no orders, no speakers, no dogs, only a terrible silence that makes me long for noise. However, at the same time I feel that I must not speak, that I must never utter a sound. There are so many spirits here, the deceased who once had bodies, lives, families, memories... now they are formless like the wind, unable to be touched or seen, but I know that they are here, and I know that I must listen. To be silent is all I have ever known, the only way I know how to mourn all that has been lost.

My foot moves of its own accord, taking the first step toward the camp.

This was the road to death, no matter which way you were sent at the end...

Ahead of us, Edward stands facing the entrance, quietly conversing with a tall, dark-haired man clad in a neat brown suit and coat. Though he stands slightly off balance, favoring his left leg, his posture is rigid and commanding. Even in discomfort, likely from some injury suffered years ago, he stands with discipline and authority that isn't befitting of a mere guard. There is something strange about this man, something controlled and yet exhausted, something familiar...

No, it couldn't be. I stomp the tinge of hope away. *No, he would have run, he would have escaped. Only a fool would have stayed.* Closer and closer we draw, one hesitant step at a time until the soft squelching of the mud beneath our shoes alerts them to our approach.

They turn to greet us.

And the entire world grinds to a sudden halt.

A soundless void fills my ears and the air is torn abruptly from my lungs. Steel-blue eyes lock with mine, the same eyes that once watched over me protectively from a distance, that begged me to go on living another day, and now gaze stunned back into my own. It doesn't matter how he's aged, I need no further proof of who he is, not even the long scar on his left cheek.

His eyes brim with tears, he struggles to speak, and then breathes a single word like a prayer. "Hodaya..."

Air at last fills my trembling body and I gasp, flecks of white light dancing before my eyes, tears burning down my face. "Alaric!"

His arms are around me a moment later, holding me up from the ground before my legs fail, his embrace so crushing it's as if someone were trying to pry me away. I worry for a moment that I may suffocate him with the deathly grip I have around his neck, but he doesn't seem to mind, and buries his face in my hair as he weeps. "You're alive, you're alive, my God! You're alive!" he rejoices over and over again, whispering his relief like a mantra.

"I didn't think... you said..." I sob, gasping between words I can barely form. "I-I never thought I would see you again."

"Neither did I," he whispers, drawing away just enough to look upon me.

"But how?" I clutch his coat, afraid to let him go. "You—you're here! What—how?"

"My brother fled when Germany surrendered, and left new

documents for me too," he says. "I've been Hans Hoffmann since the end of the war... from the letters, I didn't realize you... Basia? She's Bayla... and you. You're Halina?"

"I changed our names too..."

To escape, to forget, to move on... it seems that we've both been running from the past for a long time... and somehow it brought us right back here...

His fingers brush away my tears, cradling my face with such gentleness and reverence it's as if I were the most precious thing in the world. "You have no idea how happy I am to see you."

I smile as I have not done in a long time. "I think I do."

His own smile full of joy and relief warms my heart, and, if there is anything other than Bayla I would have lived to see, it is him. One shaking hand moves to his pocket, but the other remains securely around my back, unwilling to let me go after so many years apart.

"I found these by the train the night you arrived, just before I saw you at the crossroads. I'm so sorry I never gave them to you then, but I was afraid. I knew you would want them, and if you'd been caught with them you would have been killed," he murmurs, producing several slips of paper from his pocket, the edges worn from years of handling. "They only would have been confiscated from *me*, but... I didn't want to raise your hopes only for me to lose them. I swore to myself that I'd give them to you when you survived, but then we were evacuating and I was panicking and I forgot to do that. I've carried them with me every day since, telling myself that you're alive out there somewhere, and that one day I'll give them back to you."

He carefully places them into my hand, and the world grows faint as I feel the familiar texture brush against my skin. Smiling up at me from the first slip of paper is a couple, a woman nearly identical to Bayla in her youth and a man who gave me everything from his eyes to his heart. The photograph of my parents on their wedding day. I shuffle through the others:

Bayla in my arms as a baby, the family portrait before the invasion.

I stare for a long time at this picture, the only image of our entire family together, Bayla's hands in Mama's and mine, Papa at my side, his head turned just slightly as he smiles fondly at his girls. The entire world seems to ache as my heart does, empty as the bitter wind and yet overwhelmed with grief, and their loss stabs deeper within my soul in a single instant than I've ever acknowledged in seventeen years. I can hardly believe it is real, that this was ever truly a moment in time, immortalized in our happiness, the loving completion of our once unbroken family.

They were real... all the shattered fragments of memories I've suppressed and forgotten, my family and friends long gone from this life... they were real. They are *real.*

Alaric's hands move gently to mine, steadying my quivering fingers as I struggle to reveal the last delicate photo, and a breathless sob escapes my lips.

Naomi.

Our hair curled in matching styles, which we rarely did as the days grew bleaker, we sit with our arms linked, smiling for Papa behind the camera while we hold our chocolate. Even in black and white, her eyes glint brightly with a beautiful, internal light. Kind and forgiving as I remember she once was, her angelic smile shines brighter than the sun, and I know for certain that she was an angel sent to make this world a little less dark.

"No one blames you."

So vivid is the memory of her voice, I could almost believe she's right behind me, whispering the same words of comfort she once said a lifetime ago as she held me in her arms. I wanted so badly to believe her, for the gnawing guilt to dissipate from my heart, but to this day there has never been any relief from the burden of Noam's death. And all the others—my parents, my friends, she herself—never once has there been anyone I've blamed more, anyone I've loathed more than myself.

"It wasn't your fault."

Oh, Naomi, my dearest friend... I know that is what you would say to me now. First you would tell me there's nothing to forgive, then you would hug me and dry my tears. You would never blame me... no one would.

Noam was so kind, such a loving boy, but he wanted me to run. He would rather I have run away that night than die with him.

Mama and Papa loved their daughters more than anything in the world, more than themselves. If they had known what would happen to us, both of them would have gladly given their lives to ensure we lived. Their hearts would break if they could see me now, how I have hated myself for losing them, settled their deaths on my own shoulders.

Levana and Chasha were sweet and hopeful, no matter what became of them in the end. Chasha would despise the world for the injustice done to her, but never me. There was no hate anywhere in Levana's heart, only faith, and somehow I think she wouldn't hate even her killers.

And Naomi... She is the one who would have consoled me every day for the rest of our lives if she had lived, never would have let me blame myself as I have done in the isolation of my mind.

"You can't blame yourself anymore."

"I won't, Naomi," I whisper to her picture, the only image of my friend that exists in this world, the only proof that she was more than an angel. "We made it... it's tomorrow..."

Like shackles broken from my body, an enormous weight falls away, and I feel lighter than air. My freedom never began with liberation or with my return to the remnants of our home. It begins now, with my own acceptance. I breathe deeply the autumn breeze, my first true breath of freedom, and it is still painful, but forgiveness is now weaving its gentle, soothing binds through the cracks in my soul.

Somehow, the sun seems a little brighter, the day a little warmer, and, standing in the shadow of the place that stole so much from me and millions of others, I know I am no longer a prisoner to its hell.

This is another world. Another life... for both of us.

I turn my gaze up into Alaric's endless blue eyes, leaning further into his warmth as his fingers softly rub circles over the small of my back. At last, I recognize what it was I saw in his face all those years ago—what I see now, the devotion and tenderness, the sadness, fear, and hope, the longing for my life and happiness to go on—and I feel my heart lighten as he smiles tearfully at me.

Love.

Somehow, the words he never spoke to me, every gentle, hesitant touch, are clearer now than glass. Somehow, as he watched me from afar, saw his own life, regrets, and love reflected in me every day I went on living for Bayla, he came to care for me more than I was capable of understanding at the time. How could I have known? In this place, there was nothing but survival, nothing but my sister, but now... now we are equals. We are a man and a woman as we once were for just a few moments so long ago.

A muffled breath draws our attention, and I suddenly remember that we are not alone. Just behind us, Bayla has leaned into Edward's arms, tears of shock and joy glistening down her cheeks as she recognizes Alaric from my painting. There is no judgment in her eyes as he holds me, no resentment, no disgust, only pure, genuine hope as she gazes at me.

Take this chance, please find peace, her eyes beseech me as they've done a thousand times over the years, and this time I am certain I am ready. I am ready to remember, to face the past, to forgive, to move on, to let my heart heal.

Alaric's calloused fingers brush the hair from my face, caressing the dark locks lovingly, and I slip my arms around him, hoping he can see the newfound emotion filling my heart without words. A look of disbelief crosses his features, and the spark of light in his eyes speaks of such overwhelming, yearning hope that my breath catches, and I tighten my grip in reassurance. As I lean against his chest, feel his lips brush in a tender kiss on my head, I am warm in a way I haven't felt since before the camp.

We are all free. I survived. Bayla survived. And now, Alaric is here too, alive, returning the broken pieces of me I thought I'd lost forever, and, for the first time in a long, long time, I know for certain that everything is going to be alright.

A LETTER FROM S.E. RUTLEDGE

Dear Reader,

I am very grateful you decided to read *A Promise to My Sister*. This story is one that I have wanted to tell for many years and I sincerely hope you enjoyed it. The experiences of the thousands of men, women, and children who endured the concentration camps during the Second World War are as terrible as they are incredible, but I feel their stories must be told and learned from. If you want to keep up to date with my current releases, you can sign up at the following link. Your email address will never be shared and you can unsubscribe at any time.

www.bookouture.com/s-e-rutledge

I would like to note that, in order to avoid fictionalization of real prisoners of Auschwitz, the tattooed number given to a fictional character in this book begins with the letter A. This practice of tattooing inmates with letters before the serial number did not in reality begin until 1944—much later than Hodaya and her family arrived—and the serial numbers with these letters reached 30,000 at maximum, unlike the numbers given to Hodaya and Bayla.

Some people like Sergeant Gerhard Kurzbach and SS-Haupsturmfuhrer Mengele were real, and I have done my best through extensive research and survivors' accounts to represent them as accurately as possible. While the characters of Alaric, Hodaya, and her family are of my own creation, I wrote each of them in portrayal of real survivors, perpetrators, and those who were complicit in order to capture the reality of their suffering, their inner turmoil, and, above all, their strength and endurance.

Thank you again for reading *A Promise to My Sister* and I hope you loved it. If so, I would love to read your review and see what you think.

Thank you,

Savannah

facebook.com/savannah.rutledge.18

instagram.com/s.e.rutledge

x.com/SE_Rutledge

ACKNOWLEDGMENTS

I would like to begin first by thanking my wonderful editor, Lucy. She has been incredibly supportive from the very beginning. Her guidance has helped me in shaping this story to its full potential and encouraged me to become the best writer I can be. I would also like to thank the Bookouture publicity team, who have been very supportive and welcoming along this new journey for me. I am very grateful for the opportunity to work with them now and hopefully in the future on more projects.

I am beyond grateful to my mom and dad, who have always supported me in my dreams, and who tell anyone whether they be family or stranger that their "amazing daughter" writes books! They are always the first to hear about my stories, which are often long tirades I'm glad for their patience in listening to, and have never stopped encouraging me to continue writing.

To my best friend and sister, Felicia, I want to thank you for all your love and support over the years. You've always been there for me and I am glad to have you in my life.

I am also very happy to have my little brother's support. Although Kenny and I have very different hobbies and he is inclined toward motorcycles the way I am toward writing, he always finds the time to ask me about what I'm writing now and what I will write in the future.

A special thank you to Shelby, Sasha, and Arshia, who were the first to read Hodaya's story and gave me wonderful feedback and more confidence in myself.

I would also like to thank the many English and history teachers I've had throughout the years. They have all encouraged me in their own ways to pursue my love of both subjects, and have made me strive to better myself and my skills.

Finally, I want to extend my gratitude and respect to all those who lived the stories we now tell today. Words alone cannot express the extraordinary strength and courage of those incredible individuals. It is through suffering, bravery, and sacrifice that transcends age and generations that we can learn from them, and which connects us all through love and understanding in a way that is too powerful to name. Their lives and stories, the happinesses and tragedies, the failures and triumphs, continue to inspire us all and teach us every day the wonderful value and preciousness of life.

PUBLISHING TEAM

Turning a manuscript into a book requires the efforts of many people. The publishing team at Bookouture would like to acknowledge everyone who contributed to this publication.

Audio
Alba Proko
Melissa Tran

Commercial
Lauren Morrissette
Hannah Richmond
Imogen Allport

Cover design
Debbie Clement

Data and analysis
Mark Alder
Mohamed Bussuri

Editorial
Lucy Frederick
Imogen Allport

Made in the USA
Monee, IL
24 August 2024

64512684R10201